Malvern College

A 150TH ANNIVERSARY PORTRAIT

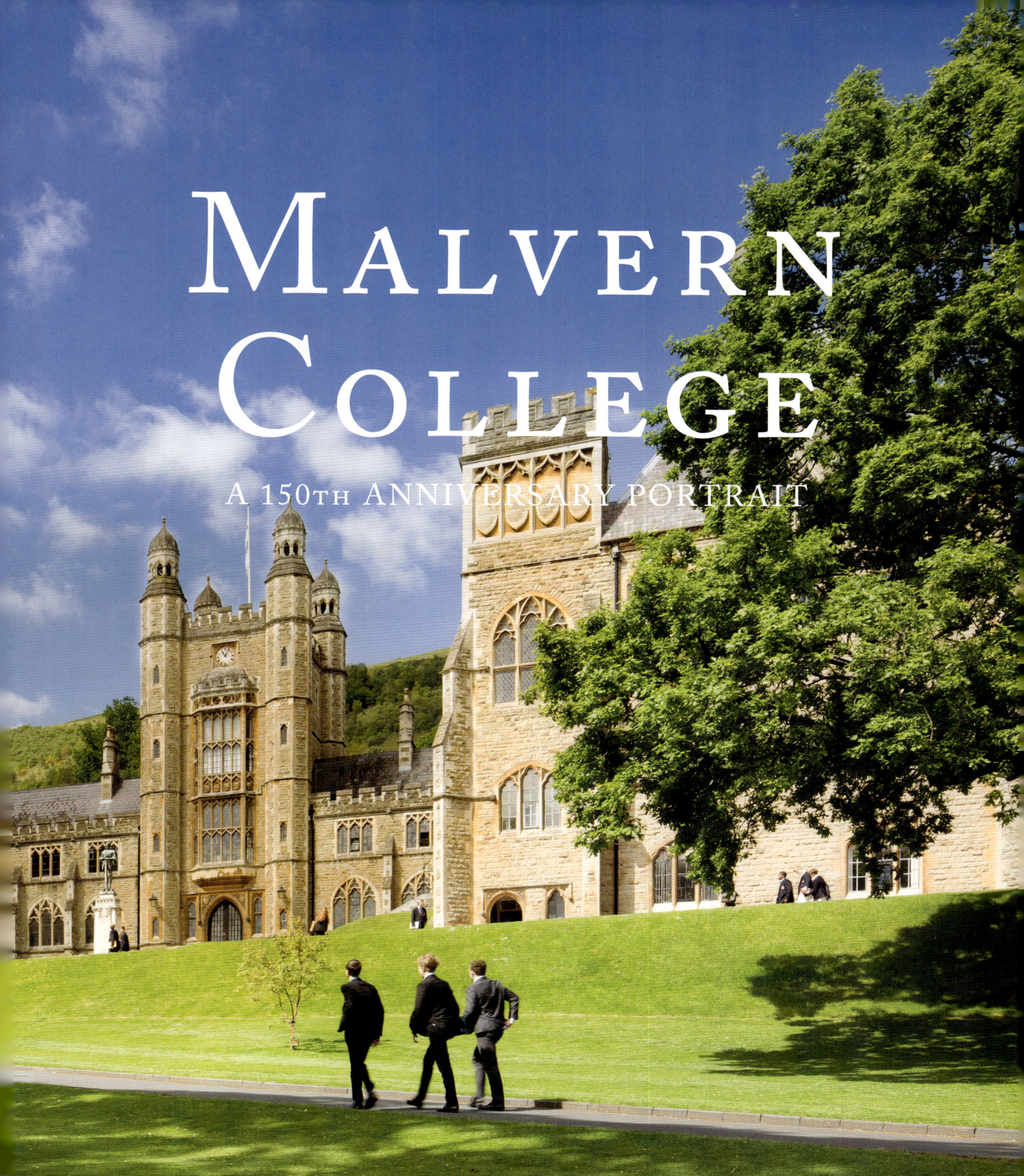

Malvern College

A 150th Anniversary Portrait

Published in Great Britain in 2014 by Shire Publications Ltd,
PO Box 883, Oxford, OX1 9PL, UK
PO Box 3985, New York, NY 10185-3985, USA
E-mail: shire@shirebooks.co.uk   www.shirebooks.co.uk
© 2014 Malvern College.

All rights reserved. Apart from any fair dealing for the purpose of private study, research, criticism or review, as permitted under the Copyright, Designs and Patents Act, 1988, no part of this publication may be reproduced, stored in a retrieval system, or transmitted in any form or by any means, electronic, electrical, chemical, mechanical, optical, photocopying, recording or otherwise, without the prior written permission of the copyright owner. Enquiries should be addressed to the Publishers.

Every attempt has been made by the Publishers to secure the appropriate permissions for materials reproduced in this book. If there has been any oversight we will be happy to rectify the situation and a written submission should be made to the Publishers.

Surprised by Joy by C. S. Lewis © C. S. Lewis Pte. Ltd. 1955. Extracts reprinted by permission.

A CIP catalogue record for this book is available from the British Library.

ISBN-13: 978 0 74781 305 7

Editor: Ruth Sheppard

Indexer: Zoe Ross

Designed by Ken Vail and typeset in Gill Sans and Adobe Caslon Pro.

Printed in China through Worldprint Ltd.

14 15 16 17 18   10 9 8 7 6 5 4 3 2 1

Cover image: Doors of Main Building.
Title pages image: Malvern College, May 2014. (Fernando Manoso)
Contents page image: Malvern v Shrewsbury, Blenheim Palace, 1940.

To my parents Edward William Allen and Louise Florence Allen who among so many gifts gave me a love of history, and to Ralph Blumenau who taught me the art of teaching it.

Contents

Acknowledgements	7
Foreword	9
1. Foundations	11
2. Making a school, 1865–91	19
3. Christian gentlemen and the playing fields of Malvern, 1892–1914	31
4. 'With a wider vision and a self-trained mind', 1914–37	43
5. 'We have not faltered nor failed', 1937–53	55
6. The new Elizabethans, 1953–82	75
7. Remaking a school, 1983–2008	95
8. Good teaching and sound learning	111
9. Look forward in faith	131
10. Prefects, fags and rebels	143
11. From Canning Town to Ghana	161
12. For Crown and country	169
13. The sporting life	185
14. Life in abundance	209
15. Embracing the future	229
Appendices	
1: The Houses of Malvern College	240
2: Wider still and wider	243
List of subscribers	251
Endnotes	253
Bibliography	266
Index	267

Acknowledgements

In the process of preparing and writing this book I have been greatly assisted by a host of Malvernians both past and present. A great debt is owed to Ralph Blumenau not only for his excellent centenary history, which has been invaluable both as a source and a model of how to write engaging history, but also for his interest, support, counsel, and contacts.

I was fortunate to benefit from the wisdom and remarkable fund of knowledge of the late George Chesterton, Alan Carter and Garnet Scott. Particular mention must be made of Pat Purcell who guided me through the musical contributions of the Directors of Music, to Roger Hall Jones for his remarkable collection of Malvern illustrations, the late Cyril Lace for his large volumes of collected Malverniana, the former College Archivist Norman Rosser for his meticulous records, and local historian, Brian Iles, who generously offered the use of his extensive collection. Helen Jones, the College Librarian, cheerfully dealt with a host of enquiries. Mike Tiley's indefatigable efforts secured for us the elusive pictures of C. S. Lewis and information on, access to, and the photographs of the Docklands Settlement. His generosity is responsible for the stunning photographs of the Church of St George and St Helena including the great west window. Roy McAdam and the Norman Mays Studio were unfailingly helpful and we have drawn heavily on the photographic skill of Mathew Lloyd. I have been particularly fortunate in the patient secretarial work of Helen Chapman. I cannot speak too highly of the support, energy, skill and good humour of Ellen Brigden, Lin Murtagh and Kiel Hanson who recorded, filed and helped select the illustrations – never was so much laughter generated by so few! The Malvernian Society office, the Development office, and the Archivist, Ian Quickfall, have been supportive throughout, and Ralph Blumenau, Martin Frayn and Paul Godsland kindly proofread early versions of the text, and Joe Gauci the last proof. Finally there could have been no better editor than Ruth Sheppard whose expertise, good sense and gentle humour was a constant support.

The following kindly gave up their time to be interviewed: Richard Baldwyn, Hugh Carson, Alan Carter, George Chesterton, Antony Clark, Professor Ken Davey, Bill Denny, John Dent, Reg Farrar, Frank Harriss, Pat Hooley, Roger Gillard, Richard Goddard, John Knee, Martin and Julia Knott, Tom Köhler-Cadmore, Rev. Andrew Law, Justin Major, Rt Hon Lord MacLaurin of Knebworth, DL, Will Morris, Tim Newsholme, Keith Packham, David Penter, Iain Sloan, Mrs Bridget Staniforth, Nigel Turner, Martin and Jane Rogers, Sheila and Nigel Stewart, James Stredder, Simon Wilkinson.

I am extremely grateful for the many Malvernians and colleagues who have contributed their knowledge, memories and photographs to this project: Philip Allen, Michaela Asamoah, Julian Bailey, Nick Baxter, Tony Beeson, Simon Bennett, Jan Bergerhoff, Anthony Bettinson, Robin Black, Peter Bowen-Simpkins, Nigel Bradford, Charles Bridge (for the Bridge family collection), David Burley, John Burton, Stephanie Cardon, Mrs Vanessa Chesterton, Robin Clark, Mike Clement, Guy Coombes, Roger Corfield, Brian Davis, Gary Donaldson, Mike Downe, Dan Eglin, Richard Faber, Geoffrey Farrer-Brown, John Fearnall, René Filho, Martin Frayn, Adam Fuge, Joe Gauci, Nigel Godfrey, Peter Gray, Rhian Grundy, Clive Haines, Mark Hardiman, Robin Harrild, Quentin Hayes, Johnnie Hill, Rory Hopkinson (for photographs of his late great-uncle J. G. H.), Alice Howick, Adam Hutsby, Louisa Jones, Willoughby Jones, David Keddie, Bert Lacey, Angela Lafferty, Sue Lamberton, Moritz Liebelt, Mrs Eve Leng, Richard Lewis, Andrew Lowcock, Adam Pharoah, Cliff Poultney, Robert Porter, Hedley Prest, Jonathan Myles-Lea, Tom Newman, Ahmed Rashid, Rob Richardson, Helen Robinson, Joe Roseman, Oliver Rundell, Jamie Russell, Mrs Ruth Scott, Anne Sharp, Roger Smith, Peter Southgate, James Stredder, Robert Stredder, Clive Sutton, Barbara Swart, Dr Mike Taylor, Richard Thurlow, Roger Tomlin, Thomas Trotter, Gavin Turner, James Vivian, Arthur Wakeley, Andrew Walker, Jonathan Wateridge, Nigel Webster, Adam Wharton, James Whitty, Tony Williams, Frank Williams-Thomas, Paul Wickes, Vanessa Young and Joseph Zivny.

Roy Allen

Opposite: The Chapel's flying buttresses and the Hills beyond. (Photograph by Jon Willcocks)

Foreword

Opposite: (Fernando Manoso)

Malvern College lies at the foot of the Malvern Hills in the heart of England – in 'Elgar country'. It exemplifies the English character – loyalty, service and responsibility. In its one hundred and fifty years it has produced men, and recently women, of outstanding character and ability who have contributed to every sphere of national and international life from the days of Empire through two world wars to the present day. This book is a fascinating account of the foundation, development and progress of an outstanding English public school. Malvern provides a well-rounded education of the highest standard – academically, artistically and sportingly. There is an absence of elitism, rather the encouragement of character and responsible leadership. These pages contain the names of many distinguished alumni who have added lustre to the name of Malvern as well as those who have supported and greatly enhanced the reputation and standing of the school. The valuable contribution of the active Malvernian Society is noted with appreciation.

The account of the years of the Second World War, with two enforced exiles, at Blenheim Palace and at Harrow, of which I have very clear memories, is of particular interest. It is a mark of the strength of the school that it maintained its unique character throughout these eventful years. The enormous contribution made by the Headmaster, H. C. A. Gaunt, and his staff and all the College servants are revealed and recognised.

Malvern has not stood still. Following the return from wartime exile, a period of necessary recovery and further development followed. The challenges of the times have been met. On the academic side the International Baccalaureate has been introduced. Twenty-two years ago, girls were admitted with great success. An extensive programme of development has been implemented including the provision of additional boarding houses, a sports centre, a swimming pool and now a new science centre. In meeting the challenges of the passing years Malvern is very fortunate in enjoying the direction of an outstanding headmaster and Common Room. As a Malvernian, I am proud to recommend this well-researched, comprehensive and thoroughly readable account of our first one hundred and fifty years.

The Right Honourable Sir Stephen Brown, GBE

1

Foundations

'To Found a College on The Model of The Great Public Schools,
For Educating The Sons of Gentlemen'

A school is inevitably a mirror of the society in which it is set. The older the foundation the more it will, over time, reflect the changes that happen to that society, and a school that has a national reach, and which educates the offspring of the influential classes will, at least in part, tell the story of what happened to that nation. It is, of course, also a story of service given, and of the formative years of generations of pupils. What follows is an account of the history of Malvern College and through its narrative we find a powerful incarnation of the forces that have transformed this country and the wider world: the power and values of the commercial middle classes, lingering aristocratic shadows, the imperial story from the heyday of Empire through to its dissolution, the profound and sombre impact of two world wars, economic and social change, new views of education, and a reassertion of Britain's European identity together with its continued post-imperial global reach.

The nineteenth century was in many ways the British century. Commercial and industrial wealth made the country powerful and influential. Britain's institutions, enshrining liberty and the rule of law together with stability, were admired by other societies cowed by authoritarianism and by those who had witnessed the recent and recurring horrors of revolution. The British Empire exported a British view, and way of doing things, to vast regions of the world. Even peoples beyond its domains envied and aspired to what seemed to be the key to material success and high civilisation. One of these exports became the English public school, which was reproduced in the dominions and colonies, particularly where British émigrés settled, and was also to attract to Britain pupils from the indigenous elites of the colonies.

The reason for this was that the public schools had acquired a mystique, and fostered a widely held belief that the triumphs of Britannia owed much to the character training provided by these schools. This would not have been a view that many would have accepted as the nineteenth century dawned. Obscure and uncertain in origins, and certainly no educational model, there was to be a transformation in the prestige of these schools leading to the public school phenomenon that exploded in Britain in the middle years of the nineteenth century, deeply affecting the fortunes of the country, and spreading its influence beyond British shores. As we shall see, this influence did not end with the dismantling of the Empire but has, in the twenty-first century, revived with large numbers coming from abroad to study in British public schools, and the 'brand' becoming highly exportable.

Opposite: Hansom's tower for the Main College Building. (Photograph by Jon Willcocks)

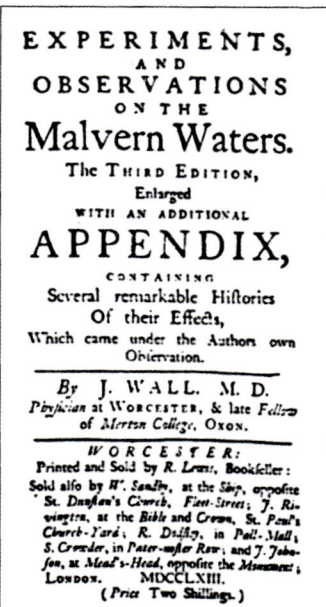

Above: Dr Wall's influential book. (The John Winsor (Harcup) Collection)

Below: Dr Gully, by Spy, entitled 'Hydropathy' in *Vanity Fair* (1876). (© The British Library Board P.P.5274.ha, Aug 5, 1876, p.90)

The public school transformation was in part an economic and a social matter. The rapidly expanding middle classes sought suitable educational institutions for their sons (and later daughters). As Gathorne-Hardy states, 'the numbers of those able and eager to pay for a public school education grew continually throughout the nineteenth century'.[1] The new middle classes may have flirted with revolution when a traditional landowning aristocracy hampered their economic or political power, but they were also powerfully attracted to the concept of social advancement. For most their wealth was a stepping-stone to status, and status came from copying the upper classes. If the old elite sent their sons to ancient boarding schools like Eton and Harrow, then the new elite wished to join in and, by necessity of numbers, they would have to create more new schools.

The middle classes might have travelled a different educational path if it had not been for the dramatic reforming zeal that transformed the traditional public schools into more acceptable educational models. The older schools perhaps reached a nadir by the beginning of the nineteenth century. Founded as charitable institutions, some as early as the twelfth century, they had become barbaric institutions, under-resourced, poorly run and with a reputation for licentiousness, boorishness and indiscipline. The curriculum was narrow and unrelated to the vast changes wrought by industrial advance and political and social change. However, headmasters like Russell at Charterhouse, Butler at Shrewsbury and most famously Arnold at Rugby 'saved the public schools as important institutions, restored to them respectability and prestige, and paved the way for an enormous increase in public school education'.[2] The Evangelical revival and the High Church movement had enshrined the ideals of the Christian gentleman, and the new centrality of Chapel in school life appealed to a deeply religious instinct in the rising middle class. Hierarchies based on merit, as expressed in the reformed prefect system, mirrored the assumptions of business hierarchy. Manly team games would train body and character, and an expanded curriculum could prepare boys for the new commercial world and feed the needs of Empire. Many of the new public schools were located in the countryside to avoid the ravages of disease and the temptations of the flesh so apparent in the urban areas. The railways offered easy access and a sufficiently expanded market to make such schools viable. The middle years of the nineteenth century saw many new schools being created to meet this rising demand. These included Cheltenham (1841), Marlborough (1843), Rossall (1844), Radley (1847), Lancing (1848), Bradfield (1850), Wellington (1859), Clifton (1862) and Haileybury (1862). In 1865 Malvern College became the latest addition to this distinguished list.

The town of Malvern had become a popular spa resort in the later eighteenth century following the publication in 1757 of Dr John Wall's *Experiments and Observations on the Malvern Waters*. By the early years of the nineteenth century the purity of Malvern's water was attracting distinguished visitors, such as the Duchess of Kent and Princess Victoria in 1831, particularly after Dr James Gully and Dr James Wilson introduced the German 'hydropathy' technique in 1842.[3] Wilson treated 350 patients in four months in his first year, and Gully – having 'a way with the great' – saw Thomas Carlyle, Charles Darwin, Lord Macaulay, Alfred Tennyson and William Gladstone pass through his hands. Charles Dickens came in 1851 to seek a cure for his wife Catherine, and he encouraged his close friend Sir Edward Bulwer Lytton to experience the treatment offered by Wilson. In 1859 the railway arrived at Malvern Link, and by 1861 included Great Malvern on the way to Hereford, bringing some 3,000 visitors a year to the town.

This expansion attracted entrepreneurs who sought to find new ways of advancing the town. One such was Walter Burrow, who was the manager of a Malvern chemists.[4] Together with his brother John, he went on to create a highly successful business bottling water from St Anne's Well. It is to these energetic and public-spirited businessmen that we must look for the spiritual founders of the College. A number of what came to be called proprietary schools had been

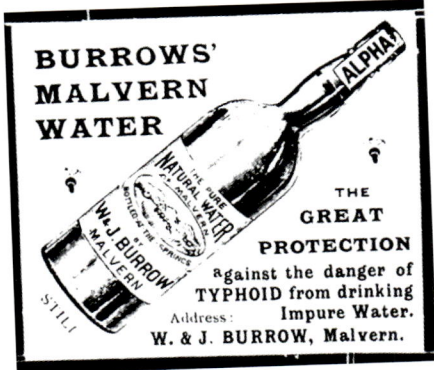

Above: Advert for Burrows' Malvern Water. Walter and John Burrow were the first advocates of building a college in Malvern. (The John Winsor (Harcup) Collection)
Left: Great Malvern railway station. (David Postle Collection)
Below: Sir Edmund Lechmere, founder, benefactor and designer of the College crest. (© National Portrait Gallery, London)

established around the country in response to a growing demand from the middle classes. These schools were founded as joint stock enterprises that issued shares to raise the capital required. They were noted for their more modern curriculums compared to the older established public schools, because they were not hampered by traditions and were thus able to adapt to the educational needs of the day. Impressed by the recent establishment of Cheltenham College in 1841, Walter Burrow 'came to the conclusion that what had proved possible at Cheltenham might be equally possible at Malvern', which in many respects had, he considered, 'advantages superior to those of Cheltenham for such an institution'.[5]

Through the agency of their brother the Rev H. H. Burrow, advice was obtained from the warden of New College, Oxford on how to proceed in establishing a school. Key local figures became enthusiastic advocates for the proposal, most notably the Rev Frank Dyson, who canvassed and won the support of The Hon. Frederick Lygon MP, son of Earl Beauchamp. Other key figures were the Lord Lieutenant of Worcestershire, Lord Lytton, Sir Edmund Lechmere, Bt., MP, Dr Gully, Canon Melville of Worcester Cathedral, who had been formerly Headmaster of Radley College, and John Lea, a partner in Lea & Perrins. Sadly, once the proposal was up and running, the role of Walter and John Burrow fades away. There are a number of suggestions they were cold-shouldered by local notables because of their association with trade. Their significant contribution only became known when John's granddaughter presented his manuscripts to the College in 1960.

The national financial crisis of 1857/8 certainly delayed progress in founding the school. The idea was revived in 1861 'largely owing to the dynamism and financial acumen' of Dr Leopold Stummes, an Austrian subject who had become Dr Wilson's partner in 1850.[6] He bought a 26-acre site and offered it for the purpose of building a school.[7] The Malvern Proprietary College Company was formed, along the lines followed by the founders of Cheltenham College,[8] and was guaranteed by John Lea to the extent of £10,000. The Hon. Frederick Lygon

Above: Dr Leopold Stummes who purchased the land on which the College is built. (Courtesy of Roger Hall-Jones (l. 1960–65))

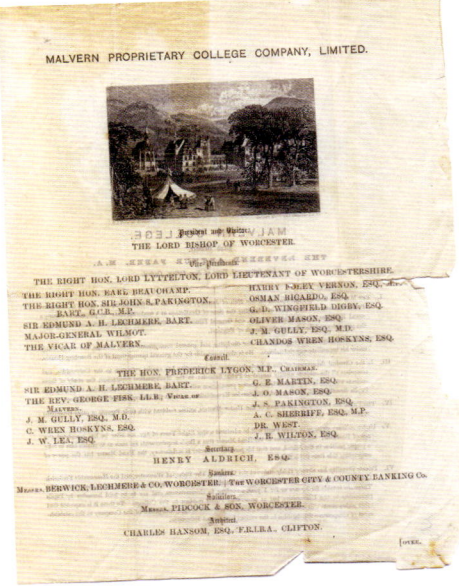

Below: Prospectus documents advertising the College.

became chairman, the Bishop of Worcester (Dr Henry Philpott) president and Dr Stummes the secretary.[9]

Rev Burrow wrote the first prospectus for the new school. Due place was given to Classics for the traditional reasons of intrinsic worth, its utility for learning modern languages and as a training of both mind and character. However, reflecting changing cultural attitudes:

> Especial regard will also be paid to those elements which are daily rising in importance, but which as yet have hardly been admitted as matters of systematic teaching. The fact that valuable civil and military appointments are now thrown open for general competition forces upon our notice the necessity of making the study of Physical Science, Modern History, and Languages, not merely a casual but an admitted and regular pursuit.

The formal foundation of the Company took place on 22 August 1862 in Dr Gully's dining room at the Imperial Hotel.[10] It was formally resolved:

> [That] a Proprietary College, to be established in an eligible situation, as nearly as possible on the model of the Public Schools for the Education of the Sons of gentlemen, at a moderate cost, is an undertaking highly desirable in the present state of education in England, and, if well conducted, likely to be successful and of great public benefit.
>
> [That] the town of Malvern, from its bracing air, gravelly soil, pure water, and convenient access by Railway, is well adapted for an undertaking of this nature.

The new College Council advertised for both an architect and a headmaster. For the former the council chose Charles Hansom[11] from forty applicants. He had built Clifton College in the fashionable neo-Gothic style. Upon the advice of the Bishop of Worcester, the College Council appointed the Rev Arthur Faber as the first Headmaster of Malvern College. Faber was aged thirty-two and a Fellow and Tutor of New College, Oxford. He had been born in India in 1831, attended both Harrow and Winchester and had gone up to New College when he was seventeen.

The Bishop of Worcester laid the foundation stone on 22 July 1863. Four hundred invitations had been sent out, and each guest was presented with 'a steel engraving of the College, beautifully executed and suitable for a frame or the album'.[12] There were toasts and speeches but Dr Gully, replying to the toast 'The Prosperity of Malvern', introduced a somewhat jarring note by berating the townspeople for having taken up only twelve of the five hundred shares: 'He could not understand how it was that the townspeople would not look beyond their noses, for with five hundred students there must be an increased expenditure of something like £100,000 per annum in Malvern'.[13]

Work now began in earnest, although the project was beset by difficulties; the original completion date of September 1864 was missed by three months, and several aspects of Hansom's plans were not built in time for the opening, including the Chapel, which was to have been located on its current site but linked to the Main Building by a covered walkway. For the next few years the Chapel was to be located in the south wing where today the school library, the Grundy, is located. The building contractors Warburton's proved unsatisfactory with a series of expensive errors that resulted in a court case. The limited share capital was insufficient to build boarding houses and the Council had to sell part of the acquired land to Lord Lygon who built a headmaster's house, which would eventually become School House, subject to an annual rent of £200. A separate company – the Building Company – was formed from among the more wealthy shareholders to build the first boarding houses. This company bought an acre of land from the Council and organised the building of houses 1 and 2. These houses were then leased

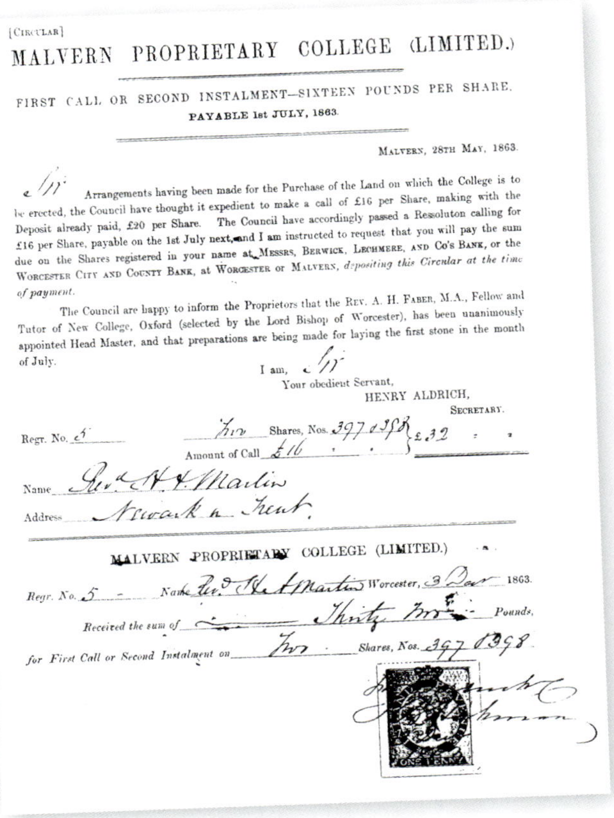

[CIRCULAR]

MALVERN PROPRIETARY COLLEGE (LIMITED.)

FIRST CALL OR SECOND INSTALMENT—SIXTEEN POUNDS PER SHARE.
PAYABLE 1st JULY, 1863.

MALVERN, 28TH MAY, 1863.

Sir Arrangements having been made for the Purchase of the Land on which the College is to be erected, the Council have thought it expedient to make a call of £16 per Share, making with the Deposit already paid, £20 per Share. The Council have accordingly passed a Ressoluton calling for £16 per Share, payable on the 1st July next, and I am instructed to request that you will pay the sum due on the Shares registered in your name at MESSRS, BERWICK, LECHMERE, AND CO'S BANK, or the WORCESTER CITY AND COUNTY BANK, at WORCESTER or MALVERN, *depositing this Circular at the time of payment.*

The Council are happy to inform the Proprietors that the REV. A. H. FABER, M.A., Fellow and Tutor of New College, Oxford (selected by the Lord Bishop of Worcester), has been unanimously appointed Head Master, and that preparations are being made for laying the first stone in the month of July.

I am, Sir
Your obedient Servant,
HENRY ALDRICH,
SECRETARY.

Regr. No. 5 Two Shares, Nos. 397 & 398 } £32 : :
Amount of Call £16 : :

Name Revd H. A. Martin
Address Newark on Trent.

MALVERN PROPRIETARY COLLEGE (LIMITED.)

Regr. No. 5 Name Revd H. A. Martin Worcester, 3 Dec 1863.
Received the sum of Thirty Two Pounds,
for First Call or Second Instalment on Two Shares, Nos. 397 & 398.

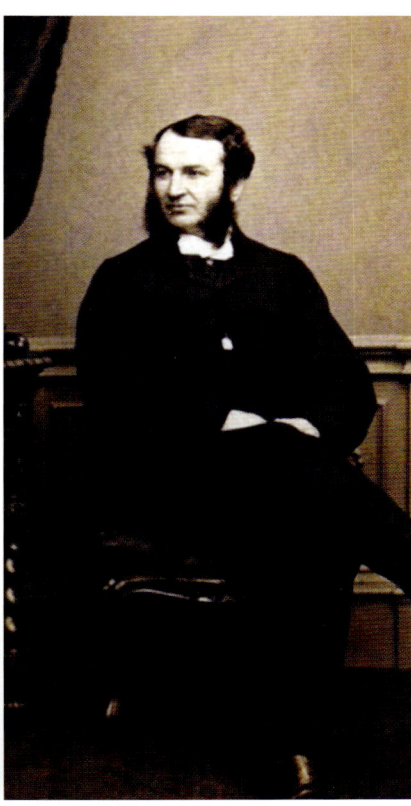

Far left: A letter requesting a payment from shareholders and announcing the appointment of the first Headmaster.

Left: Malvern's first Headmaster, Rev Arthur Faber.

to the College at a rent that delivered 6 per cent return on the investment. The College was given the right to buy the property of the Building Company within ten years (the College was not able to do this until 1877). The Building Company showed great generosity to the College as it struggled to build itself up, not least on easing the interest terms. Both the new Earl Beauchamp[14] and John Lea, the biggest shareholders, sustained considerable financial loss in order to support

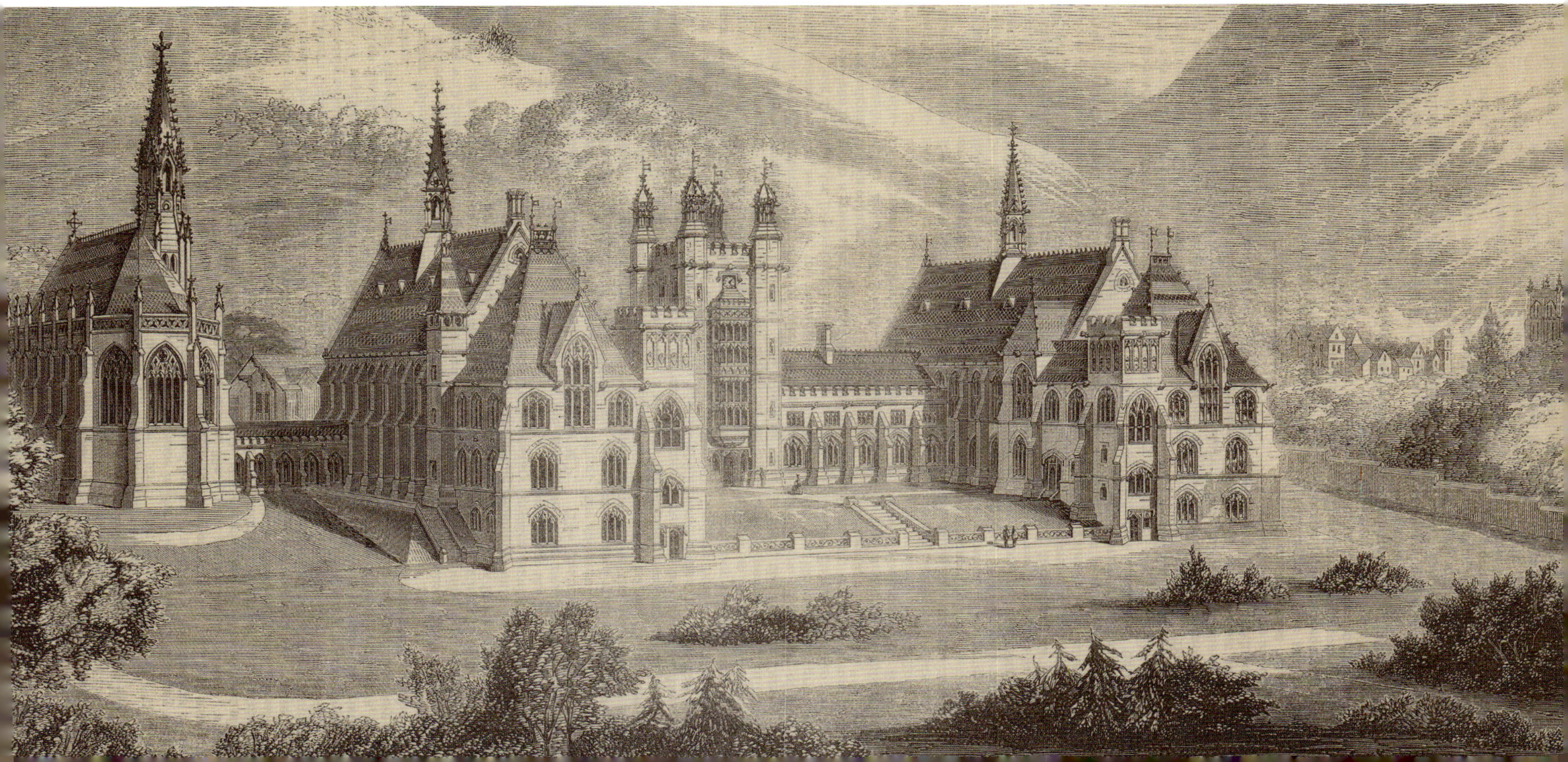

Below: Charles Hansom's original design of Malvern College. The neo-Gothic style was chosen for the Main Building. This style was inspired by medieval Christianity and was also seen as a reaction against the Classical tradition, which had become associated with rationalism and revolutionary tendencies in France and the United States. It was therefore particularly popular for new schools seeking to promote the Christian faith and traditional values.

MALVERN COLLEGE

Right: The original Main Building floor plans as they appeared in *The Builder* magazine (June 1865).

Below: Charles Hansom's design of the tower for the Main Building of the College.

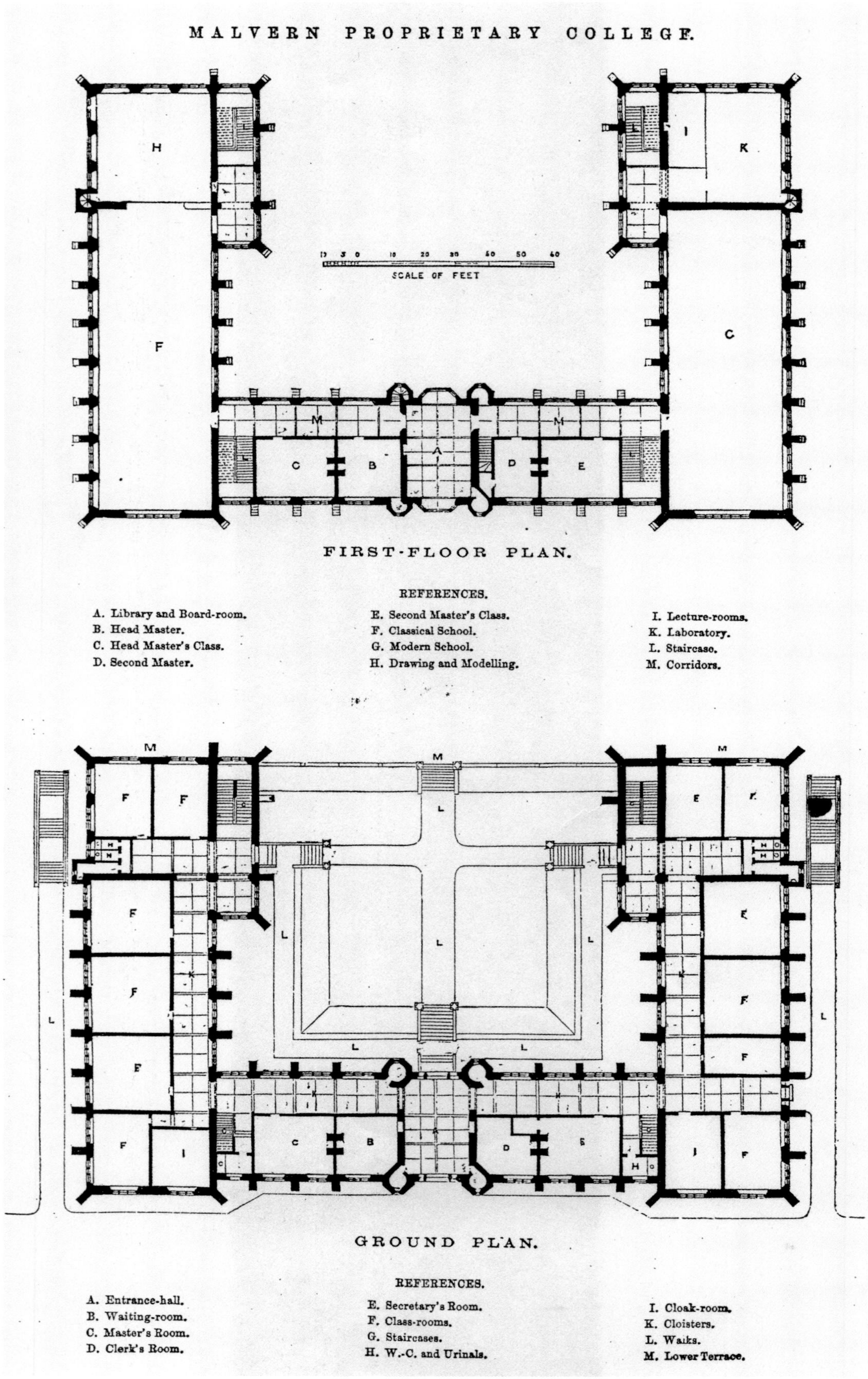

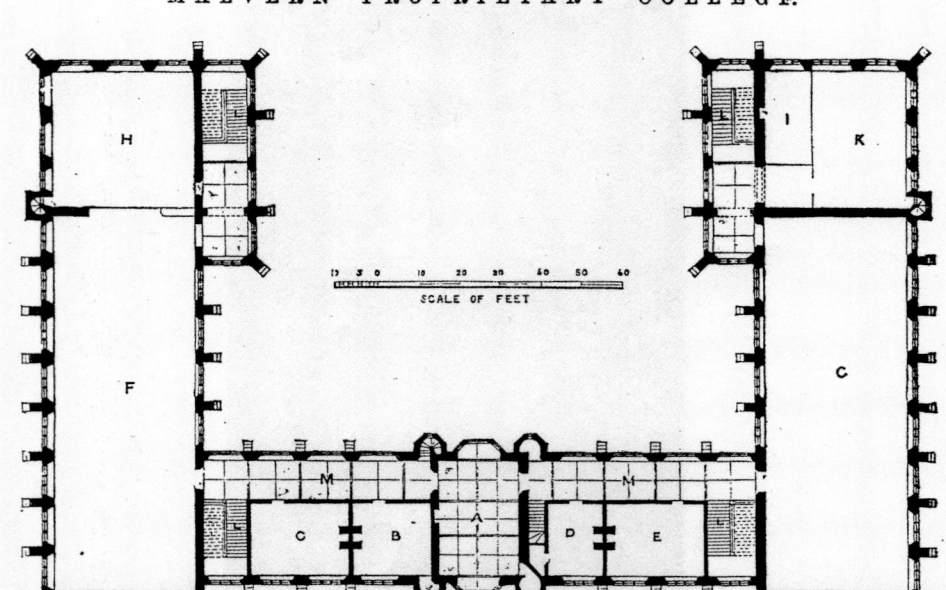

MALVERN PROPRIETARY COLLEGE.

FIRST-FLOOR PLAN.

REFERENCES.

A. Library and Board-room.
B. Head Master.
C. Head Master's Class.
D. Second Master.
E. Second Master's Class.
F. Classical School.
G. Modern School.
H. Drawing and Modelling.
I. Lecture-rooms.
K. Laboratory.
L. Staircase.
M. Corridors.

GROUND PLAN.

REFERENCES.

A. Entrance-hall.
B. Waiting-room.
C. Master's Room.
D. Clerk's Room.
E. Secretary's Room.
F. Class-rooms.
G. Staircases.
H. W.-C. and Urinals.
I. Cloak-room.
K. Cloisters.
L. Walks.
M. Lower Terrace.

Far left: The 6th Lord Beauchamp, founder, benefactor and chairman of the College Council, 1863–91. (Courtesy of The Madresfield Estate.)
Left: John Wheeley Lea, founder and benefactor. (Courtesy of Lea & Perrins)

the school in its infancy; in the words of Ralph Blumenau, 'it is no exaggeration to think of these two men as the principal founding benefactors of Malvern College'.[15]

In the year of its opening the College was described in a local guide book:

> The new College is one of the most attractive buildings in Malvern. It is situated in Radnor Road, on a gentle slope, and commands extensive views of the valley and Cotteswold range of hills on the east, and of the Malvern chain on the west. The plan is in the form of the letter E – the eastern side being left open to secure ample light and ventilation. The handsome and uniquely constructed clock, erected by Mr Skarratt, of Worcester, is an ornament to the building and a convenience to the district. The Headmaster is the Rev Arthur Faber, M.A. late Fellow of New College, a gentleman of high classical attainments, and the assistant masters are eminent for scholarship and experience in scholastic instruction. The distinction of the teachers in every department of knowledge and the hygienic advantages of the district ensure the success of this noble educational institution.[16]

Left: An early photograph of the new school.
Below: Announcement of the opening of the College, 1865.

2

Making a school, 1865–91

The school officially opened on 25 January 1865 with twenty-four boys of whom eleven were day boys.[1] There were six assistant masters. The only boarding house ready was No. 1, and the boys destined for No. 2 spent the first term in Holyrood House, later to become the Tudor Hotel.[2] The houses were entirely private ventures and the boarding fees of £60 per annum were paid directly to the housemaster with the prospect of a considerable profit once a house was full but, given the rent of £300, something of a financial embarrassment in the early days. Housemasters had to provide board and lodging, pay for a seat in Chapel for each boy and contribute to the costs of the sanatorium (housed initially on the first floor of the south wing of the Main Building). One of these founder boys recalled his first day in the new school:

Opposite: School House, 1879, entitled 'How we dressed and wore our caps in 1879'.

> I remember the 25th January very well. I was eleven years old and going to a real public school – enough to impress any boy's memory. The only house finished was McDowall's (No. 1) and about fourteen of us assembled there. It had snowed all night, and in the morning was about two feet deep and drifted against the bank in places five and six feet. We cut our way up with improvised shovels and finally got to the Coll. where we found two boys who were in lodgings with Mr. Drew, and about ten day boys. We were roughly examined and classed – I was in the Upper Fourth under Mr. McDowall – and were then given a half holiday, which I spent with a few more, wallowing in the snow.[3]

It was essential to establish an academic reputation for the fledgling school and this was perhaps Arthur Faber's greatest achievement. His 'thorough and ruthless' approach to teaching spread beyond the classroom. Requests for half-holidays to play matches had to be presented by the senior prefect in impeccable Latin. An Old Malvernian wrote in 1910:

> It fell to my lot to have to elaborate many such letters, and a difficult job it was to express in decent Latin such terms as football, fives, cricket, and so on. On one occasion I made a false concord and the half was refused, to my extreme confusion and the wrath of the school.

Although a strict disciplinarian, most notably on punctuality and handing in work on time, Faber disliked caning and insisted it was kept to a minimum. A diary extract from 1868 recorded his instruction 'that no caning should be inflicted before a communication to himself giving the name of the boy and the nature of the offence. The punishment [is] to take place across the shoulders, and without stripping of the jacket'. Given the vicious nature of corporal punishment at the time this was warmly humanitarian. Further evidence of his attitude to education could

Above: Rev Charles McDowall, founding housemaster of No. 1, 1865–74.

19

Above: School examination results, Easter 1868. Notice the description of the curriculum content.

Opposite: 'My Study' by Charles Healey (S. 1871–74).

be found in his address at the laying of the foundation stone when he declared that he wanted for his staff:

Men who would not only be masters, but who would stand in the relation to the pupils of senior friend and junior friend. There must be mutual confidence between all parties. There must be that *entente cordiale* without which no infant school could grow out of its swaddling clothes.[4]

Clearly Faber was an outstanding schoolmaster. 'His portrait shows a firm but humorous character, a sensitive and generous mouth, eyes with a sense of fun; one feels that he must have understood the young, and indeed he was "just the subject to arouse hero-worship in boys"'.[5] One of the first boys in the school wrote movingly about his:

dear old master Mr Faber. I have loved and revered him ever since. His learning, high positions, discipline, were all subordinated by his intense kind-heartedness. Boy-like, I am afraid I did not avail myself of his scholarly teaching, but I know any good honest traits I have were implanted or cultivated by his precepts and example.[6]

In the early years the school day began at 7 a.m. with an hour's work before breakfast, although in the winter only the headmaster's forms had to conform to this routine. Towards the end of his time as headmaster Faber modified this requirement during the depths of winter.[7] Breakfast was a hearty affair and house butlers would cook any food bought by the boys.

The north big schoolroom was not used for anything except to assemble in for chapel, and the south big schoolroom was the chapel. Every morning and twice on Sunday, we all fell in in twos down the big schoolroom, the masters came up the stairs from their Common Room and Mr Faber came from his private room, the second door from the stairs in the corridor, and gave the word to start. We marched down the corridor and the masters fell in at the tail of the procession. For a long time a boy called Surtees and myself were the first two boys. The order was quite accidental and depended on our various seats in chapel. Well we were both mischievous young monkeys, and our delight was to pretend the chapel door wouldn't open; when the pressure from the column became too strong, we suddenly opened the door, and about twenty small boys would fall head over heels in a heap, certainly not a dignified way of entering the house of prayer. Like all pleasurable sins this was found out, and poor Dr Wachter, the French master, was posted in the chapel to report any misdemeanours.[8]

Morning school continued to noon, with a break that saw most boys heading to 'Buggy's Bower' – a sweet shop at the rear of the still primitive pavilion. Between noon and 1 p.m. there was an hour of games, followed by lunch – which was washed down with plenty of beer. Afternoon school was from 3 to 5.30 p.m., tea was at 6 p.m., academic preparation was from 7 to 8 p.m., and then supper at 8.30 p.m. The day concluded with evening prayers. A young Old Malvernian (OM) from the 1870s recorded in his diary: 'Boys were always expected to say their prayers night and morning and I believe everyone did, and anyone neglecting to do this was jumped on by the others.'

On one of the two half-holidays there was 'impot. School' – punishments, in which passages had to be copied out in fair hand. Imposition paper had to be bought from the College porter at a penny a sheet.

The school grew rapidly, from sixty-four boys in 1866 to 190 by 1870. However, there is some evidence that in these early years life among the boys was unruly and bullying was common. In the first year of the school the younger boys in No. 1 were subject to the vicious attention of two older boys. One of the victims arrived home so ill from this torture that his parents protested and the bully was expelled. Faber had initially resisted the Arnoldian prefect system, but such incidents clearly influenced his decision to introduce the reformed system in 1868, although its impact took time to emerge.[9] The new school magazine, *The Malvernian,* declared in 1869, 'The great want of that time (a want which, we are afraid, *is scarcely even now fully supplied*) was a unanimous coalition of the seniors of the school on the side of order and authority'.

In the following years the classic features of the Victorian public school became established: a code of rules enforced by the prefects, fagging, a clear hierarchy between seniors and junior boys. By 1879 a rather perverse measurement of progress was evident when the School House custom, for new boys having to bend over with bare behinds to be shot at with catapults loaded with marbles, was reported not to be part of systematic bullying, but a one-off initiation ceremony, after which a boy was entitled to carve his name on the woodwork in the corridor.[10]

The Malvernian, issued three times a term, contained poems and essays and editorial comments that occasionally touched on national and international affairs. Domestically the tendency was against the Liberals, a theme reinforced by the voting on political motions in the Debating Society – a particular

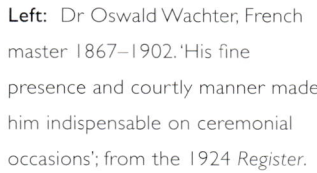

Left: Dr Oswald Wachter, French master 1867–1902. 'His fine presence and courtly manner made him indispensable on ceremonial occasions'; from the 1924 *Register*.

Below: Rev Arthur Faber as 'the early bird', 1876. Under Faber the school day began at 7.00 a.m. with an hour's work before breakfast.

MALVERN COLLEGE

enthusiasm of Faber. Hence Disraeli's government of 1876 was thought to deserve the nation's confidence, unlike Gladstone's in 1881. It opposed the extension of the male franchise in 1875 and votes for women in 1877. It also favoured the continuance of flogging in the Army in 1879, but more liberal attitudes could be found in its support for the abolition of the purchase of commissions in the Army in 1873 and in support for the government's non-intervention in the Franco-Prussian War, and for submitting the *Alabama* dispute[11] to arbitration rather than risking war. However, the dominating theme in *The Malvernian* was games, although there was the odd non-athletic intervention in the correspondence section, for instance on the degree of ritualism in Chapel, focusing on whether the chaplain should wear surplices, widely seen at the time as dangerously Catholic.

Games was to dominate not just the minds of generations of boys but was a matter of primary importance to the men who forged the new school. At its opening there were no facilities, 'only a broad sweep of turf tilted uniformly in one direction, with a slope of 1 in 15, and worse than all, no money to do anything with'.[12] This slope of the playing fields made the playing of sports like cricket very difficult. The Rev Henry Foster – 'the moving spirit behind games at Malvern between 1867 [and] 1915'[13] – complained that the purchaser of the site, Dr Stummes, 'knew probably little of cricket or other school games, nor does their importance seem to have had due weight with

Above: *Reminiscence* by Charles Healey (5. 1871–74), Head of House and School Prefect. He studied chemistry at the Royal School Weihenstephan, Bavaria.
Left: Nineteenth-century watercolour of Malvern College.

Opposite: A print of Big School by E. Burrow, published by W. H. Beynon & Co, Cheltenham in 1900. (Brian Iles Collection)

Above: No. 1 near the top of the Beacon, 1890. G. H. Simpson-Hayward (1. 1889–94) stands halfway up the tree.

those who first combined to create and launch into the world this School of ours'. Faber, a very good cricketer, met with the games masters and the cricket XI and passed a resolution 'to the effect that a level pitch was necessary to the due development of cricket'. In 1872 the Senior Turf was levelled at a cost of £1,200 met by debentures taken out by masters and their friends. The school now could offer respectable hospitality to Repton and Shrewsbury with whom matches had begun in 1871. The earliest football at Malvern was the Winchester variety but this form of football did not take root and was replaced in 1873 with association football. Rugby football had not yet made an appearance, given its association with Evangelical Rugby, which was anathema to the High Church traditions of the dominant Wykehamists on the staff.[14]

In the spirit of Victorian philanthropy the school supported a foreign mission.[15] But in 1882 it adopted the Parish of All Saints, Haggerston, in the East End of London, and contributed £80 a year to assist in the provision of a parish nurse. This started a tradition of service to the community that was to see the birth of the famous Docklands scheme and which has been, in varying forms, a constant theme in the history of the school.

The original two boarding houses, numbers 1 and 2, were quickly supplemented; No. 3 was opened in 1867 and No. 4 in 1868.[16] No. 5 (currently No. 6) was opened in 1871 under the extraordinary Rev Henry Foster. An unusual feature of his housemastership was the arrival of some Thai boys; as they could not go home during the shorter holidays Foster invited them to stay with his family. This connection brought a number of Thai students to No. 5 in succeeding generations.[17] He and his seven sons were superb rackets players and the school Rackets Courts

COLLEGE PORTERS

1869–1905	Frederick Prosser
1905–22	F. (Charlie) Smith
1922–49	J. H. Gunster
1949–72	Bob Drew
1972–85	Wilf Hoskins (a CCF instructor from 1960)
1985–2002	Ernie Whyman
2002–	Alan Wanklin

A job of great responsibility, the head porter must be approachable by pupils and teaching staff, as well as overseeing the efficient management of the daily life of the school. The first known porter was Fred Prosser (according to some reports the first school porter, from 1866 to 1869, was named Radford, but unfortunately there are no details about him). Prosser had narrowly missed winning an appointment as public hangman, a fact much enjoyed by early Malvernians; he was in office until 1905, being succeeded by Charlie Smith, who was described as 'a great character'. Gunster followed, a man of dignity and humour, and it was under his guidance that Bob Drew learnt his trade. Taking over in 1949 Drew conducted his task with genial benevolence and served the College for fifty-seven years. Wilf Hoskins succeeded him in 1972, and his guided tours for parents became legendary. In response to an enquiry from an anxious mother as to whether there was still corporal punishment at Malvern, his reply was 'Oh no Ma'am we used to have corporal punishment, but there is a new headmaster and we now use psychological methods'. Recent generations of Malvernians will be familiar with 'Ernies', early morning tasks given as behavioural sanctions supervised by the porter, which acquired their nomenclature during the tenure of Ernie Whyman. His successor has kept up this noble tradition with high competence, earthy wisdom and much humour.

Bob Drew

Wilf Hoskins

Ernie Whyman

Alan Wanklin

Left: Cricket XI, 1868. The white caps were worn by new members of the XI.

Below: Drawings of house and school colours by R. N. Redmayne (SH 1874–78).

were constructed next to his House in 1881. Foster also organised the construction of the swimming baths in 1892, and at the instigation of the boys, he founded the Artillery Cadet Corps, and was originally in charge of music. School House, still the property of Earl Beauchamp, had a chequered history but remained under headmagisterial control until the Second World War. Further houses were added periodically as numbers grew: No. 6 (now No. 5) in 1891, No. 7 in 1892, No. 8 in 1895 and No. 9 in 1898.

In 1877 the College Council adopted a coat of arms designed by Sir Edmund Lechmere that was later accepted by the College of Heralds in 1926. Arthur Faber chose the school motto – *Sapiens qui prospicit* – before the College opened; it is said to have been invented by Dr Sewell, the Warden of New College, Oxford, who offered it as a jest to Faber soon after his appointment.[18]

The finances of the school continued to be troublesome. The College owed annual rent of 6 per cent of the value of the property owned by the Building Company. With a full school this would be easily managed, but the numbers continued to be way below that desirable goal. Unlike Cheltenham or Clifton the school could not recruit many day boys given the small size of the town. Thus the young school was burdened with heavy debts and only survived through the generosity of the individuals of the Building Company. However, numbers grew and by 1873 the College for the first time showed an excess of income over expenditure; in 1876 it decided to raise money to buy up all the assets of the Building Company (which would now cease to exist) – the five houses, 25 acres of land, and the Fives Court built in 1867.[19]

In 1880 Faber retired and became rector of Sprotborough in Doncaster and later a canon of York Minster. His impact had been enormous. The young school 'had grown and prospered, numerous University distinctions were gained, the numbers rose to just under 300'.[20] In 1915 Charles Toppin wrote, 'his character dominated his surroundings to such an extent that the School was colloquially known as "Faber's School".' His contribution was recognised by electing him to the College Council and founding an Exhibition in his name; later generations commemorated him with the Faber Gate (1915) and a window in Chapel (1921).[21]

MALVERN COLLEGE

Opposite: A tribute to Rev Charles Cruttwell from his Sixth Form, 1885.
Opposite far right: A cartoon of Rev Charles Cruttwell, Headmaster 1880–85.

Above: Rev Francis Drew, founding housemaster of No. 2, 1865–81.

Below left: No. 4 showing house-colour jerseys and socks in 1874. Heath Harrison (4. 1868–76) – future benefactor and founder of a closed Exhibition at Brasenose College, Oxford – is seated front right.
Below right: No. 4, head prefect's study. (Brian Iles Collection)

COAT OF ARMS

The arms are blazoned: 'Or within two Chevronels Gules between three Fountains five Torteaux'; and the crest: 'On a Wreath of the Colours a Gryphon seiant supporting with the fore feet a Weather Vane both Stable'.

The three fountains represent the three chief wells of Malvern,[i] and may symbolise the three founts of learning, Classics, mathematics, and natural science. The five torteaux were no doubt taken from the arms of the See of Worcester in which there are ten. (They are sometimes said to represent the wafers at the Host, though their actual origin appears to be uncertain.)

The College Council selected Rev Charles Cruttwell, Fellow and former Tutor of Merton College, and a former Headmaster of Bradfield College, as Faber's successor. A scholar (he had written a history of Roman literature) and athlete, he seemed ideal but despite his many personal qualities his period in office saw a sharp decline in numbers and is generally acknowledged to be an unhappy interlude in the school's history. Clashes of personality led to a popular housemaster decamping to another school, taking a number of boys with him and ushering in a period of uncertainty. The housemaster concerned, Drew, had run No. 2 since the beginning of the school; he had been devoted to Faber and clearly did not like Cruttwell. In June 1881 the Headmaster found it necessary to report several incidents of 'insubordination' to the Council.[22] Trouble continued and Drew was threatened with dismissal. Using his great popularity he enlisted the help of parents who pressed his case with the Council, and when he was dismissed there was a deputation in his favour led by the Mayor of Exeter. The Council, significantly supported by all the other assistant masters, backed its Headmaster and there followed an exodus of some twenty-eight boys from No. 2.[23]

The consequences for the school could be seen when Cruttwell had to report a large deficit in 1881. Debenture holders had to forego interest for two years and Cruttwell had to dip into his own resources to support a master's salary. Scholarships were reduced both in number and value. By 1885 the numbers in the school fell below 200 and housemasters sought a remission of their rent; one became so financially embarrassed that he resigned his House in 1887.

Cruttwell resigned in 1885 following his marriage and appointment to a living in Sutton, Surrey. He saw six of his Classical Sixth achieve awards to Oxford and Cambridge in his last year and the *Malvern Register* records that 'under him the Sixth Form flourished exceedingly, and Malvernians of his generation are loud in their praise of his work as a teacher'.[24] However, he had not been successful as a headmaster.[25] Toppin declared that he 'was too much the scholar and too little the man of the world'. Perhaps, but what was certain was that the school was now in severe difficulties and the Council would have to find a man of exceptional abilities to turn matters around.

Fortunately for the school the Council found their man in the Rev William Grundy, Fellow of Worcester College, Oxford,

THE MALVERN CARMEN

The first Latin verse is commonly the only one sung. The English translation of all the verses follows for entertainment value.

> Exultemus, O sodales,
> Iam cessare fas novales,
> Paululum laxemus mentes,
> Dulcem domum repetentes,
>   Age, soror iuxta fratrem,
>   Celebremus Almam Matrem;
>   Quae nos ornat, haec ornanda,
>   Quae nos amat, adamanda.

Generations of Malvernians have cherished this song but few renderings could better this charming story from Andrew Lowcock:

> Not long before I went on the Bench, I was prosecuting a trial in Preston Crown Court. Defence counsel was Nick Kennedy (8. 1968–72) and the case was being tried by His Honour Judge Ronnie Livesey QC (8. 1949–54). Just before Ronnie came into court Nick and I gave an impromptu performance of the first verse of the *Carmen Malvernense*, to the astonishment of the court.

The *Carmen* in English

Ho! Comrades, hearts and voices raise,
To welcome summer holidays;
Away with books, tear up the 'scheme';
No thoughts of these to spoil our dream!
    Come, Alma Mater, let us sing
    Till overhead the rafters ring
    With her — 'tis hers — our glory sharing
    With answering love our love declaring.*

Of Thames let Eton boast her fill,
And Harrow glory in her hill;
But Malvern's mountains reach the sky,
And bounteous health her streams supply.

Whether we roam the smiling plain,
Or toil those storied heights to gain,
What fairer scene shall any find
To breed both healthy frame and mind?

Thus strengthened by our Mother's might,
Both Past and Present now unite
With loyal hearts, a vigorous band,
To spread her fame in every land.

Thorough in work and keen in games,
Nor neglecting virtue's claims,
If aught of good we here have won,
Hers be the praise and hers alone!
    Hurrah! Hurrah!
Elevens both, a cheer for you,
And for our gallant marksmen, too,
And you who guard with skill and zeal
At Prince's Court the common weal!
    Hurrah! Hurrah!
Our Gymnasts cheer; cheer them whose fame
Is to have won a scholar's name;
A cheer for all whose feats renowned
Their own and Malvern's praise resound!
    Hurrah! Hurrah!
A health to all, — the Guiding hand
And each one of the gowne'd band;
To Old Boys' cherished memory,
To all Malvernians yet to be.

*The first two lines of the chorus in Latin used to be:
    Age, fratres, (sic eamus),
    Almam Matrem canamus.

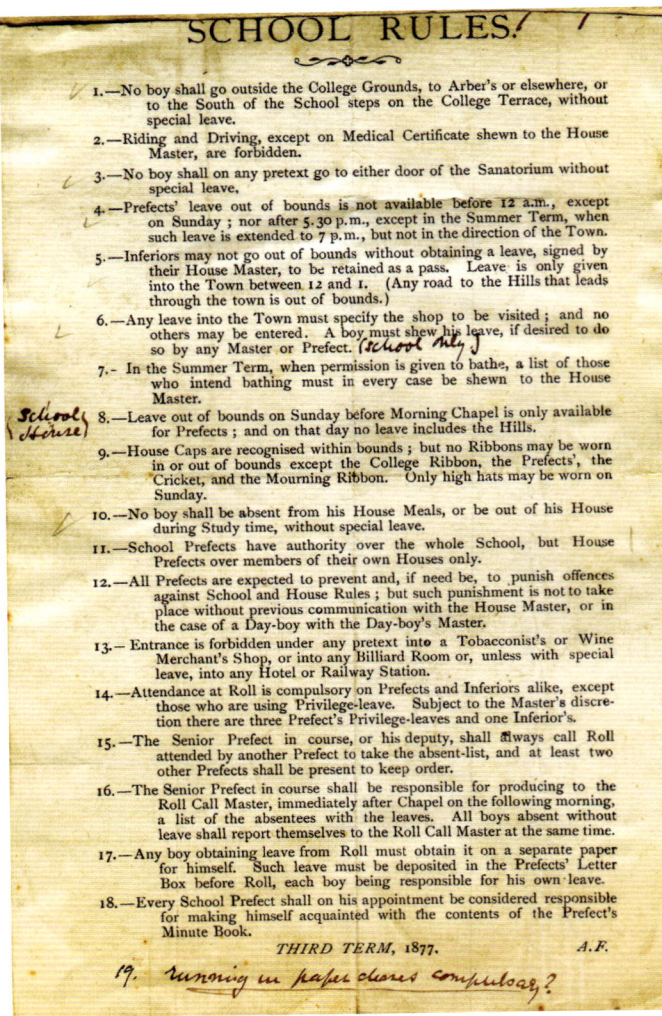

Above: School rules, 1877.

Below: No. 3 dining room (Brian Iles Collection)

a master at Rossall, and from 1880 Headmaster of Warwick School, where he had raised the numbers from eight to 124. He was a fine scholar, publishing a book of Aristotelianism in 1889, and also a superb athlete – 'as a Fives player he had few equals in England'.[26] 'An awe-inspiring disciplinarian', he made frequent use of the cane. One OM recalled the expulsion of two boys who had been seen by a master late at night in the town:

Next morning the whole School was called to Big School. Grundy and the staff, in cap and gown, came on to the platform, and the two boys were brought in, in the charge of the Corps Sergeant and stood before them. Grundy then addressed us. I forget what he said, but I knew that the crime reeked to heaven. (They had been playing billiards, in fact) And lastly … he said. "Phmm! We – do –not – want – you – amongst – us. You – can – go". (All that should be in capital letters). And down the centre alleyway they went – sort of running the gauntlet without violence. It was all very frightening to a thirteen-year-old boy, and I suppose was meant to be.[27]

Numbers, at 188, reached their nadir in 1887 and debenture holders had to be persuaded to waive interest for another ten years. There followed years of dramatic improvement – 244 in 1889, and by 1891, 323. The explanation for this improvement seems to lie with a series of measures undertaken by Grundy. In 1888 he introduced an army class shortly to be entrusted to an OM, E. C. Bullock. In the words of Blumenau, Bullock 'was an inspired and very popular teacher', who was to teach the army side 'brilliantly for forty-three years'. As early as 1892 Malvern was near the top of the list for successes in the Army examinations. In 1890 a class was started which taught book-keeping and commerce – a clear bid for the commercial and business classes so dominant in the neighbouring towns. New younger teachers were appointed: H. W. Smith, Charles Toppin, R. E. Lyon (OM), H. H. House and L. S. Milward who were to serve Malvern for many years and become characters whom generations remembered with affection. Only two of Grundy's sixteen appointments were clergymen.[28]

The school was now acquiring a clear identity and for the first time attracted distinguished visitors. Lord Randolph Churchill came to Speech Day in 1889, and the first royal visitors, the Duke and Duchess of Teck and Princess May (later Queen Mary), in 1891. The school also ditched the Winchester *Domum* for its own *Carmen*, first sung on Speech Day in 1888.[29] The academic standard of the school was not very high until Grundy's last year, and *The Malvernian* was given over almost completely to aspects of the games cult so dominant in later Victorian schools. Indeed cricket did thrive under the expert tutelage of Toppin and in 1891 the school won against Repton for the first time in thirteen years. P. H. Latham became the first cricket Blue and captained Cambridge, and in 1890 seventeen-year-old H. K. Foster played for Worcestershire against the Free Foresters, scoring 179.

In Grundy's last years as headmaster there was a restoration of intellectual interests with a new Literary Society and a revived Debating Society. There was also a sudden increase in university awards – in 1891

Left: Masters versus the school 1891, showing P. H. Latham (second left, middle row) and H. K. Foster (far left, back row).

eight were won, putting Malvern in the top nine schools in England. Dramatically the news of these awards reached Grundy on his deathbed. On 1 December he was seized by paralysis whilst playing rackets and died four days later. All the boys had to file past his corpse.

The school had emerged as a more secure, confident and successful place and Grundy was to be honoured by the raising of a memorial subscription for the school library that to this day bears his name.

Above: Rev William Grundy, Headmaster 1885–92.

Left: The Grundy Library. After the death of Grundy in 1891 a subscription list made it possible to open the first school library, which was given his name. A termly subscription of 1 shilling was made on the bill. Following the fire in this room in 1956, the Grundy was moved to its present site and this room now makes up the Economics, Politics and Business Studies area. The picture is from an etching by E. J. Burrow.

Christian gentlemen and the playing fields of Malvern, 1892–1914

Grundy's successor was the Rev Arthur Gray, former Headmaster of The King's School, Parramatta, Australia between 1886 and 1888.[1] His wife's illness forced a return to England where he taught at Clifton, his old school. Described as having something of 'the missionary about him',[2] his term as headmaster saw a continued advance by the school. A large number of university awards were achieved.[3] The Debating Society regularly attracted attendances of about a hundred and records show it refused confidence to Lord Roseberry's Liberal government and approved of the Jameson Raid.[4] This was the time of jingoism and patriotic compositions by R. E. Lyon were 'cheered lustily' at school concerts. It was a golden era for Malvern sport with cricket and rackets flourishing. In June 1897 a contingent of the Cadet Corps went to Windsor as part of the Public School Volunteers to be reviewed by Queen Victoria on the occasion of her Diamond Jubilee. However, not all was well. Despite the rise in school numbers the school suffered a series of blows with two outbreaks of diphtheria – in 1893 and 1894 – clearly linked to poor drainage in the school. Two boys died and in addition to the fear and sadness generated by the outbreak the school had to carry out expensive rebuilding of the drainage system.

Additions to the school came with the construction of the Cricket Pavilion, a new Grub Shop – both financed by the profits from the shop – and a new sanatorium. At his own expense Gray built a chemical laboratory in the same block.[5] But the greatest project for Gray was the building of a new chapel to replace the inadequate facilities in the south wing of the Main Building. In his Commemoration Speech in 1894 Gray appealed to the Malvern community 'to give us a Chapel'.[6] A chapel fund appeal was launched in 1895 with Gray personally donating £500; by 1896 the fund stood at over £6,000, and in June that year a summer bazaar was held to raise funds.

For three days the College was given over to entertaining visitors. The programme laid on by the school included a performance on the Terrace of *A Midsummer Night's Dream*; the story of *Oresteia* displayed in living tableau by the Classical Department; and a display of 'Living Waxworks' by the less classically minded. There was an Assault at Arms (a gymnastic

Opposite: The Cricket Pavilion in 1895 from a photograph captioned 'Waiting for the roller to come off?' The Pavilion block, built in 1877, has seen more changes than any other building in the grounds. It was originally constructed to include the gymnasium, workshops, laboratory, Fives courts and Grub Shop. The Grub was situated round the right hand corner and was only replaced in 1927.

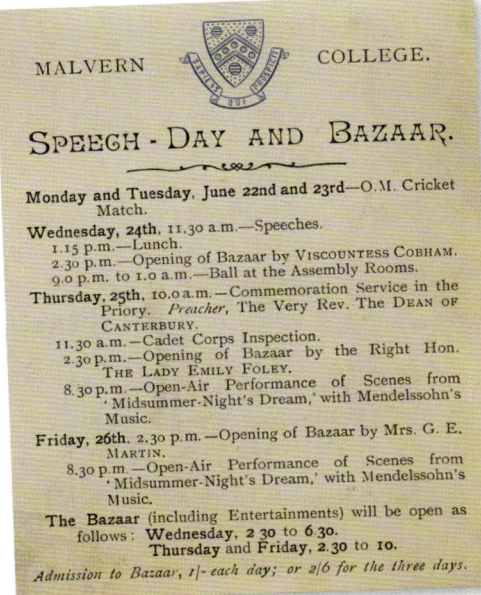

Right: Speech Day and bazaar, 1896. In the College's early years Speech Day was linked to the Commemoration of the founders of the College and became the major celebratory event in the academic year. Commem is now held at the end of the first half of the summer term and includes a service in Malvern Priory, exhibitions and performances illustrating the success of the pupils, speeches and prize-giving followed by lunch in the houses for parents and pupils.

performance), and a Café Chantant in which masters, boys, friends of the school provided music, 'although the necessary flow of conversation tended at times to spoil the enjoyment of the music-lovers'. The Art master, Mr Ehrke, who had exhibited at the Royal Academy, arranged an Art exhibition in which his own pictures were duly hung. Earl Beauchamp lent a collection of snuffboxes, and Mr Dyson Perrins a collection of curious watches. There were lectures on the 'New photography' [meaning x-rays] by the Science Master, Mr Berridge, at the end of whose lectures many visitors took a gruesome pleasure in laying bare their bones to the gaze of others'. A phonograph enabled visitors to gain amusement 'in listening to Gladstone's speech, in Edison's wonderful invention, and also in hearing the principal comic songs of the day'.[7]

Above: School prefects, 1897.
Below: Plans for the Cricket Pavilion.

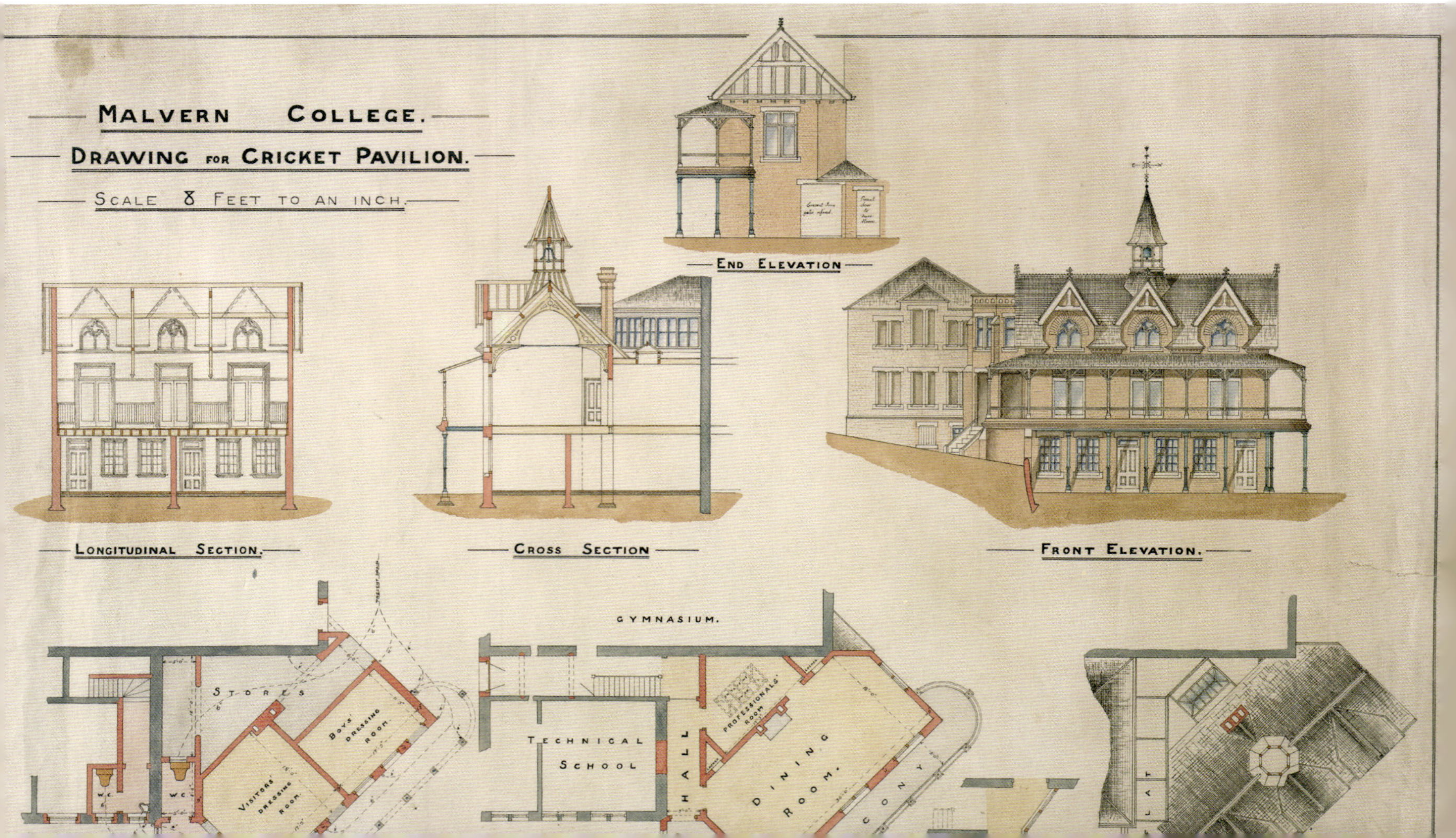

The bazaar made a profit of £1,500 and half the estimated cost of the Chapel had now been raised. Before his retirement Gray had the pleasure of seeing the plans of Sir Arthur Blomfield for a handsome Chapel to seat 650 commence. Gray also encouraged the development of a new

mission in Canning Town and, of huge importance to the school, he supported the formation in 1894 of the Old Malvernian Society.[8]

Gray resigned because of ill health in 1897. Blumenau credits him with representing much of the spirit of the late Victorian age with its 'courage, enterprise, and high moral purpose'. There is much evidence that Malvern had now acquired a unique spirit, which has endured, that Gray attributed to 'the wonderful and remarkable relationship that he had found at Malvern between masters and boys.' Indeed there seems to have been very little of the popular image of stern and remote Victorian schoolmasters. The gaiety of the bazaar scheme could never have been produced by a school whose masters were severe pedagogues. In the phenomenal winter of 1895 the younger masters could be seen tobogganing together with the boys on the glorious long run from the College building down to the railway line. There is also a warmth in the references to many of the masters both in *The Malvernian* and in the memories of OMs. One of them wrote

Above left: Junior boys in No. 5 c. 1880s/90s outside the then No. 5, which became No. 6 in 1908.
Above right: SH football XI, 1892 (Courtesy of the Hopkinson family)

Left: A parade of the Cadet Corps in the 1890s. The 9-pounder muzzle-loading guns, dating from the Crimean War, were housed in the Gun Shed (later the Caving Store, now the Porter's office) near the Chapel. The horses that pulled the guns in this period were loaned by Mr Jones, a local coal merchant. On one famous occasion when a number of cadet forces paraded in Marlborough High Street, with Malvern as the only artillery unit, it began to rain heavily. Mr Jones insisted that his horses should be covered. Much to Malvern's chagrin, the covers proclaimed in large white letters: 'JONES BROS, COAL MERCHANT'.

Above: R. B. (Judy) Porch (SH 1888–94) and J. G. Hopkinson (SH 1890–93) in 1890. J. G. Hopkinson was killed in action at Hooge on 15 September 1915. (Courtesy of the Hopkinson family)

of his shock when, in his last year at school, he was caned *for the first time*; and this incident reinforces a feeling that the discipline of the school was not based on fear. However, when beatings did take place they were often surrounded by awesome ceremony. One OM of Gray's time wrote, 'I suppose I am one of the few remaining people today who saw the last of the "Public Lickings". These were held in Big School, with the whole school present; and we stood upon painted straight lines, which kept order. The College Porter stood by the Headmaster, with the canes.'

But on the whole discipline was kindly. When a Latin master wrote on the blackboard for translation, 'Shall I stay here, or go to Philippi?' a small boy could sing out, 'For God's sake, Sir, go to Philippi!' without fear of terrible chastisement. When an influenza epidemic struck down a whole form except for one boy, the form master and his sole pupil agreed that this was no time for work and they played chess instead. A charming custom evolved in these years, which captures something of the friendliness and tranquillity of the late Victorian age. On Sunday evenings in the summer, after Chapel, while the masters strolled up and down the centre of the Senior Turf, the boys walked round and round the periphery, always one way, talking and perhaps watching the shadow of the hills lengthening over the Severn valley as the sun went down. Until James's day it was voluntary; tradition suggested that it originated to firm the turf after the original levelling of the Senior. Whatever its origins, in the reminiscences of OMs of the 1890s it simply figures as a pleasant, relaxed and sociable occasion.[9]

The new Headmaster, Sydney Rhodes James, had been a scholar at Trinity, Cambridge, captain of the Cambridge XV, assistant master and housemaster at Eton.[10] He was a larger than life character:

> thoroughly extrovert and uninhibited, quick-tempered but good hearted, with a vocabulary that amused those boys that were used to it and scarified those who were not. 'You scrubby dog; you mouldy toad; you scruffy fellow' were some of his favourite phrases.[11]

Another OM described him 'as a very virile clergyman who wore a white bowtie, and had a rather nasal twang. He was abrupt and rather slangy of approach. It was said that on one occasion a small boy ran into him in the school corridor. To the embarrassed boy James said "What's your beastly name?" To which the truthful boy had to reply, "James, please Sir."'[12]

Below: Gun squad, 1895.

Although one OM described him as unimaginative and he was said to have 'reduced poetry to prose, and Homer to a page of Bradshaw', he was an enthusiast and a passionate sportsman, regularly shooting, and playing golf at least four times a week. Certainly it was during his tenure that Malvern had its first golden age of sport. This was the era of Fostershire with all the brothers playing for the county. Malvern cricket even inspired a schoolboy story from P. G. Wodehouse, *Mike at Wrykyn*,[13] with a description that has a pleasing familiarity:

The Wrykyn playing field were formed of a series of huge steps, cut out of the hill. At the top of the hill came the school. On the first terrace was a sort of informal practice ground where, though no games were played on it, there was a good deal of punting and drop-kicking in the winter and fielding practice in the summer. The next terrace was the biggest of all and formed the first eleven cricket ground, a beautiful piece of turf, a shade too narrow for its length, bounded on the terrace side by a sharply sloping bank, some fifteen feet deep and on the other side by the precipice leading to the next terrace. At the far end of the ground stood the pavilion, and besides it is a little ivy-covered rabbit hutch for the scorers. Old Wrykynians always claimed it was the prettiest school ground in England. It certainly has the finest view. From the veranda of the pavilion you could look over three counties.

Rackets, football and golf also flourished. R. E. Foster captained England in both cricket and football and in 1905 both varsity sides were captained by OMs with five others playing in the match. Malvern produced its first Olympic gold medallist with A. N. S. Jackson's success in the 1500 metres at Stockholm in 1912. Rugby was introduced in the Easter term 1910. It was in this era that public school games became something of an obsession with both boys and masters. An OM master could remember one housemaster:

> striding up and down the touchline shouting, 'Sausages for tea, boys! Sausages for tea!' I believe he really thought it spurred his team to greater endeavour. But if your House won the Final, your Housemaster had to provide not merely sausages, but a slap-up House supper, turkey or fowl of some sort, ham, tongue and all the rest.[14]

Above: Reverend Canon Sydney James, Headmaster 1897–1914.

Below: Some notices from the Headmaster S. R. James to the school in 1900.

The extreme nature of this cult was further illustrated when School House (SH) won a House final against a favoured opponent. The Headmaster, James, enquired through the agency of a small SH boy whether he could purchase the lavish supper already prepared for the now-defeated House, to honour his conquering heroes. The boy delivered the message to the housemaster, 'Mr X':

> Mr. X flushed, got up, and said, 'did the damned fellow send me a message like that?' A pause, and then, 'Well come with me and then go back and tell him what you have seen'.
>
> Off they went through the House to a door at the back leading into the garden, where a good deal of movement was going on. Remember the match had been over a bare hour. Across one end of the garden, the gardener had been told to dig a trench, and white-aproned maids and servants were busily depositing in it the viands which should have graced the festive board at the expected House supper![15]

Another more critical voice from an OM, who had not been happy at Malvern because 'the Philistines were in their glory', nevertheless records:

> It is indeed remarkable how, in defiance of logic and inner conviction, one was elated or depressed by the results of house, but especially school matches. In my first summer term, after a good start, the Malvern cricket eleven was skittled out by Repton in the second innings for 77 runs, and decisively beaten. That day one's heart sank almost as low as it was to sink in the hour of France's fall, or when the *Prince of Wales* and *Repulse* sailed forth with high resolve, to meet a sudden doom.

However, this same critic could still appreciate the poetry of cricket, writing of the victorious school XI of 1910:

Above left: The playing fields of Malvern.

Above right: Cricket XI, 1910.

Below: Letter from Mark Vincent (SH 1898–99) to his aunt in 1898. He died from wounds received at the battle of Loos, 1 October 1915.

and those two gallant bowlers, Scott and Burton – poor short-lived Scott, victim of that earlier war[16] … Scott of the golden hair and flashing smile, fit model for Praxiteles, charging up to the wicket with godlike strides to deliver his thunderbolt, and the gentle wily Burton, with his fascinating action and subtle variation of speed and flight … with memories of the stylish Donald Knight, and the elegance and panache of the elder Naumann, his exuberant drives past cover, and his square cuts that made the boundary rails resound.

A recent biography of C. S. Lewis describes how this games cult had:

> assumed an almost unassailable position as the centrepiece of an English public school education. Athleticism was an ideology with a darker side. Boys who were not good at games were ridiculed and bullied by their peers. Athleticism devalued intellectual and artistic achievement and turned many schools into little more than training camps for the glorification of physicality.[17]

Lewis, who was no games player, reflected in his later autobiography:

> The truth is that organised and compulsory games had in my day, banished the element of play from school life almost entirely. There was no time to play (in the proper sense of the word). The rivalry was too fierce, the prizes too glittering, the 'hell of failure' too severe.[18]

Lewis's comments found more objective support in a commentary in the *Saturday Review* in 1904, which, while strongly praising the school for its adaptability, was concerned 'that the athletic is too elaborate and almost overdone, and although the scholarship list is a very fair one, the standard of work throughout the school might possibly be somewhat higher'. James was clearly sensitive to this type of accusation, saying on Speech Day in 1912, 'It makes me angry when I hear it said that Malvern is a school where too much attention is paid to games'.

The cultural side of the school seems tame in comparison. Musical life progressed somewhat with R. E. Lyon instituting classical concerts in 1906, though the repertoire and standard does not appear to have been very high. The Debating Society returned thoroughly conservative verdicts on the great questions dominating Edwardian Britain: disapproving of the formation of the Labour party and the new Liberal government, applauding the Osborne Judgement, opposing votes for women, and the over-education of the lower classes. The revived Natural History Society flourished, not least as it provided regular expeditions into the countryside where wily boys could escape supervision and 'spend a blissful afternoon eating strawberries and cream in one of the lovely Worcestershire villages.'

Towards the end of James's term numbers declined and income fell below expenditure for the first time in a quarter of a century. James attributed this fall to 'financial schemes associated with the name of Mr Lloyd George'[19] and to the lowering of the age of entry for the Army. However, other reasons may have influenced this decline. Key retirements may have reduced the appeal of some houses.[20] There was talk of a decline in the moral atmosphere, perhaps 'the evils of a monastic institution' discussed in

Above: Masters' Common Room. (Brian Iles Collection)

THE NIGHT PROWLER

Michael Arlen's account of the Night Prowler in his book "*Piracy*"[i] begins:

> There were rumours, new rumours every morning, delightful and outrageous rumours, so that the lumps in the porridge were swallowed without comment and the fish cakes were eaten without contumely. The masters looked unusually stern, but it was the sternness of thought rather than of discipline. Coll Prees went about with smiles gravely repressed and an air of being more than usually responsible for everything...
>
> For the matter was that there was some sort of night prowler about the school grounds. It would have been almost bearable if the night prowler had prowled only about the grounds, but he prowled into the Houses, he prowled actually into the Housemasters' sides of the Houses, he prowled into their studies, he sat on their chairs, he read their books, he drank their port, he tested their barley water, he smoked their cigars, he left a little neat bit of Greek verse on their desks to thank them for the same,[ii] and then, as it were for a joke, he bolted the windows from the inside, locked the doors from the outside, and left the keys in such an obvious place that no one ever found them until new ones had been made. And this went on, once or twice a week, for more than a month!

Watch was kept in the College grounds by the prefects and the police, and eventually the culprit was spotted:

> Two Coll Prees and Mr Sandys,[iii] of the Lower Fifth and the Hampshire Eleven were patrolling the borders of the Senior Turf, about which lie the main houses of Manton in the form of a horseshoe. Suddenly, just ahead of them, was seen a moving dark thing. They leapt. It ran. They chased, but the dark thing hurled down the slope from the path to the flat darkness of the Senior Turf. 'He's got running shorts', grumbled Mr Sandys, who was in a dinner jacket. 'And gym-shoes' ... Then came a laugh behind them, and again they leapt. But the dark thing grew darker and disappeared ...

Ralph Blumenau comments on Arlen's description:

> What really happened was even more amusing. The boy almost stepped into the arms of the detective, who was standing by the Armoury; but he slipped past him and ran into the darkness and along the Senior bank up to halfway, the detective after him. Having a good lead, he then turned left, straight down the bank, and made for the centre of the Senior, where in those days, because horses often got into the grounds at night, the match wickets square was surrounded by barbed wire. He reckoned that, even if his pursuer had seen him turn down the bank, the barbed wire would give him a good start if he had to go on to the Junior. Once there, he lay down flat and waited, but the detective had lost him from the start. I like the idea of the centre of the Senior Turf being the best hiding place for a fugitive.

The prowler was eventually caught. A search in the houses led to the discovery of a torch, jemmy, and a photograph of the boy in burglar's costume in his locker.

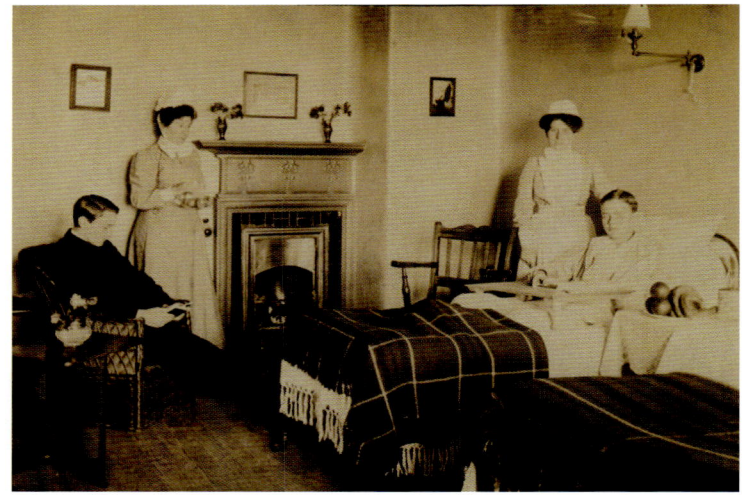

Above left: Prefects' room. (Brian Iles Collection)

Above right: The sanatorium. (Brian Iles Collection)

Below: Malvern: 'He is wise who sees ahead'. A cartoon representing the College motto *Sapiens qui prospicit*, from *The Crown*, 1908.

C. S. Lewis's thinly disguised Wyvern in *Surprised by Joy* in which relationships between boys seemed to have acquired a more sinister and much less healthy aspect. Entries in School Prefects' minutes books from 1910 to 1913 have many references to what was considered immorality, such as swearing, smoking, lewd talk, 'disgusting behaviour' and even the great sin of 'meeting and talking to girls on Sundays' for which offence two House Prefects were downgraded. The Head of School remarked that 'during the holidays he had heard of people who had refused to send their sons to Malvern because of the bad language and filthy talk which went on there'. Attempts were made to tackle these issues:

> Powell, Berry and Lea-Smith were licked for having on the previous night talked disgustingly in Powell's study.
> Burton received 4 cuts for using 'water closet' language.[21]

Expulsions were common although some miscreants survived, such as the Irish earl who sent a donkey up the aisle of the Chapel during the service and who was in the habit of carrying a revolver, 'loading one chamber only, rushing into your study, and then firing off all the others at you, so that your life depended on his counting accurately'. One who was expelled was the mysterious and successful night prowler, immortalised by the OM novelist Michael Arlen.[22]

James was a strict disciplinarian but it is notable that he felt it necessary to control the use of caning by prefects. In a letter of 1907 he wrote:

> No prefect in any circumstances has the right to cane a boy without letting you or me know that he proposed to do so. No prefect may cane a boy privately, i.e. without it being done in the prefects' room and with the consent of the Head of House. No prefect has the right to cane a boy even if leave has been obtained from you or me, if the boy chooses to appeal to me. That right of appeal must not be forgotten. In dealing with the use of the cane we must be very careful, or weak or irresponsible prefects will turn into bullies.[23]

This was clearly effective: one OM[24] recalls that he dreaded coming to Malvern having been told to expect many beatings, but 'that prophecy was completely falsified in reality as, being a more or less peaceful personality, I was never beaten by anyone during my whole time. Of course, there was beating both by masters and prefects but it could easily be escaped if you happened to be a normal citizen of the school'.

Left: Malvern's victorious tent-pitching squad, Farnborough 1910. Olympic Gold medallist A. N. S. Jackson (SH 1905–10) seated on right.

The Boer War furthered the process of Britain ending its policy of 'splendid isolation', and as the new century dawned she began the fateful engagement with the tensions that were going to lead to the First World War. Military matters grew steadily in importance and the public schools reflected this trend with, in Malvern's case, 'ceaseless encouragement' from James for the military corps.

James had intended to retire after fifteen years but extended his tenure to see through the new constitution of the College:

> But in the autumn of 1913 I sent in my resignation, to take effect at Easter 1914. I chose Easter because I thought that my successor would find the machine running smoothly in the last term of the school year, would be able to see what changes he would like to make, and would have the long summer holidays in which to work them out.

Unfortunately in the long summer holidays the First World War broke out.

Below left: The Natural History Museum in the upper floor of the south wing of the Main Building. This room was formerly used as a sanatorium until the early 1890s, then an art school and subsequently divided between classrooms and the Upper Grundy. (Brian Iles Collection)
Below: Wills's cigarette cards c. 1906.

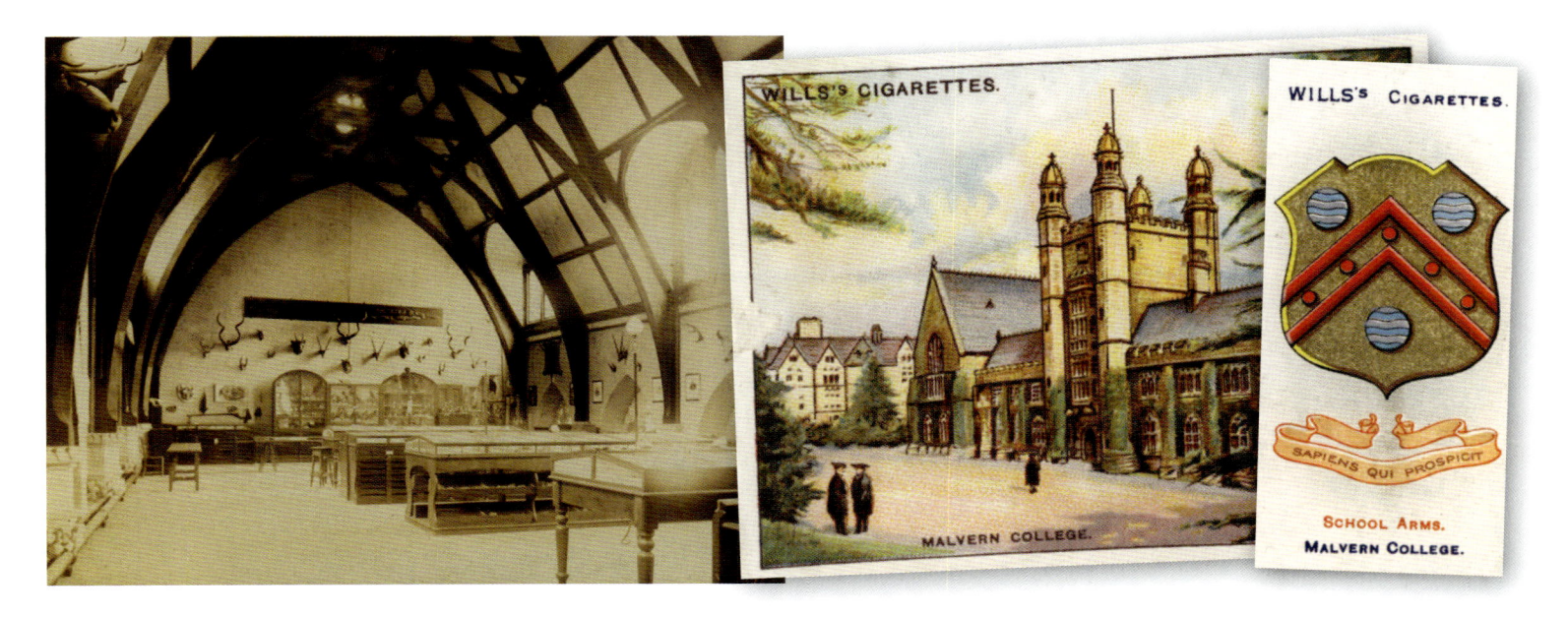

THE FOSTERS AND 'FOSTERSHIRE'

The Reverend Henry Foster and his sons, 1905.

The Rev Henry Foster was a master at Malvern from 1867 to 1915. He and his wife Sophia had seven sons, all of whom played cricket for Worcestershire, hence the nickname 'Fostershire'. The sporting tradition of the family became celebrated, and on the occasion of their diamond wedding anniversary in 1931 the King and Queen sent a telegram expressing the hope that Mr and Mrs Foster 'might long be spared to their family, whose marvellous record has long been the admiration of all lovers of games'.[i]

All seven sons were in No. 5, the Malvern cricket and soccer elevens, and in the rackets pair. The three who went to Oxford – Harry, Tip and Geoff – collected between them no fewer than eleven Blues. Five of the brothers played for the Gentlemen.[ii] The family scored a total of 42,000 runs in First-Class cricket and between them they captained Worcestershire in fourteen seasons. On the rackets court the family won ten amateur singles and twelve doubles titles.[iii] They won the Public Schools doubles titles on three occasions.

H. K. 'Harry' Foster (1873–1950; 5. 1884–92) was the first captain of Worcestershire when the county assumed First-Class status in 1899, handing over to his brother, Tip, the next year, but then in 1901 took up the reins until 1910 with one further year to come in 1913. To quote from Wisden: 'At his best he would not have been out of place in a Test match,' but he never did play for England, though he played for the Gentlemen on seven occasions. He made 29 centuries and his two highest scores were 216 against Somerset in 1903 and 125 against Warwickshire in 1904. For three years he sat on Test selection committees. The H. K. Foster cup is the most prestigious rackets event that a schoolboy can win and is played annually at Queens. He was awarded the MBE during the First World War.

W. L. 'Bill' Foster (1874–1958; 5. 1887–92), went from Malvern to Woolwich and became an officer in the Royal Field Artillery. He fought with distinction in the Boer War and won the DSO in the campaign against the 'Mad Mullah'. His duties as soldier allowed him only one full season with Worcestershire – their first as a First-Class county – in 1899. He headed the batting figures with an average of 42 in that year. A rare achievement took place in the Hampshire match in 1899 when W. L. (140 and 172 not out) and his brother R. E. (134 and 101) both scored centuries in each innings.[iv]

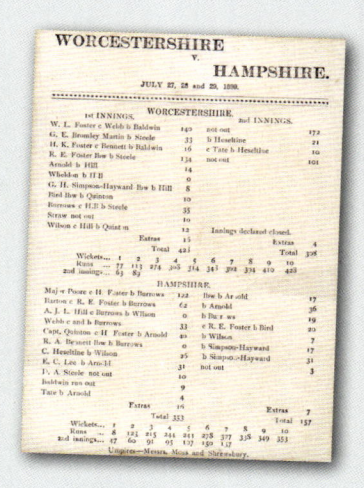

Harry K. Foster (5.1884–92) leaning out of scoreboard.

Above left: W. L. (Bill) Foster (5. 1887–92).

Above right: R. E. Foster and W. L. Foster, double century scorers in the Hampshire match, 1899.

R. E. 'Tip' Foster (1878–1914; 5. 1887–96) was the outstanding cricketer in a family of distinguished players. After 1900, when he captained the county, he played only when business commitments allowed. Despite these demands, he had the gift of taking up a bat and finding his true form at once. In his first match for Worcestershire in 1905 he scored 246 against Kent and repeated this score in August 1906 against Somerset, again without practice. His Test career is described on p.188. After his great innings in Sydney he was having a net on the Senior and the whole school, who were supposed to be in lessons, were watching from the corridors of the Main Building. A huge cheer went up when he was bowled by his sister Jessie, who was said to be a county-class bowler, having spent many hours in the nets bowling at her brothers. He excelled particularly with his driving and he was also said to be a great exponent of the late cut. He also played soccer for England. Diabetes forced him to seek a warmer climate in South Africa but that failed to provide the recovery he hoped for and he died at the age of thirty-six, just a few years before doctors began to be able to treat diabetes with insulin. An obituary described him as 'one of the finest all-around athletes the world has produced'.

Tip Foster cartoon illustrating his representation of England in both cricket and football.

B. S. 'Basil' Foster (1882–1959; 5. 1892–1900) was 'probably the least talented cricketer amongst the brothers'. He only batted eleven times for Worcestershire although he played frequently for the MCC and later transferred his allegiance to Middlesex. He developed an interest in drama following a school production of *A Midsummer's Night's Dream* and became a successful West End actor taking such lead parts as the title role in the Ian Hay and P. G. Wodehouse comedy *Leave it to Psmith*, which opened at the Shaftesbury Theatre in September 1930. In 1939 he became manager of the Richmond Theatre. He was a fine footballer, rackets and tennis player, often playing with the future Edward VIII who became a close friend after they met in the Royal Flying Corps.

Basil S. Foster.

G. N. 'Geoff' Foster (1884–1971; 5. 1896–1904) was a stylish player whose record for Worcestershire was a noteworthy one. He first played in 1903, played fairly frequently in 1907 and 1908 and had his fullest season in 1910; thereafter business commitments only allowed him occasional holiday appearances. He scored seven centuries for the county, his highest score being 175 (out of 463) made in 1913 against Leicestershire in only two hours and twenty minutes. E. W. Swanton in an obituary wrote that Foster gained Oxford Blues in cricket, soccer, rackets and golf.

Geoff N. Foster (5. 1896–1904).

M. K. 'Maurice' Foster (1889–1940; 5. 1901–08) played for the county in 1920, but business abroad allowed him to make only a few appearances for Worcestershire until he took over the captaincy in 1923 for three years; he also played regularly in 1926. Wisden says, 'he was typical of his famous family in the strength of stroke play produced by the powerful wrists and forearm always associated with those who are proficient at rackets. His forcing shots on either side of the wicket were brilliant. He could field anywhere, saving many runs and hold the most difficult of catches'. In June 1924 he had a purple patch when he scored 157 against Sussex, 138 against Kent and 125 against Somerset. In 1926, his best season, he emulated the feat of his two brothers twenty years before by making a century in each innings against Hampshire.

N. J. A. 'Johnnie' Foster (1890–1978; 5. 1903–09) went out to Malaya as a rubber planter, and therefore was only able to make a few appearances for Worcestershire; indeed his nine innings were played in 1923. He was one of the courageous British expatriates who suffered with fortitude the horrors of Changi gaol during the Japanese occupation of Malaya in the Second World War. He achieved much in the encouragement of cricket in Malaya. On one occasion he led a scratch team of the Federated Malay States in the defeat of a full Australian touring side, which had just returned from a winning Ashes series in England. This result led press agencies, in their disbelief, to ask for confirmation.

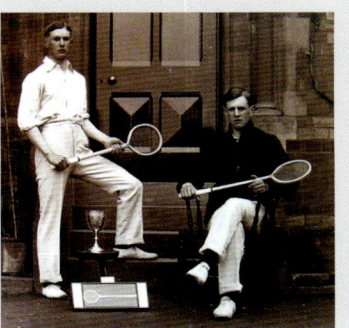

It must not be forgotten that there were three Foster sisters: Mabel, Jessie and Cicely. All were games players; Cicely played golf for England. Jessie was said to be the best bowler in the family; she also, incidentally, was the mother of Johnnie Greenstock, who later played for Worcestershire.[v]

N. J. A. 'Johnnie' (5. 1903–09) and Maurice K. (5. 1901–08) Foster.

The Reverend Henry Foster and his family, 1891. Back row, from left to right: Harry (H. K.), Tip (R. E.), Bill (W. L.). Middle row, from left to right: Basil (B. S.), Mabel (later Mrs Bullock), Mrs Foster, Jessie (later Mrs Greenstock), Johnnie (N. J. A.), The Rev Henry Foster, Cecily. Front row, from left to right: Geoffrey (G. N.), Maurice (M. K.).

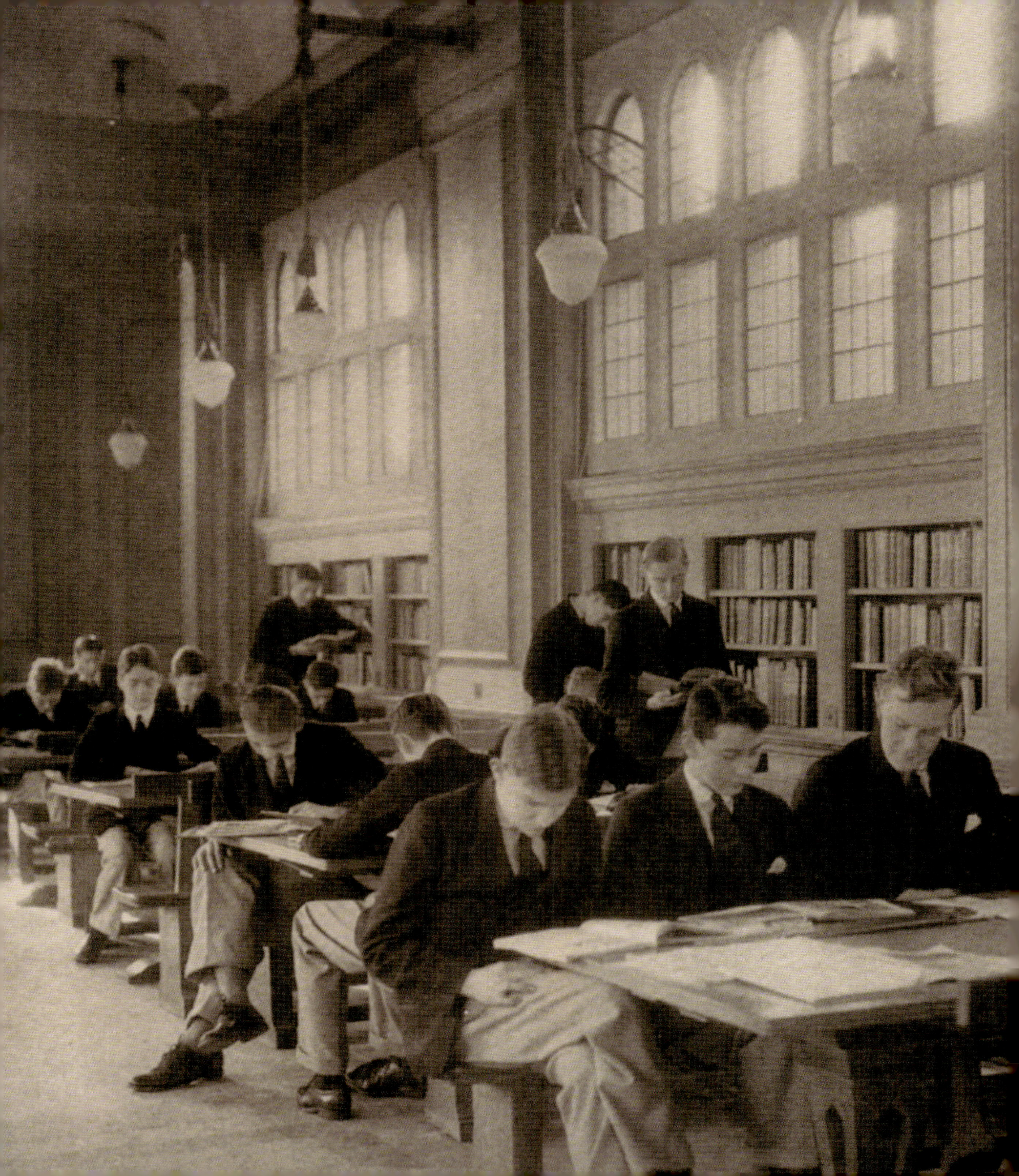

4

'With a wider vision and a self-trained mind', 1914–37

Frank Sansome Preston was the first lay Headmaster following the withdrawal of the constitutional clause that required a headmaster to be a clergyman. Although not in Holy Orders, Preston was an active lay preacher and a member of the Church Assembly. Boy and housemaster at Marlborough, and a distinguished classicist at Pembroke College, Cambridge, he came to Malvern with a vision 'about the nature of the good life and the kind of education that will best help to make boys realise it':[1]

> He strove on the one hand to create a balanced atmosphere in which respect for games did not swamp respect for things of the mind, whilst on the other he set his face against the growing tendency to regard education as a preparation for a job rather than as a preparation for life. He had the fastidious outlook of a natural aristocrat. The despoliation of beauty, whether of language or of landscape, was abhorrent to him; with materialism in any form he was totally out of sympathy; and he disliked most of the cultural developments of his time.[2]

He was to prove one of the great reforming headmasters, a task that required tact as well as vision. He was not to be the last headmaster who had to overcome ingrained conservatism which militated against much-needed progress. When he came to Malvern he was the youngest member of staff and found opposite him, at housemaster meetings, individuals who had been in post for over thirty years. His first Senior Chapel Prefect recollected being told:

> 'There will be many changes, which neither you nor the Prefects may like, but I will expect your co-operation and loyalty. And of course you can rely on mine.' This idea of co-operation between Headmaster and Prefects embarked on an enterprise, and the sense that we were being treated somehow as equals was something new to us. This was a complete contrast to the gloriously autocratic approach of Preston's predecessor, and to many of us it became the significant fact in the new regime.[3]

Another recalled Prunk (as the boys called Preston) 'as a model of a great Headmaster, international caps in two games, an athlete, tall, handsome, a beautiful speaking voice, a just and fair man and happily married.'[4] He further recalled how:

> Every Sunday, before Chapel, the Senior Prefects would foregather in the Grundy Library with Prunk. We would discuss the topics of the day, and then he would read to us some prose or

Opposite: The Memorial Library. For several decades this fiction library was a sanctuary where Junior boys were safe from fagging.

Above: Mr Frank Preston, Headmaster 1914–37.

43

poetry. His beautiful voice gripped me as well as his choice of books. Walt Whitman really got me round the throat. It sure did make an impression. That was sixty years ago and I still remember.

Preston's first years as headmaster were dominated by the First World War, which, apart from the emotional impact, saw dramatic changes within the school as staff joined up, the Combined Cadet Force (CCF) assumed even greater significance and boys frequently left early to volunteer for the services. Numbers dropped from 456 to 400 within a year. A serious staffing shortage had to be met by retired teachers, and the medically unfit; records also show that at one time 'mathematics was taught in the Sixth Form by the wife of a solicitor who had been called up, and French by a lady whose finishing school in Paris had closed down.' The strain of constant reorganisation resulted in Preston taking a term off under medical supervision.

The impact of this period of uncertainty and improvisation on the boys was often negative. Prefectorial authority was put in the hands of younger boys and a sense of insecurity affected the academic ethos and discipline suffered. The prefects' minutes book saw a decided shift from the usual issues of smoking and high jinks to matters concerned with 'bullying, general indiscipline and an unhealthy moral atmosphere.' The impact of food shortages and rationing led Preston to comment that 'the cheek-bones of the adolescent boy were unpleasantly prominent.' Letters from the front appeared in *The Malvernian* usually, within the bounds of censorship, on military matters, some with patriotic bravado, 'The OMs hope to raise a footer team in Berlin before the season is over'.[5] Others were more in touch with school matters, as when a master was reprimanded for suggesting in an earlier edition that there was little point in playing rugby for only half a term. A serving OM from the Somme wrote, 'Rugger must stay. What a confession of weakness to give it up now.' The impact of the war was felt in other ways, 'with two corps parades a week, turning out ammunition in the Engineering Shop and supporting the Malvern Y.M.C.A. Hut near St Omer'.[6]

The Debating Society showed considerable engagement in the moral issues presented by the war, with motions on whether nations were entitled to advance their own interests at the expense of other nations, whether reprisals were justifiable or submarine warfare could be defended. However, some prejudices remained strong; in 1918 the motion, 'That, in the opinion of this House, women should be relegated after the war to their proper position', was carried overwhelmingly.

Below: School House, 1914. F. S. Preston, Headmaster in his first term, with J. B. Porch to the right. C. S. Lewis can be seen on the third row, third from right. (Used by permission of The Marion E. Wade Center, Wheaton College, Wheaton, IL)

At the end of the war the school, like much of Europe, was struck by Spanish influenza. One OM recalls spending Armistice Day ill in bed 'and the only bit of excitement on that day was provided by an enterprising railway porter who pushed a wagon over a fog signal in the sidings near No. 7 to produce a suitable explosion to celebrate the occasion.'[7] Another recuperating boy, D. R. Nieper, presumably hearing the same signal, immediately strummed out the National Anthem on the piano and, upstairs, 'the feverish but excited boys stood on their beds in their pyjamas and sang the anthem to the piano below.' *The Malvernian* editorial commented, 'the influenza germ was able to produce greater changes here in a week than the Kaiser and his forces in four whole years'. Preston recalled:

Above: The Hunt comes to Malvern, 1920s. (From the collection of Richard Russell Corfield (4. 1924–29), courtesy of his son Roger Corfield (4. 1963–67))

> One day only 25 boys attended for School and Chapel, and eleven masters were still standing to teach them. Possibly will-power helped the survivors. The Army Entrance Examination was on at the time and one Woolwich candidate, a future distinguished general, when walking down College Road was greeted by the enquiry, 'How are things going, Wansbrough-Jones?' 'Very full of brandy, Sir' was the retort.

Alcohol was clearly felt to be a medical tool. Another OM recalls that he, and three other boys who had been very ill, were invited by their housemaster:

> through to his dining room, where he gave us each a good glass full of port as an extra pick-me-up. I have disliked port ever since! Confined to the House we were allowed, as a special concession, to play cards.[8]

The situation deteriorated when the school medical officer succumbed and no local doctor was available, leading Preston to appeal to the War Office. He received the heartening reply, 'Capt. West, R.A.M.C. from Leeds, seconded to your contingent to join this evening':

> He arrived about nine o'clock, and I accompanied him with a hurricane lamp while he made a tour of every House and the Sanatorium in the blackout. This he finished soon after midnight, and early the next morning organised the work throughout the School, concentrating the pneumonias, where moveable, in the Sanatorium.

One boy and two masters, including the much-loved H. W. Smith, died during the epidemic. Smith, in failing health, had spent:

> hour after hour, in his room in South Lodge, whose walls were literally papered with photographs of his old pupils, working through the long casualty lists to find the names of Malvernians, a task to break the heart of any devoted schoolmaster. Preston paying tribute in Chapel described how he had offered to relieve Smith of the burden of his work only to be

THE MALVERNIAN SOCIETY

An Old Malvernian Society (OMS) was first proposed in June 1894 and came into being in 1895 with an initial forty members. The declared purpose was to financially assist the school and its work, present prizes, books and objects of interest, provide the funds for an OM Register and 'generally encourage[s] social intercourse amongst OMs and good feelings between past and present members of the School'. Initially the headmaster was the president of the society but Preston thought this inappropriate and handed the post over to Sir Paul Lawrence in 1920, who was the first OM chairman of the College Council.

The first gift from the OM Society to the College of a cricket roller, 1896.

The first gifts came in 1896: an exhibition of £15 p.a. for the son of an OM, an annual science prize of £5 and 3 guineas for sports prizes and a cricket roller. 'Few people could have guessed what great things were to flow from these beginnings, though an investment of £1,000 by a wealthy ship owner, Heath Harrison (OM of 4. 1868–76) to provide a Scholarship to Brasenose was a sign of the generosity with which many Old Malvernians were to come to the help of the school in future years.'[i] In the same year the Society committed itself to providing an organ for the new Chapel. In 1902 the first 'improvement scheme was sponsored by the Society' which saw the building of a second rackets court, a gymnasium, and more fives courts, a store, a gate lodge and later a covered rifle range. In the new century the Society steadily acquired the outstanding shares, which was achieved between 1905 and 1928. Much credit is given to Henry Kempson (an OM and master), variously secretary and treasurer and 'a genius with figures, who had the gift of thinking in terms of years and not simply in terms of the annual balance sheet.'[ii] He pioneered the consolidation of the debentures with the Society acquiring as many as possible, with the advantage that the income now went to the Society, rather than to outsiders. Other sources of income were nomination fees on shares held by the College, profits from the school store and shop, legacies, and subscriptions.[iii] Kempson served for thirty-four years with exceptional commitment and loyalty to the school.

After the First World War the society was closely involved in raising funds for the school's memorial to those who had been killed: the statue of St George, the oak panels in the north chancel, and the Memorial Library. The society office was appropriately placed in the new building. In 1924 charitable status was achieved through the incorporating of the society into a company dedicated to educational and charitable ends and the title Malvernian Society was adopted.

The list of gifts and grants to the College from the society, or from individual OMs, is quite remarkable, and this is not an exhaustive list by any means:
- The purchase of SH from Lord Beauchamp in 1921.
- The Firs Estate 1924: the fine house and 35 acres were acquired in large part to prevent speculative residential building that would have seen the encirclement of the school by the town.

Henry Kempson (4. 1881–85).

'WITH A WIDER VISION AND A SELF-TRAINED MIND', 1914–37

- New doors from the Main Building leading into Chapel and into the Quadrangle.
- Levick Sports Awards and Malvernian Society All-Rounder Awards.
- Substantial grant towards sports complex and new boarding houses in 2008.
- Malvernian Society Assisted Places Scheme.
- Approximately half the required funds for the new Razak Science Centre.[iv]

Outstanding work has been given by a succession of Society officers, most notably R. B. (Judy) Porch, described as 'the friend and counsellor of all who knew him' who held every office in the society, serving a remarkable total of fifty-six years. When Porch took over as chairman in 1946, he was succeeded by Cyril Lace (S. 1917–22) who 'was meticulous and methodical' and successfully supervised the centenary appeal and the acquisition of the last of the debentures. Lace's successors – Brian Jacomb, George Chesterton, John Blackshaw, Michael Eglington and Syd Hill – have continued to answer the calls for more and more financial help from the College. As we have seen, the society and OM Club have sponsored a host of sporting activities for members in cricket, football, golf, shooting, court games and sailing. A Freemason's Lodge was also instituted in 1922. In recent years a host of new initiatives saw the society attempting to branch out to a wider section of the OM community. Regular House reunions, professional networking evenings, subject dinners and receptions in London and the very popular 'Malvern in London' gatherings in the Cittie of Yorke pub, High Holborn, have led to a much more inclusive and vigorous society. All OMs are now automatically life members of the Malvernian Society.

Perhaps, most significantly, the society now works closely and harmoniously with the College's Development Office, established in its present form in 2009, to ensure the highest standards of care and opportunities for its alumni and the maximum fundraising support for the College. Philanthropic support from OMs and Friends of the College has been increasingly important to the College, and many recent projects might not have taken place without this financial help. As such, the Development and Malvernian Society Office now plays a crucial role in the advancement of the school.

R. B. (Judy) Porch (SH 1888–94) 1901, teacher, housemaster and OM secretary. The steps up to the Main Building were named in his honour at the time of the centenary. Note the old crocketts bat; specially made these could be bought in the Store. Crocketts was a form of cricket played in the house yards.

- Purchase and refurbishment as teachers' accommodation of 1 College Grove, Radnor Lodge, Ashfield and Fosmo.
- The Grub, 1926.
- The Preston Science School and subsequent additions.
- Building of a bursar's house in Thirlstane Road.
- Headmaster's House.
- Acquisition of all the original shares of the College enabling the Royal Charter to be achieved.
- Purchase of the outstanding debentures.
- Sporting sites and equipment: tennis courts in the Firs, the Hooper Stand and Roger Harvey houses on the football fields, filtration system for the swimming baths; refurbishment and lighting of the Rackets Courts.
- Floodlighting in the Chapel, clergy desk and seat.
- Second World War memorials.
- A host of necessary repairs following the return of the school in 1946.

Above: The College's Jubilee dinner in Big School in 1925. The school had not celebrated the fiftieth anniversary of its opening as it fell during the war and so the Diamond Jubilee in 1925 had added significance. Ten of the boys who had entered the school in its first term were still alive and on 25 January the school sent to each the following telegram: 'Headmaster, Masters and Boys of Malvern College send Greetings on her 60th birthday to the ten Survivors of her first term's entry.'

told, 'It is my deliberate choice to drop nothing. I doubt any serious risk: anyhow, I have a right to do as I please, and as, I think, duty bids'.[9]

The immediate post-war period saw a steady increase in numbers and the school, led by the Old Malvernian Society (OMS), sought to consolidate the financial situation by buying up the debentures of the school and steadily paying off the debts. The decision of Earl Beauchamp to sell School House caused a major crisis for the school, which was unable to find the funds to buy it. Fearing a major loss of accommodation the College Council purchased the Monastery[10] for a very much smaller sum although in the end, after complex legal ramblings, the OMS was able to purchase School House for the school.[11] The OMS became ever more significant, taking on responsibility for paying off the remaining debts by 1932. Under its auspices more property and land were acquired: an additional football field, the central plot of the Lees, 1 College Grove – all in 1923; the Firs Estate was acquired the following year. In 1927 the new school shop was opened. Designed by an OM, Howard Robertson,[12] it has been described as 'the most elegant building in the grounds'. Hard tennis courts and squash courts were built in 1927 and 1933. The school crest was officially approved and registered with the College of Heralds as a coat of arms.

The most significant constitutional change in the school history also occurred in this period: the granting of the Royal Charter. This had long been desired for reasons of cultural prestige but more significantly so that the school would not be taxed as a trading concern. The conditions for this enhanced status required financial soundness and that the institution ceased to be run for private profit. The Royal Charter was granted by the Privy Council in 1929.[13]

A striking picture of Malvern in the 1920s emerges from the following account:

> Term always began on a Friday and ended on a Tuesday some twelve weeks later ... there were no exeats, except for the gravest family emergencies. Those arriving from the South had the benefit of four extra coaches added to the 4.45 p.m. train from Paddington. On the Saturday, exceptionally one got up later at 8 a.m. had breakfast at 8.30 and then spent the day unpacking the trunk which together with a tuck box, had been sent 'luggage in advance', and getting organised – perhaps moving into a new study, pinning cretonne on the walls, buying a lampshade and bargaining for a chair or a cupboard from others who had them to sell ... Throughout the term, except for games or 'volls' [voluntary runs] the only wear was ties and

stiff collars, black coats, grey trousers (prefects could wear striped ones) and black shoes or boots. On Sunday, school prefects wore morning coats. Casual clothes were unknown and the only pullovers or sweaters were the white ones needed for games and volls. House caps were always worn in the grounds, and black and white speckled straw hats (bashers) with House colours on the band were worn outside the grounds.

Up town was strictly out of bounds except on some weekdays between the end of morning school about 12.20 and lunch at 1.15. Pubs, hotels, cafes and eating places were all out of bounds, unless with parents or relatives. A fixed one-shilling (5p) pocket money a week was issued by Housemasters and charged on the termly bill. It sufficed for some modest purchases of food and drink at the 'grub', and perhaps a magazine, but tea in the tea room at the new grub when it opened about 1926 was out of the question, except perhaps when one was flush at the beginning of term or after the visit of parents or relatives.

One of the best features of Malvern was the study system (even though in School House five new boys had to share a tiny study) and the cubicles that divided up the dormitories, and it seems a pity that these were done away with after the war. They afforded a measure of privacy, which was as welcome as it was rare in the public schools of that day. Each cubicle contained, besides the bed, a 'coffin' (an oblong box on legs which contained shirts, collars, underwear, pyjamas etc) and a washstand, with jug, basin and jerry. Hot water could be obtained from a sink along the corridor, and after use the washbasin was emptied into the jerry and left for the maids to deal with when they had made the beds. In School House, at any rate, one bathroom containing four baths allowed sixty boys a bath once a week on a rota with three sessions on each of the five evenings, and these became an agreeable social occasion. In addition the changing room offered one bath (reserved for prefects and the good at games) and a few defective showers for the rest. A bootboy cleaned boots and shoes, stoked the boiler, and hauled trunks in and out of store at the beginning and end of term.

Again then as now, societies for this and that rose, flourished and died … [such as] the Archaeological Society which had little to do with archaeology but provided the excuse for

Above: The Grub in break in the 1920s. This photograph admirably illustrates the world of petty privilege in the 1920s and 1930s. It is almost possible to assess the period these individual boys had been in the school. Rounded collars were obligatory for the first two years, all jacket buttons had to be fastened for a year, one hand in a trouser pocket was permitted after three terms, and both after six. The ordinary House cap is shown on the far right, and the House colour cap in the middle.

Left: The Grub.
Opposite: This cartoon appeared in *The Beacon*, for a period a light-hearted magazine produced termly. The custom since 1922 used to be that everyone doffed their caps or hats when passing the war memorial.

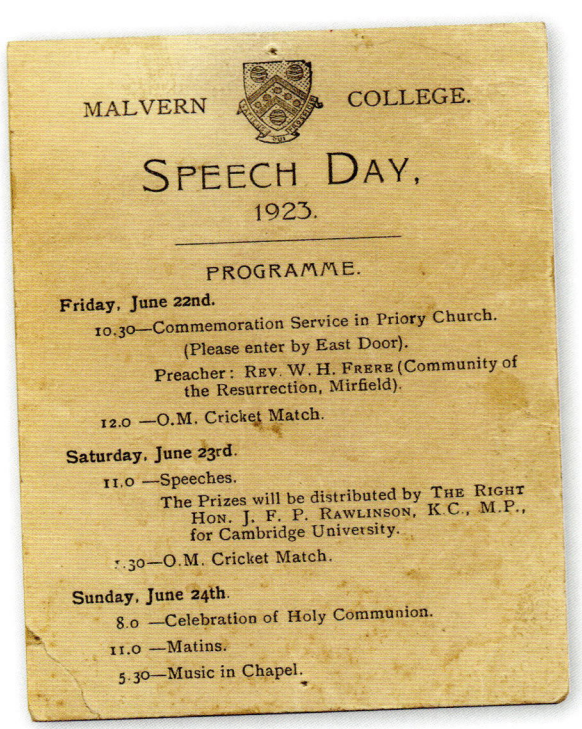

Above: Speech Day programme, 1923.

Below: Dormitory cubicles. It was a feature at Malvern until the Second World War that nearly all boys slept in their own cubicles. There was one cold and one hot tap on each floor.

trips into the country on summer Saturdays on bicycles or in masters' cars to look at a church perhaps and afterwards bathe in the river Severn.[14]

A contemporary reports an interesting social change:

A marked change from my father's time was the use of Christian names. From his own experience, he warned me solemnly that I must never let anyone know my Christian name. When I first came Christian names were not used but by the time I left it was becoming rather smart to use them among Seniors.[15]

The Great Depression hit Malvern, and all such schools, severely. Numbers fell heavily from 577 at the beginning of the school year in 1930 to 465 three years later. Masters agreed unanimously to a 5 per cent cut in their salaries in order to provide a fund to enable boys who would otherwise have had to leave to remain at the school, and the careers of over forty boys were thus saved. Early leaving again became a problem.[16]

Despite these concerns the inter-war period did see decided advances in the breadth and quality of the intellectual training offered to the boys. Preston was concerned about both academic mediocrity and insufficient breadth. The spirit in which he engaged with this challenge can be found again in his own words:

If the charge of over-athleticism was true, what should a Headmaster do? … The only hope was surely if possible to restore the balance and to discourage the disease in its worst manifestations … It was, I felt, only possible to wean the average boys from regarding almost with idolatry those who possessed a natural flair for games and treating as VIP the school colours of the past, if one could arouse his interest in other directions and widen his horizon. It was for this reason that, as soon as the end of the War made it possible, I set myself both by direct and indirect means to provide facilities for cultural needs as well as alternative occupations. A memorial Reading Room and new tennis courts could equally serve my purpose, and it was from this point of view that I valued alike a Dramatic Society and a biological laboratory.

The School had a glimpse of my mind when I ruled that in future the Sixth should share with the School Prefects the privilege of entering the School Buildings by the central steps. This was a symbol the dullest mind could understand.[17]

He worked hard to improve the teaching of science and achieved the building of what came to be known as the Preston Science School as well as a general broadening of the curriculum. Significant developments occurred outside the classroom in these years that greatly broadened the horizons of Malvern boys. School music flourished in the more suitable premises of the former Monastery.[18] The once-vigorous Debating Society declined in these years – one of its last significant meetings approved the November Revolution in Russia. Preston was somewhat nervous about political discussion that involved masters. A temporary replacement took the form of a school parliament opened by the headmaster (acting as the sovereign) with boys providing a speaker, prime minister, who headed a coalition government, together with leaders of the Liberal, Independent Conservatives and Labour parties. Vigorous debates occurred on the question of disarmament and Ireland with the government achieving comfortable majorities.[19] Later debates considered education, the estrangement between Britain and France, and the British occupation of Egypt.

Left: The Preston Science School.

A Discussion Society thrived with fortnightly meetings in which papers were read and considered by boys and some masters. From March 1920 until 1936 the society produced a literary magazine, *The Beacon*, with John Wheeler-Bennett as its first editor; House magazines like School House's *The Magpie* reappeared; and *The Malvernian* became a more stimulating publication. In the words of Ralph Blumenau, 'the editorials, which had once been mere catalogues of the term's weather, games, and principal events, all of which were recorded in other parts of the magazine, began to take on the appearance of leading articles, a little sententious at times, but with some claim to thought and style.'

Drama also emerged as a significant feature of school life in these years and many societies flourished: Play-Reading, Wireless, Railway, Photographic, Mathematical, *La Société Française*, Laletes (discussion group for the Fifth Form) and the English club.[20] A flavour of the latter's influence could be found in the Christmas term of 1932 when it produced 'two debates, a play reading session, an Eisteddfod evening, a mock session of the League of Nations, and a evening of Modern Verse, Grave and Gay'.

Given this plethora of activity there seems little doubt that Preston's aim of widening the boys' interests was being achieved. At Speech Day in 1933 he said. 'I believe in these days it is even more important to educate for leisure than to educate for salesmanship. I believe that a person who knows how to use his spare time never wastes any time.' Significantly of the six university award winners in 1932/3 five were Heads of House and only one of these was a good games player:

> Since no Housemaster or Headmaster would want to appoint as Heads of Houses boys who did not have considerable

Below: Cartoon from the Preston papers.

MALVERN COLLEGE

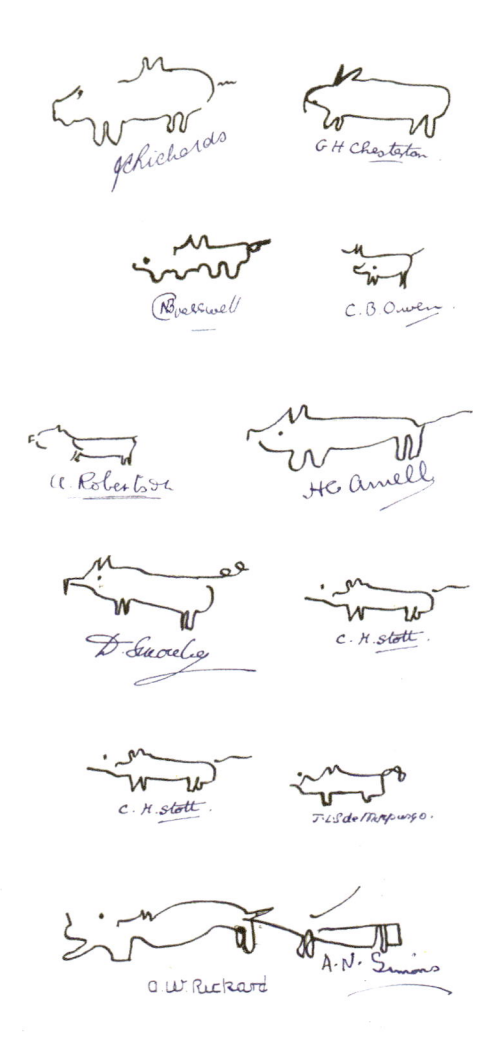

Above: A selection of 'Preston Pigs'.

standing in the eyes of the school, this suggests that boys were now ready to follow the lead of seniors who were not necessarily distinguished on the games field.[21]

Beyond these very public images of a reforming headmaster we gain a glimpse, from a boy's perspective, of a headmaster who inspired awe and some affection:

> The Headmaster appeared a somewhat stern and withdrawn figure though it was well known that he knew every boy by sight and name. New boys were invited to tea by his wife who formed a collection of 'pigs drawn with eyes shut' by every boy entering the school which, by now, must be an interesting collectors' piece. Those leaving, were entertained to dinner by the Head, who regaled us with verses of his own composition, mentioning each of us in turn, and, showing both a nice turn of humour and knowledge of our individual characters.[22]

Preston feared that the spirit of public service was being endangered by economic and political changes and above all by a growing materialism. In 1929 he used Speech Day to appeal to parents for a renewal of the spirit of service:

> Is there not a danger of the public school man becoming a little too self-centred?
>
> I am appealing to you that as you have sent your sons to a public school, you will not expect the school, to train them to regard the world as a very pleasant playground in which life's work was to obtain a sufficient amount of this world's goods and to have all its delights, but to bear and share responsibility side by side with others with a wider vision and a self-trained mind.

To that end he encouraged schemes like the Duke of York's (the future King George VI) camps aimed at bringing working-class and public school boys together. Gordon Dashwood described the experience:

> My last term, summer 1933, was especially nice for me. 'Prunk' summoned me and a friend, and asked us if we would honour the school and go to the Duke of York's Camp at Southwold on the Suffolk coast. We went, 200 public school boys, 200 young artisans from all over the U.K. under canvas with catering by Harrods. For two weeks we played, we sang, we ran, we made friends. We were honoured by the Duke of York staying with us, along with Olympic athletes, like Lord Burghley. The Duke was just one of us and enormously popular – his daughters must have adored him.[23]

Right: The Headmaster, F. S. Preston, dined out every leaver and delivered his farewell speeches in verse in the style of different poets.

Far more boys joined in the annual hop-picking camp that the School Mission organised for the people of Canning Town. The school continued to support the Mission with boys travelling to London for weekends and the organisation of a series of football matches. Under the charge of Kennedy-Cox the mission spread to the much wider Dockland Settlement. He spoke to the school each term on Mission Sunday and raised substantial amounts of money through collections.

In 1936 Preston felt it was time to retire and he did so at Easter in 1937. Ralph Blumenau writes:

> Masters and boys alike remember him with a kind of awe. Personally Preston was rather remote – he never addressed either a boy or a master by his Christian name – but everyone remembers him as a man of great wisdom. His greatness consisted in the ability to combine deep convictions with an open mind.

One of his pupils in the Classical Sixth wrote:

> Afterwards we would recall the dry comment, always kind, on, say, the bad end to a promising innings or the oracular hint at some piece of translation so good that it failed to conceal the crib behind it. In such small ways the mask of austerity would slip, and the approach to sympathy and counsel be forever open.

In a fine and moving obituary in *The Malvernian* Preston was described as:

> one of the last survivors of the generation of Public School Headmasters responsible for transforming the curriculum and to some extent the character of the Public Schools in the 1920s and 1930s. Preston at Malvern in a characteristically unobtrusive and unpublicised way developed a school which had, before 1914, been notable mainly for athletic successes and the rather narrow scholarship of the Classical Sixth into a community of much wider interests, in which not only were science, modern languages, and other academic subjects taught with much better equipment and to much higher standards, but music and art were encouraged not only for the gifted but for the average boy'.[24]

Above: Some masters of Malvern depicted in *The Sketch* magazine, 1936. (© Illustrated London News Ltd/Mary Evans)

Left: 'Some Touch Line Impressions.' From left to right: F. S. Preston, H. G. C. Salmon, W. W. Lowe, E. C. Bullock.

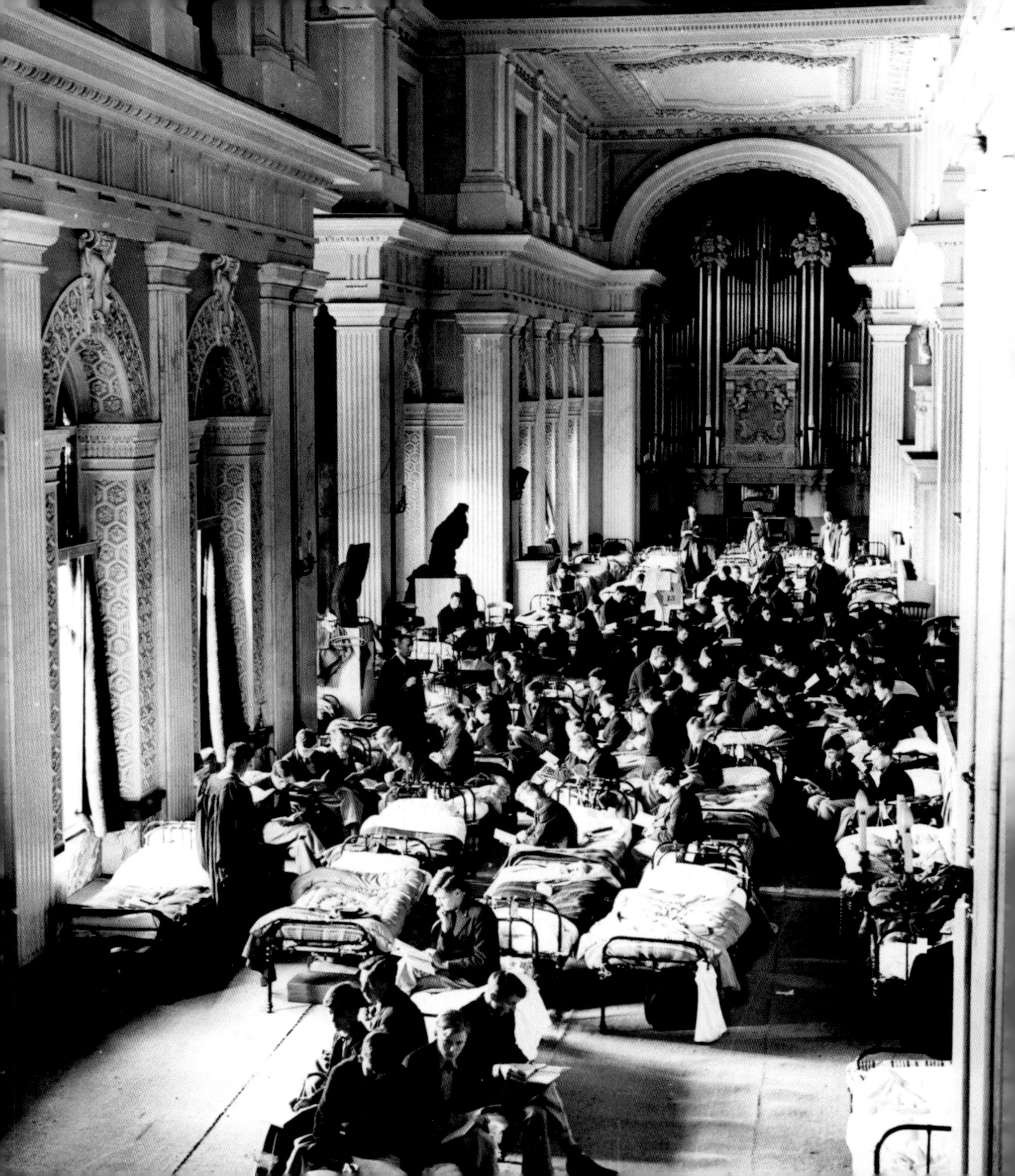

5

'We have not faltered nor failed', 1937–53

Malvern's new Headmaster, Tom Gaunt,[1] had been educated at Tonbridge and became a scholar of King's College, Cambridge, where he achieved tennis and hockey Blues; he also played cricket for Warwickshire.[2] Before coming to Malvern he had previously taught at King Edward's School, Birmingham and at Rugby.

> Behind the headmasterly façade was a person of distinct and varied talents, with a degree of shyness in his nature and with a gentle and humorous disposition. He was a sensitive scholar who loved English (his Shakespeare classes were specially memorable) and he was an accomplished writer of verse.[3]

From the first his headmastership was overshadowed by the developing crisis in Europe. In his report to the College Council in October 1938 Gaunt reported that masters were being instructed in air raid precautions 'with a view to their being in a position to train boys later.' In November *The Malvernian* editorial noted:

> It takes more than the imminence of war to unsettle Malvern for any length of time. It is true that a little excitement pervaded the atmosphere; a few of those over eighteen wandered about, vainly trying to obtain reassurance about the age for joining up; digging became more than a dilatory pastime for those bored on a Sunday; but for the most part everything went on just the same. The signing of the Munich agreement was heralded with joy and an extra half-holiday.

Unbeknown to these cheerful editors a darker scenario was under way. Gaunt was to write in detail about the coming events in his book *Two Exiles*, published after the Second World War. He records the air of gloom in the summer of 1938 and the various approaches made to him by schools seeking alternative venues in the expectation of imminent hostilities. After the relief of Munich, Gaunt felt able to relax and sweep 'the entire contents of my desk with a supreme gesture into the waste paper basket', until he received a fateful letter:

> On Boxing Day 1938, among a number of envelopes containing Christmas cards one letter stood out among the rest. It was pale bluish grey, and was marked on the outside 'Secret and Confidential' and bore the crest of His Majesty's Office of Works on the back of the envelope. Speculating rapidly on what signal honour I was about to be asked to accept, I slit open the envelope. Inside was a second sealed envelope, this time marked 'SECRET. To be opened

Opposite: The Long Library served as a dormitory for School House and most of No. 1 during the school's time at Blenheim Palace, Woodstock, Oxfordshire. SH also used it for House prayers, with the opportunity to use the organ too good to miss.

Above: Mr H. C. A. Gaunt, Headmaster 1937–53. Drawing by H. A. Freeth.

only by H. C. A. Gaunt, Esq., M.A. Headmaster of Malvern College'. I complied. It contained a letter from Sir Patrick Duff, Permanent Secretary to the Ministry of Works, informing me that the Government 'having had under consideration the question of earmarking a number of large buildings outside London for national purposes in the event of war, and I am afraid it is my ungrateful duty to let you know that Malvern College is one of those earmarked.'[4]

In April 1939 Gaunt, accompanied by the vice-chairman of the Council S. P. Richardson, went to see Sir Patrick Duff, who almost casually mentioned that he had that morning received a letter from the Duke of Marlborough, offering Blenheim Palace to the government if war should break out; 'But I suppose it would not be large enough for what you want!' Gaunt immediately asked to see the palace and the duke hosted him the following day.

Despite the evident problems of locating the school in the palace Gaunt accepted the offer, not least to prevent the opportunity being taken up by some other institution. Some reassurance about the capacity of Blenheim to meet the needs of the school emerged when the duke hosted a ball for a thousand guests to celebrate his daughter's eighteenth birthday. The catering equipment installed to meet the requirements of 'this last great European ball' was left in place in case it was needed.

EXILE TO BLENHEIM

The final countdown to war began on 1 September when Germany invaded Poland. On the same day officials from the Office of Works (later Ministry of Works) arrived at the College to prepare it to host the Admiralty. After the horror of Guernica a profound fear had developed in governing circles about the possible impact of aerial bombing were war to break out. Much planning went into how effective administration could continue if London were laid to waste. Therefore when the school was requisitioned, the plan had been to evacuate the Admiralty to Malvern if it were impossible to operate from London. 'In that case the First Lord of the Admiralty, from September 1939 to May 1940, Winston Churchill himself, would have occupied the School House drawing room as his private office, and the Preston Science School would have served as chief Signal Station for our fleet and merchant men all over the Seven Seas.'

Gaunt summoned the staff back to Malvern[5] and preparations for the move began and with considerable urgency once the requisitioning order was issued on 7 September.

At Blenheim moveable treasures were put into storage, but the duke allowed tapestries and pictures to remain on the damask walls of the state rooms (although protected by boards), and the 200-year-old parquet floor was covered with linoleum and coconut matting. The eighteenth-century curtains had to be protected with canvas covers, pads were fixed to mahogany doors, and the enormous windows (some in the Great Hall and the Library reached a height of 60 feet) had to be provided with black-out. Local firms contracted by the Office of Works moved material from Malvern:

> At Blenheim we had to be ready at all hours of the day to direct the contents as they arrived at the palace steps to their proper destination, and the final blow came when on the second day the men announced that they had received orders to dump the vanloads on the steps and return to Malvern with the utmost speed. This meant that the whole of the fifty-five vanloads had to be carried bodily, to the places assigned, by members of the teaching staff, the Office Staff, the Ground Staff, the Domestic Staff and any others whose services could be obtained, during a period of ten days from breakfast time until dusk.

In the middle of all this 'an official at Malvern announced that he had instructions from London to commandeer the whole of our beds and bedding! It was only after I had myself telephoned the ministry in London that this order was rescinded'.

The kitchen installations in the palace ran on petrol gas, which was likely soon to be unobtainable; so a gas main had to be laid from the palace to Woodstock, a distance of about a mile. A gang of masters began to hack through the limestone to dig a trench for it until a firm with a pneumatic drill could be secured. Boilers, pipes, racks, basins, lighting, ventilation fans and a host of other things had to be installed; sixty WCs were built outside – 'sixty glorious rears' as the boys would later call them.[6] Finally sixteen large huts were erected in the main courtyard to provide classroom accommodation, although they were not finished until three weeks after the boys arrived; 'During that time half the boys would go for walks while the other half were taught in the dormitories, where an almost surrealist juxtaposition of iron bedsteads, gowned pedagogues and baroque gilt met the eye.' John Lewis recalls:

Above: The house huts built in the main courtyard of Blenheim Palace were used for teaching, but the boys were also taught outside in fine weather.

> For most of the first term, lessons were conducted seated on beds in the dormitories. Meals were taken, seated by Houses, in the Great Hall in the entrance to the palace. My seat was adjacent to an Epstein bust of an earlier Duke, behind which I used to keep my weekly copy of *The Spectator*. By the second term, house huts were built in the Great Court for living in, one for each House, and also used for teaching purposes. A hall was built in the stables, which could be used for assembly meetings and for examinations, as well as concerts and plays. Rehearsals were held for a performance of the *Messiah*, later to be given in Oxford. Religious services (and confirmations) were held in Woodstock Parish Church.[7]

The school functioned as best it could – centralised housing and eating reduced the sense of being attached to a House and the boys had to become adept at living out of trunks under their beds – but there was a general feeling of excitement and adventure. The editorial of the first *Malvernian* at Blenheim caught something of this feeling:

> Few in number must be the editorials penned in a bathroom; very few in number those penned in a palace; and unique must be that penned in the bathroom of a palace. For the first time therefore in the history of school magazines, we are in a position to put forward a convincing claim to originality in an editorial. For the bathroom at Blenheim (there are many of them) constitutes a precious oasis of peace and quiet; and therefore was the environment in which this was penned – pencilled rather, for ink is taboo at Blenheim. We have all by now endured an experience which, whether we have enjoyed it or not, has been of exceptional educational value. And most of us have enjoyed it.

The calm beauty and spaciousness of Blenheim Park and the grandiose conception of the palace itself made an impression on the boys. One wrote poetically about their 'first glimpse of the beech-girt lake, grey blue in the early sunlight, its waveless surface gently veined by the fussy paddling of myriad coots; and those quiet half hours, construing Sophocles astride a leaden sphinx, a dumb creature proud in her impassivity, amid the sunlit splashing and green formality

Above: Boys walking in the main courtyard at Blenheim Palace.

of the Lower Terrace'. The view down the long avenue to the Column of Victory 'added to a sense of history to which the nation was being roused. And in the very cold weather during the Lent term, the scenes of skating on the frozen lake while the sun was setting behind a screen of frost-bound trees had a tingling beauty of their own.'[8]

The severe winter of the Lent term proved difficult. Although the palace was comfortably warm, the heating in the huts was not good and boys, wrapped in coats and rugs, came to lessons to find that icicles had formed under the corrugated iron roofs during the night. As the temperature slowly rose, they melted and dripped onto the forms below.

> We wrestled with Euclid and Virgil huddled in overcoats and mittened hands in the poorly heated wooden huts built in the main courtyard to serve as classrooms. The lake froze over, and intelligence that the Duke's teenage daughters had taken to the ice inevitably led to a rush for the skates.[9]

Influenza struck, with 150 boys out of 400 struck down at one point. Anxious to avoid dispersing the school Gaunt battled on, assisted by the heroic ministrations of the school doctor, Dr Elkington, who although sick himself 'never deserted his post, and, though hardly able to stand, continued throughout to attend to his patients'. Gaunt also recalled the use of a new drug, M&B

Above left and right: Improvised teaching environment. Note the tapestries in the left photograph.

693, an early antibiotic that was effective in preventing and treating the onset of the dreaded pneumonia.

In April and May 1940 the Phoney War came to a dramatic end with the German occupation of Norway, Denmark and Holland, the capitulation of Belgium, the miraculous evacuation from Dunkirk, and the collapse of France. The descendant of the victor of Blenheim became Prime Minister:

> Night by night, almost hour by hour, we listened to the grim catalogue of events in the Great Hall, in House huts, in dormitories and in the open air. The voice of Mr. Churchill sounded only too clearly the peril with which we were now faced; and that same voice steeled in the heart of the youngest boy the determination that, come what may, there would be no faltering.[10]

The grave national danger saw the formation of the Local Defence Volunteers, later called the Home Guard. The school received its first taste of what must have seemed real war when boys and masters formed contingents, which patrolled the grounds at night. Fire-watching on the roofs of the palace was organised. In June a Canadian armoured division was housed in the park which was 'festooned with camouflage nets over guns, anti-aircraft batteries, armoured cars, lorries and tanks; while vast spaces were covered with the tents, kitchens, stores and military equipment of six thousand men'. The Canadians stayed for ten days during which the school entertained some of the troops with an open-air concert and many boys learnt to play baseball. One OM recalls that on the Canadians' first night in Blenheim 'they drank all the liquor in Woodstock, posted sentries and shot a cow – she failed to answer their challenge'.

Nothing dimmed the instinctive mischievousness of young boys. One OM remembers 'sneaking down the corridor and stealing some of the Masters' beer, which was stored in a barrel down the corridor from our bedroom. I didn't specially like the beer but it was exciting to sneak through the quiet palace in the early morning light.' The same miscreant recalls:

> The most exciting adventure was one summer's afternoon. On a challenge it was my task to scratch my initials in the gold ball that sits at the top of the palace above the front door. I climbed up a whole bunch of stairs through the inside of the building, never running into any adults. I didn't know which way to go, but 'up' seemed to be the way. When I opened the door I was on a huge slate roof below the apex with the ball. I found a bit of old nail and climbed a slanted rook to lightly scratch JK in the lower side of the ball.[11]

BLENHEIM DIARY

A remarkable series of diary extracts by C. H. Silver (2–2/6. 1939–43)[i] sets the strange conjunction of what was happily still a boy's world against the background of the high drama of 1940:

Friday May 3rd
The Headmaster gave us a short address, urging us to keep up a steady cheerfulness. We ought not to let our hopes be buoyed up by a single victory, or be depressed by a single or even more reverses. He said this with reference to our recent withdrawal from Norway.

Monday, May 6th
By the way last night we had an air raid practice. First we went up to the dormitory and stood by the side of our beds with our gas masks. Then, when the gong was sounded, we followed No. 8 down into the basement and stood in our positions. We did that twice.

Thursday May 9th
A large political storm took place in the House of Commons last night and yesterday. The Government got a majority of only 81 votes, which just stopped the resignation of Chamberlain. Nevertheless, there are many demands in today's edition of the *Daily Mail*. Churchill made a speech in defence of the government's action concerning Trondheim … We had fielding practice after tea.

Friday, May 10th
The weather is just as fine today, but startling events have been happening elsewhere, thanks to that amazing man, Adolf. At the breakfast table, I first learnt that Germany had invaded Holland, and it is surprising to see the overwhelming difference it made to our conversation. Instead of the usual petty quibbles that so often get discussed, such major issues as the next premier and the next step in the situation. There are now reports that Brussels has been bombed and that Switzerland has been subjected to the same treatment … Ian and I went for a ride on our bikes … up the road beyond the column – we saw a block of stone … on one side the coat of arms of the Marlboroughs, on another 'Dieu defend le droit…'

We were allowed to listen to the 9 o'clock news in the house hut after prayers. We heard Mr Chamberlain saying he had resigned, and that Winston Churchill was going to be premier.

Sunday, May 26th Day of National Prayer[ii]
At this morning's service the church was literally packed. There were so many people that we had to squash ourselves in, and make use of the seats by the choir stalls to make room for them. Even then a number had to stand at the back

The news is still pretty serious … Today they denied that Calais had been taken by the Germans, and we are making desperate efforts to close the gap between the allied armies, through which the Germans are pouring mechanised forces.

Thursday, May 30th
Half-holiday for cricket, Ian and I went to the lakeside, nearly all the tadpoles have disappeared. The news is still very serious. So far as I can see, the BEF[iii] will be lucky if it gets out of Flanders intact. The fleet is guarding Dunkirk, and the army is doing a withdrawing movement under cover of the RAF and fleet. The Air Force has accounted for a great number of German planes.

Friday, May 31st
I went for a walk to the bridge. Several boys were doing rifle drill: the sight almost made me laugh seeing Mr Cosgrove and Mr Cobb firmly grasping a rifle along with the boys … The news is still very bad. Our troops have suffered what can only be called a defeat. The BEF is being evacuated in all sorts of ships.

Tuesday, June 4th
We are still holding Dunkirk, but nearly all the BEF has come back. Paris has been bombed. During Hall Sells came and told us very briefly that, at very short notice he had been called up into the Air Force. As a result he was leaving tomorrow.

Wednesday, June 5th
There is scarcely more than a wisp of cloud in the sky – This afternoon I played cricket … I said goodbye to Sells … Dunkirk is now in German hands and all the BEF has been evacuated. Apparently we have lost 30,000 men in this business … During supper Sarah and Caroline, the Duke's two eldest daughters, came round the tables to collect for the Red Cross.

In the beautiful summer of 1940 'cricket took place on the Great Lawn and swimming in the Lake' while the great struggle in France reached its sad climax and the country braced itself for what Winston Churchill called the coming Battle of Britain. It was at this moment that the school was allowed to return to Malvern.

The period of the Phoney War had given the Admiralty the time to build and equip vast underground shelters in London as well as a mass of hutments at Malvern, which would enable it to return the College to its owners in September. It still wanted to keep some of the school buildings, notably No. 1, No. 2 and No. 5, to house some of the personnel of HMS *Duke*. This was the name given to a conglomeration of buildings which had been put up on the southern

Left: Morning 'breathers' before breakfast in the courtyard.

end of the football fields and which was an initial training centre for the Navy. Certain other buildings – the Main Building, the Pavilion, the Monastery, the Museum, the Grub Shop and the Porter's Lodge – would be returned on the understanding that they might be required at forty-eight hours' notice if a crash evacuation of the Admiralty from London had to take place before all the new hutments were completed at the end of October. The temporary loss of the three northern houses was not a serious matter. Since the school was so depleted in numbers, it could only help to have them occupied by a rent-paying government department; and if worst came to worst and the crash evacuation did take place, the school could manage in the houses that remained to it for the few weeks until the hutments were completed. In March 1940, therefore, Gaunt had been able to announce that the school would return to Malvern in

Left: Malcolm Staniforth starts the 440 yards. The lawns on the south front of the palace lent themselves well to cricket, football and athletics.

Above: Letter from David James Bridge (5/7. 1937–41) from Malvern College at Blenheim Palace to his mother. (Courtesy of Charles Bridge (SH 2006–11)/ Bridge family achives)

September, although he had to write to parents in April about the inevitable redistribution of boys that would now be necessary.[12]

The time came to say goodbye to Blenheim and there was a little ceremony. All the boys autographed a book, which was given to the duchess, and the duke made a speech in which he thanked them for not having broken up the place.[13] Very little damage was sustained, perhaps the most famous being when a cricket ball shattered one of the original windows in the Long Library – unusually travelling from inside to out! The culprit was ordered to apologise in person to the duke, who seemed 'even more nervous than I was and covered in embarrassment he simply asked me to try and not do any more damage'.[14] Lewis recalls, 'at the end of our stay, at a final prize-giving, the prizes were distributed by the lovely Lady Sarah Churchill to whom 400 schoolboys were devoted. Luckily I received two leather-bound books for the Mathematical Essay Prize and the Malvernian Society Physics Prize and I was able to speak to her and to ask her to sign the two books. What a climax for my stay!'

The school returned to a profoundly different Malvern. Gaunt commented:

> I doubt whether many other towns outside London contained so great a variety of men and women of different countries meeting frequently together. The Belgian army had its headquarters in the Abbey Hotel, the Records branch of the Polish Navy and a small

contingent of Greeks were in the town, and on occasions we had visitors from Yugoslavia, Norway and Holland at some of the dances and parties which were held. For a short while a contingent of Canadians were at the Malvern House hotel, while Americans and Australians were frequent visitors. Crown Prince Paul of Greece, while staying with Lord Beauchamp at Madresfield, visited the College Chapel for Evensong one Sunday, spoke to the school afterwards and presented two books to the Library.

British soldiers were much in evidence and the Naval Initial Training Centre used No. 2 as their Officers' Mess. Also in the College, at No. 5, the Free French cadets had arrived. These patriotic French boys had cycled to the coast or had escaped through Spain when the Germans invaded France, and then crossed the Channel in fishing vessels, or by air; one even made the hazardous journey in a canoe. The Free French Army in England wanted to train about fifty of them for commissions and Gaunt was asked whether Malvern could accommodate them; the Ministry of Works released No. 5 and the French boys arrived in January 1941. 'Their red walking-out cloaks were soon a familiar sight, and the school saw a good deal of them, for they used classrooms, the Gym, and the playing fields. They took part in the School Sports in March and joined a number of other activities. General de Gaulle came to inspect them in September 1941, unfortunately when the school was on holiday.' Thirty-five of the sixty-three who had been trained at Malvern later died when they returned to France with the Army of Liberation and led the newly raised, enthusiastic, but untrained militia into battle.[15] A memorial seat on the Grub lawn was unveiled in 1949.

In January 1941, the College hosted the Malvern Conference, a meeting organised by the industrial Christian Fellowship to discuss the 'proper attitude of the Church of England towards the problems of the post-war world', particularly social and economic problems. Originally intended to meet in London in November 1940 it was postponed because of the heavy bombing of the Blitz. Gaunt, who had been invited to the original meeting, was asked whether it could be held in Malvern, and from 10 to 13 January the school hosted a series of distinguished Anglicans. The meetings were chaired by Dr Temple, the Archbishop of York (and later Canterbury), and included such interested laymen as T. S. Eliot and Dorothy Sayers. The conference met in Big School and its members slept in cubicles and took meals in the dining halls of School House, No. 3, No. 4 and No. 6. Reflecting on the great Labour victory in 1945, and the introduction of the Welfare State, Gaunt was perhaps correct to conclude that the final document of the conference 'exercised considerable influence on recent political trends in this country.'

The school tried, as far as possible, to return to normal although the atmosphere remained tense. Gaunt reported in March 1941:

> This term practically all the boys over 17 are serving in the Home Guard, in close cooperation with the town … The dispositions and duties of the Home Guard in case of invasion are already made known to Captain Salter who is in charge. Several exercises by night have been undertaken to accustom boys to the conditions of the blackout.

As the war darkened with the intensification of the Blitz on London, the ritual of listening to the nine o'clock news was universally observed. George Chesterton remembered one night vividly: 'He [Chesterton] and the others were fire-watching from the top of the Preston Science Building and they observed with a mixture of fascination and horror a conflagration in the sky somewhere north-east of them. They firmly believed that Birmingham was ablaze. In fact it was Coventry.'[16]

The House system was fully revived, although with the continued requisitioning of No. 1, No. 2 and No. 5 the boys were combined with No. 8, No. 6 and No. 7 respectively. An important

Top left: Free French cadets marching back to No. 5, 1941/42.

Top right: Free French cadets at Malvern, 1941–42.

Bottom left: Memorial plaque to the Free French cadets who fell in the liberation of France. (St Edmund's Hall)

Bottom right: Memorial to the Free French cadets unveiled in 1949.

change had been initiated at Blenheim with housemasters now becoming salaried, as with central feeding it was no longer possible for them to run their houses as private commercial propositions, in the way they had done since the school had been founded. The College Council had thus added to their financial burden at a time when the steady fall in numbers was causing grave concern. The trend had started before the war but the uncertainties and economic privations of the long conflict aggravated the problems. At the beginning of 1939 Malvern numbers were down to 430, lower than during the worst of the Depression years. At the move to Blenheim they were 398, 357 upon returning to Malvern, and down to 336 just before the second evacuation. This was not because of significant withdrawals, rather a lack of new entries.[17] The Council minutes of the summer of 1941 went so far as to say, 'if the numbers of boys in the future were to fall seriously, it might be thought expedient to explore the possibilities of amalgamating with another school'.

EXILE TO HARROW

On 25 April 1942 Tom Gaunt returned from his Easter holidays to discover that two government officials had spent two hours inspecting the College buildings and left without any explanation. A similar event had occurred at St James's Girls' School and Gaunt decided to seek clarification from the Ministry of Works in London, although he could hardly believe that Malvern would be subjected to a second evacuation:

> At the Ministry I began by apologising for troubling them over what might be a silly scare, and until that very moment I was half expecting to be walking out of the building ten minutes later with a sense of having been idiotically disturbed by the whole affair, but with a happy reassurance in my mind once again … I need not have troubled to apologise: within two minutes it became obvious that the situation was extremely critical, if not already past repair. I was told that owing to an unexpected development in the course of the War a certain vital Government department had been compelled to move their establishment elsewhere immediately; that this was a War Cabinet decision, and that Malvern College had been selected as the most suitable premises in the country.

Gaunt quickly came to the conclusion that the 'only conceivable solution was to join up with another school'.[18] Given that most schools were full he contemplated an approach to several schools in the hope that each might 'take one or two of our Boarding Houses with their Housemasters … in this way some kind of continuity would have been possible. And there would have been a nucleus from which to build again when, after an unknown number of years, we would return to Malvern'. A visit to Rugby offered some consolation along this path and Gaunt returned to Malvern for an emergency meeting of housemasters, one of whom mentioned that Harrow was much reduced in numbers and might be able to accommodate a few houses or even the whole school. The idea was not initially attractive – Harrow's numbers had of course fallen because of its close proximity to the London Blitz – 'nevertheless the idea was to grow during the next few days', not least because the school might be able to remain as one.[19]

On 30 April Gaunt went to see Mr Butler in the House of Commons and was told the reasoning behind the decision.[20] Earlier that month there had been a special commando raid upon Bruneval, on the coast of France, where a German radar station was situated. The crucial discovery of the raid was that the Germans intended to carry out a heavy attack by aircraft and parachutists upon the Telecommunications Research Establishment (TRE) at Swanage during the next full moon:

> The news had at once been communicated to the War Cabinet, and the Prime Minister had instantly given the order that TRE was to move immediately with the least possible dislocation of their vital work: they were to choose the place and accommodation best suited to their needs, and every other consideration, public or private, was to give way to this overriding necessity.
>
> TRE needed certain special geographical features for their work, including fairly high hills, a wide range of vision, proximity to an aerodrome [the airfield at Defford was used] and, of course, a secluded place of comparative safety; in addition there must be buildings which could be very speedily converted into the laboratories and research workshops which were needed, and grounds on which new buildings could be built. A large school or institution was clearly suitable, provided that it were in the right place, and the Ministry of Aircraft Production authorities, under whose auspices TRE worked, at once consulted the Board of

Right: Unloading at Harrow.

Education. Of all the schools in England two were pre-eminently suitable, Marlborough and Malvern, and of the two Malvern was preferred.[21]

Following this informative meeting Gaunt set to work to save his school. He received a positive response from some parents on the prospect of a move near to London. On 1 May a telephone call followed to Mr A. P. Boissier, the acting Headmaster of Harrow:

I outlined briefly the facts of our requisition; I made plain the plight we were in; I asked whether it were possible for Harrow to accommodate one or two of our Houses or even the whole school; and I ended with the words, 'Can you do anything for us?' He had listened to my recital in silence, and his reply was brief, 'I think so; come and have lunch!' How characteristic of the man those words were, I was to learn later!

Harrow was also in grave difficulties with falling numbers and considerable overheads. As Christopher Tyerman points out in his history of Harrow School, 'the governors could not afford to keep the school open; nor could they afford to close it'. This conundrum was resolved by the arrival of Malvern College in the summer of 1942 paying rent for the houses they occupied. Ironically, 'Harrow's near dissolution had provided this opportunity for survival, its emptiness allowing space for Malvern to live, work, worship, and play'.[22]

That afternoon Gaunt and Boissier made plans in the latter's study, and after a period of consultation Boissier said he could eventually offer Malvern five houses; but only one, Rendalls, was actually vacant at that time. The Coldstream Guards were in Westacre; the Ministry of Health had a hospital in Newlands; a London insurance company was renting Deyncourt, and Bradby would have to see its Harrovians distributed to other houses. Mr Butler moved fast to vacate the houses used by government departments and persuaded the insurance company to do the same.

Further amalgamation of the Malvern boarding houses was now necessary and the surviving houses and their new charges took the name of the housemasters.[23] Gaunt's work as a headmaster had become so heavy that he gave up School House to D. W. Erskine. So ended the long tradition by which the headmaster had always been a housemaster.

Meanwhile back at Malvern the school was packing and moving out while TRE was moving in. Some thirty-eight railway containers and fifteen vans moved most of Malvern's necessities. On 28 May Malvern was ready to begin a new phase of its existence, which was to last for nearly four and a half years.[24]

In his first address to the school in Harrow Chapel Gaunt struck a reflective note:

> Let us consider this catastrophe in its right perspective, against the broader background of the war. Compare our sufferings with the perils and privations which our brothers are facing on land, sea, and in the air. Consider the lives of those who fought at Singapore or who withdrew fighting week by week along the roads of Burma. Picture for a moment what our allies have to face in France and Poland and Greece. In the larger picture of the war our sufferings and difficulties seem a small part.
>
> But if against the vast canvas they seem a small part, they are not an insignificant part. I am sure that when the whole story of our evacuation can be told – and it cannot be told now – Malvern College will be found to have played an honourable and vital part in the winning of the war.

It was the intention of both schools that they should retain their separate identities. Gaunt recalls that the Senior Chapel Prefect wrote down a list of customs that the school had observed at Malvern – 116 of them – as a way of preserving the individual identity of the school.[25] There was therefore no amalgamation of the teaching or of the games. Inevitably there were compromises to suit the new conditions. Initially both sets of prefects had equal authority over members of both schools, there were joint chapel services, the Malvern version of Matins and the Harrow form of Evensong. The schools shared the sanatorium, the teashop and the library as well as combining their choral societies. An OM recalls:

Left: The Malvern notice boards at Harrow.

Above: While at Harrow the College welcomed a number of distinguished visitors. This photograph shows an assembly, quite possibly one that was addressed by King Haakon of Norway in June 1943. (Courtesy of Mrs Helen Jones, the College Librarian, who inherited the photograph from her father T. G. Darby (3. 1942–46) who was present.)

> When I arrived as a new boy at No. 5/7 of which Mr R. Colthurst was Housemaster; we occupied two buildings which were private houses which had been adapted – one in which we lived and another, about 100 yards away, where we went to have our meals. Few staff were employed and junior boys had to undertake a wide range of tasks, including 'blacking out' the windows in case of air raids, a range of domestic chores, including washing-up, laying tables for meals and never-ending cleaning.[26]

Despite some tribal tension, the evacuation proceeded with relatively little disharmony between the boys of the two schools. This may have been assisted by what an editorial in *The Malvernian* called the 'urgency of war'. Air raid sirens were frequently heard and the masters and boys shared fire-fighting duties. One Malvern boy recalls:

> It was not until 1943 that we had our first real taste of enemy bombing with a firebomb raid on the Hill. Malvern squads did yeoman service fighting fires in West Street, under the direction of the Headmaster, and a No. 3 squad extinguished a fire in the chapel. Damage to school property was amazingly light, but the 'Grub' was badly hit, a bitter blow to all.

On the morning of Ash Wednesday, 22 February 1944, it was a Malvern master who raised the alarm to enable the fire-watchers to save the principal school buildings from being destroyed by a major fire started by an enemy incendiary bomb. One Harrow master said: 'Malvern College could not have done more for its own buildings than it did for Harrow.' The Prime Minister, himself an Old Harrovian, assisted the feeling of camaraderie when he spoke at his old school:

You have visitors here now in the shape of a sister school – Malvern. I must say I think this is a very fine affair – to meet the needs of war, to join forces, to share alike, like two regiments that serve side by side in some famous brigade and never forget it for a hundred years after.[27]

There were decided advantages in the proximity to London, not least in the relative ease in obtaining distinguished visitors. Mr Butler agreed to come to Malvern's first prize-giving 'on the hill' in July 1942. Gaunt wrote:

Mr Butler's willingness to accept this invitation at what must have been one of the busiest times of his life (so far) was most deeply appreciated, for it not only confirmed the debt which we owed him, but also signified to the world at large that the prosperity of Malvern was treated with real concern by the Government even amid the more serious affairs of 1942.

In June 1943 the Headmaster reported visits by Sir Archibald Sinclair,[28] King Haakon of Norway and Major Attlee, the Deputy Prime Minister, and by December there had been visits by Sir Walter Monckton,[29] Quintin Hogg[30] and the Archbishop of Canterbury. Herbert Morrison, then Home Secretary, spoke to the school in February 1944; 'all these glimpses of men who were at the centre of the great events of the time gave these occasions an even greater sense of immediacy that they might have had in quiet Worcestershire.' Gaunt formed a discussion group, which he invited distinguished men from various walks of life to address. Cultural and educational trips to London were frequent and there was a revival of the connection with the Docklands Settlement, which had suffered badly during the bombing; three of the settlements were a total loss, and there was a great shortage of staff. Some twenty boys went to help the Mission in the summer of 1942, and in June 1943 the school hosted some 120 members of the settlement.

Gaunt reported in June 1945 that VE Day had been celebrated with much 'festivity in the Town, in some of which our boys took part. I am glad to say that their conduct was exemplary, and won much high praise from the townspeople themselves. A weekend holiday was granted.' John Burton recalls:

In my third term on VE Day we were allowed time off and could join the celebrations in the town. Somewhat later Winston Churchill came to attend a Harrow School function at the Speech Room. Two friends and I decided to go to where he would probably be and saw him emerge from the Headmaster's House – accompanied by the Head. He seemed amused by the presence of three Malvern boys and we were convinced that he winked at us, which of course made our day.[31]

During their time away, nostalgia for Malvern gave way to a concern that the familiar and defining patterns of behaviour beloved of many Malvernians would be lost forever. Indeed when the school did eventually go back there were only four boys who had been at the school before its move to Harrow. Gaunt was not a natural conservative but 'after the turmoil and changes of two exiles, he was looking longingly for the stability which old-established traditions might give'. So from 1943 to 1946 successive editions of *The Malvernian* printed accounts of school customs.

Prominent among these time-honoured conventions was the rule that School House had the sole use of the path leading down from their yard to the Pavilion; that No. 1 did not subject the new boys at the end of their first fortnight to the rather terrifying ordeal that took place in other houses of being examined by the prefects on the customs and slang of the

Below: Telegrams received on the occasion of the College returning to Malvern.

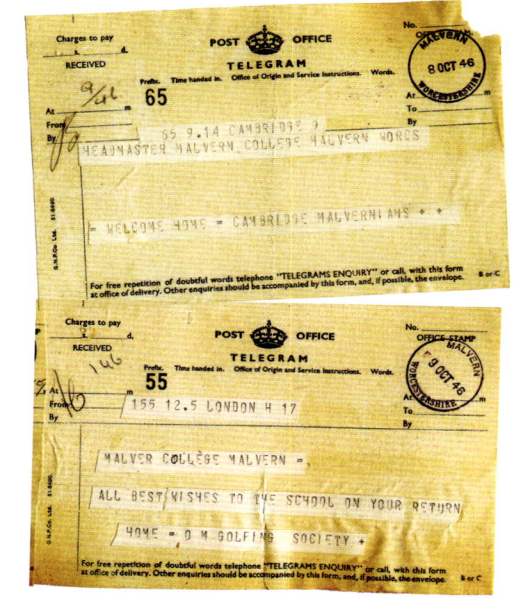

Right: 'Back Home'. Summer at Malvern; No. 6 boys in 1949. (Courtesy of Peter Southgate (6. 1946–50))

school, but instead made new boys stand on a table and sing a song; that No. 6 inherited from Toppin's day the privilege of sitting on the Senior itself, instead of on the bank, to watch matches; that on the command of the Head of House, No. 8 would go for a walk round the garden just before bedtime on fine summer evenings; that No. 9 considered it a tradition to have only OM housemasters, that it enjoyed sole use of the Monastery garden, and was the only house to frown on 'house-bangs'.[32] Among other traditions that were valued was an elaborate code enforcing the hierarchy of boys' lives, 'the right to walk about with one hand in your pocket (except when passing School Prefects) if you had been at the School for one year, and to have both hands in your pockets after two years; the right to sport a white handkerchief in your breast pocket after three years and to wear floral decorations after four, and a host of other sartorial rules'.

The editorial of March 1946 provided a reminder of school rules before the imminent return to Malvern:

> There should be no necessity for some unsuspecting member of the Lower School to be told off for walking up the main steps and past St George. On the first Sunday of the new term, everyone should know that the whole school waits in Houses on the Terrace before morning Chapel. No boy should walk past the Masters' Common Room with his hands in his pockets. No one should be ignorant of the traditions and privileges of the seniors. All should know that only members of the Eleven and School Prefects may walk across the Senior; that in the summer term the whole school walks twice around the Senior after evening Chapel; that during matches the school sits in Houses on the bank, with the Seniors at the top and Juniors at the bottom.

There was some reaction to this litany in subsequent editions of *The Malvernian*; some supportive, like a well-known OM cricketer who wrote 'I am one of the many old boys who hope desperately that the new Malvern will do its best to reach back over the last few ghastly years and try to touch the unseen hand that guided the school before its day in exile'; some critical, like a letter that complained about why a young boy in the XI should be given privileges denied to a young boy in the Sixth Form. In a later edition one correspondent retorted:

> May Malvern be restored home purged of bad traditions, enriched by new traditions. A tradition must stand or fall by itself. If it is backed by sound reason then it will live; but if it needs reactionary propping up by people no longer at the school, then it deserves to die.

The school's legal contract with Harrow provided that Malvern's tenure would come to an end within one year of the end of hostilities with Germany. Harrow nobly did not enforce this provision when it became apparent that the TRE would take much longer to vacate the school. This was a real financial loss for Harrow who had to turn away potential pupils. The end of the war brought a happy rise in boarding school numbers: Malvern was down to 268 in January 1944 but reopened 'at home' with 402.

In order to thank Harrow for their hospitality Malvern presented their hosts with what has become known as the Malvern Clock. Inscribed in a stone plaque below the clock is the school motto and a further Latin text translated as:

> The Council of Malvern College had this clock set up in the year 1950 – remembering the hospitality received on this hill over four years 1942–1946 and so many acts of kindness.
>
> Whatsoever hour God shall have blessed you with, take it with a grateful hand.

The school eventually returned to Malvern in September 1946 – a year after originally planned. It took a question in the House of Commons and the intervention of the new Minister of Education, Ellen Wilkinson, to force the pace, and even this was only a partial derequisition. However, Gaunt was able to announce:

> For a term or two the scientists of T.R.E. will be working in the College grounds, in nearly all the temporary buildings which they have erected and in some of the College buildings. We shall have to put up with the minimum of redecoration, with such things as open dormitories, and even with unpartitioned studies for the time being ... But we shall be back at last – back to our home and familiar surroundings – back to the open hills – back, pray God, for good!

Some boys had had their first glimpse of their school when the TRE allowed some of Overbury Harvest Camp to visit in the summer of 1945:

> A few of us, of course, needed no directing, but the majority were complete strangers to the place. We first went over the School buildings and were allowed into some of the rooms, notably the Sixth Form Room, which is being used as the Superintendent's study. Next we

Above: The Malvern clock at Harrow.

Left: Walking around the Senior after evening Chapel c. 1948. This custom evolved in the nineteenth century quite possibly as a way of flattening the Senior Turf. It became a much-loved time of sociability. (Courtesy of Peter Southgate (6. 1946–50))

Right: The visit of Field Marshal Bernard Montgomery to the College in December 1950.

> went into the Chapel and were convinced that our memories of its beauty were not exaggerated … we were not allowed into any of the Houses, but from the outside, at least, they looked the same as ever. When we reached the Senior, the members of the Cricket XI present, in defiance of all notices, walked onto it, but a policeman soon turned them off … everywhere we went, we encountered policemen, very odd bits of apparatus, and miles of barbed wire … We were all very grateful to the Superintendent for allowing us to go 'home' for an hour.

The first years back in Malvern saw a sharp rise in numbers – over two hundred in the first two years, and a steady increase after that. The increase was needed, for there was a very large overdraft at the bank awaiting government compensation.[33] It was a period of rapid inflation and the school was as ever dependent on the Malvernian Society, this time for the extensive repairs to school buildings. An interesting event occurred in 1948 when Malvern hosted two German boys for a term under a scheme sponsored by Robert Birley[34] to bring some sixty 'carefully selected German boys' to be guests in English schools.

The rapid increase in numbers meant that Malvern became an unbalanced school – initially very young and then top heavy with seniors, and the need to recruit led to a fall in entrance requirements. It has been suggested that cumulatively this led to 'an unusual amount of rule breaking and unpleasant incidents', although some had a decidedly Monty Python flavour:

> This term X was dismissed from the prefectorial body for being an inadequate Prefect. He and an Inferior broke into one of the magazines in one of the quarries, using a jemmy to force the lock. He took from the magazine 25 sticks of gelignite and 13 detonators which he brought back to the House and kept in his Grub box.[35]

> I remember one Derby Day when most of No. 6 were standing in the House corridor waiting to be beaten for gambling on the race. X after taking all the bets in the first place, was walking up and down the line of us taking bets on how many strokes we would each receive.[36]

Left: *Classic Travel, Great Malvern* by Eric Bottomley GRA, depicting the connection between the College, the steam railway and the Morgan Motor Company. (Eric Bottomley)

Although, given the entry, academic standards were not strong, there was still much intellectual and cultural activity with a plethora of new and old societies thriving. Choral music and drama revived and the quality of the now termly *Malvernian* improved. Games initially suffered from the relative youth of the school but in 1949, in A. H. Chadder's last year in charge of football, the XI won all four of its school matches. Football Blues were still won and one George Chesterton achieved a cricket Blue before coming back to Malvern in 1950 to teach and run the cricket. In the Ledder (see Chapter 13) of 1951 R. H. Chadder of School House discovered a new route, which enabled his House to achieve seven of the nine Ledder caps. In Gaunt's last report to the Council he recorded that the Coronation exeat had been 'greatly enjoyed by boys and staff alike. A large majority took part in the Abbey service and procession on Television, and evidently have been greatly impressed by it.'

Finally in 1953 Tom Gaunt also retired and subsequently took holy orders.[37] His headmastership had been the most extraordinary and exhausting of all the tenures of the office. He had coped with pre-war economic difficulties, two exiles involving four moves for the school, and then the economic and political uncertainties of the post-war world. It was hardly surprising that he became wedded to re-establishing a settled order of things in his final years. The school owes much to his fortitude and great labours on its behalf. A former pupil remembers his acts of kindness, not least when Gaunt discovered that the boy would spend much of the summer holiday on his own while his parents were abroad and so invited him to join a climbing expedition to Switzerland.[38] A charming final image captures this rather elusive personality:

> Mr Gaunt and I met one afternoon, walking on a hill path. He stopped, smiled, asked my name and House, and was so charming to me, and such a perfect gentleman, that over a period of 50 years I still remember every word he said. I was in my first term then, and to have a polite civilised conversation with anyone in authority was a surprise and a novelty. He wished me well and went on his way. He left the College at the end of the Christmas term, and many years later I read in the *Telegraph* obituaries that he had died, and felt real sadness and regret.[39]

Below: Sir Godfrey Huggins, 1st Viscount Malvern (3. 1898–99), Prime Minister of Southern Rhodesia 1933–53 and of the Federation of Rhodesia and Nyasaland 1953–56. He presented the prizes at Commemoration in 1953.

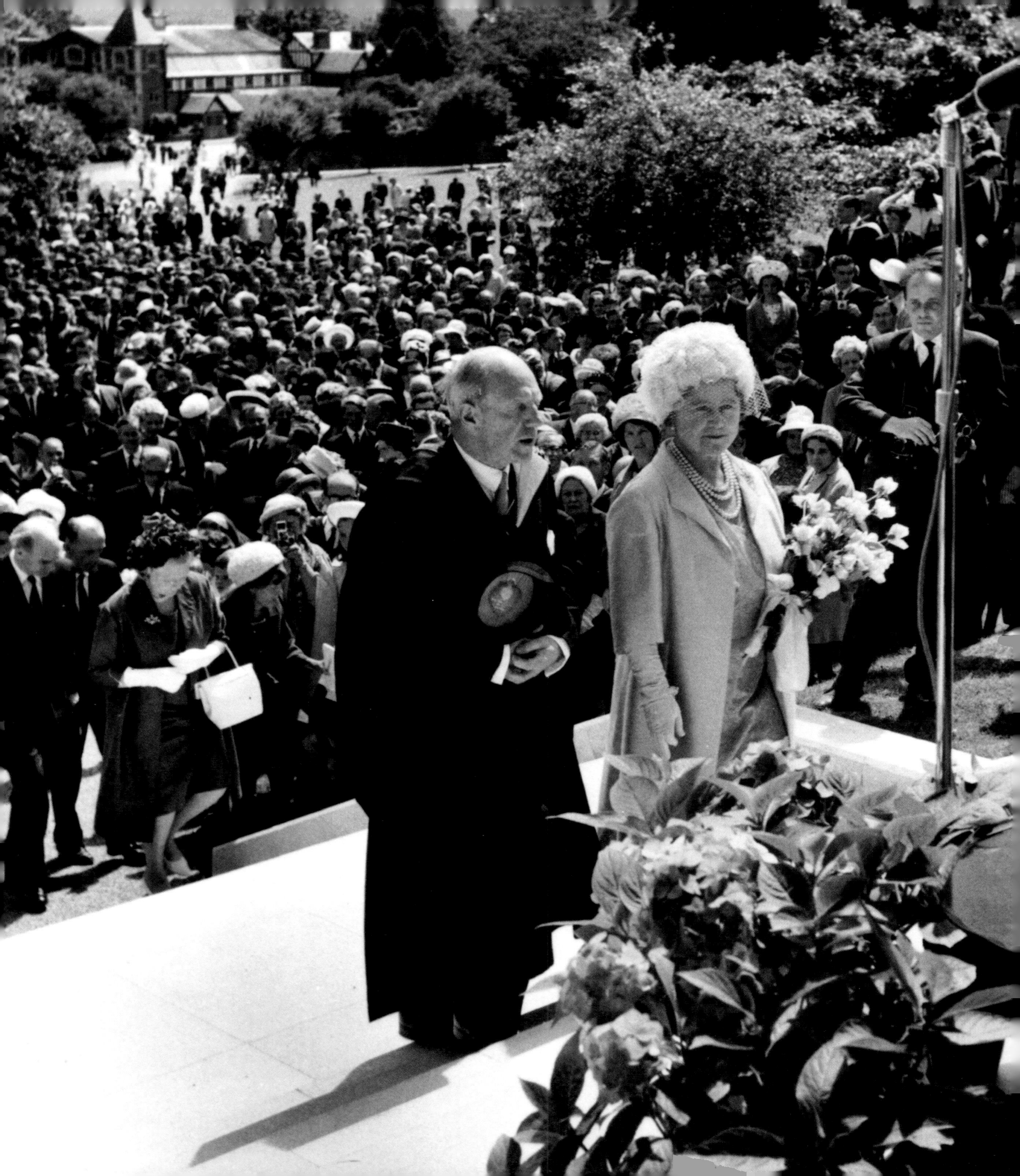

6

The new Elizabethans, 1953–82

With the crowning of the young Queen Elizabeth II in 1953 it became fashionable for a while to talk about a new Elizabethan age with pleasing echoes of the glories of the first Elizabeth, when England saw a growing pre-eminence in Europe, the beginning of a great empire, a flowering of literature and a buccaneer adventurism. The new age, it was widely predicted, would echo and surpass that of the new queen's noble predecessor. Donald Lindsay's headmastership began in 1953 and Martin Rogers saw the Queen's Silver Jubilee. Of more significance is the fact that Malvern, like so much of British society, went through the disillusionment that followed this early optimism and then the beginning of a profound reorientation of the school which, like the country, remained indebted to its past but also began feeling its way towards a new vision. This was in many ways closer to the real world of the first Elizabeth when a nervous, divided country struggled for survival in a hostile world and yet managed to emerge strengthened and vigorous.

Donald Lindsay was educated at Clifton and Trinity College, Oxford. Subsequently he taught at Manchester Grammar School, lectured in education at Bristol University, became the senior historian at Repton, and served as Headmaster of Portsmouth Grammar School for eleven years. His career at Malvern was to be distinguished and an early indication of Lindsay's character and strengths comes from the memoirs of the Old Malvernian Sir John Wheeler-Bennett. He had not greatly enjoyed his school days and left in 1920 determined never to return. However, his opinion was changed after hearing the new Headmaster speak at an OM function that he had reluctantly attended out of obligation to an old friend.[1] He recorded that to begin with it was a 'dreary' occasion, but his disappointment was to vanish when the Headmaster spoke, earning Wheeler-Bennett's praise:

> 'as one of the 'best *ex tempore* speakers I have ever listened to.' With the ability of an actor manqué, Lindsay 'soothed the fears of the Philistines with glowing tributes to the school's past and present athletic triumphs … spoke in praise of the standards of scholarship, resisting the temptation to suggest that they might be higher … then, venturing on more dangerous ground, said boldly that public school education should provide opportunities for the athlete and the scholar and also for the artist, the boy who could seek and find expression in the world of arts and craftsmanship'; that and interest in music, drama, painting, sculpture or photography was not something 'different', to be ashamed of, but rather that it was to be accepted as part of school life. Wheeler-Bennett was delighted. 'Here was someone who talked my language and shared my belief that in a public school the needs and interests of mind and body were catered for in balance and perspective.'[2]

Opposite: Donald Lindsay with Her Majesty Queen Elizabeth, the Queen Mother during the College's centenary celebrations in July 1965.

Above: Mr Donald Lindsay, Headmaster 1953–71. (John Farebrother)

Right: CCF parade, 1958. (Courtesy of Gavin Turner (1. 1954–58))

Below: 'Cold War warriors'. (Courtesy of Richard Lewis (SH 1955–60))

In a glowing character description for the centenary history of the school, Ralph Blumenau described Donald Lindsay:

> He is perhaps the first headmaster since Faber with a twinkle in his eye. He takes his work seriously, but himself not at all. He leads by encouragement. He drives neither his staff nor his boys; fear and awe are not weapons in his armoury. It is characteristic of him that he wants boys sent up to his study for good work and not for bad work; and because it is so clear to everyone that he prefers to praise rather than reprove, his criticisms, when they do come, are all the more effective. He is the least aloof of headmasters, and by his own example has softened the rigidities of a public school hierarchy from the Headmaster's study right down to the smallest fag. The seriousness underlying these attitudes is concealed behind a screen of irreverent wit and light-hearted humour. He is incapable of making a dull speech or of preaching a boring sermon. In fact, he conceives the combating of dullness, apathy, or mere routine as one of his chief functions.[3]

There is little doubt that Lindsay achieved this last objective. A flavour of his inimitable style comes in the recollections of his last Senior Chapel Prefect:

> DDL is talking in a lengthy fashion about some new rule which has already been accepted. I remind him of the Games committee meeting. He replied, 'I suppose that means you want me to stop. I can't understand you. What are you here for, if not to listen to me? You don't know what's good for you, Go!'
>
> While watching the match I am joined by DDL who points out some boy doing something 'illegal'. I turn to a passing school prefect and hand on the task. The Head observes, 'I'm glad to see the chain of delegation still works. It is only by delegating that one can be lazy and still get the job done.'[4]

In the summer of 1917, **Sir John Wheeler-Bennett** (5. 1917–20) joined Malvern[i] where his ambition to become a historian 'took shape and meaning'. In April 1916 a German bomb had exploded in the schoolyard of his preparatory school pitching him 'down the stairs and into oblivion'. The shell shock left him with a permanent bad stammer and a series of nervous disorders. With his poor health and the knowledge that his dream of becoming a soldier was 'unrealisable', he became even more determined 'to find out why and how things had happened in the past and might well be repeated in future'.[ii] Continued ill health meant that he did not follow his brother to Oxford. He was an enthusiast for the new League of Nations having been deeply impressed by seeing President Wilson in London in 1918, and after school he joined The League of Nations Union. Financially independent, he became an inveterate traveller, meeting virtually everyone of importance, and established his own information service on international politics. Living in Germany from 1927 to 1934 he became a friend and confidant of a wide circle of politicians both in Germany and beyond. An authority on German and diplomatic history, his most significant works were *The Forgotten Peace*, a study of the treaty of Brest-Litovsk, and *The Nemesis of Power*, a study of the German Army. He advised the British and American governments on the German resistance to Hitler, assisted the British prosecution at the Nuremberg Trials and edited *Documents on German Foreign Policy* after the war. He was historical adviser to the Royal Archives from 1959 until his death. He was a Tutor at New College, Oxford, and was a founding Fellow of St Anthony's College, Oxford. He was asked by HM The Queen to write the official biography of her father, the late King George VI, who along with Sir John had been treated by the Australian speech therapist Lionel Logue, on whom Sir John commented 'I can never forget or be too grateful for the change he wrought in my own life'.[iii] Deeply impressed by Donald Lindsay, he was persuaded to become chairman of the Malvern College Council and presided with patrician elegance over the centenary celebrations in 1965. In 2000 the College honoured his memory with the establishment of the Wheeler-Bennett Society, a Sixth Form scholars' society.

(Courtesy of the family of Sir John Wheeler-Bennett)

Wheeler-Bennett Society meeting.

This spirit of mild absurdity clearly runs through the Lindsay years. The much respected and ever entertaining John Farebrother, housemaster of No. 6 and in charge of the CCF, had the task of preparing the boys for the annual inspection by imitating the reviewing officer. A colleague described seeing all the boys in serried ranks, standing to attention. As Farebrother went past, he spoke to each cadet in his line and, watching from afar, it seemed that each boy soldier doubled up in hysterical laughter in response to the jovial asides.[5] A common theme of school life was the staged rivalry between senior masters – a source of endless entertainment to the boys. A new master teaching in the Main Building was surprised to hear a thud on a nearby door and upon investigation found it to be a rubber-tipped arrow fired by Farebrother at the door of the revered Malcolm Staniforth.[6] The exchange of arrows provided joyous entertainment for those boys who witnessed it. This was the time when the same two housemasters took their rivalry to a new level when one, together with his senior prefects, broke into a rival house to steal all the sporting trophies and displayed them in his dining room, from which the irate victim had to collect them the following day. A former pupil remembered participating in another apparent feud:

> There was always great rivalry between Norman Rosser and 'Jock' McNevin. The latter's classroom in the Science block overlooked the Geography school. On one occasion I was asked to make some hydrogen sulphide in a Kipp's apparatus. This is a simple mixture of ferric sulphide and a weak acid and the resultant gas is extremely pungent, smelling strongly

Above: The Headmaster, Mr D. Lindsay, with the Senior Chapel Prefect (left), Michael J. Theobald (5. 1953–58), and the Junior Chapel Prefect, Robert T. Collet (8. 1953–58). Photograph taken in 1958 and published in *The Illustrated London News*. (© Illustrated London News Ltd/Mary Evans)

of rotten eggs. The apparatus has a fine nozzle ideally shaped to fit through a keyhole. I carefully carried this down to the door of Mr. Rosser's classroom and, in full view of the science block, delivered a large quantity of this noxious gas and then departed to watch the results. As you may imagine it caused uproar at the time but whether Norman Rosser ever repaid this 'gift' I never learnt.[7]

Lindsay certainly led from the front. He appeared in the Masters' Shrove Tuesday Review in 1957 and 1962 as the prima ballerina in a *corps de ballet*[8] composed of all the heftiest members of staff. One colleague recalled a moment of stunned silence as the boys tried to absorb what they were seeing before their descent into howls of laughter.

A common theme in many recollections of the school during these years was of a welcoming and friendly Common Room. A symbol of this attractive atmosphere was the Masters' 'Bottling' Club, which saw members of the Common Room bottling wine or fortified wines from large kegs transported from foreign vineyards. For many years this pleasing activity took place in the cellars of No. 8. It was invariably an increasingly libidinous and jolly evening. It was of course known to the boys, who took a healthy interest in the stories that circulated about their pedagogues letting their hair down. The resident tutor[9] of No. 8 recalls coming down to breakfast after one such bottling session to discover 'an unusual buzz of animated conversation. On enquiring, I was informed that the senior boys in the House had been taking bets the previous evening as to which member of staff would be the last to depart. 'Who was it? I asked. 'Who do you think sir?' they replied. I hazarded a guess, only to be told: 'Wrong, Sir. It was the Headmaster, and he seemed to have had a very good evening!' On one occasion a great barrel of sherry fell off the transport and masters could be seen attempting to stop its increasingly rapid acceleration down the slope by No. 8 and even more engagingly trying to save some of the spilling contents with whatever receptacle came to hand.[10]

However, Lindsay had serious business to transact. Upon his appointment it was clear to him that Malvern needed to raise its academic standards after the inevitable fall brought about by the war and the necessary rapid expansion since the return from Harrow. He was convinced that in the more challenging post-war circumstances Malvern, and indeed all public schools, would only survive by giving absolute priority to academic work. The changes in educational opportunity introduced by both the wartime coalition and the post-war Labour government would mean that far more students would be able to apply for the great universities, and the meritocratic sentiments of a more egalitarian country would make formal educational achievement much more important. The days when public school boys of only moderate academic attainments could enter universities were numbered. In his first report to the College Council Lindsay was stark:

> The standard of academic achievement and the amount of work done by boys is not good enough for a school of Malvern's standing.

He recommended a long-term plan involving four aspects: an increase in lessons and preparation time; the encouragement of masters to recognise the importance of mastering the technique of their job in the form-room; a sufficiently generous salary scale to attract first-rate men to Malvern; and most important of all – the raising of the standard of entry.

Salaries were paid a term in arrears to the discomfiture of many newly appointed masters. One young master went to the College clerk seeking help, to which the response was, 'So you want to join the half term club' – a secret deal by which a number of young masters received an advance on their salary. Shortly afterward the College Council met with anxious staff to discuss salaries. In responding to the request for monthly payments the vice-chairman of the council reminded the masters that they were fortunate to be teaching in a school where the view was worth £200 p.a. One of the more vociferous replies pointed out, in robust language, that it was not possible to live on a view![11] Lindsay persuaded the council to end the archaic system by which each master negotiated his own salary and introduced a universal and much improved scale. With the great expansion of education and much wider career opportunities this would be the only way of securing men of the academic calibre to lift the school's performance. A key part of Lindsay's strategy to lift academic standards was his power of recruitment and appointment. He strongly backed innovative teachers, like John Lewis and George Sayer, who could teach well, connect with the wider intellectual world and win sponsorship. He promoted those he found to be able, and he spent much time in recruiting to the school bright, young academic teachers.

Lindsay also worked on changing the attitude of the senior boys by continual personal exhortation. Two additional periods were added to the weekly timetable, more Hall time was created,[12] and monthly report cards were introduced. In 1955 the entry standard for Common Entrance was raised and standards predictably rose – in one year the number of O level passes increased by 20 per cent and continued to improve in subsequent years; by 1960 45 per cent of the school was in the Sixth Form compared to 34 per cent in 1939.[13] A level results improved and some years yielded impressive university awards. In 1957 departmental inspections were introduced in which Her Majesty's Inspectors spent a day or so 'listening to the teaching and discussing with masters individually and collectively, their problems'.

The more expansive view of education that dominated the vision of Preston was also a central concern of Lindsay, who believed that high academic standards should not be achieved 'at the expense of the full life, whose realisation must always remain the chief aim of a good education'. Co-curricular activities became ever more numerous.[14] In 1956 a move was made to stimulate the younger boys with the creation of the Ferrets where new boys would be provided with a

Above: House breakfast in the 1960s. (© Michael Ward / ArenaPAL)

Below left: Boys leaving the new Science block in 1958. The older Preston Science Building can be seen to the left. (© Illustrated London News Ltd/Mary Evans)

Below right: Nuffield learning. (© Michael Ward / ArenaPAL)

George Sayer came to Malvern in 1945 and ran the English department until his retirement in 1974. He formed a strong friendship with C. S. Lewis (who had tutored him at Oxford) and J. R. R. Tolkein, both of whom regularly visited George in Malvern. He developed a reputation for profound scholarship, affable eccentricity and great personal warmth and kindness. One former pupil writes:

> I was privileged to be taught English by George Sayer for a year. I doubt that the dear man adhered too much to any concept of syllabus; being fond of any literary or grammatical red herring that his class would frequently throw in his direction. Knowing that he enjoyed being sidetracked, we did just that. In his magisterial and benign fashion he would deliver a worthy, energetic and fulsome explanation of the newly arisen question, which usually had nothing to do with the subject that we were supposed to be learning about. The most important thing that I recall of his lessons was that he managed, through a boundless, infectious enthusiasm, to imbue me with an insatiable appetite and love for literature. That indeed was a magnificent gift. I am sure that there are a multitude of his former pupils who are grateful, well-read and articulate recipients of his legacy.[i]

(© Michael Ward / ArenaPAL)

Other former students write that his greatest gift was his determination that we should 'engage with ideas',[ii] how 'George taught him a love of language and literature'.[iii] Jeremy Paxman remembered 'the most wonderful, inspirational teacher who was a profoundly decent and compassionate man' and 'the sort of teacher you dream of having'. Choosing George Sayer as his most influential teacher, for a national campaign advocating the teaching profession, he remembered his infectious enthusiasm and his style of teaching as an object lesson in how praise gets results. Essays would be returned covered in witty, encouraging comments in red ink, along with blots of marmalade and paw prints; 'Dear boy, I'm so sorry, the cat seems to have walked all over this'.

programme that introduced 'to all the activities and interests which Malvern has in store for them'. In typical style Lindsay introduced this new scheme as follows; 'I am informed by naturalists that a ferret is an animal given to periodic bursts of intense activity followed by long periods of lethargy. This seemed not inappropriate as a description of a young boy.'[15] For senior boys the College also became a pioneer for the new Duke of Edinburgh Award scheme and another innovation was Arduous Training weekends in the Brecons followed by the annual Cairngorms camps in the holidays.

Donald Lindsay encouraged a civilised vision of the role that games should take in a school. He said at one Speech Day:

> We are very fortunate at the moment in those masters who are in charge of games. They possess two essential but rare qualities in those who devote themselves to training boys to play games – a sense of proportion and a determination that games exist to be enjoyed by those who play them. Games at Malvern are neither a burden nor a compulsory religious exercise: moreover, the boy whose abilities lie elsewhere is not an outcast.

Ian Beer records a delightful vignette of DDL's management of the sporting life of the school:

> Another aspect of College life in which he took much interest, but in which he had little expertise, was sport. Although in his youth he loved tennis and badminton he delegated sport in the College to others and simply listened. On appointing a new cricket professional he rightly sought the advice of George Chesterton and asked him what professional question

should he ask? George suggested, 'ask how important is the back lift in batting?' The right moment came at the subsequent interview: 'How important' said Donald, most knowledgeably, 'is the uplift in batting?'[16]

Drama blossomed in this period not least because of Lindsay's love of the theatre. An initiative from School House in 1960 led to the annual House Play Competition, and expeditions to the theatre at Stratford, Birmingham and Cheltenham became a regular feature of school life. *The Malvernian* became more of a vehicle for the literary works of the boys with essays, poems, and accounts of school trips. House magazines blossomed intermittently. But perhaps the most pronounced cultural change was the growth of interest in the arts. The corridors of the Main Building 'were ornamented with paintings and murals tending towards the fauve and with sculptures tending towards the abstract. These forms of art duly provoked discussion, controversy and growing interest in the school'.[17] Choral music went from strength to strength. In 1955 the Remembrance Day service was broadcast from the Chapel. From 1957 onwards the College combined each year with one of the girls' schools for the choral concert at Easter. Slowly contact with the girls' schools grew with debating, drama, and from 1961 dances, making the school 'a little less monastic'.

Lindsay was anxious to ensure that the boys in his charge had a greater understanding of the outside world. In his speeches he reminded them that the world did not owe them a living and he instituted fortnightly Sixth Form lectures from speakers 'with forthright views'. He promoted weekend exchanges between boys from Malvern and boys from the maintained sector. A key change was the ending of the Mission in Canning Town in 1957. In its place came a scheme of voluntary service in which boys visited and assisted the elderly or the disabled in the town, or provided manual labour for the tending of the Malvern Hills.

Donald Lindsay proved adroit at gently civilising the rather archaic structures he inherited. He disliked beating and did his best to avoid it. One OM recalls that he was summoned to the headmaster's study for the expected caning after he had disobeyed a headmagisterial order about fooling around in gym. He had compounded his offence by giving a false name (Smith) to the warrant officer in charge:

> At the due time I arrived at the door, knocked and entered. 'Ah! Smith' he said, 'at last we meet. I have been wondering about you. We have no record at all of you attending Malvern.

Left: Skiing. 1950s style. (Courtesy of Richard Lewis)

Above left: Junior dormitory, 1960s.
(© Michael Ward/Arena PAL)

Above right: Dormitory high jinks.
(Courtesy of Gavin Turner)

Who are you?' 'Pegrum,' I replied meekly and trembling all over. 'Oh yes the boy who messed around in Gym, contrary to my instruction. Well, Pegrum, now that we know who you are, I'd like you to bend over the arm of that chair and put your arms on the seat.'

I did as he asked and he moved to my front where he swished the Headmaster's cane, which had suddenly materialised in his hand. 'Three, I think. Do you not agree, Pegrum?' 'Yes Sir', I mumbled, 'No, I mean no, Sir', I blurted. 'Three it is then', He said as he disappeared behind me and I clenched my buttocks. Thwack! Thwack! Thwack! Oh, the pain. My clenched buttocks hurt from the clenching, but not from the beating. Donald Lindsay had beaten the back of the huge leather chair, not my bottom. I could not believe it. 'Right Pegrum, let that be a lesson to you.' 'Yes Sir,' I said in disbelief, 'thank you Sir, thank you.' I backed towards the door, turned and left.

Outside three of my friends were gleefully grinning at me as I pretended to hold my backside in feigned agony. 'Was it hard?' 'Did it really hurt?' 'Are you OK?' All the questions under the sun, but I never said a word. Suddenly, I understood what Donald Lindsay was all about and from that day onwards I had the highest regard for the man.[18]

Despite such inspired leniency Donald Lindsay could certainly command more traditional respect. After the half-term break in 1965 the train from London bringing Malvern boys back to school saw a graphic example of bad behaviour when a boy firing an air pistol narrowly missed a distinguished academic at Oxford station. The whole school was summoned to Big School and Lindsay walked onto the stage, kept the assembly standing and berated the school so effectively that 'you could have heard a pin drop'. One master said that he, along with the whole community, was made to feel thoroughly ashamed of Malvern College. The whole school was gated and the Christmas house suppers were cancelled with all the boys having to write an essay instead.[19]

The traditional hierarchy of the boys' world changed a little. In his final section on the school as it approached the centenary Ralph Blumenau wrote:

> The new boys' exam has ceased to inspire terror; fag calls have been restricted to certain times of the day; beatings by prefects are extremely rare and can only be given with Housemasters' approval; bullying is checked as soon as discovered. For some time prefects' meetings still gave a great deal of attention to the dress rules by which the seniority of a boy could be recognised. At one meeting in 1961 most of these were swept away. In the centenary year the

old school uniform with its black jackets will disappear altogether, to be replaced with grey suits and house ties. The straw hats or 'bashers' will go at the same time.

A few years later he was able to record further change:

[Prefects'] authority now weighs more lightly on the younger boys; personal fagging had gone, and in the Headmaster's words the prefects regard themselves 'less as policemen and more as welfare officers'.[20]

With the election of a Labour government in 1964 the long simmering political threat to the public schools led to the establishment of the Public Schools' Commission, under Sir John Newsom, charged with advising 'on the best way of integrating the public school with the state system of education'. Donald Lindsay, as chairman of the Headmasters' Conference,[21] led the charge against the first tranche of proposals that came out in July 1968,[22] determined to defend the right to enjoy independence for both parents and schools. Lindsay, a master of political astuteness, set the tone for relations between the independent sector and all future governments. He concluded his address to the 1968 conference: 'Please trust us to help. We will go as far as we can to meet national needs so long as we do not betray what we believe to be of lasting value in our schools. We would like to continue this dialogue with you, to work with you in laying the foundations for the future. The HMC has not slammed the door'. Ian Beer was to state that Lindsay 'helped preserve the freedom in education the independent schools enjoy today'.[23] The reports of the Public Schools' Commission satisfied nobody. The commission itself was deeply divided. The radical Left simply wanted abolition which ran against public opinion; the mainstream Left could not make up its mind if it wanted to invest public money in supplying places in boarding schools. The independent sector was hostile to the specific proposals and predictably the whole venture was torpedoed by the financial restraints confronting the government in the late 1960s.[24]

Donald Lindsay had a great gift for capturing the moment and all who remember him describe the pleasure of listening to his speeches and sermons. A fine example came on 30 January in a tribute to Sir Winston Churchill, who had died a few days before:

Today our service is one of thanksgiving not of mourning. There is nothing tragic in the death of an old man of ninety whose mortal body had for some years become a woefully inadequate dwelling place for the superb spirit within it. No Christian can ever regard death as the worst which can befall a man. In Churchill's own words on his late master, King George VI: 'In the end Death came to him as a friend.'

Thus our purpose this morning is to mark our belief that, under God, to no other single man is so much owed by so many. That you and I live out our lives as free men; free to do the right as we see it, free to speak the truth as we see it, free to

Above: The old Terrace.

Below: Malvern 'gentlemen' at Commem, 1960. (Andrew Irwin (S. 1956–61))

THE CENTENARY

The College's centenary was celebrated in some style in July 1965 with a visit from Her Majesty Queen Elizabeth, the Queen Mother and the recently retired Prime Minister, Harold Macmillan. Ralph Blumenau's *A History of Malvern College, 1865–1965* was published for the anniversary. After reading out a loyal address to the Queen and Her Majesty's reply, Sir John Wheeler-Bennett spoke:

> Five score years ago our founding fathers in their wisdom purchased a parcel of land with one of the fairest views in England and built thereon a school. From that school beneath the shadow of these majestic hills, have come forth generations of boys who have lived lives here and passed on to the greater world beyond. This never ceasing, ever flowing stream of young life is in itself inspiring; an inspiration to those of you who teach and to those of us who govern, to give each generation the very best that is for then available.
>
> Sir, those years of the mighty past were enriched by many splendid virtues, which we can ill afford to ignore or neglect today. There were for example, the virtues of leadership, of preparation for a part in the service of the country, and, when we had an Empire, Malvernians did not shirk their share of its burden; there were the virtues of comradeship and of self – a sacrifice which found its ultimate utterance in the fact that during the two World Wars nearly seven hundred old boys of this school laid down their lives. It is these virtues, I believe, these golden virtues, that we should cherish and retain.
>
> And how to face the future? Here I would offer the counsel of one whom I am proud to remember as a brilliant pupil of mine some thirty years ago. I speak of President John Fitzgerald Kennedy. Had Jack Kennedy not been stricken down by the assassin's bullet at Dallas, Texas, he would have given a speech next day at the neighbouring city of Austin, and he would have spoken these words: 'This is a time for courage and a time of challenge. Neither conformity nor complacency will do'.

Donald Lindsay's speech clearly stated his educational vision and the sense of his achievement. Imagining the return of Faber and his colleagues to Malvern he believed that:

> Two things would, I think, strike this band of kindly ghosts as they take stock of us – mere numbers and the richness of life which Malvern can today offer. Mr Faber's six assistants have today become fifty-five and the original two dozen pupils are now six hundred strong … Those masters who today are privileged to serve Malvern are a good centenary vintage – never corked and only on the rarest and most justifiable occasions, bottled.
>
> I believe that it is the wonderful richness of school life today, which would most astonish Arthur Faber. Games have always

THE NEW ELIZABETHANS, 1953–82

been held in high regard at Malvern (but they are) no more important than all the other sides of school life, which together contribute to producing a balanced education. Music, painting, sculpture, pottery, printing and woodwork; the activities of innumerable societies; arduous training in the Brecon Beacons, in Snowdonia or the Cairngorms; the opportunities offered by the Duke of Edinburgh Award Scheme; sailing and canoeing at Defford; and the joy which the instructed countryman gains in our exquisite nature reserve at Hope End – in all this lies true education for it is life in abundance.

Harold Macmillan concluded an elegant speech with timeless educational advice:

Nevertheless, whether in the arts or in the sciences, there is surely another aspect of education which cannot be altogether put aside. Learning for its own sake; for the poise and intellectual confidence, which it gives to the sincere student; the respect of knowledge and culture for their values – all this can and should be preserved.

I was an undergraduate at Oxford … I remember attending at least the first of a course of lectures in 'Greats' given by one of the leading philosophers of Oxford. I have always remembered his introductory words:

'Gentlemen I welcome you. I think I should say something before we begin. It is about your future. Some of you when you leave the university will no doubt become civil servants at home; some may go to serve in India or the Colonies; some will go into the Church; some will go into business; some will live as country gentlemen, with the appropriate duties to their station; others – perhaps – will become schoolmasters; others, again, university dons. Except for this last class, which I trust will be small; nothing that you will learn from me will be of the slightest practical use to you – save only this. If you work hard, and pay due attention to your studies, you should – in after life – be able to know when a man is talking rot. And that, in my view, is the main purpose of education'.

Former Prime Minister Harold Macmillan, Headmaster Donald Lindsay, chairman of the College Council Sir John Wheeler-Bennett and the Bishop of Worcester the Rt Rev Lewis Charles-Edwards.

Her Majesty Queen Elizabeth, the Queen Mother with the Senior Chapel Prefect A. D. Roberts (8. 1960–65), the chairman of the College Council Sir John Wheeler-Bennett, and the Headmaster Donald Lindsay.

Above: Malcolm and Bridget Staniforth.

believe what we wish to believe; is, I repeat, under God, due to Winston Churchill more than to any other man.

So to the God who created and sustained him and into whose nearer presence Winston Churchill passed last Sunday morning let us give humble thanks. And as we remember with gratitude this incredible life, let us show forth not only with our lips but in our lives our determination to be strong in the Lord and in the power of His might; to take unto us the whole armour of God; so that, like Winston Churchill, we too may be able to withstand in the evil day, and having done all, to stand.[25]

There is a warmth of references by OMs to the masters who were now nearing the end of their careers. The first is to the 'eccentric and amiable Eb Kennedy, famous for the slang and nicknames he invented and his "pay or play" system of classroom discipline based on fines and tossing a coin for "double or quits" – who nevertheless aroused my interest in Julius Caesar's tactics in the Gallic Wars and the fates of the characters in Ovid's *Metamorphoses* and who left me feeling very well-disposed towards the study of Latin.'[26] Another is to the 'gentle, whimsical, and shrewd' Lewis Dodd, an excellent housemaster, who also organised the centenary celebrations with skill, tact and evident success.[27] A third is to Malcolm Staniforth, a much respected housemaster whose love of cricket and sporting enthusiasm was echoed by the boys in No. 3, who also delighted in the warmth of his wife Bridget. He was to serve both Lindsay and Rogers with distinction as second master.[28]

As his headmastership reached its closing years Donald Lindsay could reflect on considerable progress in Malvern's academic reputation. In 1969 some eighty Malvernians went on to university, about half of them to Oxford and Cambridge, including thirteen award winners – more than had ever been achieved in Malvern's 104-year history.[29] In practically every field of academic study there had been dramatic changes in teaching methods with much more emphasis on active investigation rather than the passive reception of knowledge. This was perhaps most marked in the sciences 'where Malvern boys have the advantage of working in what are almost certainly the best-equipped laboratories of any school in England'. Beyond the academic the school was more open and intellectually and culturally lively than it had been in 1953. Music, always strong in the choral tradition, could now boast two flourishing orchestras and a large military band. The corridors of the school were 'alive with paintings and drawings, sculptures and pottery'. The drama competition was well entrenched and the CCF now provided a variety of activities which boys could choose, from car maintenance to cooking.[30] In this area a typically inspired appointment made a great difference to the life of many boys: Kevin Walton, a war hero and explorer, was recruited to give engineering lectures, and organise sailing expeditions to the Western and Northern Isles:[31]

> I went on them given the alternatives offered by the CCF and ended up going sailing every year with him – and then visiting the islands again and again. He had achieved so much and it was quite something to be encouraged by someone like him.[32]

The school was more outward looking. Voluntary service took boys into the local community. Every boy in the first year of his Sixth Form spent four days at Coventry Cathedral seeing what the cathedral regarded as the Christian approach to an industrial society. Malvern was the first public school to embrace the Duke of Edinburgh's Award Scheme. The domination of house life was mitigated somewhat for the Sixth Form with the birth of the Long Room Club, which in 1966 could report eighty-five members from the Upper Sixth who would be allowed limited quantities of beer while socialising on certain evenings.[33]

The outward reach of the school found expression in some unusual ways. Some enterprising boys in No. 1 and No. 5 saw a business opportunity in selling potatoes in Worcester's housing estates. The successful enterprise came to the attention of the authorities when the boys used the College printing press to print handbills and inadvertently left some behind. They were buying the potatoes wholesale, weighing and bagging them on a weighing machine in the CCF stores, then distributing them using a car kept illegally in a Malvern car park. A CCF officer had seen them at work and had accepted their story that it was part of a biology project. The dénouement came when the housemaster of No. 1 lay in wait in the car park in the dark and switched on his headlights dramatically as the suspect car arrived, only for boys other than those suspected to emerge from it. Realising that the game was up, they explained that they were helping out the real miscreants who had examinations that day and did not want to let their customers down![34]

Above: A study in headwear, 1965. (© Michael Ward / ArenaPAL)

To earlier generations Malvern was famous for excelling in two or three sports, cricket above all, together with football and rackets. By the beginning of the 1970s they had been joined by a very large number of outdoor activities from tennis to sailing; and the watching of school matches had become a voluntary activity. An editorial in *The Malvernian* in March 1970 stated:

> No longer does one have to have considerable prowess on the games field to be anyone. The obscurity of the intellectual and the artist is virtually over. Sport is no longer the only path to popularity and fame. Sport over the last decade has been slowly assuming its rightful position and boys have been accepted even though their talent lies elsewhere. This has also given the less gifted sportsmen a chance to flourish in other fields without the perpetual confinements of compulsory games.

Preston would have rejoiced.

Donald Lindsay had presided over a gentle revolution steered with subtle skill by his theatrical, benign and supremely intelligent personality. One OM who disliked Malvern intensely found Lindsay 'an altogether admirable figure, he left the school a far more civilised place than he found it'.[35] He described him as 'a fine orator and a good teacher, funny and approachable'.[36] Another wrote:

> DDL was one of the few people I have met whom I have regarded as truly inspirational. I saw quite lot of him as a College Prefect, and even more, in my last term, as Junior Chapel Prefect, and I always left any meeting with him feeling better than when I arrived. Over 27 years as a barrister and nearly 12 as a judge I have listened to an awful lot of speeches, and he was one of the best public speakers I have ever heard. He had a knack of communicating instantly with his audience and possessed a wonderful sense of humour.[37]

There is warmth in nearly all the memories of Donald Lindsay and his time as headmaster, an enjoyment of the man and his magnificent performance but also great admiration for what he achieved. The dramatically improved academic status of the school, the entrenchment of a wider view of education, and the steady erosion of the more brutal and archaic aspects of the boys' lives undoubtedly support the judgement that he was one of the great post-war public school headmasters.

The appointment of the new Headmaster, Martin Rogers, coincided with a period of profound social change in Britain. The victory in the Second World War, the building of the welfare state and the romance of the new Elizabethan age had faded somewhat as Britain's diminished world role became apparent. The idealism associated with the welfare revolution of the late 1940s also faded as crime rose and social disintegration grew in the cities. Above all Britain's economic performance seemed to have relegated it to the role of the 'sick man of Europe' with strikes, inflation, persistent regional unemployment and relatively low growth rates. A growing familiarity with the rest of the world through the advance of television and easier travel highlighted how far Britain had fallen in comparison to its neighbours and also served to weaken the insular self-confidence that saw Britain as home to all that was good. The inevitable result was a persistent questioning of familiar assumptions that underpinned much of British life.

The world of education was particularly affected by this mood with widespread criticism of the eleven-plus examination, the growth of comprehensive schools and aggressive assaults on all forms of elitism. This was already having an impact on the wider public school world as the 1970s dawned although inevitably it was more apparent in the cosmopolitan centres. Martin Rogers recalls that after his experiences at Westminster, Malvern seemed to be set in an earlier epoch. He approached his new school with a quiet determination to modernise and further civilise. Inevitably there would be resistance. What emerged at Malvern, as in many other schools, was something of a culture war between various schools of thought favouring change and those who clung to traditional values and institutions. It would take decades for this clash to be in large part resolved and, in classic dialectical form, for a new synthesis to emerge that perhaps satisfied a larger constituency than might have seemed possible at the height of the conflict.

Donald Lindsay had in many ways transformed the school most notably in its much greater academic profile; however, Martin Rogers felt that the school still had an excessively traditional air. There was an all-male teaching staff, overwhelmingly recruited from Oxbridge, and still, of course, heavily imbued with the military experiences of the Second World War. The school was, as with most public schools, single sex and there was little formal contact with the neighbouring girls' schools. The School and House Prefect system was still thriving, and group fagging and beating were still normal parts of school life.[38] Sport was still largely dominated by football and cricket. The CCF was compulsory. Music and drama were valued but for many remained marginal activities. Many boys were happy in the school but the house structures had changed little and the dominance of the housemaster and his prefects could still make life difficult for some.

Public schools had gained a great advantage from the changes afoot in the maintained sector. As the grammar schools fell in swathes to the new bright hope of the comprehensives, many middle-class parents sought to protect status and academic teaching for their children. The later disappointments

Below: Skittish prefects in the mid 1960s. (© Michael Ward / ArenaPAL)

with the new system created a growing demand for traditional teaching and high academic standards. In many ways the public schools were able to reach out to this constituency and to expand their academic profile (which had often been rather limited). This put a premium in a highly competitive market for proof of academic worth. This encouraged a search for inspiring academic staff and changes in curriculums, teaching methods, facilities and school structures.

Martin Rogers was ideally qualified to lead Malvern in these more challenging times. He was the first Malvern headmaster to cross the academic divide between science and the humanities having, after Oundle, studied natural sciences and history at Cambridge. Moreover, he was the first to have studied abroad, at Heidelberg, and he had also some experience in industry. He had taught chemistry at Westminster School and was master of the Queen's Scholars.[39] Although inheriting a successful and popular school – there were 586 boys in the school when his headmastership began – the new Headmaster was only too aware of the challenges that had emerged from the wider state of British education particularly in the independent sector. He consciously sought to follow what he saw as a progressive agenda in Malvern. Having introduced Sixth Form bed studies to his house at Westminster, and seen the notable improvement the change made to social and academic attitudes, he sought to follow the same path at Malvern. Initially there was little enthusiasm – 'absolutely no interest, not a single Housemaster wanted study bedrooms – modern idea, absolute nonsense'[40] – but once George Chesterton embraced the idea a programme of conversion began. A successful appeal launched in September 1981 raised the necessary funds to provide every boy in the Sixth Form with a study bedroom.[41] In its own way this was to provide a radical departure, encouraging the relative independence and individuality of sixth formers in sharp contrast to older ideas of a communitarian culture. Like his predecessor, Martin Rogers disliked caning and it was during his headmastership that this time-honoured punishment finally came to an end, not by a central ruling but simply becoming unfashionable. An OM recalled being beaten for smoking two weeks after arriving at Malvern in January 1976, and again in 1978 after being drunk:

> The reason why this latter incident may be of historical interest is I was never again caned and nor were any other boys, to my knowledge, in either School House or elsewhere. All subsequent tobacco and alcohol enjoyment on my part was met with a fine and a ritual gating. By the time I left in 1980, caning had become a rare and fading badge of honour from a bygone era. I have often wondered therefore if I was the last boy to be caned at Malvern College![42]

Above: Mr Martin Rogers, Headmaster 1971–82.

Below left: Senior dormitory, 1958. Note the lack of privacy and cramped conditions. (© Illustrated London News Ltd/Mary Evans)

Below right: Bed-study revolution, 1980s.

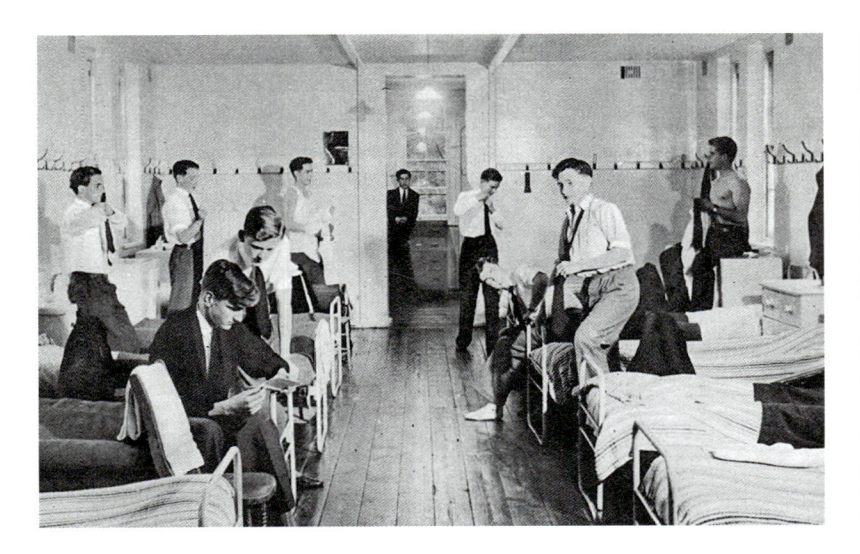

THE DUKE OF EDINBURGH AWARD SCHEME

From 1954 onwards senior boys at Malvern were sent on expeditions all over the neighbouring counties with certain tasks to perform within a limited time and all requiring a good deal of resourcefulness. The report of these tests in *The Malvernian* caught the eye of the authorities responsible for working out the schemes for the new Duke of Edinburgh Awards and consequently Sir John Hunt invited Malvern to be one of the first schools to try out the schemes before they were launched officially. Therefore Malvern can pride itself on being an initiator of this hugely successful international enterprise. The successful participation of the College owes much to the dedicated work of the supervisors, in particular Richard Goddard who ran the programme from 1966 until 2000. He was also the national adviser for independent schools to the award scheme.[i]

Above: Martin Rogers greeting the Duke of Edinburgh who was visiting the College in connection with the award scheme. Richard Goddard, the College supervisor of the scheme, is on the far right.

Another major change, both physical and educational, came in the sporting arena. Most public schools were building new sports centres where a wider range of sports might be offered and with a stronger emphasis on all pupils finding some athletic endeavour that they could follow. Again, this was something of a contrast to the dominance of the team-game culture begun in the mid nineteenth century and which had come to dominate not just school sport but also the wider sporting culture of Britain and its Empire. This tradition was associated not just with physical health but also with the virtues of manliness, loyalty and character. The newer sporting culture reflected the not always attractive cult of individual fulfilment, concerns about the unhealthy lifestyle of so many youngsters and the national concern to emulate the sporting triumphs of other countries where physical training and education seemed to be the key to Olympic and international success. Martin Rogers was concerned about how many boys were 'slipping through the net' of the more traditional games programme and wanted a complete rethink of the organisation of sport at Malvern. So for the first time a Director of Physical Education was appointed who was given the brief of creating a physical education programme for all boys. Rugby, now to be the dominant sport in the Lent term, achieved equal status with football and cricket. These developments coincided with the building of a new sports hall that would provide facilities for more indoor activity.[43] The sports hall was opened by Lady Holland-Martin in October 1977 and survived until replaced by the much more elaborate sports complex in 2010. There were inevitable concerns about these developments with the fear of the diminution of the more traditional games and the ethic that went with them.

Another avenue that would in time profoundly change the school also gathered pace. Almost imperceptibly girls, from neighbouring girls' schools, started to appear on campus to be taught in some Sixth Form subjects. Starting in 1972 with some twenty-one girls attending some lessons and using library facilities, by 1977 the number was seventy-three and by 1981 ninety-one. This suited the local girls' schools where small sixth forms made a wide range of subjects impossible and also satisfied a growing sense that some degree of co-education, at least in the classroom, would be popular with parents. Financially this enabled the girls' schools to attract parents with the promise of a wider curriculum and, of course, it brought in useful money and numbers to Malvern. A staff committee appointed by Donald Lindsay to consider Malvern in the 1970s had supported full co-education, but such a move was premature as it would have been very unpopular with the neighbouring girls' schools and there was little enthusiasm for such a move from parents, the OM Society and some of the teaching staff. While single-sex schools were financially viable, there would be little prospect of change. An advocate of co-education recalls the early problems:

> As for the mixed classes, the boys were scarcely gentlemanly. On the first morning they occupied all the seats round the outside of the classroom so as to corral the girls in the middle – one of the problems for many years was that the girls were always very few in number, which made a naturally intimidating experience even more so. I soon put a stop to that, and arranged the seating in such a way that rows from the back to the front of the room alternated between boys and girls. I gathered that some boys spread the rumour that I was trying to match-make.
>
> The boys continued to do very little to make the girls feel welcome; and one day, when the girls were kept up at Ellerslie for some reason or other, I took the boys to task. A pimply boy said, 'Well, Sir, you will agree that they are hardly God's gift to men' – expressing the widely felt disappointment that the Ellerslie girls were not a particularly glamorous lot. My reply was obvious: 'And what exactly makes you think that you are God's gift to women?'
>
> Common Room was not very much better. When the girls or their women teachers were discussed, the air was often thick with contemptuous male chauvinist comments; and no attempt was made to provide the girls with a place where they could spend break or an interval between classes; and the very few women teachers who taught at the College in those days were almost ignored in the Common Room.[44]

The 1970s also saw the beginning of a new approach to pastoral care. The traditional pattern placed this area entirely in the hands of the housemasters with *in extremis* support from the chaplaincy and the medical staff. Most houses had acquired a team of house tutors chosen by the housemaster who would assist in running the house in various ways: taking over for a night's duty, coaching games and being another adult presence in the community. But there was growing demand from sixth formers for more informal contact with the teaching staff and for the house to be less central in pastoral matters for the older pupils. An initial experiment allowed Lower Sixth boys to choose a tutor, usually someone who taught them, who would meet them informally from time to time. It was as yet very unsystematic and the responsibilities were not entirely clear;

but it proved a popular development, which would in time evolve into a central theme of Malvern life much praised and admired by parents, students and school inspectors. Significant changes also began in some of the boarding houses. Prefect punishments declined and in at least one house came to an end.[45] The same house chose to elect their Head of House – the franchise being given to all the boys. A greater informality was apparent and much more emphasis was put on training the older boys to manage the communal needs of their house. These changes produced considerable tension with understandable resistance coming from those housemasters and others who thought contemporary fads were undermining good discipline and time-honoured customs.

Academically the school flourished. Oxbridge success remained notable and O level and A level results were generally very good. Towards the end of his headmastership Martin Rogers was able to announce that Malvern would participate in the new Conservative government's Assisted Places scheme 'designed to help the sons of parents who could not otherwise afford to send them to the best independent schools.'[46] The scheme was implemented in September 1981 and was to prove popular; it enabled the school to benefit from the considerable academic abilities of the pupils that the scheme attracted.

The new building programmes of the Rogers years reflected the direction in which he wished the school to move. Apart from bed studies and the new sports hall, the most significant addition was the Lindsay Art Centre. At the time it was considered to be one of the most impressive art facilities in the public school world. Towards the end of his headmastership work also began on turning the old gymnasium into a fully equipped theatre.[47] These developments reflected perhaps the most notable and long-lasting achievements of the post-war era – the great advance of the arts at Malvern.

Below: Common Room, 1977.

Martin Rogers had long been interested in bringing the world of school and industrial enterprise closer together:

> Coming from industry into a school environment I found that there was at the time an almost complete ignorance of, and even hostility towards, business. School seemed to be quite out of touch with the way in which wealth is created and what industry is about. It worried me that people could be so out of touch with the real world and I decided to do something about it.[48]

To this end a Redman-Heenan fellow was appointed to improve the understanding of and the links with industry. Industrial conferences for the Lower Sixth became a regular feature of life. Work experience was encouraged and a form of leadership training that owed much to management selection procedures was introduced for both the masters and boys. This did not prove popular with senior masters who thought their wartime and National Service experience was quite enough training for one lifetime. The 'misery produces strange bedfellows' aspect of the training at Symonds Yat had one endearing outcome when the housemasters felt that they needed to develop a stronger common bond in the face of headmagisterial fiats, and so was born the famous Flymo meetings[49] in which the creation of a team spirit owed rather more to the libationary generosity of the rotating hosts.

A committed Christian, Martin Rogers was also anxious to bridge the divide between science and religious belief. He actively supported his chaplains, Tim Wright and Ian Ogilvie, in their attempts to make Chapel more intellectually vibrant and a forum for challenging ideas. Distinguished outside speakers came on many Sundays and there was a reorientation of the weekly Chapels away from repetitive liturgy towards more stimulating sermons from members of staff, boy-led services and more contemplative worship using music, drama, readings and mediation.

Martin Rogers chose to retire from Malvern in 1982 to become Master of the King Edward VI foundation in Birmingham.[50] A civilised and sensitive man his headmastership had seen the arts flourish, the physical, and to some extent the social, structure of the boarding houses modernised, and an academic liveliness that reflected the new generation of masters appointed during his term. It would be fair to say that for the more 'liberal' elements of the Common Room progress was too slow, whilst for the more senior elements many of the new initiatives and attitudes seemed misplaced and were thought to be undermining the essence of the school. To balance such views and in a competitive world to keep the school afloat required great skill. It was undoubtedly a mark of his success that during his tenure pupil numbers were never fewer than 580 and reached 617 in two years (1976 and 1980). Pointers to the future could be seen in the tripling in the number of day boys (twenty-one in 1972, sixty in 1981) and in the steady increase both in the numbers of girls attending Sixth Form classes and the range of subjects that they now studied. In a valedictory tribute *The Malvernian* commented: 'The phrase "caring community" may be a cliché but it is pleasant to live in one and the fact that we do is due, as much as to anyone, to our outgoing Headmaster.'[51] The chairman of the College Council bade farewell in these words:

> bringing to his task a calm and understanding authority, he has successfully maintained the standing of Malvern as one of the country's leading independent schools. Academic standards have been enhanced, the widest of interests encouraged, and the material amenities of the school significantly improved by important development programmes. His achievement is to leave the school full and flourishing and ready to meet the demands of the eighties.[52]

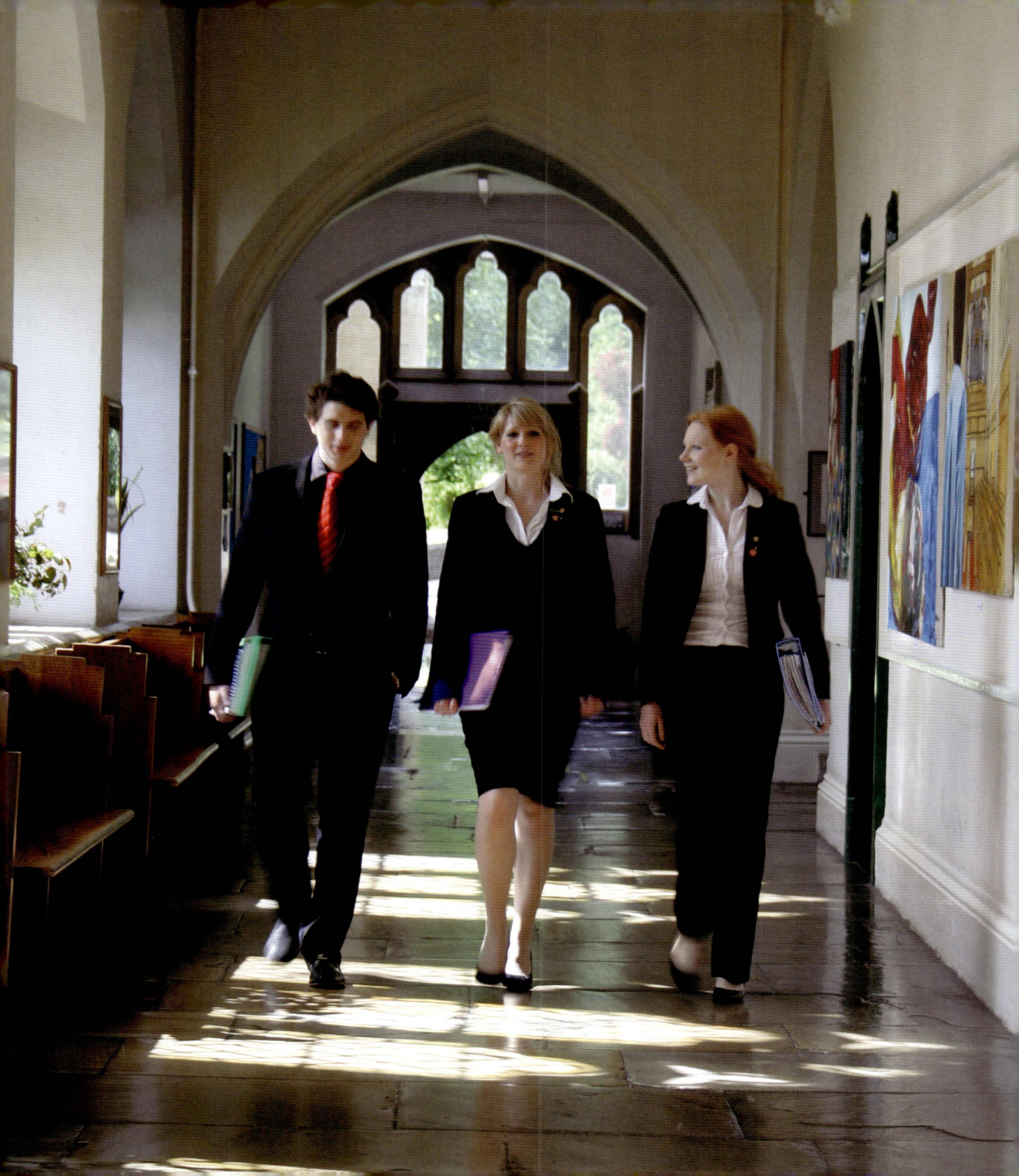

7

Remaking a school, 1983–2008

The new Headmaster, Roy de Courcy Chapman, was the rector of Glasgow Academy. Educated at Dollar Academy and St Andrew's University, he had taught at Marlborough where he had been Head of Modern Languages and the officer commanding the CCF. The chairman of the Council reported that the Council had unanimously selected him from a large field of candidates and described him as 'having abundant energy and an easy and direct approach. He is a strong but not heavy disciplinarian.' Before his arrival in January 1983 there was an interregnum of one term when the second master George Chesterton ably led the school. Roy Chapman appeared every inch a traditionalist but it was during his headmastership that the most dramatic changes came to the College. By his retirement in 1996 the school was co-educational, and increasingly global in its outlook with the International Baccalaureate established as an alternative to A level. The old school prefect system had been abolished and the school elected a Sixth Form Council.

The man himself was difficult to read. Energetic, sprightly in manner, and crisp of speech he gave little away, but exhibited a remarkable memory. His enigmatic mode of address when discussing 'problems' became even more complex by a tendency to elaborate metaphors. This caused great amusement to his new colleagues, but he was respected and admired for his effective decision-making and grasp of the essentials of leadership. Discipline, widely seen as rather slack when he took over, was certainly tightened and pupils came to fear the dramatic interviews that followed their offence. A consummate actor, he would affect great fury, interrogate with a skill from which Scotland Yard could have learnt much, and pronounce sentence with the solemnity of a hanging judge. What pupils did not see was the twinkle behind the glint and the peals of laughter that would often precede or follow the performance. He certainly enjoyed the foibles of the young as much as any schoolmaster.

The difficult financial climate at the beginning of the 1980s certainly affected Malvern, as did later downturns in the early 1990s. Competition for a declining cohort of potential students pushed all schools into a consideration of how best they could improve their appeal. As the decade advanced, this led Malvern to embrace the International Baccalaureate and also full co-education. The IB had been around for a number of years – taught at Atlantic College and Sevenoaks – but had hardly entered the mainstream of British education.[1] It did, however, have two major attractions: its breadth, and its appeal to foreign students. In the 1980s and 1990s there was much discussion about the narrowness of British sixth-form education particularly in comparison to that of economic rivals in Europe and beyond. The IB kept more academic options open and was seen as both broad and rigorous. In time the politicians would reflect the changing mood and embrace the changes to A level that saw the introduction of the AS/A2

Above: Mr Roy de C. Chapman, Headmaster 1983–96.

system with the intention that students study a wider range of subjects in their last school years. This in turn would lead to a vigorous counter-argument that A-level standards were being weakened and a growing demand for strong academic courses out of the reach of politicians. Ironically, as this introspective debate raged, British public-school education became increasingly popular on the Continent, particularly in Germany. Starting as simply a desire to fill a fallow year, and improve English, this quickly grew into an enthusiasm for the more traditional approach to learning that many Germans found in British boarding schools. A major restraint on this potential market was the unfamiliar A-level qualification that limited access into the German university world. The IB in contrast was acceptable and fitted more neatly into the wider range of subjects studied in continental countries both up to and in the equivalent of the Sixth Form. It was also recognised by nearly all European universities. Roy Chapman recalls that he started to consider the possibility of bringing the IB to Malvern in 1990: 'I thought the IB could be the unique selling point which had so far eluded us. I raised the possible introduction of the IB with the Council and was authorised to explore it further with the appointment of René Filho as Director of IB from September 1990'.

He could have found no better champion for the IB than this much-admired lively Head of French, who had taught at the College since 1974. He became a passionate advocate for the educational advantages of the still unfamiliar course and in a series of presentations persuaded members of the College Council and the heads of the academic departments to initiate the IB at Malvern. It duly started in the autumn of 1992 with just six students, running as an alternative to A level – a policy that has continued. By 2010 there was a rough parity of numbers. The introduction of the new A levels in 2000, and much bad publicity about poor A-level marking, persuaded a significant number of pupils, and their parents, to embrace the new course. This coincided with a dramatic increase in the number of pupils joining Malvern in the Sixth Form, compensating for the smaller numbers coming in at the traditional age of thirteen. Many of these pupils, both British and from overseas, came specifically to study for the IB. This gave Malvern a crucial advantage in a difficult period of financial, demographic and political pressure.

Below: The Chapman Technology Centre.

As part of a general reconsideration of Malvern's educational programme it was decided to create an innovative GCSE curriculum which would involve pupils studying humanities, science, a modern foreign language and a 'practical aesthetic subject' (music, art, drama and technology) as well as mathematics, English and religious studies. To accompany this scheme it was decided to build a technology block, which was completed in 1992 and named the Chapman Technology Centre.

In the year that the IB was introduced Malvern went fully co-educational, with girls joining the school at thirteen and the creation of the first two all-girl houses – Ellerslie House (originally located on the former, site) and No. 6. Since the early 1970s when girls had first been taught at the College, the numbers had grown significantly and were now to be found in virtually every discipline in the school. Female teachers were now a familiar aspect of the Common Room. Social activities had also grown and two girls (both the daughters of housemasters) had even been allowed to become members of the school: Julia Harvey and Camilla Nicholls.[2]

According to Roy Chapman's account, the process that led to the eventual merger started when 'a chill wind was about to blow concerning the September 1989 entry'. He recalled being approached by the Headmistress of Ellerslie and the Headmaster of Hillstone about the possible 'pooling of purchases. It was not too difficult to see that the hidden agenda was a concern that their numbers were also down and that they were looking for ways of cutting their costs'.

The situation was attributable to a number of national changes. A 40 per cent cut in those members of the armed forces entitled to the Boarding School Allowance, a cut in the actual BSA contribution, and a growing unwillingness of international companies to subsidise boarding fees all threatened a key element of fee income. The crisis in Lloyds of London hit hard as a number of parents, and grandparents, had been funding their children's education from the money they had made at Lloyds. Initial lump-sum payments for fees were declining and the income from long-term insurance policies was failing to keep pace with rising fees. The fear (soon to be realised) that a future Labour government would end the Assisted Places scheme was also a factor. In addition parents were increasingly choosing schools close to their homes so they could see more of their children, a social change that particularly affected 'rural boarding schools that were furthest away from the great urban centres of population'.

Hit by falling numbers there was every prospect of Ellerslie going the way of so many other small single-sex schools and closing. This would have not only been a sad event in its own right but given the significant number of Ellerslie girls who were taught at the College it would have had an impact on Malvern's finances at the very time of a major recession and general falling demand. Locally the collapse of any of the four girls' schools[3] might have had an impact on the College because many parents desired to send sons and daughters to the same town. Equally the collapse of one of the local 'feeder' prep schools would have hit the school hard. For some schools, economies could be made, by moving along the local day school path. However, Malvern College would find this difficult because it was surrounded by day schools with whose fees it could not realistically compete.

Roy Chapman recalls that the idea of a tri-partite merger came to him at the end of August 1990 when he balanced the evident concerns of Ellerslie and Hillstone with the need to ensure the future numbers of the College. Because the idea of amalgamating the three schools was 'so potentially explosive', he felt caution was essential. He initially consulted two 'key people whose judgement and confidentiality I trusted completely: the Bursar (John Hunter) and my Second Master (John Blackshaw). Both were positive and encouraging'. Further consultation followed with the two heads, both of whom 'were quite shaken by the extent of my very tentative proposals', but who came back with their blessing in principle for further discussion. An approach to the chairman of the College Council, Sir Stephen Brown, and the vice-chairman, Mr Tim Scriven, was greeted with more reserve, although permission was given to work out more details and to present it to the General Purposes Committee, the Council 'think tank' three weeks later.

The Headmaster duly wrote what he called 'a seminal paper of vital importance in the history of the mergers'. In his preamble he explored the general crisis in recruitment described above, and concluded:

> We are almost certainly heading for a trough as far as independent education is concerned. However, as has happened so often in the past, the independent schools will bounce back in due course as the swing of the pendulum moves back again. Independent schools need to make provision both for the difficulties which lie ahead and for the period of expansion which will inevitably follow for those who have survived as a result of forethought and prudent management.

He went on to say that 'the warning signals of deep trouble from Ellerslie and Hillstone are too deafening to ignore'. In rejecting what he called 'tinkering and planned procrastination' he suggested the possibility of an education for children aged eight to eighteen using the College

Above: René Filho, Head of French and pioneer of the Malvern IB, on tour.

site as the core; Ellerslie would disappear except as a house, and its former location would become the site of the new co-educational preparatory school. The merger would be accompanied by the introduction of the International Baccalaureate. Chapman hoped all would be in place by the autumn of 1992.

Malvern College would be the dominant partner throughout because of its relative strength, which enabled it to be 'in the position to dictate proposals which represent our best interest'. The General Purposes Committee agreed to recommend to the full Council that a joint working party be established. The Council agreed to this proposal but the Headmaster was anxious:

> My muted euphoria after the General Purpose Committee because the first hurdle had been cleared was followed by massive frustration that the issues at stake did not seem to be regarded by others as pressing as I regarded them. I was very conscious of my ideal time frame and I thought there was a distinct possibility that what appeared to me almost like procrastination could lead to the ultimate failure of the Grand Design.

There followed a period of cloak and dagger meetings veiled in complex security. It quickly became clear that legal problems regarding the trusts of Hillstone and Ellerslie would not cause difficulties, that Malvern College stood to gain valuable assets and that the Royal Charter would have to be amended. It was clear that most of the concern and discussion related to financial rather than educational matters. Professor Ken Davey[4] was given the task of presenting a full report to the General Purposes Committee in March 1991. The general conclusion was that the best option was a full merger of the schools. This was approved by the full Council meeting on 9 March 1991. Chapman recalls the feeling of this historic meeting:

> Gradually, gradually, I could feel the initial doubts and suspicions begin to give way. More than one person said that change appeared inevitable and that now might be the optimum time to make it.

Below: *The Malvernian* celebrates co-education.

The timetable for announcements now became a priority. Local prep schools, newspapers, parents, staff and the boys in the College were all informed during the last week of the Lent term. The school was told between two performances of the Masters' Review; a sketch involving co-education was received very differently on the second night. The only moment of resistance was some obvious dissatisfaction from some boys in No. 6 when the Headmaster announced that their house would become the first campus girls' house (the other would be on the old Ellerslie site). A predictable comment came from a member of another house to the effect that 'No. 6 was a girls' house already'. Tension eased when the Headmaster responded to a request by the No. 6 Hundred[5] that they should be allowed to remain together for their Sixth Form years. This was to prove possible by utilising the Hampton site when the merger was implemented.[6] One member of No. 6 would not leave the matter and spent the Easter holidays contacting eminent former members of his house to seek support. This included the then Speaker of the House of Commons, Sir Bernard Weatherill. Chapman recalls that the latter contacted him and then responded positively when given the background and facts. There was further resistance from a number of Old Malvernians but most came around to accepting, albeit reluctantly, the necessity for the act.

Over the next year and a half the details of the new school were agreed through a series of Common Room meetings and some seventeen working parties. The second master, John Blackshaw, presided over this process of preparation most effectively, leading one senior colleague to recall that his work was 'outstanding, there was not a thing he didn't think of'.[7] Given national and social trends, familiarity with a largely mixed Sixth Form, and the remarkably effective planning by

ELLERSLIE

It was in May 1922 that I arrived at Cherbourg with my vanload of furniture, private and scholastic, together with Elsie Harley, a housemaid, her brother as gardener, and in a few days time Miss Scales, who was my right hand and Senior Music Mistress. It was a lovely time of year to start my school in Malvern where I had taken over the Senior House of a Preparatory School known as Abbots Hill, from an elderly Principal, Miss Lloyd Jones.

So begins Miss Sayle's account of the creation of the new school with twenty-four girls and four members of staff. Within a year she had added Ellerslie 'with its pleasant house and grounds' to Cherbourg and the school started to grow, adding a science school 'thanks to Mr Berridge of the Malvern College for Boys who so kindly volunteered to direct the plans', together with a gymnasium, swimming baths and a preparatory school located in Hampton House. By 1931, with 100 girls in the school, an assembly hall and a chapel – the normal accoutrements of a boarding school – were in place. The school had a deeply Christian tradition. Outward-bound activity, centred on the Girl Guides, was an important element of the education offered.

The Second World War saw an increase in numbers, as more and more parents sent their daughters away from the urban bombing. By the end of the war the school had grown to its maximum size of 135 and Southlands had been added as a Senior house. When its Silver Jubilee was celebrated in 1947, the school was flourishing. In 1954 Miss Sayle handed over 'my private school to Ellerslie School Trust' and in 1957 she retired, handing over control of the school to Miss Prior, who recalled:

> She had left me a wonderful school; numbers were small, only 89 girls, but the site was perfect and the peace and beauty of the gardens and the serene and unhurried atmosphere in which the girls lived provided a background for education not easily found elsewhere.

Miss Gladys Sayle, founder of Ellerslie School, receiving Mrs Christopher Soames, who visited Ellerslie to make an appeal on behalf of the Church Army.

A new library was established as a memorial to Miss Sayle and new buildings included laboratories, a geography room, a new School House, dining hall and music block. Common Entrance was taken and Ellerslie was accepted into the Governing Body of Girls Schools. Day boarders appeared, and by 1964 the numbers had reached 200. The school became more academic, with Jane Styles gaining the first Cambridge place. This coincided with growing cooperation with Malvern College, initially for sixth-form science subjects and later more extensively; there were also joint dramatic and musical productions and social interchange. By the mid 1970s there were 270 girls in the school and in 1971 Mrs Margaret Thatcher, as Secretary of State for Education, laid the foundation stone for new classrooms at Hampton. In 1974 Miss Prior handed over the reins to Miss Pamela Binyon 'whom I had taught years ago when she was a very naughty little twelve year old. I knew that the school would be safe in her hands'. In the next few years Chesfield was acquired and a 'multi-purpose Hall in 1980 aptly named the Margaret Prior Hall was built enabling the old gym to be converted into a fine art room'.

Martin Rogers suggested that the two sixth forms should work even further towards joint teaching. This slowly evolved and continued apace under Roy Chapman until there was joint teaching or learning in all subjects.

> I often wondered how much closer the two schools would grow in the future: with hindsight I can see the 'joint teaching' period as a bridge period, forming one of the foundation stones of the merger, although I do not think that this was in anyone's minds at the time.

By the end of her time as headmistress Miss Binyon could reflect on 'an increasing number gaining Oxbridge successes in subjects spread across the curriculum but also an increasing number gaining places in county sports teams or excelling in drama or music and the Duke of Edinburgh Award Scheme'. The last headmistress of Ellerslie was Mrs Baker, who presided over the merger. Although the former buildings have gone, the spirit of Ellerslie lives on, not least in the newly built boarding house of that name. The House displays many photographs and memorabilia from the old school.

Council and Common Room the whole process was accomplished with speedy efficiency and to general acclaim. The Director of Studies at the time remembers a Common Room meeting when an expert on co-education 'came to tell us how to make ready – each thing he mentioned, I thought "yes that's covered"'.[8] The new school came into being in September 1992 consisting of 526 boys and 145 girls. Hillstone had a total of 101 – thirty-eight girls and sixty-three boys, with a further thirty-five in the Pre-Prep.

The new housemistress of No. 6 was Sue Lamberton and she recalls the birth of the new House:

Above: A cartoon of the 'disciplinarian' Roy Chapman by Jonathan Wateridge (2. 1985–90), 1986.

> It was with a high degree of nervousness that I obeyed the summons to go to Roy Chapman's study one afternoon in September 1991. I had only been a member of Common Room and a Tutor in No. 1 for one year. What infringement of the rules had I committed? Wisely he invited me to sit down before asking me if I would like to become the first woman Housemistress at the College. I was surprised, thrilled, delighted and scared but, after long and serious discussions with my husband, I decided to accept. It was without doubt one of the best decisions I have ever made.
>
> The weeks in the summer of 1992 leading up to the arrival of 65 girls cannot be adequately captured on paper. Suffice to say that anxiety, tension, hard work by builders and a concerted effort by virtually the whole of Common Room meant that we were within a gnat's whisker of being ready on the great day. Study carpets were laid, urinals were ripped out, showers and individual bathrooms went in, and I, meanwhile, recruited vigorously. The Head of Science hung the curtains and put up pictures, the Head of Classics assembled bunk beds and a prospective house tutor unpacked my kitchen belongings. We rapidly discovered

HILLSTONE

Hillstone was founded in 1883 by Miss Chaffer in Hillstone House, after which the school was named; reportedly 'it was quite a by-word in Malvern in those days to see the line of carriages on Monday morning all down Como Road bringing the boys back after their weekend at home'. In 1899 the school was taken over by the Misses Lord with only three boarders and four day boys, no gas, no bathroom and oil lamps only. The school was advertised 'for small boys first leaving home' who would be given a thorough grounding for the public schools and the Navy. By 1918 the first headmaster took over, the Rev Alfred Hooper, and enrolment reached eighty-six by 1931. There was a steady expansion of facilities and, before the Second World War, Hillstone was considered to be one of the best-equipped prep schools in the country. In the post-war period under the guidance of firstly Christopher Torrance (known as 'The Liberator') and then Roger and Anne Gillard the school became a model of a civilised, happy and academic preparatory school. However, in the uncertain economic times of the 1980s the viability of the school could not be guaranteed. An initial proposal to amalgamate with The Downs School in 1986 was frustrated by a lobby of parents but by the early 1990s Roger Gillard sought a merger with Malvern College, the destination of most of its pupils. So it came about that this highly regarded and successful school became part of the greater educational project born in 1992.

that we had no storage space in the dormitories, no completed common rooms and no carpets on the private side. But we could cope with these minor deprivations.

No. 6 took as its mantra the quotation from war-embattled *Rosie the Riveter*: 'We can do it' and do it they did! The united joy in the house when a girl came top in the Mechanics Examination was terrific. Did I notice a change in the College as the girls settled in? Of course. Over time girl/boy relationships normalised. The boys began to see the more academic girls as a challenge and eventually accepted them as their peers, not bodies to be assessed. It helped that in 1998 No. 6 sent four girls to Oxbridge. When I left the house in 2002 co-education was a given, never to be questioned.'[9]

The learning curve for the boys was at times sharp. Angela Lafferty recalls returning Remove examination papers at the end of the first year of full co-education. 'A boy's hand went up, a bright chap whom I had first met when taking J. B. B.'s French set the previous term, now in my first mixed Remove German set. "Please can you check my total mark?" I did so and it was correct. "Why did you need it checked?" I asked. "I was sure it wasn't correct. SHE (indicating the girl sitting next to him) got more than me."'[10]

The former Hundred of No. 6 became the first occupants of Hampton together with their housemaster Richard Goddard,[11] and when No. 4 became a girls' house the same pattern was followed under Trevor Southall. When No. 3 followed there was now a shortage of boy places in the houses so it was decided to continue using Hampton as an overflow house. It started with twenty boys with Dr Richard Witcomb as housemaster. The boys of No. 3 mostly went to SH with a few joining Hampton, which by then largely consisted of new boys – not a very satisfactory situation as they did not readily mix with the rest of the school. This arrangement continued until the end of the summer term 1997.[12]

More than twenty years on, the success of co-education was evident. Three aspects can be highlighted. Academic standards greatly improved by having a wider potential, and at all levels – GCSE, A level, IB and Oxbridge – the girls gave a powerful lead more than proportionate to their numbers. The academic staff quickly noticed that the more serious approach of the average girl impacted on the boys and in class having the 'feminine' point of view gave a much-needed balance – the quality of discussion particularly in the humanities greatly improved. That the arrival of girls 'soothed the savage breast' was also evident – no teacher was naive enough to assume that all girls spread kindness and good will; indeed the verbal brutality of an embittered girl could shock even the most primitive male – but in the round the girls would not tolerate the excesses of rampant oafishness that all-male communities can give rise to. The affectionate nature of the community certainly increased and the growing naturalness of relationship became a marked feature of the school. The greatest dread of those uncertain about co-education – of distracted and lovesick boys and girls and still worse dangerous liaisons – proved largely groundless. Roy Chapman reported that he had had to expel a number of boys for sexual misdemeanours before the merger but none during his remaining years. The third area of note was the huge contribution that the girls made to the arts: music and drama acquired a new depth and distinction. This further reinforced the trend begun under Lindsay of these areas acquiring a status formerly reserved only for games. The successful transition to a fully co-educational school also owed much to the remarkably talented housemistresses who presided over the first girls' houses. The energy, warmth, humour and good sense of Sue Lamberton (No. 6), Helen Robinson (No. 4) and Angela Lafferty (No. 3) were inspirational and they made fine role models for the new Malvernians. The work of the female deputy heads was also vital in easing inevitable tensions and in showing hesitant males how to be robust with erring girls. Lindsay Kontarines and Angela Lafferty provided master classes in good sense, high standards and explosive mirth.

Above: John and Mary Blackshaw. J. B. B. was housemaster of No. 5 and second master; he greatly assisted the merger in 1992.

Above: Mrs Lindsay Kontarines, the first female deputy head, in 1992.

Above: Mrs Sue Lamberton, housemistress, No. 6, 1992–2002.
Below: Mrs Eirian Hart, housemistress, Ellerslie House, 1992–94.

The 1980s also saw a renewed debate about the quality of pastoral care at Malvern. During the Rogers years a social sixth-form tutor system had emerged, proving popular with the boys and generally appreciated by the Common Room. With the arrival of a new college chaplain, the Rev Keith Wilkinson, who had been a chaplain at Eton, a further reconsideration was undertaken. The chaplain thought Malvern could benefit from aspects of the Etonian tutorial system which provided a strong pastoral bond between teachers and their charges. While appreciating the strengths of the traditional House system there was growing concern that some boys found themselves isolated, unhappy or insecure, particularly if they found their year uncongenial or simply did not form a good relationship with their housemaster or the house tutors who invariably were seen as allies of the man who appointed them – the housemaster. There was also a feeling that house life could be too insular for sixth formers who wanted wider social contacts and greater stimulus from teachers they valued. A Tutorial Committee[13] recommended a thorough overhaul of the whole pastoral care system. In addition to the House pastoral system, pupils would now have a school tutor, who could be another adult to whom they might turn; given that tutor groups would have pupils from different houses, this also enabled them to mix with contemporaries outside the house more easily. In the Lower School the school tutors would be allocated but in the Sixth Form the pupils would choose them. The proposals met stiff resistance in some quarters, especially from many housemasters, with strong feelings that it would undermine the special relationship between housemasters and pupils, create tensions between members of staff, clashes of authority, confuse parents and pupils and even invite popularity contests between potential tutors.

Despite all these reservations the system was introduced in 1985 and became one of the most cherished parts of the College, later to be much praised by various inspectors. In its first year in operation the Headmaster praised the new system for 'enabling us to see below the placid surface, we have been able to identify a significant number of problems and respond to cries for help which might otherwise have passed unnoticed.'[14] Although subject to human frailty, in time it became deeply appreciated by all involved in pastoral care – at the very least a fail-safe mechanism and more often an easer of tensions, a builder of confidence between adults and students, and the creation for many pupils of a vital and important relationship that fulfilled the highest ideals of pastoral care very much in the spirit of Faber's original hope: 'men who would not only be masters, but would stand in the relation to the pupils of senior friend and junior friend'. In the modern setting of co-education that innocent comment has proved to have much to commend it as the ethic that has inspired pastoral care at Malvern. The school has been greatly enriched by the involvement of virtually the whole staff in the tutorial system bringing in a range of expertise, human sympathies and good will that has made the Malvern system admired beyond this community.

The traditional school prefect system had, in the opinion of many, rather lost its way by the end of the 1980s. Increasingly stripped of real power in the school the post was prized more for its status and limited privileges. There were clear abuses by some unsatisfactory appointees and the horse-trading between housemasters became unseemly. In 1992 the new Senior Chapel Prefect, Adam Fuge (2. 1987–92), proposed that the whole system should be abolished and replaced with an elected School Council. There was surprisingly little resistance and by the following year the council was in place, elected by both the students and the Common Room. Heads of House continued to be appointed by housemasters although increasingly this included some process of consultation or election. The Senior and Junior Chapel Prefects were still appointed by the headmaster again following some process of consultation. The new Sixth Form Council performed a number of functions, most notably organising charity events, school socials and representing the student body to the headmaster.

During the Chapman years other initiatives were to bear much fruit. In his first year a new scheme was introduced in the Lent term to enable all Lower Sixth pupils to gain practical work experience. The new registrar, Pat Hooley, undertook a number of initiatives to bring pupils to the school. 'Young Malvern' was also introduced in the summer holidays of 1985 in which children between eight and thirteen would spend a week or two using the school facilities for an activities holiday. This in time became very popular and led to a number of local children eventually joining the school. With the decline of the traditional preparatory-school entry Hooley was instrumental in developing the Sixth Form entry which went up from a handful to over fifty new students annually – many of them from Germany – in a couple of years. This innovation served the school well in these difficult years both for enrolment and in the quality and enthusiasm of the new intake.

The Malvernian continued to echo both national trends and the particular concerns of the school. There could certainly be no question that the school had a vibrant intellectual culture, at least for those who sought it. During these years many distinguished figures trod the boards in sixth-form lectures, Chapel or addressing academic societies like the newly created Weatherill Society or the more established History and Lucretian societies. Professor Moelwyn Merchant gave the Lent talks in 1984 and subsequently became a great friend of the school; Sir John Harvey Jones continued the interest in industrial links; Sir Roger Young and Rev Tom Hodgson gave challenging views on modern Christianity and Professor Kalistos Ware introduced the increasingly fashionable world of Orthodoxy. The British commander in the First Gulf War, Sir Peter de la Billière, spoke to an enthusiastic audience in 1995; and Jeremy Paxman, the Torquemada of *Newsnight*, reappeared in his old school.

Perhaps of greater significance than the formal lectures was the sense of a more outward-looking generation far more engaged with the contemporary concerns than early generations. Articles, often based on interviews conducted by boys, appeared in what increasingly became a highly literary *Malvernian*. The arts were strongly represented with youth culture, Francis Bacon, Quentin Tarantino and Sir Michael Tippett coming under the spotlight together with reviews of artistic visits abroad. Political issues ranged from the world of the Speaker, interviews with MPs to the need to prepare pupils for democratic leadership. The global reach of the school was increasingly evident through perceptive accounts of French exchanges, sporting tours to South America and South Africa, Poland, the Middle East, Mexico and Auschwitz-

Above: Mrs Helen Robinson, housemistress No. 4, 1993–2004.
Below: Mrs Angela Lafferty, housemistress No. 3, 1995–2006, and senior mistress 2006–2010.

Left: Co-education in action twenty years after the merger. (Photograph by Philip Hollis)

Above: Adam Fuge, Senior Chapel Prefect (2. 1987–92), with Lord Weatherill (6. 1934–38) and Headmaster Roy Chapman, in 1991.

Below: Commem picnic in the 1980s.

Birkenau. Film and play reviews abounded. Editorials became forthright and confident in both criticism and advice. There was much approving comment on the changes to leadership patterns in houses and the school, on co-education and the International Baccalaureate. Teachers and pupils exchanged views and were much more open about political and religious themes than would have been possible in earlier times. Hardly an area of school life was not subject to examination, often critical. Such openness and freedom might disturb and, at times, descend into adolescent fripperies, but it impressed with its liveliness, wit and engagement. Most would see it as a sign of a healthy educational atmosphere. Discipline had moved almost exclusively to masters with a great reluctance by senior pupils to exercise the kind of supervision perceived as normal a generation before. The nature of offences changed – much less on clothing regulation, idleness and insolence to seniors, much more to do with the perennial problems of drinking and smoking. Drugs and sex appeared occasionally. There was a whiff of the rebellious nature of the times with an underground magazine, *The Mauler*, making an appearance. It suffered the fate of many such magazines; initially a witty critique, it descended into such bad taste that the pupils themselves rejected it. Petty vandalism occurred usually at the end of term and on one occasion 'So What' was inscribed on the Chapel wall in what seemed indelible paint. It was encouraging to find that the body of pupils were as disgusted as the adults.

In 1994 Roy Chapman was honoured with the chairmanship of the Headmasters' Conference. As his tenure at Malvern reached its closing years he could reflect on a range of remarkable achievements. The school was now fully co-educational, it was academically livelier than at any time in its history and it was increasingly international. The long process of rethinking the form and style of leadership and the relationship between pupils, and between masters and pupils, had produced in effect a new school. Chapman's skill in advocating and advancing the merger puts him in the top flight of Malvern headmasters. He was also a good Burkean, allowing necessary change while maintaining a disciplined and effective institution. His enigmatic personality left no doubt who was in charge and the respect in which he was held was powerfully exhibited when he addressed a farewell school assembly. A spontaneous standing ovation notably led by the pupils was a moving and appropriate ending to a most distinguished headmastership.

His successor Hugh Carson took over the College at a difficult time. The national trends identified in Roy Chapman's pre-merger analysis were becoming acutely apparent. National boarding was in sharp decline, ever-increasing fees were reducing the intake and economic and political uncertainties were making the future look decidedly insecure. With the victory of New Labour in the general election of 1997 old socialist hostilities to independent schools reappeared and the first target was the Assisted Places scheme. Apart from the loss of talent and the distressing removal of a ladder of opportunity for such pupils, the school also had to find ways of replacing nearly a hundred pupils supported by the scheme in the school (representing about 17 per cent of the senior roll) – no easy task given the general circumstances that the country found itself in. It was a mark of Hugh Carson's success that this threat to the school was overcome.

Above: Pupils and masters of the College gathering for a school photograph in the 1980s.

Hugh Carson had been educated at Tonbridge and served in the Army before studying history and politics at Royal Holloway, London. He had been a housemaster at Epsom and Headmaster of Denstone College. His wife, Penny, whom he had met when they were both serving in the Army in Germany, was a distinguished historian of India. He struck a familiar note when in an interview given to *The Malvernian* before his arrival he felt that his greatest achievement at his previous school had been 'successfully to redress the balance in the school by creating an atmosphere in which, although sport was obviously still of consequence, those who had academic and aesthetic abilities were shown no less respect'. He hoped to apply the same principles to Malvern and stated that 'the aesthetic subjects and sport enabled pupils to keep fit, healthy and happy'. This should be achieved through encouragement because force usually led 'to stubbornness'. Another key part of his educational vision was the importance of the spiritual dimension and he sought to make Chapel a place 'to which people would enjoy going and in which they are actively interested.'[15]

After a number of meetings with the new Headmaster one distinguished former member of staff described him as undoubtedly the nicest headmaster he had known at the school. A gentle and unassuming manner belied an astute mind and one not incapable of necessary ruthlessness when required. In his early days Hugh Carson decided to follow individual pupils around for a day to their lessons, meals and sports. One new sixth former from Germany found himself rather dreading the daunting prospect of being so accompanied. A day or so later he told his tutor that the experience had proved surprisingly congenial and how touched he was to find a gift of Pevsner's guide to Worcestershire on his desk a couple of days later – he had briefly mentioned his interest in architecture and old buildings to the Headmaster.[16] A younger pupil floundering in his attempt to retrieve his dropped books and papers found the Headmaster helping him. Both were fine examples of the civilised ripples that became a feature of school life in the next ten years. Although instinctive, this style was also an act of policy as the new Headmaster felt strongly that encouraging civilised behaviour was the mark of a good school. A tribute at the end of his headmastership recalled that 'in all his dealings with pupils, Hugh always treated them with dignity and respect which maintained and enhanced Malvern's reputation', best summarised in a quotation from the inspection report: 'Pupils' behaviour is excellent; they have very positive attitudes towards each other and show pride in their College and their work, and relationships among pupils are very friendly and supportive.'[17]

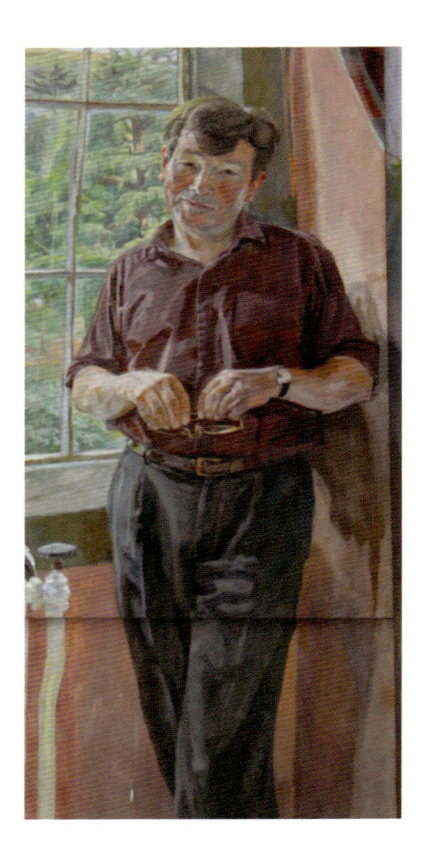

Yet he was certainly not a 'pushover'; 'occasionally the eyes would flash and the wise would back away from that particular discussion.'[18]

Early on in his headmastership Hugh Carson could take pleasure in a further extension of the school's facilities when, due to the generosity of an existing parent, the former Catholic church of St Edmunds was acquired for the use of the school. The church building was adapted to provide an excellent facility for concerts and lectures and the basement area was converted into a new Sixth Form Centre complete with bar, dancing area, table football, billiard table and widescreen television. Lord Hurd opened the new complex in the spring of 1998. This centre became of great importance in the social life of sixth formers. Open twice during the week and every Saturday, it became the focal point for youthful exuberance, and just occasional excess, breaking down barriers of house, gender and nationality. A Lower School version was created in the Grub. These innovations, together with tutorial outings and cultural trips, transformed the school into a much more relaxed and open institution.

It was during this period that the international nature of the school became more apparent. Hugh Carson was able to report in 2000 that Malvern was 'an English school with an international dimension'. A celebration of this was held at the end of the Lent term when the pupils organised what became known as Culture Shock 2000, which celebrated the diversity of the school with sixty-six pupils representing over twenty-five countries. There was a splendid bazaar-like atmosphere as visitors enjoyed decorative displays and crafts, performances of traditional music and dancing and national foods and beverages.[19] The Belgian ambassador to the United Kingdom and the senior advisor to the World Bank opened it and the hall was packed, with over £1,000 raised for Amnesty and orphaned children in India.

In the same year the success of the IB was evident – in 1999 there had been thirty-six candidates, all of whom passed scoring the equivalent of ABB at A level. In 2000 there were 100 students studying for the IB and by the new academic year there were more students studying the IB than A level. Carson was determined to further strengthen the academic achievement and reputation of the school. He founded, and hosted, a sixth-form scholars' society, which was named the Wheeler-Bennett Society, honouring one of the most distinguished academic Old Malvernians. Lower Sixth pupils were recommended by heads of the academic departments (and the retiring cohort) and when selected had the opportunity to present a paper for discussion. The papers produced give an insight into concerns and interests of the intellectual elite of the school, from Steiner education to the drama and literature of the ancient world, quantum physics to Hegel's philosophy of history, sustainable democracy to the futility of feudality, the energy dilemma to neo-colonialism in Africa, and the Arab Spring. A junior version for the Lower School was also launched, named after Malvern's first Nobel Prize winner, Aston. A new magazine, *Inklings*, was funded to allow a wider circulation of challenging articles by students, staff and the wider Malvern community. Scholars' lectures were introduced, roughly one a term. In 2004 the topics included 'Iraq – a commander's perspective' by a serving brigadier who was also a parent, a lecture on sports history and the aftermath of Soviet communism by Professor Selezneva, another parent. The Lucretian Society continued to flourish, meeting six times a year with the intention of introducing to pupils a range of scientific and industrial issues. The 2004–05 series included speakers on rocket science, Darwin, chemistry in the clouds, and explosive events on the sun. Likewise theatrical productions and the musical life of the College demonstrated a breadth and quality that stimulated and impressed.

The form of leadership of the College underwent something of a revolution during this period. From the earliest days the College Council appointed the headmaster, the bursar and the school doctor. The headmaster was supported by a second master, in

Below: Portrait of Hugh Carson, Headmaster, 1997–2006, by Daphne Todd.

Below: Sir Ghillean Prance (l. 1951–56), former Director of The Royal Botanic Gardens at Kew, visiting speaker in 2002.

THE BURLEYS

The Burleys became one of the most popular and familiar aspects of school life for some eighty years (1930–2010). Mr Harry Burley took over the job of haircutting for the boys from a Mr 'Sham' Bruton, the groundsman/handyman who had a room next to the old swimming pool. Mr Burley and his staff moved around from House to House in the evenings and as well as cutting hair took with him some stock from his salon. Top sales went to soap, shaving cream, razor blades, combs and collar studs. In 1935 his two sons, Stanley and Dennis, started working alongside him, but only Dennis survived the war to come back to work at the College. In 1964 Dennis was joined by his son David, who writes:

> College was then coming out of a life rather like *Tom Brown's Schooldays* with a very definite hierarchy amongst the boys and fagging still very much the norm. All this changed quite quickly under the modernising influence of Headmaster, Donald Lindsay. The school became very much more outward looking and soon there were even lessons with girls from and at other schools. Fashion in hair styles changed with the traditional 'short back and sides' of the 1930s giving way to flowing locks, and then a cropped style with the school having to intervene to prevent excessive shortness. By now most sales were body sprays, hair gel and Dax Wax.
>
> The forty-six years I worked at College were most interesting and enjoyable and the boys definitely helped to keep me young. I was very moved to have a farewell evening at School House with a cake and presentation of House Colours, which were also awarded by Number 2. My wife Janet and I were invited by the Headmaster, Mr Antony Clark, to Chapel and presented with an excellent picture of cricket on the Senior and also a compass to assist in our travelling around Europe, and so ended an era.

The Burley generations; left to right: Dennis, Harry and David Burley.

effect a deputy who would assist in the day-to-day management of the school and deputise when the headmaster was away. From time to time the second master might find himself the acting headmaster, in times of illness or during interregnums. The second master also acted as the Head of the Common Room until, in the 1980s, the teaching staff preferred the option of electing their own presiding officers. When the College went co-educational, a female additional deputy head was appointed. With the growing complexity of the school a senior management team was created with a number of deputy heads responsible for the academic, pastoral and logistic sides of the school. The bursarial department also increased to include expertise in human resources, marketing and development. Following a series of 'brainstorming' Common Room sessions to explore the direction Malvern should take, regular appraisal was brought in for all members of staff, including the headmaster, as a way of furthering the quality of teaching and as a conduit for ideas.

By early 2000 the economic pressures on the independent sector were increasing, with fees rising rapidly to cover a rising cost base that had to address, amongst other things, growing pension costs and extensive employment, health and safety regulations as well as the loss of the Assisted Places scheme. The resultant financial squeeze on the College became acute. Two day-houses were created, for boys in No. 5 and girls in No. 8, to market the school to local parents. Neither would survive long; with a boarding-school infrastructure, fees simply could not be reduced to match those of more established local independent day schools. It became apparent that the best marketing strategy for Malvern was to emphasise its nature as primarily a boarding school. The Headmaster led a highly successful appeal in 2000 raising over £1 million, which enabled the College to build a modern all-weather pitch, and the Pavilion was extensively

Below: *The Malvernian* featuring House ties and pins in 1999.

THE DOWNS SCHOOL

Founded in 1900 by Herbert Jones, the headmaster at Leighton Park School, as a preparatory school for boys, it opened with four pupils and slowly expanded, with forty pupils by 1918. In 1920 Jones was succeeded by his second master, Geoffrey Hoyland, who had married into the Cadbury family and used the family's wealth to expand and improve the school. Hoyland built new buildings, introduced student self-government and an innovative curriculum with an emphasis on science and the arts. Under his supervision, the pupils built and maintained a miniature railway, the only one in any English school at the time, which still survives to this day. Among the notable masters he hired were Maurice Field, who taught painting to a number of notable English artists, including Lawrence Gowing, and W. H. Auden. Frazer Hoyland succeeded his brother Geoffrey as headmaster in 1940. He increased the school's emphasis on music and drama, making this Quaker-influenced school a beacon of civilised and progressive education.

In the late twentieth century the school became co-educational and added a nursery, kindergarten and pre-prep school. In 2008 the school merged with Malvern College Preparatory School, on The Downs' existing site.

Famous old boys include Lawrence Gowing, painter; Alan Hodgkin, neuroscientist and Nobel laureate; Richard Mason, novelist; Drummond Hoyle Matthews, geologist and marine geophysicist; Frederick Sanger, biochemist and the fourth person to become a double Nobel laureate; historian A. J. P. Taylor; Michael Yates, television designer; and actor Will Merrick. (Bottom photograph by Larry Bray)

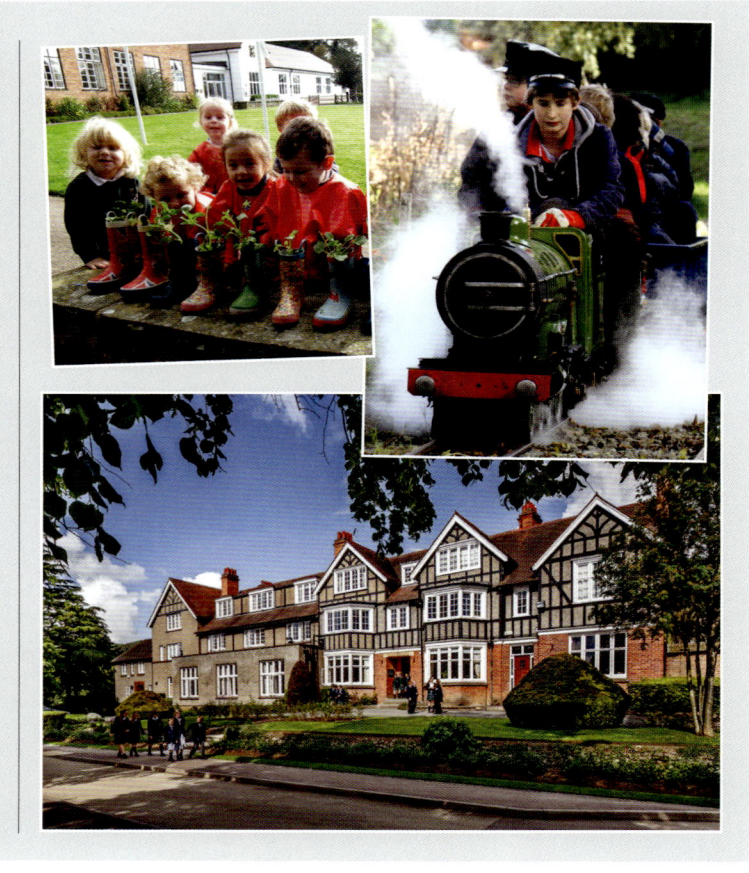

Below: *Distractions*, 2003, by Emily Webb (3. 2002–07).

renovated, eventually becoming the Carson Centre.[20] Limited budgets meant that at this stage little more could be done to expand or modernise the school's facilities, although Carson insisted that what money was available should be used to improve the houses as much as possible. However, the economies made over the previous twenty years to the detriment of the fabric of the College's extensive estate were now coming home to roost. Quite simply, Malvern had to invest or risk declining rapidly.

Following the retirement of the then chairman and treasurer, and the appointment of Lord MacLaurin as chairman and Robin Black as treasurer in 2003, significant changes were made to the management of the College with the elimination of the historic Council committees and the creation of a new management board, similar to the board structure seen in most public companies. At the same time, discussions began on the shape of an investment programme in the College that would eventually prove part of the most extensive investment in the College since the early building programme of the 1890s. One of the proposed changes included an attempt to save money by ending House eating and establishing central catering, but it was defeated by vigorous opposition from the Headmaster and many parents.

A further major initiative, aimed at strengthening the school's preparatory school base, came with the decision to merge Hillstone and The Downs at the latter's extensive and beautiful site in Colwall. The

College Council agreed to a far-reaching investment programme in the Colwall site partly funded by the sale of the former Ellerslie school buildings, which then housed Hillstone, and a very generous donation of £2 million to the College from the Malvernian Society. The new school opened in September 2008.

Examining *The Malvernian* during these years gives much evidence of a vibrant, outward-looking and mature school. As ever the school attracted a range of distinguished speakers. Henry Metelmann, described aptly by *The Malvernian* as 'a living witness to history', shared his moving memories of growing up in poverty in Weimar Germany, his infatuation with the Nazis and his terrible disillusionment in the bloodshed of the Eastern Front. John Simpson reflected both on his career as the BBC's foreign correspondent and on the human rights aspects of his job. A surprising visitor was the new Labour Secretary of State for Education, David Blunkett, who simply wanted to learn more about the school and came away deeply impressed, concluding that he would dearly like to transport the school to his own Sheffield constituency. Jeremy Paxman again returned to his old school to discuss his new book *The English* and charmed all those that he met with his very un-*Newsnight* manner. The range of school trips would have stunned previous generations. Every year saw major expeditions involving large numbers of pupils and staff: all of the Foundation Year to the First World War battlefields and often half the Removes to Normandy; history of art trips to Florence, Rome, Venice, Amsterdam and Paris; study trips to the European Parliament, Cyprus, Paris, NATO headquarters and to the Model European Parliament in Lisbon; climbing expeditions to the European summits and the Haute Route in the Alps; Classics trips to Greece; and Spanish trips to Andalucía. Further afield there was a natural history expedition to the Amazon, a cricket tour of South Africa and a cultural tour to China.

Hugh Carson retired in 2006. The school owed him much. In 1997 the future had not looked bright for the College, but ten years on the numbers had stabilised, the school was in surplus, academic standards and the arts had flourished and the school was attracting excellent pupils from all around the world. The professional role and opportunities for advancement for women had been greatly expanded. A major school inspection coincided with his last year and the inspectors were so impressed by what they found in Malvern that they made no recommendation for improvements – an extremely rare conclusion. 'The leadership of the College is good; it is caring, committed and experienced and is well supported by the governing body; it has moved the College forward considerably over the last ten years'.[21] They were particularly impressed with the pastoral side of the school and the excellent relations between staff and pupils, together with the excellent teaching to be found in so many departments. There could be no better tribute for a retiring headmaster.

The shape of the investment programme and the discussions on future direction of the school were now progressing but final decisions would have to await Carson's successors. A brief interlude occurred with the appointment of David Dowdles who, with the strong support of Lord MacLaurin and the Council, promoted the first stage of a dramatic plan to greatly develop the school's sporting and boarding facilities. Dowdles' early departure and the interregnum of his deputy, Sarah Welch, did not deflect the grand scheme. With the appointment of Antony Clark in 2008, which will be covered in more detail in Chapter 15, matters could advance with vigour.

Above: Mr David Dowdles, Headmaster 2006–07.

Below: Joy at Commem, 2008.

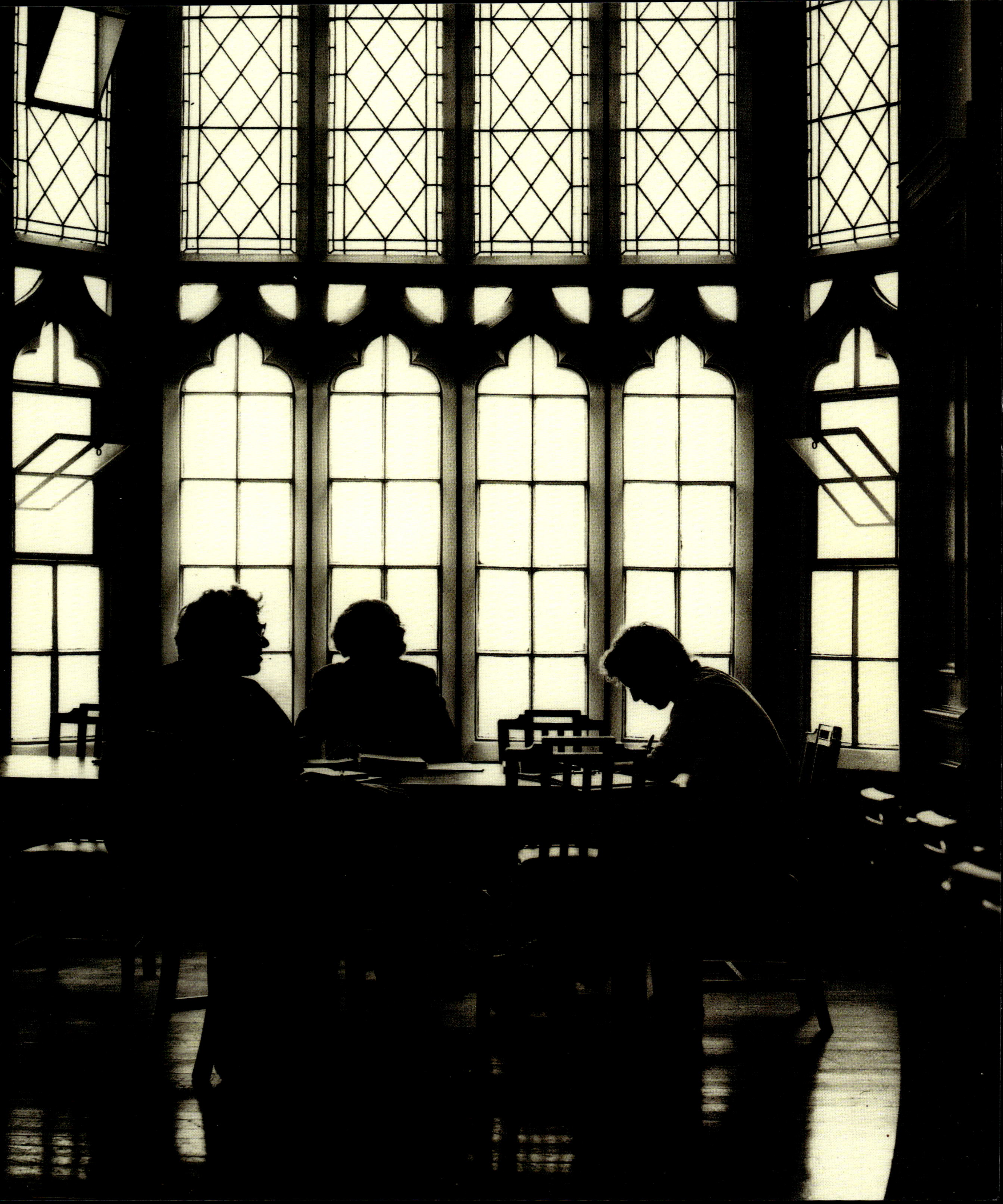

8

Good teaching and sound learning

The founding fathers of the College realised that for it to be successful it would have to establish a strong scholastic reputation, which meant, in the nineteenth century, a strong Classical tradition and the ability to win awards to Oxford and Cambridge. But it was also clear that from the beginning Malvern showed its capacity to adjust to new educational needs. In the earliest statements are references to the mercantile interests and it is striking how wide a range of subjects was offered to the boys studying in this mid-Victorian school.

The curriculum for the first boys in the school, who were divided into three forms, consisted of Classics, mathematics, French, German and music. In 1867 Faber added English literature, modern history and composition. It was possible to study chemistry outside the curriculum but, until 1887, at extra cost. On offer, no doubt influenced by Britain's imperial role, but apparently not taken up, were Sanskrit, Hindustani and Persian.

By 1870 the school showed its confidence by accepting outside examiners (there were as yet no public examinations by which a school could be judged) and rejoiced in the first awards to Oxford and Cambridge. As a token of academic strength, extracts from Greek, French and English plays were performed on Speech Day. However, an early concern was whether Malvern was attracting enough boys with scholarly potential. As a significant number of boys 'destined for Mercantile pursuits left the school without reaching the highest forms', it was felt necessary 'to take measures to attract to the College a larger number of pupils destined for the Universities'.[1] So, for example, from 1870 the sons of clergymen were offered reduced fees in the hope that such boys, coming from academic backgrounds, would create 'adequate competition amongst the Scholars'. The policy seemed successful – after 1872 there was never a year without university awards (the range was from five to ten awards).[2] As ever money was a constraint, the first *Malvern Register* of 1894 reflecting that any assessment of Malvern's 'intellectual distinctions' must take into account that the school was unable to offer the number of scholarships available to 'the rich foundations of the older public schools'.[3]

Arthur Faber can be credited with much of this early success. An OM who entered the school in 1875 described him as 'one of the best and most delightful of men. We of his form loved him, with a love tempered by awe. He was a fine scholar and taught us out of the bare text. He construed Homer and Virgil like a poet, and his English Literature lectures made one a lover of the subject for life. He was a tall and impressive figure. If he was called out of class on business, he would invariably return jingling his keys, to warn that he was coming.'[4] His successor Cruttwell was also an able Classical teacher, and Grundy expanded the academic range of the school and appointed a number of outstanding masters. Unsurprisingly, in the later years of the century the academic strength of the school developed strongly.

Opposite: The Classical Sixth Form Room. John Hart conducts a Classical tutorial. (© Michael Ward/ArenaPAL)

Above: 'One of the best and most delightful men': Rev Arthur Faber, (Staff 1865–80) teacher and Headmaster.

In his centenary history of the College Ralph Blumenau singles out **Harry Hammond House** (Staff 1890–1928) as the key to the strength of Malvern's scholarship results:

> He had curly brown hair, bright blue eyes, which were often cast ceilingwards, and the general appearance of a superannuated cherub. This aesthetic, highly impersonal individual, with his scholarly stoop, high-pitched voice and occasional spoonerisms, lived in his own world and was impervious to his surroundings. It was the world of the spirit, the cult of beauty, which really mattered. He conducted us through his beloved *Georgics* with a light of ecstasy in his eyes. The Gold Treasury was his constant companion. His exquisitely neat handwriting denoted the life long Hellenist; the taste and elegance of his Greek iambics could scarcely have been surpassed.

He also ran a flourishing Literary Society, which met in his house (No. 4) to read plays. He ran his house for thirty years and by his retirement had successfully trained nearly 130 Classical Scholars and Exhibitioners. 'He lived to a ripe old age, and at ninety-three saw through the press a book of 'versions' of his own compositions in Latin and Greek.'[1]

The oak panelling in the Sixth Form classroom is dedicated to his memory. The Greek inscription reads 'HARRY HAMMOND HOUSE. A memorial to the teaching of a man rich in knowledge stands this work of a skilled master carpenter'.

The First World War had serious implications for the standard of teaching. Teachers of serviceable age and appropriate fitness joined up and their places were taken by 'the physically unfit or the over-aged, or worse still, by inexperienced enthusiasts who had always believed that they had a flair for teaching and grasped eagerly at an opportunity to prove the fact – it usually proved to be an illusion.'[5] No doubt this contributed to the unhappiness that John Wheeler-Bennett felt during his days at school, leaving in 1920 in his own words as 'a critic, a sceptic and a rebel, determined not to return there under any circumstances.'[6]

However, the same author praised the broad sweep of his historical education and the joys of historical literature that contributed to his 'itch to become a historian'. And it was still possible for a boy to lose himself in the joys of reading. Wheeler-Bennett recalls 'becoming drunk on a solid orgy of verse', which began with Keats, Shelley and Byron, and continued with Tennyson and Browning, leading on to Rudyard Kipling, James Elroy Flecker and Rupert Brooke.

> In the peace of the school library, on Sunday evenings in the summer before Chapel, I would climb into a window-sill and sit entranced, now with the treasures of my current poet, now with the beauty of the view before me, stretching with lengthening shadows over the Vale of Evesham across the wooded slopes of Bredon and The Rhydd – as lovely an expanse as anywhere in England.[7]

According to Preston the intellectual breadth and quality of teaching were causing concern even before the privations of war hit the school. He recalled the rather mediocre offering he discovered upon his appointment:

> The curriculum in vogue at Malvern in 1914 appeared to me hardly to respond with the ideas being worked out elsewhere in what was the dawn of the age of transition. It was conventional and adequate only by Victorian standards, and even then narrow and uninspiring.[8]

Opposite left: The Grundy Library.
Opposite right: The Council Room as a classroom in around 1912, later panelled in memory of Charles Toppin, and now the headmaster's study. (Brian Iles Collection)

GOOD TEACHING AND SOUND LEARNING

According to Blumenau the most beloved of the non-athletic masters was **Harry Wakelyn Smith** (Staff 1885–1918), nicknamed Smugy, or Smewgy, according to C. S. Lewis, who paid this tribute:

Smewgy was 'beyond expectation, beyond hope' … He was honey-tongued. Every verse he read turned into music on his lips: something midway between speech and song. It is not the only good way of reading verse, but it is the way to enchant boys; more dramatic and less rhythmical ways can be learned later. He first taught me the right sensuality of poetry, how it should be savoured and mouthed in solitude. Of Milton's 'Thrones, Dominations, Princedoms, Virtues, Powers' he said, 'That line made me happy for a week' … Nor had I ever met before perfect courtesy in a teacher. It had nothing to do with softness; Smewgy could be very severe, but it was the severity of a judge, weighty and measured, without taunting …

He always addressed us as 'gentlemen' and the possibility of behaving otherwise seemed thus to be ruled out from the beginning … His manner was perfect: no familiarity, no hostility, no threadbare humour; mutual respect; decorum. 'Never let us live with *amousia*' was one of his favourite maxims: *amousia*, the absence of the Muses. And he knew, as Spenser knew, that courtesy was of the Muses.

Thus, even had he taught us nothing else, to be in Smewgy's form was to be in a measure ennobled. Amidst all the banal ambition and flashy splendours of school life he stood as a permanent reminder of things more gracious, more humane, larger and cooler. But his teaching, in the narrower sense, was equally good. He could enchant but he could also analyse. An idiom or a textual crux, once expounded by Smewgy, became clear as day. He made us feel that the scholar's demand for accuracy was not merely pedantic, still less an arbitrary moral discipline, but rather a niceness, a delicacy, to lack which argued 'a gross and swinish disposition'.[1]

Another OM recalled:

When he was particularly pleased with the work of any of his boys, he would send them to the Headmaster 'to be praised', as he put it, to the embarrassment of the Headmaster, and still more to the boys themselves, whose discomfiture he rendered absolute by presenting each of them with a buttonhole full of flowers, a 'badge of honour' which had to be worn in Chapel.

He was devoted to Malvern and its boys; and when he died in 1918, during the influenza epidemic, he left a book to each boy who had passed through his form and who was still at the school. He too has a room panelled in his memory. On the panelling is a tribute in Greek, which translates as:

This stands as the memorial for the man who
Having spent most of his time teaching here
Charmed with his meekness the minds of boys so that they wished
To cultivate the flowery precinct of the Muses
Although Fate has brought an end to his charming work
This man lives on with an immortal name

THE LEWIS CONNECTION

In 1909 a Northern Ireland solicitor, Alfred Lewis, made the decision to send his elder son Warren (Warnie) to Malvern College. Warren's younger brother 'Jack' (C. S.) followed in 1913.[i] Thus began the long and extraordinary connection between the Lewis family and the College.

Warren settled into the school happily and always remembered it with affection, despite not being allowed back for an extra term to prepare for the Army entrance examination having been caught smoking. He went on to a military career and became a distinguished historian of seventeenth-century France.[ii] He was to edit the family papers and was described by his brother as 'his dearest and closest friend'. C. S. Lewis, however, did not enjoy his time at Malvern and left after only one year. He was later to write in his autobiographical *Surprised by Joy* of his dislike of the sporting culture represented by the 'Bloods' and clearly felt alienated from his schoolfellows. However, in later years he paid warm tributes to his teacher H. W. Smith, who developed his love of the Classics and of English literature. According to his close friend and former pupil George Sayer, Lewis came to regret his attacks on his old school, even going as far as saying that they were exaggerated. A recent biography suggests that much of his unhappiness was related to the circumstances of his mother's death and intense homesickness for his beloved Northern Ireland. He initially found England ugly and longed for the glorious landscapes of County Down. However, this same writer describes how the young Lewis acquired a much more positive view of England when Harry Smith invited him and another boy to drive into the country where Lewis discovered 'an enchanted ground of rolling hills and valleys', with 'mysterious woods and cornfields'.[iii]

After his year at Malvern Lewis was privately tutored and later wounded fighting on the Western Front. He entered into a pact with his close friend Paddy Moore that if either of them were killed, the survivor would care for the deceased's surviving parent. Lewis fulfilled this pledge and entered into a deep friendship with Mrs Jane Moore that survived until the latter's death. Her daughter Maureen would later marry Leonard Blake, the Director of Music at Malvern from 1945 until 1968. Lewis then followed a brilliant academic career at Oxford, being elected in 1925 as a Fellow and Tutor in English literature at Magdalen College, a post he held until 1954 when he accepted the new chair of Mediaeval and Renaissance literature at Cambridge. After adolescent atheism he became convinced by Christianity, partly influenced by his friendship with J. R. R. Tolkien and reading G. K. Chesterton, and became its greatest modern literary advocate with popular books like *The Chronicles of Narnia*, *Mere Christianity* and *The Screwtape Letters*. He was a founder member of Inklings, a discussion group that included Tolkien, and met in The Eagle and Child pub in Oxford. When George Sayer became Head of English at Malvern, Lewis and Tolkien became regular visitors.

In November 2013 C. S. Lewis was honoured, on the fiftieth anniversary of his death, with a memorial in Poets' Corner in Westminster Abbey. Representatives from the College, including the Headmaster, attended this tribute to one of its most illustrious sons.

Warren Lewis (left) and Blodo Hilton, both dressed in Officers' Training Corps uniforms, Easter term 1913. (Used by permission of The Marion E. Wade Center, Wheaton College, Wheaton, IL)

Detail of School House photograph, summer 1914. C. S. Lewis middle row, centre. (Used by permission of The Marion E. Wade Center, Wheaton College, Wheaton, IL)

C. S. Lewis at his desk in 1960. (Used by permission of The Marion E. Wade Center, Wheaton College, Wheaton, IL)

He goes on to describe an excellent Classical side where the small numbers received careful and individual teaching, which enabled Malvern to achieve a sound university scholarship record. He remembered four excellent Classicists, one historian (taught by a part-time specialist) and one mathematician. The top set in science consisted 'chiefly of would be medicos and practically no university candidates'. A Modern Fifth Form saw some entries for the School Certificate and many more entered for the London Matriculation. In the days when it was still possible for many boys to enter Oxford and Cambridge with what today would be viewed as woeful academic abilities, the form master allegedly prepared them by reading 'aloud the crib for the set books at either university alternately'. Finally there was the army class top set which prepared boys for the Woolwich list.[9]

> The general impression given was that Malvern in its Upper School provided an educational system that made it possible for boys to pass the necessary preliminary examinations for the services and the professions and also for admission to the universities at the low standard demanded in 1914, and for gifted boys to obtain scholarships in Classics, and occasionally in Mathematics – in other words, gave parents the facilities of a good coaching establishment.

Above: Francis William Ashton (2. 1891–93) won the Nobel Prize for Chemistry in 1922, for his invention of the mass spectrograph in 1919. Aston was a Fellow at Trinity College, Cambridge, and Fellow of the Royal Society. (© National Portrait Gallery, London)

If this was the Sixth Form, it was much worse in the Lower School 'where the expectation was that masters would exact a quota of industry and maintain (with occasional exceptions) excellent discipline'. Preston was deeply concerned about Malvern's reputation for over-athleticism and the narrowness of the educational experience of so many of the boys.

Academic innovations came fast and furious. Preston invited inspections from the Board of Education for the first time, Higher and School certificates were introduced, and above all there was a great extension in the facilities for teaching science. The old Radnor stables were converted into a science block in 1920 but in 1934 Preston raised the possibility of a new building with the Council who, reflecting the uncertain financial position in the Depression years, concluded that the money would have to be raised by an appeal. OMs and friends of the school raised the necessary sum of £21,000, and in 1938 the new Preston Science building was opened by the former Prime Minister, Earl Baldwin.[10] Other academic innovations included the introduction

Left: Science laboratory in 1912. (Brian Iles Collection)

One of the most outstanding masters to serve the College was **John Lewis** (2/6. 1937–42), who returned to Malvern in 1946 and was to serve as senior science master for twenty-eight years and as housemaster of No. 8 from 1961 to 1976. He was first and foremost an inspiring and gifted physics teacher and was largely responsible for the creation of a new approach to science teaching, Nuffield Science, which emphasised the importance of 'hands on learning' through experiment. His pupils loved his teaching, one recalling:

> 'Johnny Lou' taught us with a mixture of practical work and witty, but crystal-clear explanation, as though he was a detective masterfully unravelling a complicated mystery.[i]

He was a great publicist for the new science and achieved national and even international prominence as the associate director of the National Physics Project, as British representative on the Physics Committee of OECD and in 1988 as chairman of the Association for Science Education (the professional association for 16,000 science teachers). He had previously been appointed secretary of the International Union of Pure and Applied Physics's Commission on Physics Education. In 1989 the International Council of Scientific Unions[ii] appointed him the secretary of their committee on the Teaching of Science. A mere schoolmaster had never occupied either of these posts. In his last years of teaching Lewis pioneered the Science in Society project aimed at showing the relevance of science to daily life and industry and also developed the 'Malvern Diploma'. Put simply, he inspired generations of pupils and put Malvern on the educational map – and he still found time to found and run The Malvern Swordsmen.[iii]

(Courtesy of Berrows Newspapers)

of Spanish, specialist biology and a Business Fifth. If the aim had been to expand the intellectual range of Malvernians, Preston could take justifiable pride when fourteen Firsts won by OMs at Oxford and Cambridge in 1929 and 1930 were taken from seven different faculties.[11]

The Malvernian provides a fascinating insight into the intellectual life of the school on the eve of the Second World War. A discussion society came to the conclusion that 'some form of Communism was in the remote future possible, and even desirable'. A school lecture in October 1938 was on 'A Year of the War in Spain' by a Captain Wintringham, who was the officer commanding the British Battalion of the International Brigade. It was reported that some pupils had attended the League of Nations Union Summer School in Geneva where the Headmaster Mr Gaunt was one of the wardens. The December editorial rejoiced in the free speech enjoyed by Malvernians in contrast to 'the German or Italian school boy, smarting under a supposed wrong, who must remain silent'. The Allison Society saw a staged reading of *Journey's End*. The French play was Molière's *L'Avare*.[12] In May 1939 psychoanalysis was the subject in the Discussion Society and an exhibition of furniture was held in Big School accompanied by a lecture by Dr Nikolaus Pevsner on contemporary design in building and furniture.

The outbreak of the Second World War interrupted this proud progress. Perhaps due to the complexities of war – younger teachers called up, the sense of impermanence generated by two exiles, the poor conditions at Blenheim, the anxiety of the times – there is a decided sense of a sharp decline in teaching standards and the quality of learning in these years. George Chesterton recalls that his form master at Blenheim:

> only bothered with the boys who were academic and really wanted to learn. I did not count myself among their number. He couldn't have cared less whether you did any work or not.

> This suited me down to the ground. He was lazy, I guess. For example, first period in the morning was obviously too early for him – he seldom turned up![13]

Upon the first return to Malvern matters did not improve: 'It has to be said that I don't think I was well taught – ever'. The boys idled away the 'indescribably boring' mathematics lessons by playing a form of ping-pong using a metal bar across the ceiling as a substitute net:

> Every so often, predictably enough, the ball would be missed and it would bounce over desks and up to the front where [the master] was busy writing up problems on the board. Either he would not notice or, more probably, would affect not to notice ... 'If you were bright and you were particularly interested in the subject, then I'm sure you would have got all the teaching and attention that you needed.'

Gaunt was clearly aware of the deficiencies in classroom teaching, but as Andrew Murtagh puts it, 'at a period in the school's history when it was not at all clear whether civilisation as they knew it, let alone Malvern College, would survive, he had to busy himself with more pressing concerns.'[14]

When the school finally returned from Harrow in 1946, the most urgent problem was to build up numbers and it is clear that academic standards did not notably improve for some years. Gaunt was worried about examination results, not least when 30 per cent of boys left without the School Certificate. At Christmas 1949 he remarked that 'there were only five boys whose reports could be termed excellent'. In 1951 Gaunt reported to the College Council that a recent school inspectors' report had criticised a lack of intellectual excitement among the younger boys and a certain dreariness in the teaching. He attributed this to the number of boys who in more prosperous times would not have been accepted into the school and who had to be drilled through the School Certificate: 'This has no doubt led to a growing attitude of despair on the part of both master and boy, which has become somewhat widespread', although both he, and

Above: The economist James Meade (8.1921–26), in 1990. During the Second World War Meade became a member of the Economic Section of the War Cabinet Secretariat and in 1947 became the professor of Commerce at the London School of Economics, during which time he wrote two books, *The Balance of Payments* and *Trade and Welfare*. From 1967 to 1974 he was senior research fellow of Christ's College, Cambridge, winning the Nobel Prize in Economics, with Swedish economist Bernie Ohlen, in 1977, for work in the field of international economics. (© Liam Woon / National Portrait Gallery, London)

Left: Richard Walwyn captivates.

the inspectors, stressed that this did not apply to the Sixth Form. One master recalled being given the famous 100X, a class of thirty-one boys who had all failed O level Maths at least once, in his first term. Two sets of about sixty were kept down to go around the Hundred again because of insufficient passes.[15] An obituary tribute concluded that Gaunt 'shared Preston's aim for, and would applaud Lindsay's achievement of, a return to really competitive academic standards, but he was robbed by circumstances of the satisfaction of seeing much concrete progress in this direction.'[16]

The transformation in Malvern's intellectual hinterland and academic profile began during the headmastership of Donald Lindsay. He was acutely aware of the need to advance the quality of teaching and achievement if the school was to survive in the more egalitarian and competitive post-war world.

There was much to build on, not least a long-standing academic tradition in Classics and mathematics, which, even in the thin pickings of the post-war years, provided intellectual challenge for the most able under the scholarly influence of George White and Ralph Cobb.[17] But the wider reformation began in science. The building of the Preston Science School before the war had greatly increased the significance of the sciences in the school and, by 1958, some 60 per cent of sixth formers were doing science subjects – up from 40 per cent ten years before.

The science curriculum was modernised under John Lewis, a most able teacher of physics, who became the senior science master in 1955, and was later described as 'one of the principal instruments of Donald Lindsay's radical policy of pointing Malvern towards the twenty-first

---

After a distinguished war in which he was awarded the Distinguished Service Cross, **Tony Leng** (Staff 1954–88) was recruited to Malvern to run the Modern Languages department, which he was to do with distinction for twenty-seven years. A gifted scholar and teacher, he had the capacity to stimulate the brightest linguists and coax the hopeless through the required public examinations. Under his leadership Malvern became one of the first schools in the country to build a language laboratory. The department also became a powerhouse of academic achievement. His notes on the back of envelopes became legendary but behind the apparent chaos was a sure direction and a profoundly scholarly man. His reports were perceptive and he didn't waste words: 'Silently successful', 'Uncomprehending', 'Fidgets well'. His letters of appreciation after being entertained were often poetic and always stylish.

He wrote superbly funny ironic accounts of incidents in the school and in retirement of the foibles of his neighbours. Humour and mischief were great weapons in his armoury. To John Blackshaw about a boy in his house he wrote:

> Would you please arrange for him to have a lecture from some authoritative person on the birds and the bees, and by extension the dire risk involved in prostitution, a feature of life of which he seems not to know the existence?

The boy obviously learned fast:

(Photograph by George Chesterton)

> I invited X – actually he asked himself – to my home Saturday morning to see Jacques Tati. He didn't come, but as I hurried home to put the film on, I saw him tucked away by the fence outside No. 8 with a young lady. When I got home the other boys were already there and one of them said, 'X sends his apologies and regrets he cannot make it.' I felt like saying: he's making it very nicely thank you.

A wise, kind and thoughtful housemaster he showed a deft touch in handling difficult boys, particularly intelligent ones. Two boys who wrote to Radio Luxembourg bemoaning their frustrated state at a boarding school were overwhelmed by a mountain of mail 'which he placed between them' at breakfast. They were made to reply to each letter – 'a clever punishment, particularly since some of the letters enclosed photographs or showed a degree of familiarity with the adult world that they themselves did not possess.' When he sent some miscreants for an early morning run he drove to pick them up fearing they would miss breakfast.

After a post-teaching stint as librarian he spent a fine retirement engaged in painting, writing, enjoying his family and a fount of simple acts of kindness.

Reg Farrar (Staff 1949–85) joined the staff after Army service in India and gaining his degree at St John's College, Cambridge. Alan Carter summed up his outstanding teaching career as follows:

A schoolmaster who has been enjoyed by pupils and colleagues alike but, of course, his most outstanding contribution to the school has been his teaching of mathematics. He took over the department from Ralph Cobb in 1962 and continued the tradition of the highest scholarship. The record of the Maths department in achieving Scholarships and Exhibitions at Oxford and Cambridge and in gaining A grades with distinction at A level is second to none. Such a success is due to Reg's inspiration. First and foremost he is a teacher of calibre who insisted on the highest standard and is dedicated to scholarly attitudes. He is an individual concerned for his pupils, and they have, over the years, demonstrated their affection and admiration for him. No Mathematician could ever forget Reg's crumpet parties. The greatest thing about Reg is that even in the same breath as praising his skills and dedication as teacher and academic (he is a by-word throughout the country) we can all smile because of some moment of fun he has given us. Unpretentious, unpompous, modest and kind – in the strictest confidence a lovely character.[i]

Hilarity was never far away. On one occasion, in SH, he brought the house down when a pressing appointment led him to leave lunch early, which he did on all fours 'so as not to draw attention'. His submarine impersonations and jaunty hummed snatches of Mozart enlivened his lessons and appropriately his former pupils and colleagues gave him membership of Glyndebourne as a retirement gift.

(Photograph by R. Sherwood (3. 1981–86))

century suitably equipped with a broader and deeper scientific education.'[18] He became chairman of a national government-supported committee to update the teaching of physics. Much of the experimental work for this was done in the College laboratories, and Malvern 'was one of the thirty schools in a pilot scheme for teaching a new syllabus which included aspects of modern physics not hitherto taught at schools.'[19] This innovative work led to the development of Nuffield Science, an attempt to encourage 'learning through experiments' rather than the more didactic approach then in favour. Lewis was a superb fundraiser, acquiring grants, mainly from the Nuffield Foundation, for curriculum improvements, and the newly established Industrial Fund for the Advancement of Scientific Education in Schools for improvements in buildings and facilities. Grants enabled a modern extension to the Preston building in 1958, and a second floor was added two years later, which included the Salter Lecture Room.[20] It was significant that on Centenary Day, 25 January 1965, the school celebrated with the opening by Sir Bernard Lovell of a third extension to the Preston Science School. The chairman of the College Council, Sir John Wheeler-Bennett, said: 'Malvern College, over and above its other considerable achievements, has become one of the leading science schools in the country'. He went on to praise: 'the truly splendid work which our Senior Science master, John Lewis, has done here, work which has fired the imagination and the discipleship of so many.'[21]

Lewis's widespread connections assisted the Science department in other ways; for example, Birmingham University provided an electron microscope. He also pioneered support for preparatory schools' science teaching, greatly assisted by a grant from Esso; the national teaching materials, which were largely written by the College science staff, led Malvern to become the leading school in influencing scientific teaching in the preparatory sector not least through the residential courses provided by the College for hundreds of preparatory school teachers. The Science departments were also in the forefront of A-level examining in all three of the natural sciences.

Ralph Blumenau (Staff 1958–85) was recruited to Malvern with a view to running the History department, which he was to do for nearly thirty years up until his retirement. A superb teacher, he exuded intellectual excitement and had the great gift of being able to explain complex ideas simply. An intellectual powerhouse, he saw a steady expansion in the popularity and success of the History department. His Lower Sixth forum and Upper Sixth Socratic Society had pupils writing, introducing and discussing academic papers, which certainly stimulated the more able scholars. His lecture series on the history of art became legendary and the jewel in the crown of the Sixth Form General periods.

His enthusiasm concealed a mind that intellectually was of steel, but his feelings warm and sincere, were there for us to appreciate. Such were my first impressions of the man who was to play an important role in Donald Lindsay's planned changes to Malvern's academic climate.[i]

Former pupils are full of praise:

Ralph was one of the fine young masters DDL managed to secure for the College at that time, he prepared superb duplicated hand-outs for every lesson, which we filed for exam revision later – after, of course, he had first captivated us with utterly absorbing accounts of late nineteenth and twentieth-century European history, though he never referred to the bitter personal tragedies he had experienced himself in Germany in the actual period we were studying.

Ralph would start classes talking about Music, Art, Philosophy, movies, theatre and international events. His history lessons were full of such innovations. Everything I take an interest in today: writing and reading poetry, art and travelling the world to see the great museums, writing prose and journalism and a curiosity and inquisitiveness about the world and people – I owe to Ralph. He opened up intellectual doors that we did not know existed. I dedicated my last book *Pakistan on the Brink* to him as I really felt the need to express my gratitude to him for what he did for us in our youth. I tell my children that everything I am today is partly due to him and I wish they had had such an intellectual mentor at school.[ii]

The final comment on this remarkable man must be given to the man who appointed him to the staff. Ralph had expressed his regret to Donald Lindsay that, with the latter's retirement, he would not

(Photograph by George Chesterton)

have a Lindsay valedictory. Typical of the man, he did not forget the occasion and he wrote what he would have said in a charming letter:

Your appointment was one of the very best I ever made. You brought what I lacked but appreciated – real scholarship. Any good staff must have its quota of alpha minds. It wouldn't do to have 100 per cent of them – there would be no athletes to teach geography! But men like you bring quality and set standards and are invaluable.

Had I been pronouncing your obituary I would have praised the courage of a man who, newly appointed, scrapped the history text book which his headmaster had written![iii]

After his career at Malvern he wrote *Philosophy and Living* and was a popular lecturer at the University of the Third Age in London. He was awarded the BEM for services to adult education in the New Year Honours in 2014.

GOOD TEACHING AND SOUND LEARNING

Lewis was greatly assisted by the work of a number of able teachers appointed during these years. Ken Grayson, Fred Vivian-Robinson[22] and Alan Duff, described by Lewis 'as perhaps the best teacher of physics of us all' helped to develop Nuffield Physics.[23] Martin Rogers[24] wrote the Nuffield O-level Chemistry course one summer at Malvern. Michael McNevin, James Campbell-Ferguson and Colin Nicholls were members of the team that developed Nuffield A-level Chemistry and 'trialled' it at Malvern. All pupils entering the school had long studied physics and chemistry, but under the influence of Arnold Darlington[25] biology moved from being a subject studied only by potential medics to being included in all pupils' education. Darlington was a captivating teacher who spellbound his classes both in biology and with his tales of gruesome murders about which he was something of an expert. Mention must also be made of Richard Walwyn, who was not only a gifted teacher of physics, but became responsible for the introduction of ICT into the mainstream of the educational and administrative life of the school.

Lewis was succeeded as Head of Science by a series of distinguished teachers – Michael Shepherd, David Penter and Chris Hall – all of whom kept Malvern science in the forefront of national developments and maintained the high profile within the school that was so much part of its academic renaissance.[26]

The other area of growing excellence was modern languages under the inspired Tony Leng, who taught French and became Head of Languages. Another grant from the Nuffield Foundation enabled Malvern to become, in 1963, the first public school to have a language laboratory, enabling much more rapid individual linguistic progress.[27]

The success of Lindsay's innovations became apparent in the growing numbers of able scholars attracted to the school and a steady rise in academic standard at all levels. By 1969 Lindsay was able to report the greatest number of Oxbridge scholarships that the school had ever seen. Three outstanding masters have received universal praise from those fortunate enough to be taught by them. George Sayer and Reg Farrar were both recruited by Tom Gaunt, and Ralph Blumenau by Donald Lindsay. All were to play a significant part in Malvern's revival as an academic school and all three were to become beloved and greatly admired by their pupils.

The masters chosen by Gaunt and Lindsay to revive the academic life of the school also contributed to a steady undermining of that scourge of public schools, Philistinism. One distinguished OM of the 1950s described both boys and most masters as 'aggressively disinterested in the arts', and even the few who were more positively inclined regarded 'anything from the twentieth century both difficult and culturally dangerous'.[28] Even traditional classics were subject to absurd prejudice. When the Choral Society proposed to sing Brahms' German Requiem, anti-German feeling erupted only to be quelled by Lindsay publicly announcing that the Brahms was a special favourite of his and how much he was looking forward to the production. Almost imperceptibly things began to change. An art fund allowed the school to purchase a considerable collection of lithographs, prints and paintings from contemporary artists which were displayed in corridors, classroom and in the boarding houses.[29] Orchestral music began to develop and theatrical productions became more frequent and more adventurous. The building of the Lindsay Art Centre, and the later transformation of the old school gym into a theatre, marked a significant change that mirrored the growing prestige of these areas in national life. Some masters opened up the world of art and music through their lessons and even the décor of their rooms. Donald Lindsay gave unstinting support to these culturally uplifting moves. An OM recalls a range of experiences that 'stocked my imagination with riches that have stayed with me' such as visiting Deerhurst ('a magical Anglo-Saxon church') with George Sayer, and 'the deep spiritual experience of attending the three-hour Good Friday service in Tewkesbury Abbey' with his housemaster:

Above: Light switch in Classical Sixth Form room.

There were, in fact, many experiences of this kind – if you took advantage of them. Two of the last, and greatest, of these for me were singing with the Choral Society in Bach's *St. Matthew Passion* and attending the first night of Benjamin Britten's shattering *War Requiem* in Coventry Cathedral.[30]

The 1970s witnessed a continued strength in the academic life of the school. The numbers of scholars remained high, as did awards to Oxbridge. John Hart's Classics lessons remained a joy and a source of endless entertaining stories. As if it were necessary, he proved his intellectual eminence by victory in the BBC Mastermind competition in 1976, leading to the renaming of the end of the Christmas term's quiz as the Hart General Knowledge Quiz.[31]

New trends did emerge. Martin Rogers introduced a new form – the Foundation year – in which all boys would begin their school career. The more able could take O levels in certain subjects, such as Latin, maths, English and French in the Remove and then spend their time in the Hundred as members of the so-called 'Lower Sixth' where they prepared for sixth-form study or took 'AO' examinations.[32] The scholars would complete A-level courses at the end of the VIC and then embark on four terms of Oxbridge preparation in their chosen discipline while usually adding a further A level or two. Teaching became more focused on enquiry and discussion. Early forms of coursework (before the genre became an intellectual quagmire) encouraged much more individual study. More attention was paid to the process and technique of learning and study skills entered into the experience of all, with gifted presentations pioneered by Martin Frayn. During the Rogers era efforts were made to bridge the gap between academic study and the world of work, particularly industry, through visits to factories, industrial conferences and work experience schemes.

Another notable change accompanied the growing numbers of girls in the school:

> In those days almost all boys were still addressed by their surnames. In the small third-year Sixth some masters would change over to using first names; and the process of changing over always seemed rather awkward and embarrassing. In girls' schools, however, it was almost always first names that were used; and before the girls first arrived, I had told the boys that therefore I was going to address them by their first names also. I didn't actually know the first names of many of the boys in my class – that was still quite usual in those days – and some of them seemed almost embarrassed to give them, especially if they were in the slightest bit

Above: John Hart, senior Classics master and victor in Mastermind and *Pepper v Hart*.

PEPPER v HART

John Hart made national headlines, and legal history, when he led an appeal against a tax ruling that he thought to be unjust. In 1992 the long-running legal saga of *Pepper v Hart & others* finally came to an end. It started in 1984 when the local inspector of taxes assessed ten masters for income tax on the benefit of the reduced fees they paid for their sons. In John Hart's words:

> This we thought was wrong in law, and our appeal was upheld by the Special Commissioner of Income Tax, but when the Inland Revenue appealed in turn their view was upheld by Mr Justice Vinelott in the High Court, and then in the Court of Appeal. Our counsel had said from the start that the case had 'House of Lords potential', and so it proved – not once, but twice! What made legal history was the fact that, in the second hearing, seven Law Lords decided to dispense themselves from the ancient rule of practice that forbade reference to Parliamentary proceedings in Hansard. As a Treasury Minister had made it explicitly clear, in the relevant debate in 1976, that people in our situation were not meant to be caught by the tax, we were home and dry – 7-0.

Alan Carter (Staff 1960–97) took over the English department upon George Sayer's retirement. Universally acknowledged as one of the most gifted teachers in the school, his dramatic style could enliven the dullest text. Perhaps his greatest gift was that most difficult of all pedagogic skills: allowing a class to reflect and reach their own conclusions, gently prompted, but never cajoled:

> He drew from us vociferous explanations, comments and opinions, even as he chalked unattributed poems up on the blackboard before our very eyes; read us Spenser's *Faerie Queene* with a stylish Middle English accent; approached every lesson with mischievous humour, stimulating us to read, analyse, discuss, champion or doubt, disagree, laugh, take sides passionately.

One OM recalls that Alan Carter, together with his 'co-conspirator' Dale Vargas,[i] also influenced sartorial taste by raising 'our limited awareness of contemporary male '60s fashion, with their almost daily displays of striped and subtle coloured shirts, well-cut corduroy and woven jackets, slimline trousers with slanting pockets and trouser ends (MOST DEFINITELY without turn-ups) above elegant shoes (often laceless such as Chelsea boots) with colourful silk Italian narrow ties or bow ties and sometimes complemented by a colourful silk handkerchief emerging from the top pocket.'

unusual. How stuffy many aspects of public school life still were in those days! The Science Department had of course also introduced first names in the mixed forms; but I was the only member of staff who at that time decided that I would address all boys by their first names: it suddenly seemed almost more artificial to call the younger boys by their surnames. I found that it made a small but really quite significant difference to the atmosphere in the classroom; and I am glad to say that, even before Malvern went wholly co-educational, the use of first names throughout the school had become the rule.[33]

In the 1980s the school readjusted its academic profile. While science remained strong both in recruitment and results, the literary subjects and social sciences grew stronger. By the 1990s Malvern could no longer be defined as primarily a science school; greater numbers were pursuing other subjects with a growing achievement of fine academic results in the arts and social sciences. These subjects increasingly dominated Oxbridge places. Between 1989 and 2014 the top five subjects for which places were won were History (51), PPE & Economics (40), languages including Classics (40), Maths and Engineering (34) and sciences (27).

This movement was a national trend, but at Malvern it owed much to a newer generation of heads of department and teachers. John Venning (who took over the English department in 1984) induced creativity from his scholars that led not only to fine academic results but also to genuine excitement. He was in every sense a presence, much enjoyed by his pupils, who rejoiced in his stylish, dry mordant humour. In his first lesson with the scholars he announced that he would leave the room for a while so that 'they could talk about him'. The polymath John Knee, who succeeded Reg Farrar, was widely considered by the pupils to be a genius, a view reinforced by his brilliance at chess.[34] Malvern was one of the first schools in the country to start a Business form and in the post-war years this evolved, under Jim Bolam, into the Economics and Politics department. His successors Simon Wilkinson, Martin Frayn[35] and Stephen Holroyd presided over a great expansion in the numbers of pupils studying these subjects and their growing, valuable contribution to the intellectual life of the school. The Languages department acquired a series of dynamic and colourful characters. Both René Filho and Paul Godsland brought brilliance to the French department together with, respectively, Gallic and Geordie charm; Richard Hookham brought an irrepressible liveliness and commitment to Spanish teaching and David Matthews presided over this empire with studied unflappability and good sense working closely on the growing links with Germany. Among the great characters of this generation mention must be made of Douglas Mensforth, an iconoclastic English teacher whose readings of Chaucer and Milton became legendary. He managed an effortless transition from his early fearsome image represented by his nickname 'Dracula' to a benign lover of cats, charming his German students in their own language, and sporting a striking array of contemporary T-shirts.

A remarkable generation of literary and artistic OMs emerged. Distinguished artists included Julian Bailey and Jonathan Wateridge. Giles Foden became a household name after the success of *The Last King of Scotland*. James Delingpole, Oludiran Adebayo, Miles Hordern and Horatio Clare were part of this Malvern golden age. Among historians Dominic Sandbrook achieved the double honour of proving both a distinguished academic historian and a popular television presenter. Notable academics emerged with the class of 1984 boasting two professors from among its ranks: Simon Caney in political theory at Oxford, and Christopher Whitty in tropical medicine in London.[36]

The introduction of the National Curriculum and 'double award science' in the late 1980s made a re-evaluation of the Lower School curriculum necessary. Breadth was continued, in that all pupils took GCSE examinations in (as well as maths, English, science and, for some, Latin or Greek) a modern foreign language, a humanity (in addition to religious studies) and a 'practical-aesthetic' subject (chosen from art, drama, music and technology). The academic profile of the College was also affected by changes in the management structure.[37] For the first time a director of studies was appointed to supervise all aspects of the curriculum; this post was first held by Frank Harriss, formerly Head of Chemistry, who proved a master of handling the avalanche of national initiatives and the matrix of issues raised by the merger, and above all showed diplomatic finesse in handling heads of department, teachers and the pupil body. The outward appearance of St Francis, self-effacing and mild-mannered, concealed a Machiavellian skill in moving colleagues in the direction he wished them to go. He was succeeded by Joe Gauci

Right: Spanish enthusiasm: Señor Richard Hookham.

GOOD TEACHING AND SOUND LEARNING

Left: The joy of learning. (Photograph by Jon Willcocks)

in 2005, who brought remarkable administrative gifts to the task combined with Cromwellian steeliness when required.

The introduction of the International Baccalaureate in 1992 opened a new chapter in the academic life of the school. After an uncertain start it steadily increased in popularity, not least because it made possible the recruitment of able pupils from European countries who would have been wary of the unfamiliar A-level system. In a time of growing uncertainty about the future and quality of A-level courses and grading, the IB won support from a wide stratum of British pupils as well. The results were remarkable and the sense of academic energy released by sets of intellectually hungry entrants to the Lower Sixth transformed life in the Sixth Form.[38]

The steady improvement in IB results over the years was a consequence of a highly dedicated and experienced teaching staff. After René Filho's launch, the task of administering the course fell to John Knee and then Peter Gray, both men of great ability, professionalism and tact. Several teachers trained as IB workshop leaders and examiners. The school hosted several IB special-interest groups and welcomed visitors from schools in the UK and abroad. The increase in the number of pupils allowed the school to expand the number of subjects offered. It became one of very few schools in the world to be able to offer the further mathematics course (surely the most demanding of all IB courses). Design and Technology was introduced as an A-level subject in the 1990s coinciding with the building of the Chapman Design and Technology Centre (rather aptly on the site of the last remaining huts from the TRE) and was now offered for the IB. Philosophy appeared in 2008. Elements of philosophy had been part of the Religious Studies A level and it was, of course, central to the Theory of Knowledge course. The enthusiasm and stimulating teaching

Below: IB studies. (Photograph by Jon Willcocks)

Right: The Chapman Design and Technology Centre – achieving the vision.

of Dr Robin Lister and Rev Andrew Law made this new addition both possible and popular. Additional courses added recently include Sport and Exercise Science (piloted at Malvern) and Environmental Systems and Societies. Malvern's continuing commitment to breadth was also evidenced by the fact that it offered visual arts, theatre arts and music as elective subjects. By 2012 it was evident that there was an accelerating trend for Malvern students to apply to and study in the USA, leading the school to appoint a teacher in charge of supervising their applications.[39]

Most traditional subjects thrived in the lively intellectual climate. History continued to combine popularity with the excellent scholarship that produced the school's strongest Oxbridge successes. In this gifted department mention must be made of the captivating Alan Smith of whom an inspector, who had watched his GCSE history lesson, said, 'for those pupils nothing

Right: Learning by experiment. (Photograph by Jon Willcocks)

existed beyond his words'. The English department flourished under Peter Chappell who also did much to revive debating. Classics, now under the skilful management of Richard Thurlow, received a fillip from the arrival of German students where classical languages had remained a compulsory part of their gymnasium education. German and Spanish flourished, as did economics for a generation seeking understanding of the endless flow of economic news and perhaps the hope that it would lead to the path of riches. The proof that all change comes from below could be seen in an upsurge in interest in Mandarin, leading at least one recent Senior Chapel Prefect to begin learning the language in addition to an extraordinarily heavy programme. Holiday and gap-year expeditions to China to master the rudiments of the language started as a novelty and then became a familiar option to consider.

Teaching changed beyond all recognition. A range of differences would strike a visitor from pre-war Malvern. The classrooms are cheerful, decorated and full of technology. Students (for that was now their normal nomenclature) sat in seminar positions rather than serried ranks. Discussion and interaction were the norm; vigorous engagement and debate were the stuff of most lessons. As one boy put it, 'intellectual curiosity thrives and the teachers actively stimulate this; they are also happy (mostly) to be disagreed with.' Laughter and exchanged witticisms were common. Textbooks and computer programmes were sophisticated. Research presentations were central and discussion of internal assessments, extended essays or the Theory of Knowledge[40] presentation permeated the air – more reminiscent of a university than the Victorian schoolroom. A purposeful informality dominated the relationship between teachers and students. No teacher would survive who was not master of their brief and who could not engage and interest their charges. Students prized professionalism in their teachers and held the highest respect for those who wore their learning lightly but had something interesting to say. A sense of common purpose was generated by looming examinations.

One German/Spanish boy remembered his early days at Malvern:

> Classes were, compared to Germany, much smaller. I was thus quickly struck by the feeling that every student was an important member of the class and that one had a much more personal relationship to the teacher. On the other side, I found the teachers far stricter and it took me some time to adjust to that. As an example, during the second day of classes, one of my teachers gave an energetic speech about the importance of having the top button closed and

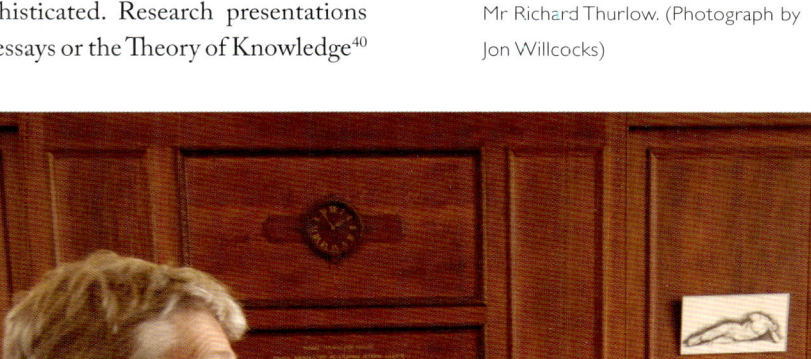

Above: Debating: making a point. (Photograph by Jon Willcocks)

Below: The Classical tradition with Mr Richard Thurlow. (Photograph by Jon Willcocks)

MALVERN COLLEGE

Right: Malvern's entry to the Engineering Education scheme 2007, in which the team presented to HRH Princess Anne, Patron of WISE (Women in Science and Engineering). The project incorporated the idea of Electromagnetic Levitation (April 2007).

the tie properly attached to that final button. I could not resist laughing although as inconspicuously as possible. This, however, was naturally seen, which led to the rhetorical question asking whether I had actually laughed. Being direct (as many Germans are), I simply answered with 'Yes'; resulting in him asking the same question again, this time, more loudly. My answer was the same, as I did not know what exactly I was doing wrong by being honest, until it was made clear to me that responses given by students would have to end with the word 'Sir'.

It became clear to me that although the student–teacher relationship was much more personal than in Germany, the respect students showed to their teachers was higher too. But more importantly, it was mutual respect, which enabled the creation of a unique atmosphere in classrooms, which every student and every teacher shared.[41]

Right: Modern Upper Grundy.

GOOD TEACHING AND SOUND LEARNING

The pursuit of academic excellence remained constant, but considerable procedures were introduced to enable more pupils to learn effectively. There was a dramatic change in attitude and opportunities for those who once would have been labelled 'slow' or incapable. Advances in understanding the nature of dyslexia and the manifold problems of how children learn transformed the lives of many. An outstanding learning support department screened all pupils, and guided and supported those who needed different modes of study. The results for many of these young people were nothing short of remarkable. In the 1980s it was still possible for a master to dismiss dyslexia as a middle-class excuse for laziness; twenty years later a more sophisticated understanding was enabling children who would have suffered years of humiliation and failure to study at the best universities.

A fine example of modern teaching was illustrated by one inspired English teacher who decided that the best way to absorb her pupils in Joe Simpson's climbing tale *Touching the Void* was by taking them out of the classroom and onto the climbing wall. She said: 'It is very difficult for some children to visualise text and therefore a story can remain closed to them. We're in a privileged teaching environment where we have both a climbing wall and an outward bound instructor, so it struck me that we could take the book out of the classroom and bring the story alive.' After visualising the text's landscape by creating a model of the mountain outside the classroom, complete with fissures and crevasses, pupils received climbing instruction to give insight into the technical features of the text. They also watched a recreation of the moment Simon Yates had to cut climbing partner Simpson's rope. In full mountaineering gear, the instructor cut the rope tied to a Sixth Form volunteer, who fell safely from a balcony to a crash mat. 'I can honestly say that the cutting of that rope was one of my most satisfying teaching experiences in a long time because in that moment, the words on the page came alive for the class in a way that invigorated all our subsequent work on the text.'[42]

Teachers were beset with initiatives from government reports, examining boards and the latest trend usually acquired in the ubiquitous round of the new industry of INSET (in service training). The ideas ranged from the useful to the trite and absurd. The fable of the emperor's new clothes came regularly to mind and should of course be learned by rote by all new teachers as an inoculation of sanity as they embark on their careers. However, a greater professionalism in training and supporting teachers and assessment of each teacher's performance undoubtedly helped to raise standards. Inspections came regularly and it was to the credit of the school that on all occasions there was little but praise for the intellectual atmosphere, creativity, and achievement of the student body and unstinted praise for the outstanding relationship between teachers and students.

Above: Mrs Alison Higgins (Staff Ellerslie and then Malvern College 1992–2010). (Photograph by Jon Willcocks)

Below left: Touching the Void.
Below right: Poppy Donaldson (4. 2007–12), a talented young writer, had her short story published in *The Cry of the Wolf and Other Short Stories* after winning a prestigious competition organised to coincide with World Book Day 2009.

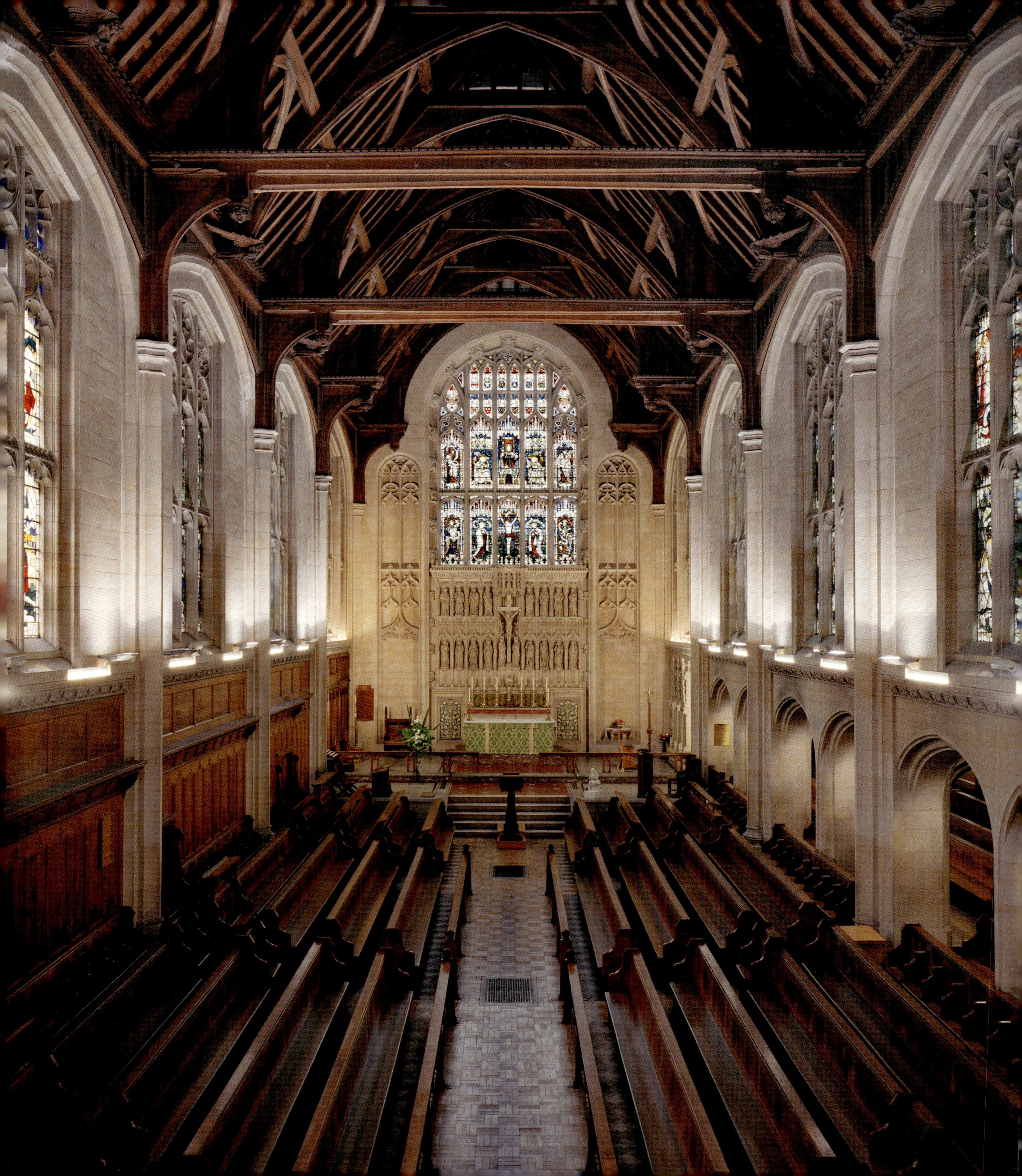

9

Look forward in faith

The older English public schools often started as religious foundations with preparation for the clerical life as a central objective. After the years of decline the Arnoldian revival returned powerfully to this theme, not so much to foster men of the cloth but to endue young men with the moral foundations that would make for a Christian gentleman. From the beginning Malvern followed this pattern. The choice of neo-Gothic for the Main Building was inspired by the attractions of the Age of Faith associated with Gothic architecture. Two figurative carvings of a soldier and a cleric grace the main entrance. All the early headmasters were in holy orders, as indeed were most of the teaching body. The teachings, worship and practice of the Christian faith run through the entire story of the school. The Chapel has been the focus for some of the most moving episodes in the school's history, both national and individual, and it is here above all that generations of Malvernians have confronted the great questions of their own existence. Most will have been bored, provoked, moved and stimulated in equal measure. For many the group identity and the joy of communal singing abide as their lasting memory, for others a word, reading or moment of transcendence transformed their lives. Perhaps it is therefore no surprise that it is Chapel that exerts such a powerful memory in the mind of many Old Malvernians.

Charles Hansom's original designs for the College included a chapel linked to the main school by cloisters. A shortage of funds prevented the implementation of this design and for the first thirty years of the College's existence Chapel services took place in the south wing of the Main Building. Under the headmastership of Gray a chapel fund was established in 1894 in order to finance the building of a chapel. In stirring words Gray spoke of his proposal on Speech Day:

> A Chapel we must have here. We cannot do for your boys here what we long to do for them without a Chapel, a Chapel worthy of the school, of its beautiful buildings, worthy of its reputation and of its fame. Everything else has been provided: in every other respect I think I may say the school is almost perfectly equipped. The Chapel alone is left – the highest and noblest: the crown of all is left to be the last of all. Our Chapel, as it stands, is miserably inadequate. There is bare accommodation in it for our boys, little for our Masters and their families, none for visitors, none for our servants. Our Chapel is, as it stands, I trust, what every school Chapel ought to be, the very shrine and centre of all its life, the pivot round which all revolves. But if our present Chapel is this, what might not a worthy Chapel be? What a power, what a potent force in the moulding and fashioning of these young lives which we send forth every year to influence – as Christians, as useful citizens, as high-minded, God-fearing gentlemen

Opposite: The College Chapel looking east, designed by Sir Arthur Blomfield and opened in 1899. (© Alastair Carew-Cox (7. 1975–80))

Above: The old Chapel in the south wing. Masters and wives sat under the canopy on the left. The pulpit was later given to the College Mission Chapel in Canning Town.

MALVERN COLLEGE

Top right: The west elevation and cross-section for the 1895 plans for the Chapel.

Below right: Plans for the extension on the southern elevation of the Chapel.

– the national life of our beloved England. Ladies and gentlemen, I appeal to you, and through you, and from you, to all who care for this great School, all who love it, to give us a Chapel.

As we have seen, the money was quickly raised. Sir Arthur Blomfield[1] was employed as the architect and wisely he made allowance in his design for a possible extension to the south. Sadly Gray had to resign on the grounds of ill health before his beloved project could be completed. Gray's successor, S. R. James, saw the completion of the Chapel, and he wrote in his autobiography:

> When I came to Malvern the walls were about ten feet above ground – that was in September 1897 – and we moved into the new building in March 1899. It was then quite bare internally, seated with chairs, and without the panelling, which was to line the walls below the windows. To

watch the additions to its completeness and beauty, which were quickly made one after another, was of absorbing interest, and no one could have done better or more conscientious work than the builders, Messrs Collins and Godfrey of Tewkesbury, or the sculptors, Messrs. Martyn of Cheltenham. Their workmen seemed to be inspired by the same spirit which animated the medieval craftsmen.

In 1899 the new Chapel was opened and dedicated by Bishop Perowne of Worcester. The Perpendicular style was steadily embellished over the years with the addition of the reredos, seating and panelling. The sedilia and the east and west windows were installed as memorials to the Malvernians killed in the Boer War. The Old Malvernian Society gave the organ. After only nine years it proved necessary to extend the south aisle, creating more than a hundred extra seats.

Left: Sir Arthur Blomfield's architectural drawing which appeared in *The Builder* in April 1898. It was also displayed in the Royal Academy.

MALVERN COLLEGE

CHAPEL WINDOWS

From the north-west

The Advent window (1914)
In memory of W. H. B. Evans (6. 1896–1901) Senior Chapel Prefect and a distinguished cricketer who was killed flying with Colonel Cody in 1913.

The Nativity or Christmas window (1935)
In memory of Rev Henry Foster, housemaster of No. 5 1871–1908, father of the famous cricketing Fosters.

The Epiphany window (1921)
In memory of Rev Arthur Faber, the first Headmaster (1865–80).

The Lent window (1936)
In memory of the Rev S. R. James, Headmaster from 1897 to 1914.

The Holy Week window (1903)
In memory of Rev William Grundy, Headmaster from 1885 to 1891.

The Easter window (1902)
Dedicated to the memory of the seventeen Malvernians who gave their lives in the Boer War. The window in the West End (1903) is also dedicated to them.

The Epiphany window.

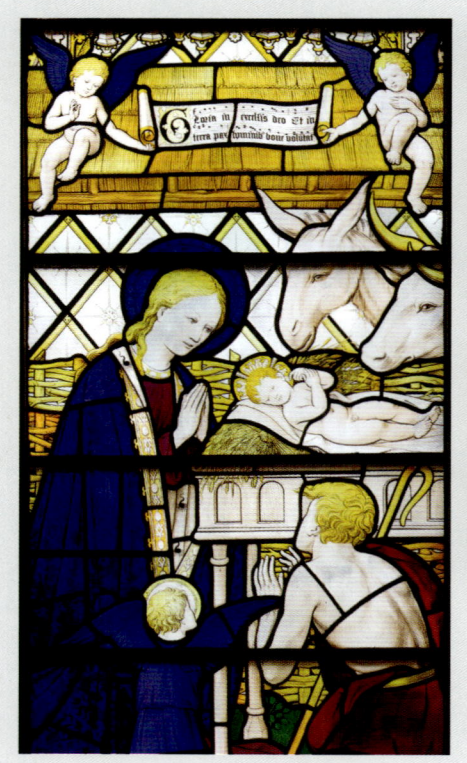

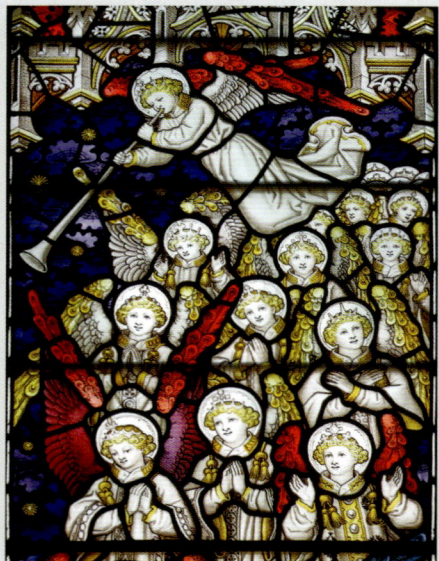

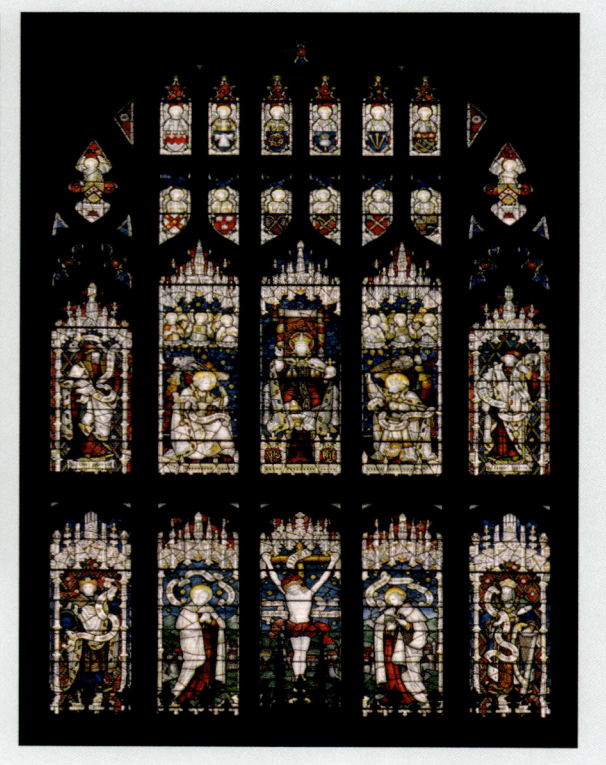

Above: Detail from the Advent window.
Left: The Nativity window.
Right: The Easter window.

(Photographs © Alastair Carew-Cox)

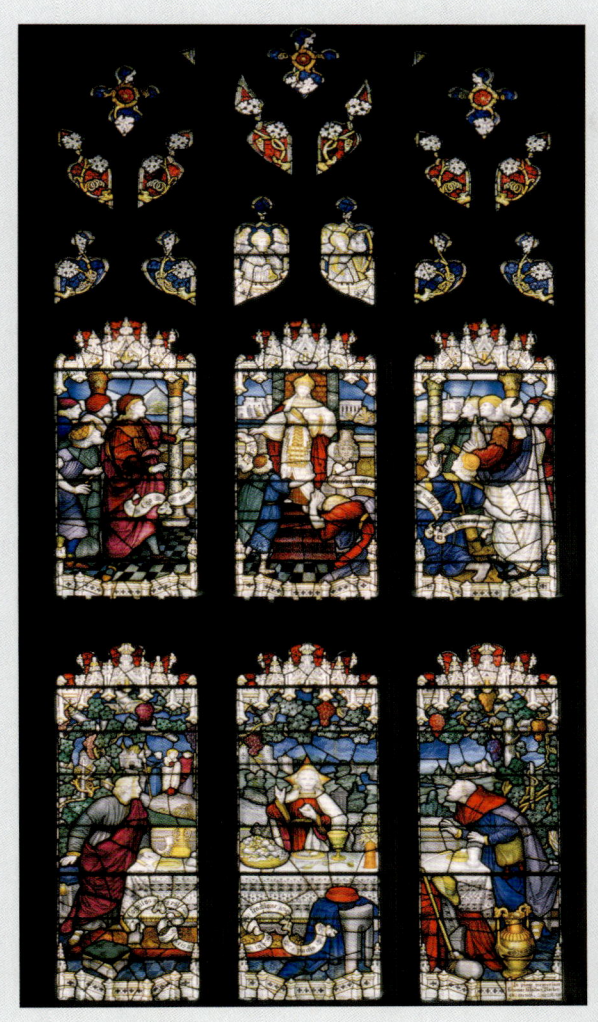

LOOK FORWARD IN FAITH

The Emmaus (Sunday after Easter) window (1903)
In memory of T. W. Barker, a boy at Malvern 1868–70, who died in 1902.
The Ascension Day window (1903)
Presented by the mothers of Malvernians.
The Whit Sunday window (1906)
In memory of L. Estridge, housemaster of No. 4 1868–78.
The Trinity window (1908)
In memory of Edward Chance, a member of the College Council.
The All Saints window (1909)
In memory of H. E. Charrington (7. 1902–07), who died in 1908.
Rabbit Hutches
Six windows of two lights. The first three commemorate Mrs Maria Faber, the wife of the first headmaster, and the next three are in memory of F. F. Bell (4. 1871–75) who died following an accident during the Easter holidays, 1875. The two other pairs are Kempe windows. The most easterly (1903) is in memory of M. W. H. Lindsey (2. 1885–91), killed in action in 1901. The next pair were finished in 1904 and commemorated the life of H. Ingleby (2. 1867–74), who died in 1900.

The Emmaus window.

Detail from the Ascension Day window.

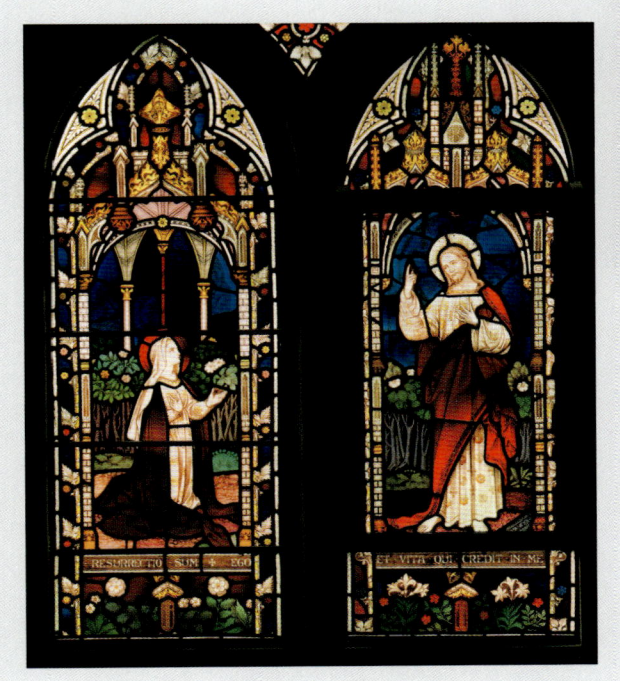

Right: Kempe signed his work with a wheatsheaf. His nephew Walter Tower, who took over the studio, added a white tower to the wheatsheaf. Both signs can be seen in the Chapel.
Left: Window commemorating the life of Maria Faber.

Above: The architect recommended the early siting of twelve carved angels which were donated by members of the College community at £10 each. (© Alastair Carew-Cox)

This work was carried out by Charles Blomfield, the son of the late Sir Arthur Blomfield, and has for generations of Malvernians been known as the 'rabbit hutches'. The money for this was raised by donations and the expanded Chapel could now seat 570.

The Headmaster, S. R. James, asked his brother, Dr Montague James, provost of King's College, Cambridge,[2] to draw up a scheme for filling all the windows with stained glass. The *Malvern College Register*, 1865 to 1914, records:

> His scheme provided that the East window and the large windows on the North and South sides should illustrate the Christian Year from Advent to All Saints Day, the upper halves of the latter windows shewing types from the Old Testament, the lower half the fulfilment of those types in the New Testament; the East window should represent the Crucifixion, and Christ enthroned in glory, the execution of the designs for these windows was entrusted to Messrs C. E. Kempe & Co, with extremely successful results.

The overall outcome has created a work of great beauty:

> In the College the glass, and particularly that on the south wall of the Chapel is, I believe, among the very finest that the studios produced. Not only is the workmanship of the highest order technically, but the range of scriptural material and originality of its depiction is breathtaking. In all, there is close on 1,160 square feet distributed over twelve windows. The east, in five lights just exceeds in area the east window of near neighbour Worcester Cathedral, these two being easily the largest Kempe windows in Worcestershire.[3]

> Characteristic features of Kempe's windows are the glowing golden-yellow and silver white, the richness of detail, the peacock-feather wings of his angels, and the tabernacle – work brightened by contrast with dark blue skies, sometimes cloudy and sometimes thickened with leaf forms.[4]

There are not many accounts of Chapel services before 1914 but an engaging anecdote tells of one old Irishman, in Holy Orders, who used to preach once, and only once, a term. 'His sermon was much looked forward to and he never disappointed the school in his choice of a somewhat uncommon text. During my time I heard him preach on the following: "Also he went down and slew a lion in a pit on a snowy day," and "It seemeth to me that there is as it were a plague in this house," and a very good sermon too.'[5]

The trauma of the First World War was reflected in the life of the Chapel. Between 1914 and 1918 week by week the casualty lists of Malvernians, killed or missing, were read out in Chapel and then pinned on the Chapel door. A vivid impression of these sombre days comes from one OM:

> Every Sunday evening the headmaster Preston read out in chapel the Roll of Honour of Old Malvernians who had given their lives in the past week. A – who used to sit at the end of the pew just below you, B – whose fag you were in your first term, C – who made that wonderful century in the Repton match, D – who had been down for the day only a few weeks ago, newly commissioned, so smart in his new uniform. Some Sundays the list was very long; after the bloodbath of the Somme it was very long. After he had finished reading we would stand in silence for a few seconds and then from the organ came the first bars of the hymns

Above: The First World War Memorial.

Below: Bronze sculpture of St George, one of the memorials to those killed in the First World War, designed and executed by Alfred Drury RA.

we came to love. Clear and strong the voices of five hundred boys would rise to fill the roof with sound. Preston, standing in his stall under the organ loft, did not sing. His hands rested on the Roll he had just read.[6]

A year after the Armistice, on 29 November 1919, a memorial service was held in the Chapel to honour their memory. *The Malvernian* reported:

> No one who was present can have failed to be impressed with the dignity and simplicity of the Service, which was in all respects worthy of the occasion. The relatives of the fallen occupied the seats in the East end of the Nave, and the rest of the Nave was filled by Old Malvernians (most of them in uniform), members of the Staff and the Prefects. The Service began with Psalm XV, sung to the Chant familiar to all Old Boys by its association with the first and last day of the term Chapel Services, and following the Special Lesson from Rev.vii.9–17 and the Opening Sentences and Prayers, the Head Master read the long Roll of Honour of 440 names, and the solo 'O Rest in the Lord' was beautifully rendered by Mrs. H. L. Brutton.
>
> Canon James's address, with its message of hope and pride, made a direct appeal to the congregation as he recalled the services of the fallen to their country and pointed out the call of duty that an England worthy of their sacrifices might be born again. At the close of the hymn 'O God our Help in ages past,' the buglers of the Worcestershire Regiment played the Last Post outside the Chapel at the West End, and following the concluding prayers for Peace and Christ's Church on earth, the Reveille was sounded outside the East End of the building. Probably nothing was more impressive in the whole Service than the sound of the bugles and the muffled roll of the drums, bringing back to mind the warfare in which those whose memory was thus honoured had offered up their lives for God and their fellowmen. The Service concluded with the Blessing given by Canon James.

The First World War cast a long shadow and in 1922 the tributes from the Old Malvernians and the school were in place. *The Malvernian* reported:

> The Panels in the Chapel and the Statue in the Quadrangle are now in position. The panels are on the north wall of the sanctuary, and on them are inscribed the names of the fallen. There are nine tablets, and the lettering in white holly wood is inlaid. Surmounting these tablets are three smaller tablets. The centre one bears a coloured representation of the College coat of arms. On one side is the date 1914 and on the other 1918. The inscription is as follows:
>
> *Here are recorded the names of the 457 members of this college who gave their lives for their country in the Great War.*[7]

On Saturday 8 July the Bishop of Worcester, who was accompanied by Archdeacon James (formerly Headmaster), dedicated the panels in the Chapel. There was a short, impressive service, the choir singing the anthem 'Comes at times, a stillness as of even'. Further memorials were later added in the ante-chapel to the 248 Malvernians who died in the Second World War, and to those killed in post-war conflicts.

A glimpse of the school's religious life can be found in this extract from an OM who was in the College from 1924:

> Close attention was paid to our spiritual welfare. A five-minute period of silence was imposed in dormitories and cubicles morning and evening for saying one's prayers. There was compulsory attendance in the School Chapel for Morning Prayer every day. Every boy had his allotted seat and every Prefect had a responsibility for a given section of seating to check for any absentees. On Sunday there was full morning and evening prayer with hymns and sermon, and led by an excellent school choir.
>
> At the beginning of my second year I was duly confirmed along with all my peers. To what extent this was voluntary I have no idea, but I imagine parents would have been consulted and expressed approval, but in due course I was summoned to the house tutor's study and given an embarrassed talk on the facts of life about which I knew absolutely nothing, and came away afterwards still little the wiser.[8]

Another glorious aside on Confirmation preparation comes from one of the No. 7 boys when the school was at Harrow. Summoned by the chaplain before the ceremony he was asked:

> 'Any questions, boy?'
>
> 'Yes sir, I am not sure about the afterlife.'
>
> 'Nor am I; ask your Housemaster. And don't put Brylcreem in your hair, it makes the bishop's hands greasy'.

After the Second World War along with every other facet of the school the mode of worship gradually changed. Donald Lindsay and his successors had little time for what they would call 'public school religion' with its dull formalities and associations with a hierarchical and rapidly disintegrating social order. Reflecting national changes in the Church of England, the Holy Communion became more central, worship less formal, and pupil initiative greater. The number of compulsory chapels was reduced. Services saw worship and contemplation through an appreciation of music, meditation and readings. In 1960 a new crypt chapel was built underneath the east end of the Chapel in what used to be a storeroom. The work on this was carried out almost entirely by boys, including the woodwork for its decoration. It has since been used for

Below: *Madonna and Child* by Cindy Jones, ceramics teacher, 1985–2011, presented to the College by Hugh Carson.

midweek Communion services, for baptisms and for a Sunday school. It also provides a peaceful place that pupils can drop into unostentatiously.

George Chesterton preached in Chapel on Sunday 5 December 1982 at the end of his short spell as acting headmaster. The sermon made a great impact and was later published in the *OMN*.[9] The first part of the sermon saw an imaginary dialogue between Chesterton and the enlivened statue of St George, which mulled over the changes he had witnessed over his sixty-year sojourn. Responding to a request for ideas for the coming service, St George replied:

> 'Well I imagine,' said George, 'that there will be the usual lesson which comes up at the end of term, the bit, do you remember, that St Paul wrote about armour. He wrote it when he was in prison in his letter to the Ephesians. He got his idea from the guard who was in charge of him, the soldier's armour emphasised his own vulnerability.'
>
> 'Are you', I said, 'in a way telling me that the boys are vulnerable and that I should tell them so? They won't like it you know.'
>
> 'No, I agree,' said George, 'but remind them that so long as they belong to a community like Malvern which exists solely to help them, they are scarcely vulnerable at all, but when they leave, and join a big firm, work on the shop floor, go into the Services, on the Stock Exchange or wherever they wind up it is every man for himself. Sadly also it is a world of violence where cruelty and murder are taken for granted; I know there was the business of the dragon, but that had to be dealt with, rather like the Falklands affair. So advise them to look forward and to take up the whole armour of God. There won't be many in Chapel who do not, to use the splendid prayer book phrase, 'profess and call themselves Christians', tell them to take up the shield of faith. Rightly they are advised to question and of course they will have doubts, but tell them not to be afraid of their faith, nor to be ashamed of it.'
>
> 'Do you think they will listen?' I asked.
>
> 'Of course there are those who sign off at once, you will never get through to them, but many will. Suggest to them that they think of me not only as a war memorial to remind them of the example of those in the past but that I am also a symbol, of the future.'
>
> At that moment the clock struck behind me, and I realised it was almost dark. I came out of my dream and looked up at St George, a figure immovable in cold bronze. I turned and continued my walk home.
>
> What then is my message to you? Look forward in faith
>
> Sapiens Qui Prospicit

Controversies swirled around the Chapel, particularly in the radical years of the 1960s and 1970s. Malvernians in more recent years have questioned compulsory Chapel, surveyed the religious feelings of the students and seen the publication of learned and deeply spiritual articles by visiting preachers, members of the Common Room and pupils themselves. If anything – despite a growing ignorance of the forms and theology of Christianity – interest in matters religious, spiritual and theological has never been more intense.

The centenary of the dedication of the Chapel was celebrated with a sung Eucharist on 1 June 1999. The former Headmaster, Donald Lindsay, gave the address.[10] After reflecting on the history of the building he concluded as follows:

Above top: Exterior of the Chapel. (Photograph by Jon Willcocks)

Above: Morning worship. (Photograph by Jon Willcocks)

Above: *Look Up*: an unusual view of the Chapel against the night sky, taken by Tim Loh (5. 2012–14). It was the winning photograph in the Malvern College Science Photography Competition, 2013.

Malvern, like many another school, was founded for the promotion of godliness and good learning. Good learning goes without question; but what of godliness? We were all born with a capacity to love and a need to be loved. I do not use the word love in a sentimental or emotional sense, but as a concern for others. A good school like Malvern is above all, a place in which we grow to maturity by developing our personal relations.

The only key to any life worth living is to be found in our relations of love with other people. Right at the heart of Malvern stands this Chapel to proclaim this. God grant that in your years at Malvern you began to find this to be true and that on your knees, in this lovely place you first caught, for a brief moment, an awareness of the Divine Glory.

In 2004 a grant from the Malvernian Society enabled the College to create and publish a school service book, which also contained hymns and a section on personal devotion.

CHAPLAINS

Before 1914 all the headmasters were in holy orders and thus presumably conducted most services. Frank Preston was the first lay headmaster and from his appointment there has been a defined post of school chaplain.

C. E. Storrs	1914	T. J. Wright	1971	A. P. Law	2002–05 (assistant chaplain 2005–07)
W. O. Cosgrove	1925	I. D. Ogilvie	1977		
R. G. Born	1945	K. H. Wilkinson	1984	T. H. Mordecai	2005–07
R. T. Holtby	1952	S. W. Lewis	1989	A. P. Law	2007–
A. Shaw	1954	B. E. Close	1996		
A. R. Thornley	1958	N. A. T. Menon	autumn term 2001 (subsequently assistant chaplain)		
J. D. Strong	1965				

It was very much the hope of Arthur Gray that his beloved Chapel would provide the core of the Malvernian education. A century on and Hugh Carson sought the same. Gray would no doubt have been shocked by the growth of secularism and the unsettled state of church matters at the beginning of the twenty-first century, but he might have been quietly pleased that the Chapel, and all it stands for, still means a great deal to so many. A recent OM wrote: 'Chapel, with its singing hymns together with the staff and our fellow schoolmates and sitting with our House, is one of the aspects of Malvern that I miss the most, since it created such a strong sense of community among us.'[11] A current pupil records that the regular singing of *Jerusalem* 'brings everyone together; there is three minutes of pride on people's faces as they put the hymnbook down and prove to their fellow pupils that they know it'. He also comments 'whether you are Christian or not there is always a moral message within the service and that message is relevant no matter what you believe'.[12]

What, then, is the role of Chapel in the second decade of the twenty-first century?

Above: Celebration of the Eucharist, 2014.

> The College Chapel is not a parish church, yet it hosts a worshipping community which extends beyond current members of common room and the pupil body. The liturgical seasons and the occasional offices are observed: pupils are baptised and confirmed; OMs celebrate their weddings; funeral and memorial services are held. But the core function of Chapel is to offer a space for regular worship and spiritual growth. The contemporary pupil body is diverse in its spiritual allegiances: there are committed Christians and pupils who are committed to other faiths. There are those who regard themselves as spiritual in a wider, non-specific sense; there are the doubters, the earnest seekers and those for whom God seems absent or irrelevant. The challenge is to speak and act in a way that can engage the whole of this broad spectrum. In this context, an inclusive approach is appropriate, whilst allowing pupils to understand that our Chapel tradition is drawing upon the wealth and variety within Anglicanism. Music and silent meditation allow common space for prayer and spiritual reflection. The opportunities afforded to pupils and staff to share their own ideas in leading a weekday Chapel presentation allow for an open exchange of ideas. This is surely not too far from the vision of the College's Christian founders, or the Gospel promise of 'life in all its fullness.' (John 10:10)[13]

It is still the place the school turns to in times of rejoicing and of sadness; hence, the request for a service when John Lennon was murdered or the stunned silence in Chapel the morning after 11 September 2001. It remains a place of pilgrimage for returning OMs and a place of wonder for visitors. Even more moving and poignant is the presence of the quiet individual lost in reflection to be found on almost any day of the week. Perhaps the essence of our Chapel lies in the words of Eliot:

> You are not here to verify
> Instruct yourself, or inform curiosity
> Or carry report. You are here to kneel
> Where prayer has been valid. And prayer is more
> Than an order of words, the conscious occupation
> Of the praying mind, or the sound of the voice praying[14]

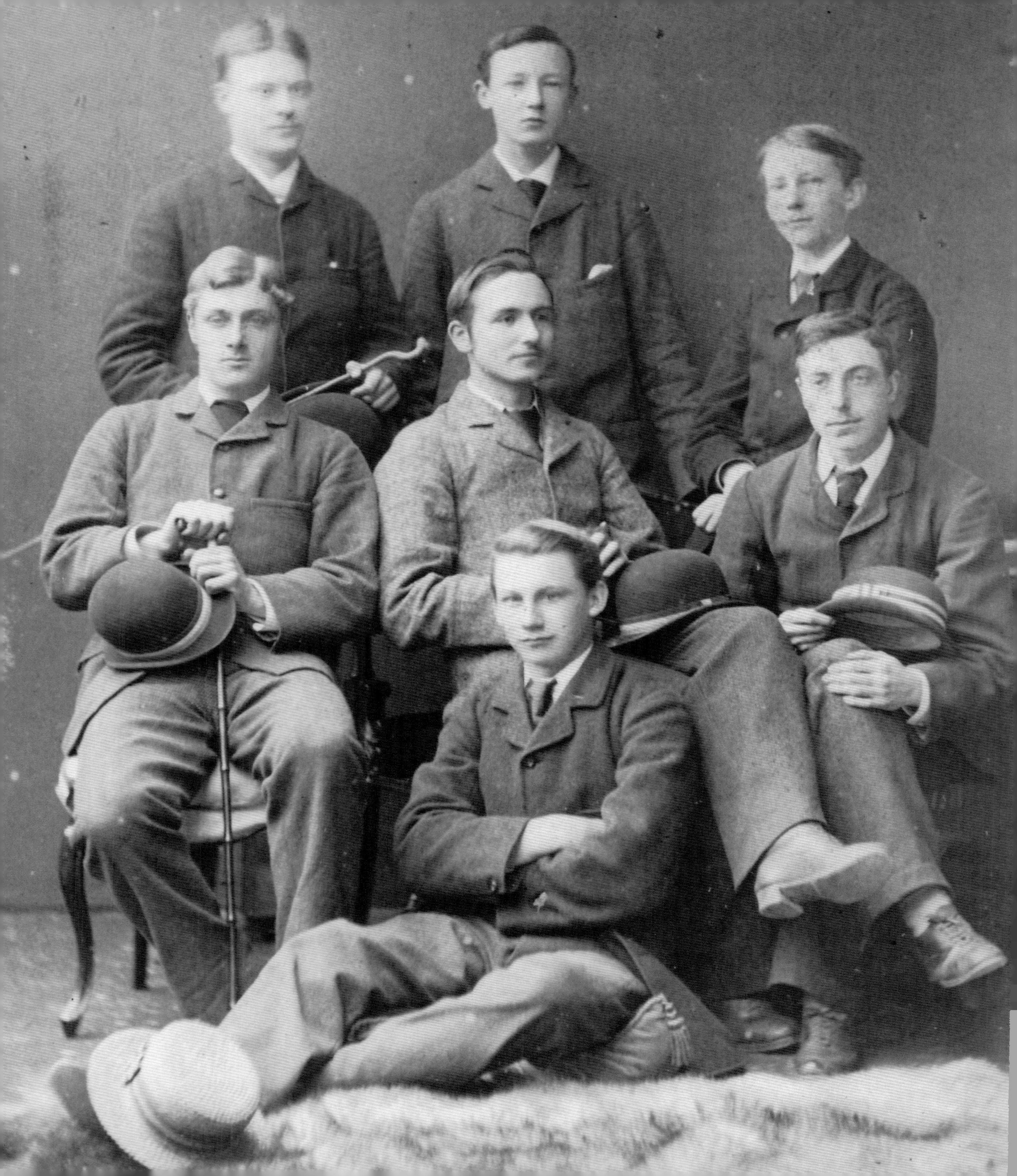

10

Prefects, fags and rebels

From the earliest days of the new public school system there was a conscious desire to train the future leaders of the country and the Empire. Central to this education was the requirement to learn to serve before you could learn to command. There was also the necessity to ensure that the reformed schools maintained effective discipline in contrast to the chaotic world of the early nineteenth century. Dr Thomas Arnold, Headmaster of Rugby, 1828–41, had addressed these needs by creating the prefect system. Senior boys who had proved their moral worth in their progress through the school were given power and responsibility for the younger boys in the boarding houses, thus creating both a disciplined hierarchy and a form of fraternal care. The younger boys would learn, through service, the various attributes that would in time make them effective leaders: responsibility for themselves, pride in their appearance, humility and loyalty. This tradition of what came to be called 'fagging' had ancient origins but the system that was to become so familiar in endless novels, memoirs and films, like so many public-school traditions, emerged in the mid nineteenth century. It quickly became the accepted social structure in boarding schools and fitted comfortably with the attitudes of Victorian society.

The Rev Arthur Faber, the first Headmaster of Malvern, was reluctant to introduce what was seen as the Rugby system but problems of both discipline and bullying in the new school brought about a change of mind. So by 1868 the essential elements of a prefect system and its supporting structure of fagging were in place and seems to have contributed to a much improved atmosphere in the school. As the years passed the system acquired its own traditions; winning both supporters and critics.

How did this social hierarchy work at Malvern? Accounts from the late nineteenth century are mixed. In an ironic aside the Old Malvernian Michael Arlen summed up the essentials of the system:

> The difference between a College Prefect and a House Prefect is that a Coll Pree can do what he likes everywhere, and a House Pree can do what he likes in his House. Inferiors can do what they like in their studies, more or less. Fags can't do what they like anywhere.[1]

C. S. Lewis cast a critical eye in his autobiography: 'Different schools have different kinds of fagging', he wrote:

> At some of them, individual Bloods have individual fags. This is the system most often depicted in school stories; it is sometimes represented as – and for all I know, sometimes really is – a fruitful relation as of a knight and squire, in which service on the one part is

Opposite: No. 3 House Prefects, 1879.

Above: School prefects in 1868.
Below: Rules and regulations, 1868.

rewarded by some degree of countenance and protection on the other. But whatever its merits may be, we never experienced that at Wyvern.[2] Fagging was with us as impersonal as the labour market in Victorian England … All boys under a certain seniority constituted a labour pool, the common property of all the Bloods. When a Blood wanted his OTC kit brushed and polished, or his boots cleaned, or his study 'done out', or his tea made, he shouted. We all came running, and of course the Blood gave the work to the boy he most disliked.[3]

But others found the atmosphere more congenial:

It was a good life at Malvern in those days … it was the fairness of everything that, above all, appealed to me. There was no bullying, the prefects saw to that; if a couple of boys were caught fighting, the scrap was broken up, and they had it out, fairly, in the reading room the same evening, with boxing gloves and a referee, with the rest of the House as spectators. Plenty of caning went on, but it was fair. There was almost a tariff for it: for example, cutting a game produced a warning the first time, three strokes the second, and six of the best for subsequent offences. Thus you knew what you were in line for, and when the punishment was over, the misdeed was forgotten.[4]

By the 1920s the system was entrenched and attempts had been made to rectify some of the evident abuses of an earlier epoch. We are fortunate to have a number of accounts by Old Malvernians from this period. A. M. Field wrote a detailed account of his time at Malvern in the 1920s, when in each house the Head of House, two School Prefects and four House Prefects would enforce discipline, and adherence to the school's code of conduct and tradition. He remembered that:

Prefects were entitled to detail a new boy as a personal fag to tidy his study, clean his shoes and perform other personal duties he might require such as making toast for tea (a privilege confined to prefects). Every boy for his first two years was eligible to be called upon for fagging duties in the house by a prefect who would stand outside the Common Room and yell 'YOU', whereupon every junior would have to respond to the call at best speed. Usually the last to arrive would be picked to carry out the chore, which might involve anything from tidying the Common Room to going to the tuck shop. Slackness in a fag's performance would be rewarded with a 'swishing', a sharp tap on the bottom with a swagger cane. Any infringement of House rules or flagrant flouting of school tradition would be punished with a formal beating. The normal form of punishment was up to 'six of the best' with the heel of a slipper. Charge and sentence would be pronounced by the Head of House and administered by one of the House prefects. A more serious offence would be punished with six strokes of a swagger cane. As far as I can remember, no beatings were ever administered by the Housemaster or any of the staff, but for a really serious breaking of School rules there might be a formal beating by the Head of School (the Senior Chapel Prefect) in the School Prefects' common room 'up coll' but this was extremely rare. For all that I have said Malvern was no 'Dotheboys Hall'.[5] Conformity to rules, and especially to tradition was exercised as much by one's peers as by the hierarchy...

At this time the dress code was strict and rigorously enforced:

Black Marlborough jackets and grey flannel trousers were worn at all times except when engaged in sport, and black striped trousers on Sundays. Prefects wore black morning coats in Chapel on Sundays. Stiff Eton collars were worn for the first two years, and from the third year onwards these could be the short pointed variety. Coloured waistcoats were not admissible, and whatever the weather, pullovers were not allowed until the third year (as I learnt to my cost when I was seen wearing one inside my shirt when changing for games. I was punished!). The top six senior boys below the rank of prefect had the role of overseeing dress and personal tidiness and given the power of punishment for breaking the rules and sloppiness. The penalty for infringement was a summons to the Head Senior Inferior's (as they were called) study and given a 'thick ear' which was a really hard slap with an open palm on the side of the face, an iniquitous form of punishment when all is considered ... It certainly maintained high standards. Another privilege of seniority was walking about with hands in trouser pockets. New boys for the whole of their first year were forbidden to put either hand in trouser pockets. After one year they were allowed one hand in pocket, and third year onwards both hands were permitted, but 'never when passing a master'. Distinctive House caps had to be worn at all times in the school grounds (except when wearing sports gear) and outside the grounds black and white straw hats with distinctive coloured hat bands were 'de rigueur' even when walking on the hills. Umbrellas were a privilege enjoyed only by prefects.

Restrictions also ensured that boys were kept away from external temptations:

No one might leave the school grounds under any pretext except for the official twice weekly period of 12.30 to 1 p.m. to go 'up town' to do any shopping, and to go for a walk on Sunday afternoons when there were very strict areas declared out of bounds which included all the built up area of town, and especially the roads surrounding the Malvern Girls' College.[6]

An OM of No. 1 recalls:

> A Prefect on waking would have his hot water brought by his fag – he did not have to be at breakfast on the dot, but could come in later – the top table for the Prefects had their tea in a pot, not an urn, and the breakfast bacon instead of being congealed on a plate was on a dish for him to help himself. After breakfast a fag would bring him his outdoor shoes and take away his house slippers; when it was time for him to go 'up Coll' another fag would be waiting in the lobby to brush him down. Lunch, however, was taken at the head of the ordinary tables as the Housemaster, his family and guests, used the top table. Unless he was in the House XIs or Rugger XV (Easter term) he could largely choose his form of exercise – yarder, fives or a run. Later in the changing room he would go to the head of the queue for a shower. Before going up Coll in the evenings in the winter terms – a tray of tea and bread and butter would arrive at the Head of House's study, which did as a Prefects' room. House tea at 6 p.m. consisted of eggs and bacon or some such dish, while everyone else had only a boiled egg. Once or twice a term, the Prefects, wearing their dinner jackets, would be invited to dinner by their Housemaster. The extra food was paid for by the Prefects directly to the House cook; I remember my father's face when asked for additional pocket money to sustain a Prefect's dignity.[7]

An OM recalled the form of briefing given to new boys by the Senior Inferiors:

> You five are now members of No. 5 House and we intend to see that you do nothing to discredit it. Take note that we will not tolerate unbrushed hair, scurf on the collar, inky fingers, ties improperly tied or not pulled up. Caps will be worn straight and not showing the lining, socks properly pulled up, and shoes clean. We do not expect to see you slouching about with your hands in trouser pockets. If you feel cold, use the pockets of the jacket. Trousers

Right: School prefects in 1932.

should be pressed to a straight crease down the front legs. Do not run to the tuck shop during break, as though you were starved. We shall expect you all to know the first verse and chorus of the School song by next week, and you will always sing up in House Prayers.[8]

By the 1930s fagging remained the central fact of a younger boy's life. Fags still sat in their studies with one foot out in the corridor so as to have a good start when there was a fag-call. They still made toast for the prefects by holding slices of bread before the gas-fire with their bare hands because the toast was not allowed to show marks of a toasting fork. 'The provision of toasting forks was mooted from time to time,' writes one OM, 'but was invariably turned down by the fags themselves as being effeminate and less capable of reducing the true toast-maker's chef d'oeuvre'.

Always lurking behind the system was the dread of the ultimate punishment – a beating. A contemporary provides a graphic account of what happened to a culprit who had offended:

> Retribution, if it followed, usually followed quickly, but never till after House prayers, that is to say, not until the victim was undressed and ready for bed, in his dormitory or cubicle. The Prefects would gather in the Pres' Room, and the junior of their number would be sent to summon the defaulter. The bedroom door would be flung open, or the cubicle curtain roughly pulled aside, and the messenger of the gods would demand, 'Smith, you are wanted in the 'Pres' Room in pyjamas!' The messenger was gone. A wan smile to one's fellows, a hasty shuffle into slippers and dressing gown, and then, with heart in throat, down the flight of stone stairs … along the by-now-darkened study passages to the shut door of the Pres' Room, a timid knock, 'Come in!' The Pres' Room seemed a blaze of light, and ranged around its walls, on which hung boards with the names of past prefects, were seated in fairly easy chairs the eight or nine prefects of the house. They seemed to be all knees and grey flannel trousers. The table, covered with a dark, ink-stained cloth, normally in the middle of the room, had been pushed to one end, and a chair with a semi-circular back was drawn up close to and facing it. The Head of House snapped out a few words of accusation and demanded to know if the victim had anything to say: but by then it did not matter. 'Take off your dressing-gown. Bend over.' It was not enough just to bend over the back of the chair. The head must be under the table and the backside facing the ceiling. The running swing with the whippy house-shoe, its body reinforced with an old table-knife and its sole hardened with such things as the flat ends of drawing pins. Perhaps there would be four or five or six strokes. Then, as one craved most for sympathy or admiration or interest, or a mixture of all three, the hardest cut of all, delivered in a tone of utter contempt: 'Get up. Get out'. There was never time to put on one's dressing-gown, but one might have been beaten again if one had left it there.

The author concludes his account: 'I bear not the slightest resentment against these proceedings, nor did they make me unhappy at the time', and, besides, he is able to say that by the time he left in 1932 there was a great deal less beating by prefects than there had been when he arrived in 1927.[9]

To a modern eye these structures and customs seem absurd and brutal. But to contemporaries the public school training was admired and prized as the ideal preparation for imperial service and indeed what was still a hierarchical professional and business world. In examining recruitment to the Colonial Service, Dr Finlay Murray emphasised that the most important attribute was not scholastic attainment but 'character' and this is what a public-school education nurtured.[10] Such schools were seen as 'adult life in microcosm'; an 'anteroom where all the essential conditions of society were experienced in miniature. Like real-world society, the School was presented as a community, some of whose members lead, others of whom follow, and all of who have responsibilities and privileges.'[11] This would prepare boys for the male-dominated and authoritarian world that awaited them. As at school the authoritarianism ahead would be mild and benevolent with the rights of the ruled majority scrupulously observed. At such schools future leaders would have to pass through 'established institutional structures and experiences before their capacity to take part in the ruling process can be judged safe.'

Such schools were felt to equip men with the necessary qualities to succeed as colonial administrators, including leadership, strong character, self-reliance, fairness and the ability to adapt. The director of recruitment in the Colonial Office from 1931 until 1948, Sir Ralph Furse, had a romantic view of public-school hierarchy and service seeing it as 'the spiritual child of the tradition of chivalry'. Seeing the Colonial Service as 'a crusading service', where better to recruit than from those institutions 'whose sole ethos had been concerned with such a spirit for generations past'. It is interesting to note that a foreign observer credited the British governors with having a good rapport with their subjects. Robert Heussler, an American academic, wrote 'that many French and Belgian administrators viewed their charges as barbaric nuisances, whereas the British District Officer would be more likely to see his as attractive children'. In this, perhaps, we can see a continuation of the prefect–fag relationship.[12]

Following the Second World War there was a steady erosion of the old system with fagging and beating eventually disappearing and the prefect system being challenged and subsequently reformed to reflect changing social attitudes and newer concepts of leadership training. However, in the years immediately after the war older ways of thinking were still prevalent. The need to recover from the traumas caused by the two evacuations led to a strong restatement of traditions and customs in order to keep alive what was seen as the spirit of the school.

During Tom Gaunt's last years the School Prefects' minutes have a strongly conservative flavour. Today the style and attitude seem strangely archaic. Prefects met regularly under the presidency of the Senior Chapel Prefect and all were referred to as 'gentlemen' and by their surnames or the area of responsibility that they commanded. The mode of discussion and language is that of men who could have been sitting in an officers' mess or a rather stuffy boardroom. Upon appointment prefects signed the prefects' book, a tradition kept since 1894, and were instructed in their duties. They were also told to keep all prefectorial deliberations confidential. The usual form was for the meeting to start and for the headmaster to join the assembled prefects after they had discussed their own business. Headmagisterial comment was sometimes directed to specific problems in need of solution, pressing matters of business or discipline, and sometimes little homilies about conduct. So in October 1950 Gaunt reminded School Prefects 'that fagging was a public service not just a tradition and the fagging should be constructive. There was often a temptation for prefects to show off and this should be resisted' but in March 1951 he 'mentioned

Below: Prefects' book, introduced by Rev Arthur Gray, Headmaster. All School Prefects have to sign this book.

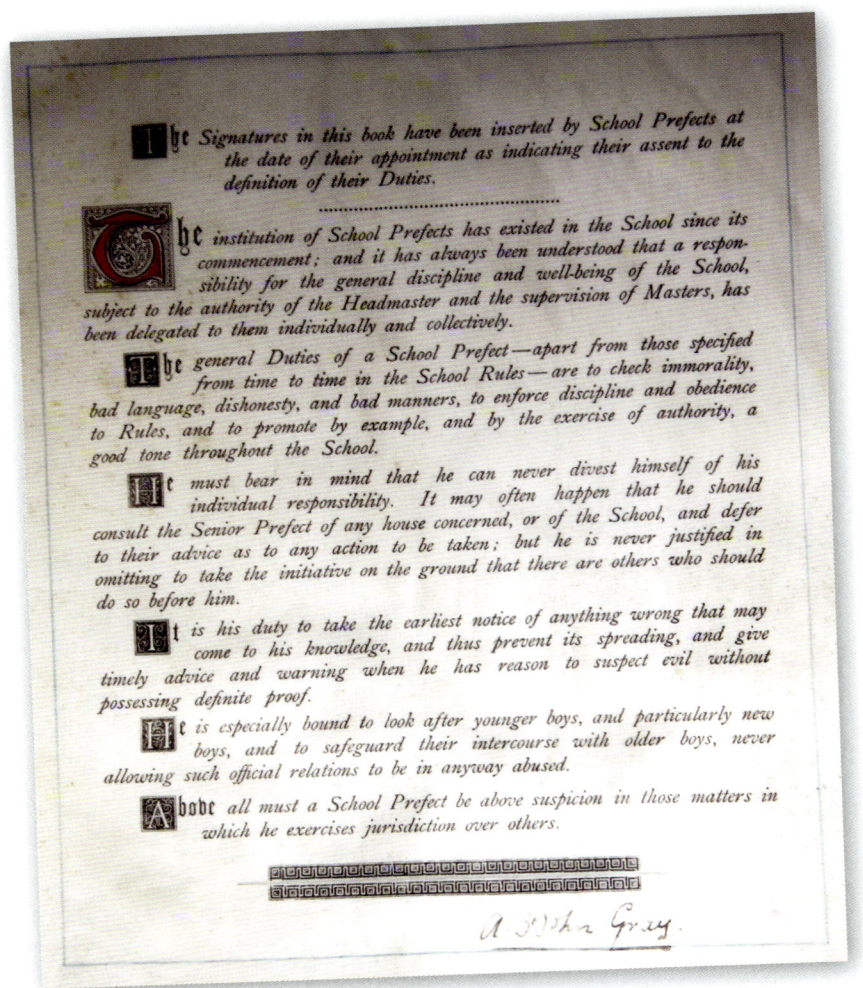

PREFECTS, FAGS AND REBELS

that if a boy gave undue trouble a prefects' caning had a surprising effect if it is necessary'.

Senior Chapel Prefects emphasised the role of their colleagues in enforcing good discipline and exhorted their colleagues to 'behave in a seemly, dignified and yet at the same time not too stuck-up manner'.[13] A typical example from January 1961 follows:

> Theobald [Senior Chapel Prefect] welcomed the new gentlemen, and explained that all business discussed was confidential. Theobald asked gentlemen to observe the rule of silence in the Grundy at all times, and to help enforcing it, and also to check talking in Chapel. Theobald asked that all Heads of Houses to ensure that everyone knew that it was illegal to pass balls on the way down to the pitches. In order to improve the appearance of Inferiors, Theobald asked all gentlemen to ensure that Inferiors had their jackets buttoned up and their ties anchored and their coats done up, or over their arms, and in particular this applied to House Prefects. Gentlemen should also prevent Inferiors from having outrageous hairstyles.

A final glimpse of the old-style fagging comes in these rather delightful accounts:

> It was while John Farebrother was Housemaster of No. 6. We had a visit from a couple of black African students from Cheltenham St Paul's Teacher Training College, whom I was

Below: Group fagging in action at Malvern in 1958, as shown in *The Illustrated London News*. (© Illustrated London News Ltd/Mary Evans)

taking round the school. At one point I took them to a Prefects' room, and they asked the prefects what the fagging system was and how it worked. 'I'll show you,' said one of them; he put his head out of the door and yelled 'FAAAAAG!!!', and a host of little boys scampered to heed the call. The two Africans roared with laughter – they had never seen anything so funny!¹⁴

Another OM remembers his first days in No. 7 in 1959:

> Each new boy was assigned a mentor from the previous year. We were required to learn the Carmen and the 'House rules'. And we needed to learn our duties as fags and what was required of us when a prefect yelled 'Fag', 'Duty Fag' or 'Special'. At the end of a fortnight, we were given a test to ensure that we knew all that was required. Of course we all passed. It would have reflected badly on our mentors if we had not. Then, on the following Sunday, we were walked up to the top of the Beacon wearing our Sunday clothes including our 'basher' [straw hat]. When we got to the top the mentor would take our offensively pristine bashers and fling them downhill as far as they could, leaving us to race after them. Our initiation complete, we were left to find our own way back to the House.¹⁵

But the stirrings of change became increasingly apparent. Britain was experiencing something of a social revolution. The Second World War was seen as the People's War fought by democracies for democracy, and the egalitarian instincts of the post-war Labour government together with the growth of classless consumerism affected popular consciousness. With the independence of India in 1947 and the rapid dismantling of the African and West Indian Empire imperial service was fast disappearing. Conscription went in 1960 and the first adult post-war generation had less time for deference. The radicalism of the 1960s slowly impacted on even the most venerable of institutions.¹⁶ Donald Lindsay sought to move the school on 'by encouragement rather than by command. For example, he did not order the prefects to make a bonfire of the quaint dress and other "privileges" they enjoyed; but he so effectively conveyed to them that they were really rather ridiculous that in 1961 they themselves decided to abolish them.'¹⁷

Below: Duty calls. (© Michael Ward / ArenaPAL)

Coloured socks, white squares, white handkerchiefs in top pockets and white shirts could be worn by all and sundry; VIB, House Pres and School Prefects could walk past the George Memorial; gloves may be worn without overcoats; One hand could be placed in one pocket after one year, and when fagging time had been completed they could put their hands in both pockets.¹⁸

However, the pace of change was slow. In 1961, when George Chesterton took over No. 5, the formal structure and style was unchanged. Taking over the house at the beginning of the summer term he inherited the previous housemaster's Head of House who would 'every night put on his tails and come through at about 8.40 p.m. before prayers to discuss the day.' Innovations were not welcome, as George Chesterton found out when he commented that he intended to wander round the dormitories in the evening to check on the boys:

For his recent biography of **George Chesterton** (SH 1936–41; staff 1950–82), Andrew Murtagh used the apt title *A Remarkable Man*. The son of a parson, George came to Malvern in March 1936 and shone at cricket, being a colour in the XI in 1939, 1940 and 1941, and captaining the side in his final year. On leaving school he served in the RAF during the war, flying Stirling bombers and seeing action, most notably in the airborne operation known as *Market Garden* at Arnhem. He then took up his place at Oxford, gaining a Blue. He came back to Malvern in 1950 to teach geography. Becoming master in charge of cricket in 1951 he remained in that post until 1965, overseeing some of the most talented XIs the school has had. Whilst he was a schoolmaster at Malvern, he opened the bowling for Worcestershire for a number of years, during which time he was selected for the Gentlemen against the Players.

He went on to become housemaster, second master and acting head before his retirement. The simple facts of his biography do not do justice to the warmth, humour and humanity of the man. He was a master of telling stories against himself, such as when an inspector came to watch him teach a divinity class in his early teaching career. The visit was unexpected and the divinity class, typically of its

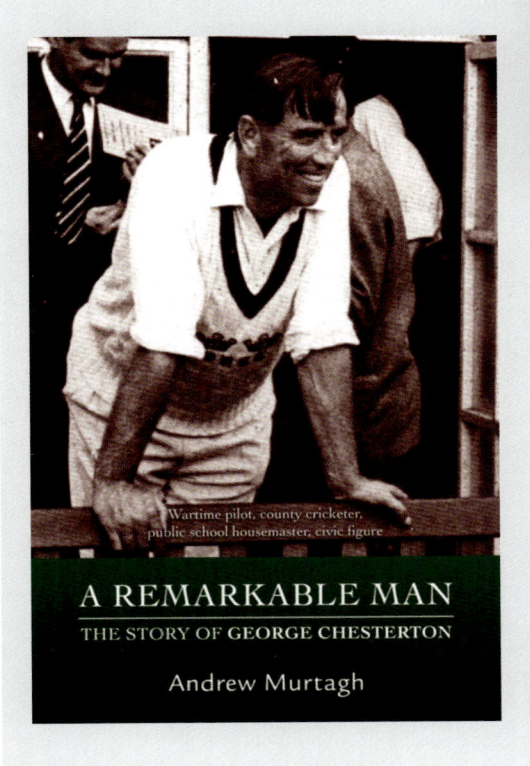

(Courtesy of British Ceremonial Arts Ltd)

time, consisted of a consideration of a Bible story. The allocated story was of the Gadarene Swine, which George claimed he had never fully understood, and when the passage was read he attempted to move on but was floored by the inspector's desire to discuss it. When George hesitated the visitor took over the class and expanded eloquently. At the end of the lesson he congratulated George for the excellent lesson and clearly reported such fulsome praise back to Gaunt that George was only saved from having to teach more divinity lessons by a fortunate increase in his geography allocation.[i]

He was a compassionate and civilised housemaster and an inspirer of generations of cricketers, a bon viveur, an appreciator of art, a conservationist and gentle patriot. He was also a very fine preacher and public speaker. He was later elected president of Worcestershire CCC. He lived to celebrate his ninetieth birthday, see the publication of an acclaimed biography of his life and to receive the MBE from the Queen at Buckingham Palace just two weeks before his death. Typically, although very frail, he insisted on attempting to stand for the National Anthem – a gesture warmly acknowledged by Her Majesty.

Above: No. 5 House Prefects with housemaster George Chesterton, 1962. The Head of House, James Stredder, is seated second from left on the front row.

'Oh you can't do that Sir.' 'Well I think I'm going to do it Robert.' 'Well, once in a while' he said and then I started going round all the studies and he very strongly disapproved of that as I think did the other prefects but they had to accept it'.

The House Prefects still largely exercised discipline, not always fairly, as GHC recalled:

On one of my first days in the House I saw a boy weeding the path in his game clothes and I said, 'Hello, what are you doing?' and he said 'Punishment, Sir' so I said, 'Who gave you that?' 'Head of House Sir'. 'What had you done wrong?' It was something petty but I thought it was sensible punishment and said, 'How long do you do this for' and he said 'Half an hour'. There was always a certain loyalty about boys and he wasn't going to let Johnson down and of course his half hour was in half-hour shifts and what I discovered was every half hour he had to change into different clothes so he started in games clothes, then into his ordinary clothes, then into his CCF kit, then into his Sunday kit. In fact he did about three hours weeding which was completely over the top.

The free for all for the older boys to punish at will had disappeared:

It was fairly regulated by the time I got there. There was a book and the Head of House had to enter every beating and say how many strokes he had given with a slipper and what the offence was. He continued during his time as Head of House to beat boys but he always had to get my permission before beating.

George Chesterton's first appointment as Head of House marked another change:

I chose a relatively young boy, James Stredder, who was very much an academic and an extremely nice boy. When I asked him to be Head of House he was amazed because he said 'I am a year younger than most of the people who were expecting to be in that position and I must warn you that, before I accept your invitation, that I will never consider beating a boy. I don't think it is right for boys to beat other boys'. I think he was rather surprised when I said 'James, that will be fine by me' and so he never did and the tradition, although it didn't die out all together, began to go and became quite a rarity. That was entirely his doing and he proved an excellent Head of House.

This decision was to have a wider impact. No. 5's Head of House eventually became the Senior Chapel Prefect. An incident in the town[19] involving some mobbing of a prefect by boys from another house led to:

a real old dust up, and John Farebrother – whose House, No. 6, was involved insisted that there should be a School Prefects' beating. James Stredder said 'No – I don't believe in beating the boys' and so John went to Donald about it and said that this boy is not doing his job but Donald supported James Stredder. He said that he is Head of School and he has thought this through and he feels that this is not the right thing to do. I should think that was almost the last occasion when they considered a School Prefects' beating.[20]

James Stredder (5. 1957–62) recalls:

> When I was Senior Chapel Prefect I actually tried to abolish beating by prefects, throughout the school. First, I asked Heads of House to carry out a 'beating survey', the results of which I took to Donald Lindsay. I remember thinking that the bizarre picture of the College that the results presented, would be seen as a 'prima facie' case for abolition (at least one House had no beating – No. 9, I think, but am not sure, and there may have been one or two others with no beating, while beatings in at least one House involved a ritual with one blow from every prefect in the house, in turn, with, but I couldn't swear to the accuracy of this – an extra blow from the Head of House) – but, in those days, Housemasters did, of course, have a great deal of room for the implementation of their own policies and, even if he'd wanted to rule out beating by boys, it would probably have been impractical for DDL to have insisted. In the case of No. 5, I was certainly the first Head of House to avoid the practice, though I'm not sure whether any subsequent HOH used it.[21]

Above: School Prefects in 1962.

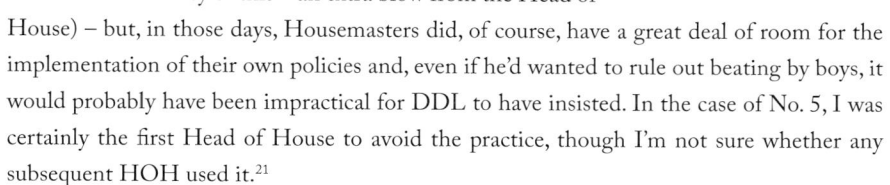

However, there was still widespread support for what was so familiar. Hence, in a survey for *The Malvernian* in July 1966 a cross-section of boys from one-third of the school rejected the idea of abolishing fagging by 165 to 5. Nevertheless, personal fagging soon ceased. The College prefects' record in 1967 refers to it having ended, and the following editorial appeared in *The Malvernian*:

> The change in the fagging system, namely the abolition of personal fagging, caused many a lump in many a throat. Yet the old image of the servile fag cleaning his lord and master's shoes, and the domineering prefect ruling by fear alone, has dated quite considerably, rather like sock suspenders. The lot of the modern prefect is a much harder and paradoxically more rewarding one. To gain respect by fear is one thing, to win it through sympathy and character is another, the experimental abolition of personal fagging in some houses previous to the central dictum, pointed to one fact – it was the bad or inefficient prefect who found it hardest to survive.[22]

Another editorial in *The Malvernian* from 1972 saw further reflections on the fluid situation:

> The rigidly divided social hierarchy of ten years ago is disappearing and as a result there is greater communication between younger and older boys; and between boys and masters.[23]

By the 1970s there was a vigorous debate about the whole nature of hierarchy and authority in the school. Although personal fagging had gone, the structures, and some of the attitudes formed in the early days of the school, had remained the same. Prefects, led by a Head of House, largely ran houses. Not all sixth formers were chosen for this role, which was seen as an honour for those who had loyally served their houses and who had the moral authority to be set in leadership positions. These prefects formed a powerful elite and they were expected

Above left: Martin and Julia Knott, who ran No. 2 from 1979 to 1991.

Above right: Pastoral care: Alan Duff in School House, c. 1980.

to distance themselves from those not in the prefect body and to adhere to a strict code of personal behaviour while enforcing the development of house spirit and high standards among the younger boys. With the assault on traditional hierarchies in wider society, and the growth of 'youth culture', it was inevitable that the prefect system would come under attack. It was lampooned in books, films such as the iconoclastic *If* and television dramas such as *Good and Bad at Games*. Educationalists questioned many of the assumptions upon which traditional boarding schools had so long operated, and a new wave of satirists often targeted public-school values, traditions and accents. It did not fit comfortably with the growing democratisation and classlessness of British society and, of course, relative British decline undermined the belief that there were natural leaders found and fostered by the glories of the old order. It is notable how the nature of the School Prefects' minutes change perceptibly in this period. The high seriousness and intensity of concern about discipline, behaviour and privilege of the 1950s and early 1960s gave way to levity, irony and an increasing lack of interest in the old expectations. Discussion increasingly turned to social engagements with the neighbouring girls' school and on one notable occasion about whether the prefects should order copies of an underground magazine from Radley.

The impact on the House system was gradual. Between 1965 and 1975 only four houses changed their housemaster and there were strongly entrenched traditional views. However, as a new generation took over, there was a decided change in atmosphere if not always in structure. The concern to eradicate bullying and the feeling that pastoral care required intense adult involvement led to the disappearance of the custom that adults were only seen on the boys' side as harbingers of punishment or sad news. Alan Duff was a model of traditional paternalistic care and his kindness and good sense when dealing with boys became legendary.[24] Martin Knott wanted 'a softer House in which all boys felt valued' and he spent 'a great deal of time and care choosing dormitory prefects' and ensuring that 'channels of communication were open'. He also carefully chose the occupants of studies, and even where boys sat at table, 'to avoid the formation of cliques'. Prefects were valued, not so much for their disciplinary skills as for their care of younger boys and for their astuteness in knowing when to involve an adult.[25] In Malvern the most dramatic reconsideration came from Michael Harvey who took over No. 3 in 1972.[26] He described the leadership training of the public schools as 'archaic', 'one that ignores the exigencies of the outside world, especially those of modern industrial management'. He described the existing system as having a series of unattractive characteristics:

The most pernicious effect was always more the actual attitude of mind that it fostered rather than the work it imposed. Fags learned to obey their seniors not out of respect for their behaviour, but because of fear of punishment or physical harassment. If anything, the system did not encourage obedience to authority. It further accentuated the social dichotomy between juniors and seniors. Because some of the chores such as the cleaning of prefects' mugs or the going on errands for prefects 'uptown' were so blatantly unreasonable, work was shirked at the slightest opportunity. Indeed, as a system for running the House, it worked extraordinarily inefficiently. In the absence of any community spirit, the fag felt he was doing jobs not for the benefit of the House as a whole and therefore indirectly for himself, but for the benefit of the prefect only.

The system also encouraged the wrong frame of mind amongst prefects themselves. Firstly, it taught them to rely too heavily on getting jobs done by threatening punishments rather than by persuasion. It also gave them far too much power – it was a system that was vulnerable to startling abuses.

By far the most serious consequence of the traditional system however was that it encouraged the complete breakdown of communication between the older and more junior boys. The prevailing attitude was that you were 'odd' or 'peculiar' if as a senior you talked to new boys … Thus there was no discussion of younger boys' difficulties, no concerted attempt to restrict bullying. Like the animals in the jungle, it was every member of the House for himself.

Michael Harvey's solution was to recast the system completely:

> Each member of the House was to be made aware of his responsibility to the rest of the community. It was the role of the prefects to accentuate this awareness and to ensure discipline not by physical coercion or constant recourse to punishments, but through persuasion and the strength of example.[27]

Below: Michael and Suse Harvey, who ran No. 3, 1972–84.

What became known as the No. 3 system quickly became an object of fascination, ridicule and, among Michael's colleagues, even some hostility. In essence the prefect system was dissolved and all Lower Sixth formers were supposed to participate in running the house working as heads of teams to attend to the various tasks that the house required. The senior boys did a day on duty supervising the younger members of the house. In time the whole house community elected the Head of House. Discussion through house meetings and through counselling sessions became central to the life of the house. Tutors were encouraged to spend as much time as possible in informal contact with the boys. These new approaches reflected similar ideas emerging in industry, politics, the armed forces and in academic thinking about leadership, where the emphasis passed from formal hierarchies to 'earned' respect, the enabling of wider participation to emancipate repressed talent, and the belief that informality improved information flow and eased unnecessary tensions. However, to many outside the house it looked anarchic and dangerous and, not unreasonably, even the more sympathetic members of staff reflected that only a charismatic and powerful housemaster could run it. It was at this time, under the headmastership of Martin Rogers, that both teachers and pupils were subject to much of this new thinking not least in the Leadership Trust's 'away days' at Symonds Yat.[28] An improbable assortment of staff would find themselves wrestling with team

Above: Mentoring, No. 1, 2014.

building and achieving tasks involving the ubiquitous barrels and planks. If nothing else it provided a fund of hilarious stories and anecdotes. In time the spirit of these changes became influential throughout the school, although the institutional form varied and changed over time.

An example of the spread of this new thinking can be found in the story of the end of group fagging in No. 8.[29] The background to this was a proposal from the relatively new housemaster of No. 8, Mr Colin Nicholls, to abolish the system. This had led to much tension between the housemaster and the boys during the summer of 1980. The new Head of House, Mark Hardiman,[30] sought to end both the tension and the practice and he sent a letter to all the new sixth formers before the beginning of term – a remarkable document:

> It would seem surprising, at first, that there was such a unanimous opposition against the abolition of fagging proposed by the Housemaster. It is, in fact, a liberal proposal. Our reaction to it was, objectively, reactionary.
>
> What I am suggesting is not simply abolition of fagging, but rather a whole change within No. 8, of which the discarding of fagging is only one part. The change will in fact involve a change of attitude and the instigation of leadership based on consultation and cooperation between everyone in the house and the housemaster.
>
> It seems to me that the changes from the old public school system in No. 8 have already taken place. The house is in a limbo created by itself – in which a move and change is not only desirable but also necessary. During the last few years, this system has by itself naturally disintegrated simply because it is an artificial institution.
>
> The whole hierarchical system – inclusive of fagging and elitist bodies of seniors and all the attitudes that go with it – is out-dated and out-moded simply by the fact we have made it so by the way we now live and think.
>
> It is therefore ironic to me that it is the housemaster Mr Nicholls who meets with such opposition to a proposal for change, which should have come from us.

Hardiman then sketched out a new way of running the house, which involved all of the Upper Sixth becoming prefects and the Lower Sixth running a series of house groups to attend to the required communal tasks formerly done by the fags. The groups would work by consultation and discussion about how best to achieve the desired task.[31] Other houses had similar experiences. A future Head of House described the rather unhealthy atmosphere when he arrived:

> In both the FY and Removes [we] lived in a state of constant defensiveness towards seniors; I dare say all the juniors did. I was always on the look out for certain members of VIC and VIB who could be relied upon to make life as difficult as possible for you if they met you in the corridor. They very rarely did you any physical harm, but they threatened by their very size to do so, while asking questions or acting in a way that they hoped would instil fear or mental discomfort.

Later, when beginning his time as the Head of House, he had become deeply influenced by the changes going on in No. 3 and elsewhere. He recalls that:

> What I wanted was for people to be more tolerant; for the prefects to be more understanding and approachable, for the whole Sixth Form to be more generous and reasonable towards the juniors, and for everyone in general to make more of an effort to make the House a happy place to live in.

In terms of structure he adopted the group system now used in both No. 3 and No. 8. Again the innate conservatism of the older boys was an obstacle:

> As I had expected, it was members of my own year who raised the most complaints about these reforms; how were they going to be able to punish people now that the old system of penalties had been systemised? I didn't like to tell them that one of the main ideas behind my changes had been the abolition of the punishment system that they themselves had been so badly abusing.[32]

By the 1990s most houses had evolved along these lines with senior boys rarely punishing, even if they had the power to do so, and more consultative structures became the norm. A new generation of housemasters had to more actively 'sell' their houses and were aware of the need to reflect wider changes in society. A greater informality was evident and a far closer supervision of the care of boys and girls at all levels of the house took place. Social events like birthday celebrations and tutorial suppers – pioneered in No. 7 and No. 1 – became common, seeing happy interaction between the pupils and the teaching staff. Discipline now came from the adults and pupils responded warmly to well-run houses like Brian White's No. 2, where rules were strictly enforced but there could be no doubting the warmth and individual attention of the housemaster and his wife. School prefects continued but came under attack both for their mode of selection, some poor behaviour that undermined their status and a growing feeling of redundancy. The dénouement came in 1991 when a Senior Chapel Prefect proposed their abolition and replacement by an elected Sixth Form council. Roy Chapman eventually accepted the idea although the Heads of Houses, and the Senior and Junior Chapel Prefects (who continued to be appointed by the headmaster) in effect kept alive something of the old school prefect tradition. Separate meetings were held between the headmaster and these 'prefects' and the newly elected Council. As the new century dawned, the influx of new pupils into the Sixth Form grew from a handful to a flood, many of them from abroad bringing with them more individualistic attitudes and wider cultural references; this further eroded the more traditional patterns of authority.

However, at the beginning of the new century there was something of a revival of more traditional forms of leadership. The headmaster had always chosen the Senior and Junior Chapel Prefects although after considerable consultation with the Common Room. Following the merger there was a necessary expansion of the head of school posts to three to accommodate girls in at least one of the top jobs, and in recent years the head of school team has expanded and each is given a specific area

Below: Leadership training by Major General Andy Salmon CMG OBE (retd). This talk was part of the programme designed to help develop the leadership qualities of those pupils that had taken over the reins of responsibility in their houses or as part of the Chapel Prefects' team.

Above: The School Council, 2013.

of responsibility. In one sense this can be seen as a return to the older models of school prefects but the process of selection and the expectations of their role is profoundly different.

Lower-sixth pupils who were invited to apply for these school positions submitted a letter explaining their motives and qualifications for advancement.[33] A series of interviews preceded the final selection. Houses also introduced more defined and directive leadership and the word 'prefect' returned. The process of selection for these prefects and the Heads of Houses became a complex mix of election and careful selection; candidates were encouraged to write letters of application, leading to interviews with house staff as well as varying processes of consultation with the boys and girls of their houses – in some houses a formal election, sometimes preceded by hustings, in others interviews with all the pupils. Pupils chosen to serve in positions of responsibility received training for their roles, considering appropriate behaviour, the art of consultation and the handling of confidences, including how to counsel the bereaved, isolated or troubled members of the school.

Some houses experimented with giving each junior member a senior student who would act as an approachable mentor. A new hierarchy of responsibility emerged with the official school tutor system enabling older pupils to learn from, and discuss social problems with, their own sixth-form tutor. A school peer mentoring system also emerged with volunteers going through a process of screening and training to enable them to offer advice and support throughout the school in educational or personal matters. The School Council became the body that oversaw charitable appeals and social events in the school.

A common criticism of the new style of leadership is that it was effective in pastoral matters but not in the assertion and acceptance of discipline. Pupils simply did not feel it was appropriate or part of their role to discipline the younger pupils, never mind their own contemporaries. Inevitably, much of this role had to be picked up by the teaching staff. In recent years there has been an attempt to rectify this by introducing new forms of leadership training for the younger pupils and developing more of a partnership between senior pupils and the adult community. There is absolutely no doubt that the cumulative effect of the dramatic changes described above is a kinder and friendlier institution where the interaction of pupils seems healthier and a better preparation for the wider society of which they are a part. This key area of school life is in a continuous process of evolutionary change and reflects more generally trends in modern society.

A happy conjunction of the new Malvernian style of leadership can be found in an account by a German girl who spent her secondary education at the College, studied the IB in the Sixth Form and became Head of House:

> Malvern also taught me how to take responsibility in various areas. The role as Head of House for No. 4 was a great opportunity for me to develop my interpersonal skills, which has been a tremendous help ever since. Living in a boarding house is an experience that I will never forget. Every time I returned to Malvern after a holiday I had butterflies in my stomach because I had missed my 'sisters' so much. Girls who came from all over the world would spice up many nights with one of their fascinating stories. Malvern taught me to have self-confidence in my own abilities as well as independence from an early age, two character traits that have helped me considerably to get to where I am today.[34]

PREFECTS, FAGS AND REBELS

A flavour of the current role of the Senior Chapel Prefect can be found in a speech given to a full school Chapel in April 2010:

> At the heart of what we do, is service: service to Malvern College, the people and the place in which we live. Part of our role is interacting regularly with the Heads of Houses, Sixth Form Council and of course with each other, to discuss areas and concerns within the College that need to be addressed, and areas that need to be promoted.
>
> We have a weekly meeting with the Headmaster and Deputy Head to discuss what is happening in the school and what needs to be done. A very important part of what we do, is representing you, and being the link between the pupil body, the staff and the senior staff running the school. We value this very highly and I myself shall be chairing the Junior School Council to hear your suggestions for how to make Malvern a better, more enjoyable place for you. All five of us shall be coming round every House as often as we can to see how everything is going, and we urge you that if there is anything you would like to speak to us about, please do. We are here to listen and to help.
>
> Our role is also not only inside the school. We shall be meeting parents, both current and prospective, and teachers from other schools, showing them what Malvern has to offer. We will be promoting Malvern as much as we can, and representing its values when we are outside the College.[35]

Below: Antony Clark, Headmaster and Lord MacLaurin, chairman of the College Council and incoming and outgoing Chapel Prefects, 2013.

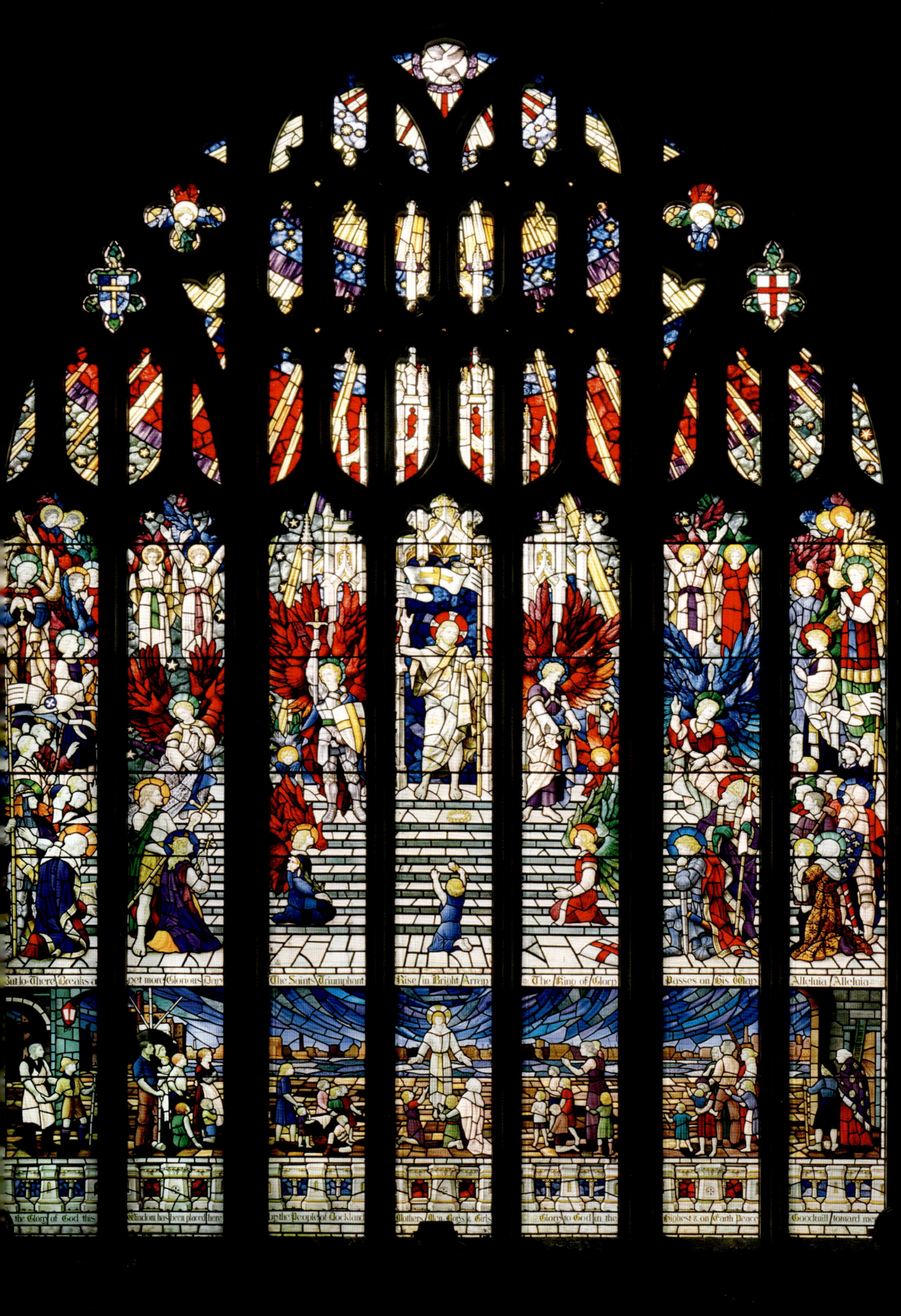

But lo There Breaks a yet more Glorious Day / The Saints Triumphant Rise in Bright Array / The King of Glory Passes on His Way / Alleluia Alleluia

the Glory of God this Window has been placed here by the People of Dockland Mothers Men Boys & Girls Glory to God in the Highest & on Earth Peace Goodwill toward men

11

From Canning Town to Ghana

The Victorian concept of service ran strong and deep. It was not, by and large, based on calculation of personal advantage, but on a high view of human purpose steeped in Christian thinking and in particular on the twin currents of Evangelicalism and the High Church movement. Both believed that 'by their works shall you know them'. The former eschewed self-indulgence in favour of the moral purity of charity; the latter sought to offer the beauty of holiness to the most barren aspects of industrialised society.

It was no surprise therefore to find that the youthful Malvern should first seek to support foreign Christian missions in 1878[1] and then the creation of the Malvern Mission in 1882, when Malvern College adopted a parish in Haggerston, Hackney, contributing £80 a year for a parish nurse. They wanted to do more and at the urging of the Bishop of St Albans and Colchester, found their answer when Vincent Street in Canning Town was identified in *The Times* as 'the worst street in London'.[2] The school transferred its activities with *The Malvernian* describing the new site 'as crowded with tenements of artisans and dock labourers . . . [requiring] mission work carried on by men of Christian principle and devotion, which may elevate, and cheer, and brighten the laborious and often dreary lives of their toilers.'[3]

Unable to find any suitable premises in that street, 'a house was obtained in Copper Street which ran parallel with Vincent Street, and the Malvern College Mission started, originally just a workman's cottage similar to those occupied by the people of the neighbourhood'.[4] The Rev Gresham Gillett was appointed as the first full-time missioner who, with funding from the College, erected a corrugated iron church dedicated to St Alban and the English Martyrs[5] and purchased an adjoining site for club facilities and a residence. A general operating fund of £200 p.a. was supplied by school Chapel donations to serve the 6,000 people of the parish 'entrusted to us.'[6] One of the missioner's activities was holding open-air meetings, going out with a cross and lamps to a different street each night. The missioner also gave a report each term to the boys at the College about the work of the mission, which saw the opening of boys' clubs, a working men's club and of a church lads' brigade, the holding of Sunday schools attended by 250–300 children, and the work of the mission nurse, who visited and tended the sick. In 1893 the prefects were so stirred that they donated £20 to the mission.

Correspondence from an OM who had volunteered at the mission impressed upon the College that: 'the great work before it in Canning Town, is to reflect something of its own life, its morals, its intellectual activity, and its athletic prowess', which will 'better the lot of the poor, and cast a ray of sunshine into their dark and gloomy homes, and bring up the little children in the light of Christianity'.[7] One OM recalled his first contact with the mission and the lives of the people who depended upon it:

Opposite: The west window at the Docklands Settlement church. (© Alastair Carew-Cox (7. 1975–80))

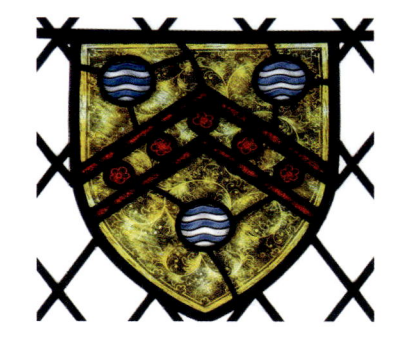

Above: The Malvern College and the See of Worcester crests in stained glass at the Docklands Settlement church. (© Alastair Carew-Cox)

> I took the school football team to Canning Town to play a friendly match against a team of Dockland boys. It was the first time a team from Malvern had done this; possibly the first match ever played by a Public School against boys from the so-called working classes. After the match was over, we were taken round to see the Mission buildings and then the homes of the boys who had been our opponents on the football pitch on the Beckton Marshes, and the conditions under which they existed. I will not say lived, for the conditions were just indescribable. It was quite possible that I might have remained in blissful ignorance, were it not for this occasion, of the meaning of 'slum' life … Fortunately I had seen the picture for myself on that day in Canning Town; an experience which I never forgot or allowed out of mind.[8]

The Malvern College Mission flourished during the headmastership of James who showed a great interest in it, and the missioner from 1905 to 1909 was G. P. Crookenden – 'probably a man after James' own heart: breezy and vigorous, possibly even a little tactless'. *The Malvernian* gave considerable coverage to its activities and it reported with pride that in mission week in 1908 the attendance at children's services rose from 400 to 800 in a parish of 7,000 people, and in the same year how the parish managed to put on a performance of *HMS Pinafore*. In 1907 the missioner brought some boys to Malvern where they played football against the College boys, went to a school concert, loved their early morning swim in the swimming baths, had a rare view of the countryside from British Camp, and attended a service in Chapel.

Reginald Kennedy-Cox (7. 1895–99) became a social worker at the Mission in 1908 following a visit to the Old Bailey when, in search of material for a play, he was shaken to his core by seeing a young sailor from the East End condemned to death for murder. He felt a burning obligation to prevent the descent from poverty and ignorance to the violence that had led to the sailor's condemnation. What they lacked most in their daily lives, he said later, was 'beauty'. If he could provide 'somewhere to meet where beauty, cleanliness, peace were to be found, then the spirit would soon grow and blossom'.[9]

He concentrated on work with the boys, dividing them up into ten houses named after the houses at Malvern (in those days both numerical and after their housemasters), keeping them busy with activities like football. One of the biggest problems was how to keep the men and women from 'getting drunk and behaving like animals'. So on Saturday evenings he organised a cine-projector at the mission to show some of the early silent films supplemented by a series of 'vulgar' turns booked from a small music-hall agent. This lasted until 11 p.m. when the pubs had closed in Canning Town. He organised a team of helpers to dissuade the youngsters from going across to the Poplar pubs which stayed open later, even going to the extent of invading some of the pubs, and then they brought the drunks home at the end of the evening.

The dockers were also provided with a hall where there 'was warmth, recreation and refreshment of a non-alcoholic kind' – a respite between their visits every two hours to the dock gates to see whether there was work. There was also a labour bureau, which succeeded in placing a very large number of the unemployed. The little corrugated iron church was now being overwhelmed by both numbers and decay and an appeal was started to raise the £7,000 needed to build a brick church. In the Christmas holidays of 1912/13 Malvern boys collected £254 towards that sum.

Kennedy-Cox did not like the title of 'mission' and decided to change the name to a 'settlement', and as they were working down by the docks, it became the Dockland Settlement. After the First World War he set about rebuilding the settlement's buildings. Joined by Captain Ben Tinton they oversaw 'the demolition of dilapidated Victorian cottages and a rebuilding of the entire site between 1924–34 on the model of an Oxbridge quadrangle, with a mock-Tudor building replicating the architecture of Lincoln's Inn'. The new buildings incorporated numerous

Below: Sir Reginald Kennedy-Cox. (© National Portrait Gallery, London)

Above left: The church at the Malvern College Docklands settlement.
Above right: Malvern College Docklands settlement: the quadrangle.

purpose-built clubrooms, residential accommodation for men and women and a theatre, which he described as 'a little building of real beauty where only Shakespeare or opera was played'. Then there was the roof garden – it had a paved stone terrace with a rose pagoda on either side, a sundial in the centre and the inevitable fountain at the end. Being above the smoke zone there was splendid view of the docks with their cranes and shipping.

Kennedy-Cox, nicknamed 'Kennedy-Cadger', was a master of acquiring philanthropic support:

> One such longstanding patron was the Sultan of Johore, a Muslim anglophile acknowledged as one of the richest men in the world. Another prominent supporter was the American tobacco magnate Bernhard Baron who donated £12,000 for the building of swimming baths[10] before funding improved premises for Jewish East End youth at the St George's Settlement in 1929. At the height of its success, the Settlement attracted over 10,000 members and its financial upkeep was supported from Kennedy-Cox's own pocket, continued support from Malvern College and the entrepreneurial cultivation of the great and the good. Fund-raising benefits included football matches by West Ham United and Tottenham Hotspur, as well as an annual 'Heart of the Empire' Ball at the Royal Albert Hall.[11]

Annual dinners at the Mansion House raised thousands of pounds and each Lord Mayor of London visited the settlement during his term in office. Kennedy-Cox toured the USA to raise money for the new chapel and an annual jumble sale in the West End raised at least £1,000 per annum. Knowing the value of publicity Kennedy-Cox also secured extensive royal patronage. In April 1930 the new church was dedicated to St George for boys, and St Helena for girls, with 1,200 people squeezed in a space for 800, with the guest of honour Queen Mary. The wife of the Sultan of Johore 'opened the chapel door with a golden key at its consecration'. The Docklands Settlement became a national movement with the buildings at Canning Town called No. 1 acting as model for ten other settlements in places like Southampton, Plymouth and Bristol.[12]

Kennedy-Cox was convinced that effective social work must have a firm religious basis. He ran eight or more services on a Sunday. None of these services lasted more than 20 minutes or half an hour. He felt it 'was desperately difficult to retain the high emotional tension which the tremendous reality of religion should engender for more than a very brief space of time'. On summer Sundays he hired bicycles and sent out groups of children to country villages with a picnic lunch and a pre-arranged service in the local church. 'The result was that Sunday after

Above left and middle: Stained-glass windows from the Docklands church, commemorating the interest of successive Lord Mayors of London in the work of the settlement, the work of the settlement's second president, and honouring local men who fought during the First and Second World Wars. (© Alastair Carew-Cox)

Above right: The St George window in the Docklands church commemorating the College's role in its building. (© Alastair Carew-Cox)

Sunday a host of very ordinary healthy boys and girls spent an energetic, clean happy Sunday and began to draw near to a, for them, often very remote God under the pleasantest auspices.'[13]

Although spared the worst of the bombing during the Second World War, the buildings deteriorated badly and the settlement ran into debt. The whole site was built on a series of small islands in the marshes intersected by subterranean streams of water from the docks. The impact of the bombing diverted these streams and the church and men's hostel began to slip and crack. The post-war years were not easy and the old activities did not attract the same support. By the late 1950s Donald Lindsay decided that Malvern should end its link with the settlement. The profoundly changed world of post-war Britain saw the intense poverty and limited opportunities of areas such as the East End of London change beyond recognition. The kind of charitable activity represented by public-school missions was also out of favour, being seen as patronising and part of the class-ridden society that the welfare state and greater social mobility were supposed to eradicate. It was also difficult for meaningful service to take place so far from the school. In its key period between the wars there is no doubt that the settlement achieved great success in promoting improved living conditions, educational advance and a sense of community. It might well be seen as a notable example of paternalistic attempts to install ideals of self-help and patriotic loyalty in a working-class community at a time when the governing elites feared the rise of socialism. However, there is little doubt that many of the inhabitants felt grateful for what was offered. An OM records recently meeting 'with two former members of the Settlement now in their 80s who were so grateful for the way in which it improved the quality of their lives during the War years that they recently took the trouble to visit Malvern during a holiday in the area and they were very impressed.'[14] One of them wrote that 'following Black Saturday when the Blitz hit the Docklands area we "were left homeless" and what followed was five years of indelible horror but thanks to Kennedy-Cox and his band we survived to tell the story.' He went on to thank Malvernians: 'their care and inspiration was immeasurable. Providence indeed'.[15]

The replacement for the connection with the old mission was local Voluntary Service – a series of schemes in which boys served their local community: visiting the elderly, decorating their homes, tending their gardens, working with disadvantaged local youngsters, creating tapes for the visual impaired, and useful conservation projects. By the mid 1970s this voluntary organisation involved large numbers of particularly Sixth Form boys. The boys ran the organisation with adult advisers and apart from the aforementioned activities it also raised money for charitable projects at home and overseas. In May 1975 the chairman of VS was able to report that 'groups help at Powick, St. Wulstan's and at Dalvington where they are in contact with the handicapped and the sub-normal; over 70 boys visit OAPs in Malvern; the decorating sections paint the houses of those who need help; boys teach at a local primary school; others make tapes of local news for the blind while we attempt to draw the attention of boys to those in need throughout the world through our Oxfam group.'[16]

The changing nature of the school – the large number of Sixth Form entrants, the pressure on time of the IB programme and legal changes – reduced some of these activities over time. Community service did continue and the IB required service hours from candidates. Language clubs in local schools became popular and so did large-scale charity events to raise money for a range of causes. The newly created Sixth Form School Council came to dominate such fundraising for a wide range of local, national and international charities. Each year they have raised in excess of £10,000 through non-uniform days,[17] an annual Sixth Form Ball, and Spring Ball for the Lower School, and selling seasonal products such as Valentine carnations and

Above: Voluntary Service: helping the community, 1980s.

Below left: The Help For Heroes Endurance Challenge, 2010. The Cadets marched 24 miles (38.6km) climbed 6,561 feet (2,000m) and paddled 21 miles (33.7km) in a total time of 16½ hours to raise money for Help For Heroes.
Below right: Simon Harwood (5. 2005–10) at HOKISA.

Above: Pupils raising money for Wings of Hope, 2012, a charity raising money for poor and orphaned children in developing countries. These girls won the award for 'Most Awareness Raised'. Projects included creating a special Jubilee card for the Queen and they attracted sponsorship from Waitrose, Holywell Malvern Spring Water and Morgan.

leavers' hoodies. There are a number of long-standing charitable links such as annual donations of £1,500 to FOAG (Farmers Overseas Action Group), £1,500 to COCO (Comrades of Children Overseas), as well as £1,500 to Hospice Care Kenya. The School Council also selects a 'charity of the year' to support and in 2013 some £3,200 was raised for Sebakwe Black Rhino Trust, which promotes the conservation of this endangered species. As well as the charity of the year, the School Council donates money to other charities which in recent years have included Cancer Research UK, Comic Relief, Children in Need, St Richard's Hospice, Acorns, Cystic Fibrosis, Get A-Head and Whizzkids. Sporting trips to South Africa have seen support given to HOKISA,[18] a charity that cares for children living with and affected by HIV/Aids, full-time and in a family environment. When a child cannot be looked after by family members or neighbours, he or she is placed via the magistrate's court at the HOKISA Home. Malvern College is now a 'Friend of Hokisa'.

In 2010 there was a new development in the tradition of service at Malvern College. Under the umbrella of the IB programme, the school organised an expedition to Ghana where students from the school would both learn about the country and complete a number of projects to help local villages. The ethos of the project could not be more removed from older conceptions of imperial service or 'doing something for the natives'. This was to be a learning and sharing experience for the Malvernians. They lived simply, following the diet and living customs of the villages in which they were hosted. The various projects were completed together with local youths and every attempt was made to build up a relationship of equals. The following is an account by a student who went on the 2011 Ghana expedition:

> When we arrived in Accra we were taken to one of the three IB schools in Ghana, called Tema International School. During our two days at the school, we came across very typical Ghanaian food, learned some traditional dances and visited a small village in which we helped in the building of a primary school. It was very easy to get to know all the students, as they all spoke excellent English and shared our interests; playing a football match greatly helped us to get to know one another. We spent eight days in a small village called Ankwanda, where we helped to paint classrooms and built a playground for the little school. We lived in tents and cooked our own food, often consisting of rice dishes with cooked vegetables. Whilst building the playground, we were greatly helped by local people with digging holes, getting rid of roots and with carrying heavy material. We were mostly responsible for producing plans for the construction, ordering the material required from an organisation called SABRE and mixing the cement. I also gave a Mathematics lesson for a class of fifteen students, which was a great experience, as I got the feeling that the pupils were becoming quite enthusiastic and I was certainly willing to give more of these lessons.

We dedicated our final week to getting to know the country better. As a group I think that we all felt that by the end of the trip we were so much closer and had learnt how to work together efficiently but also had fun at the same time. The work that we did was so enriching and the entire experience of seeing a country so different to all of our home countries was life-changing and will last in our memories forever.[19]

That the grand ideal of service continues to resonate in the lives of Old Malvernians is evident in the countless individual commitments to charitable undertakings. For some it becomes part of a greater vision; Sir Tom Shebbeare was the executive director of perhaps the most important charitable organisation in the country, the Prince's Trust, which is dedicated to improving opportunities for the deprived and disadvantaged, and then had overall responsibility for all sixteen of the Prince of Wales's charities before moving to Virgin Money Giving, another charitable fund. A key aim of these charities is to encourage self-help and enterprise, not dependency. A more recent OM has a dramatic vision to reform the whole approach of the investing community. By changing the nature of investment to long-term sustainable enterprise, he hopes to serve investors, managers and ultimately society more effectively. A fundamental aspect of the scheme is the diversion of part of the usual management fee to philanthropic causes. The vision of these men provides a stimulating alternative to failed ideological models and a political and economic system in seemingly permanent crisis.

Below: In 2010, the College began its association with Ghana. In 2013 the fourth expedition took place in the summer holidays when thirty-six pupils were involved in helping with a number of development projects as well as experiencing life in a modern African country.

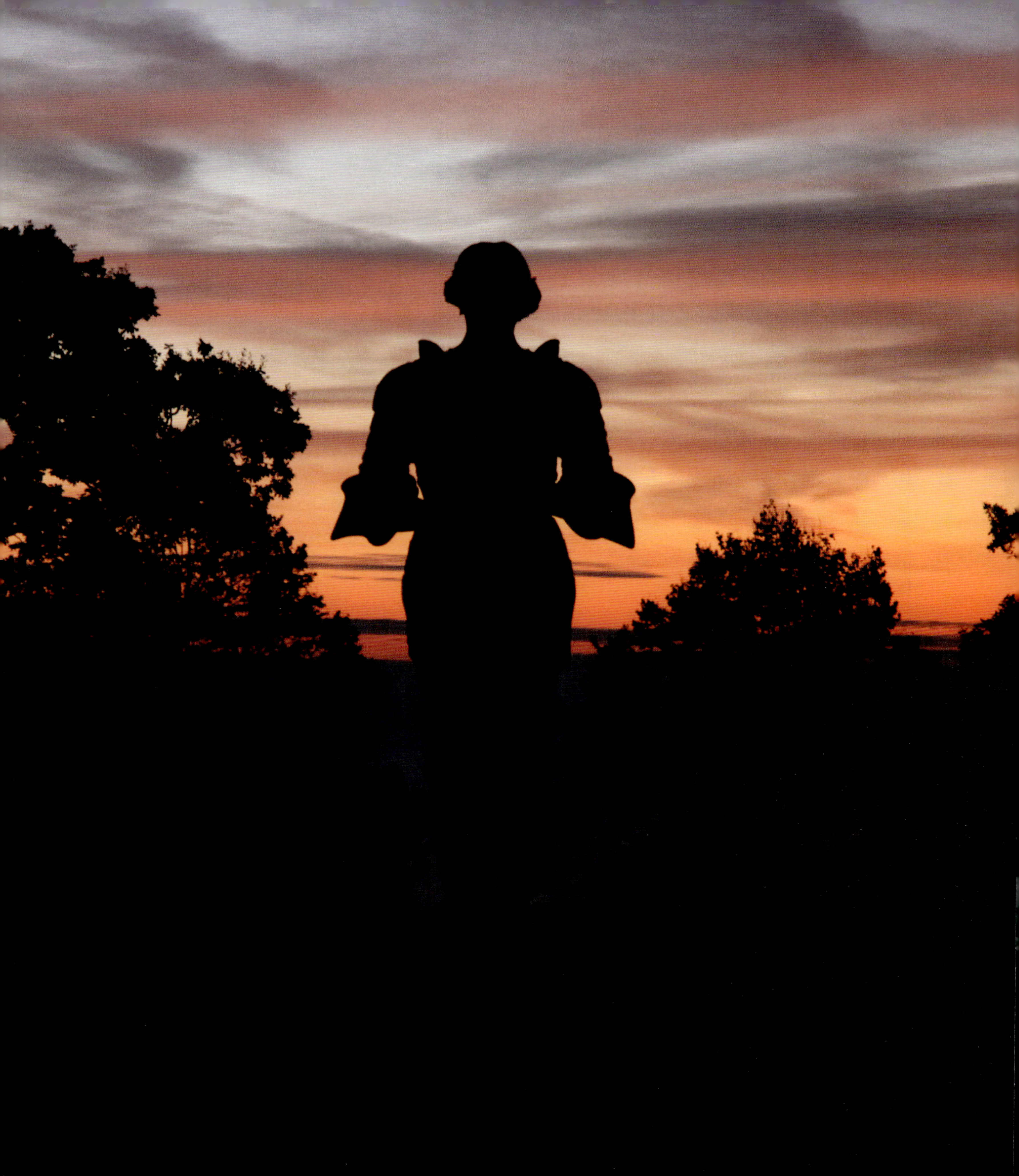

12

For Crown and country

In October 1883 the Rev Henry Foster, housemaster of No. 5, at the request of the boys in the school, started an artillery cadet corps. Only five years later an Army directive ordered schools to dispense with artillery, but pleas from Malvern to be exempt were upheld, and for twenty years Malvern was the only artillery corps in the country. As such it marched at the head of the public schools' column on the occasions when Field Days took place at Aldershot. The corps was equipped with four 9-pounder, muzzle-loading, horse-drawn field pieces. During one Field Day at Marlborough in 1895 the horses took fright and bolted through the ranks of the contingent, seriously injuring one of the gunners. In 1897 a contingent from the corps took part in a parade of Public Schools Volunteers at Windsor, part of Queen Victoria's Diamond Jubilee celebrations.

The first war that affected Malvernians was the Boer War of 1899–1902. Of the 153 Old Malvernians who are known to have fought in South Africa, several sent reports home to *The Malvernian*, which carried an article from the front line in almost every issue. When Ladysmith was relieved, the Headmaster sent the under-porter round the classrooms with the news; and four months later, when the relief of Mafeking became known, the whole school, led by B. S. Foster (whose brother W. L. Foster was one of those fighting in South Africa), broke bounds and rushed 'up Town' ('for what purpose I never discovered,' wrote one OM); and a fireworks display was held when the news arrived that Pretoria had been captured. Seventeen Old Malvernians were killed in that war; they are commemorated in the east window of the Chapel. Captain David Reginald Younger (4. 1885–90) was awarded a posthumous Victoria Cross for an action during the Boer War.[1]

By 1903 the artillery pieces were so antiquated that the War Office forbade their use. In 1908 the cadet corps of the public schools were embodied as contingents of the junior divisions of the Officers' Training Corps.[2] With a growing interest in rifle shooting, the corps, although voluntary, became very popular and in 1911 when it went to Windsor for the Coronation Review of George V, the Malvern Corps was the third largest in the country. In 1913, 435 out of the 461 boys in the school were involved. With the advent of the First World War the corps took on a new urgency. Parades were held twice a week with occasional night operations thrown in for good measure.

The last *Malvernian* published before the outbreak of the First World War has a great poignancy in the simple concerns of that generation before the devastating conflict began:

> Even the weather, the eternal fountain of complaint, has for once defied reproach. The cricket season has been a good one and the latter half of term had proved uneventful. With a word

Opposite: St George at sunrise.

Above: David Reginald Younger, who was awarded the Victoria Cross posthumously for bravery during an action near Leenoehoek on 11 July 1900. Having helped lead a party of men in dragging an artillery wagon under cover during the battle, Younger called for volunteers to bring in one of the guns. He went out alone under heavy fire to attach a rope to the gun, then beckoned men to come and help him drag it in. As they moved the gun Younger was mortally wounded.

169

Above left: The Malvern College Cadet Corps, 1885.
Above right: Cadets in action.

of good cheer to those who pass from our midst, we turn the page upon another summer term, another school year.³

The next edition told a different story:

> Those few brief months ago, it seems strange indeed to think that England was at peace with all the world, and no ordinary person had any real expectation of the catastrophe to come. But it has come, as indeed it had to come, soon or late. First in our minds must come those old boys of Malvern who are at present serving with the colours. To each and all of these, her children, Malvern extends her encouragement and her prayers, in the supreme confidence that all will do their duty in accordance with the noble traditions of the past.⁴

Like the country at large Malvern entered the First World War with patriotic enthusiasm and a flood of volunteers. An interesting example of this, together with the social impact of traditional hierarchy, comes from the obituary of the baronet Sir Herbert Archer Croft (5. 1885–86):

> When the war broke out he joined the 1st Herefordshire regiment as a private. He offered to raise 150 men on joining, and performed this task within a week. He was gazetted Captain three months after enlisting, and died of wounds received in Gallipoli in the middle of August.

The reality of conflict became apparent over the next four years as each issue of *The Malvernian* listed those killed in a Roll of Honour, often with tributes paid by comrades, commanding officers or former schoolfellows. Most obituaries included an account of the fallen serviceman's time at Malvern. Letters and some accounts of the conflict also appeared. These tributes often have a touching simplicity and reading through them brings home the heartrending sense of loss and promise unfulfilled.⁵ Of the 2,833 Malvernians known to have served in the First World War, 457 were killed – fourteen died on 1 July 1916, the dreadful first day of the Battle of the Somme – and 1,100 were Mentioned in Despatches or otherwise honoured. The following selection from the Roll of Honour contains accounts of high heroism:

Francis Edward Robinson (8. 1909–12), killed 27 October 1914:

> His brother officers have written of him with praise and affection … speaking of his wonderful calmness and pluck under fire. On the day of his death no less than five officers had been killed or wounded and he was left in command of the company; and it was while going around to see that they were safe that he met his end.

Sidney Hannaford Hellyer (5. 1904–06), died of wounds, 8 May 1915:

> A shrapnel shell burst right in the middle of our company, killing four of us outright and wounding eight, including Mr Sidney, who had his arm blown off, the other arm broke in two places, and several other wounds in other parts of his body. But wounded as he was, he would not let anyone touch him until all the others had been attended to. I have never met a braver man in my life, and our platoon owed their lives to him, time and time again, by the way he handled them.

Ambrose Childs Clarke (2. 1910–14), killed in action, 9 May 1915:

> His last thought was for others, for when his trench came under fire, he refused to take shelter until he had seen all his men were under cover. He had just got the last man to a place of safety when he was killed instantaneously. He was gazetted 2nd Lieutenant last August at the age of 17.

John Paxman Everitt (8. 1910–14), killed in action on the first day of the Somme, 1 July 1916:

> Full of grit, a thorough gentleman, with high ideals and with a cherished hope for the welfare of his School and House, he answered the call of his country in the same grand spirit that was characteristic of him throughout his school days. An extract from a letter to his mother from a private in his regiment shows in what admiration he was held by his men: 'I am proud to be able to say that he was always kind and a gentleman. I admired his principles; he was well liked and admired by his men, and what few of them remain join me in sending our deepest sympathy in your sad bereavement'.

Edward William Burke (2. 1911–15), killed in action, 14 September 1916. The Burke Military Prize was founded by a bequest from him:

> In the seven weeks he was out, he made many flights over the enemy lines and won a great name for himself, as he was absolutely without fear. His pilot records the gallant way in which he died: 'I selected him as my observer before the others as he was one of the very best. We and another machine were somewhat behind on a reconnaissance when a strong hostile patrol came up and attacked the other machine. As the pilot was young and inexperienced I turned to help him. We kept off the enemy, your son fighting like a hero. It was then that he was hit. He became unconscious but he recovered consciousness, and no sooner had he done so than he started working his Lewis gun, and actually fired another drum of ammunition before again losing consciousness. Your son was dead when he reached the ground.'

Richard Bernard, Earl of Shannon (SH 1911–15), killed in action, 13 April 1917:

> Shannon was a thorough Irishman, high spirited, venturesome, and independent. He was one of those boys who are more likely to find scope for full development of their qualities in later life than at school, for his bent was towards Natural History, sport, and all kinds of machinery, rather than games and ordinary school work. Entirely fearless, he was certain to make his mark in the war, and no member of his family could have better right to have borne its motto: *Spectemur agendo*.

Having been recommended for the Military Cross for his gallant actions on the 9th April when, with the loss of all the other officers, he took command of his company and led it right through until he captured the final objective where he dug in. He showed the most marked courage, coolness and leadership in very trying circumstances … I sent him down on the 10th and had his wounds dressed. But as we were so short of officers he came straight back like the gallant little sportsman he was. On the 13th he commanded this company, with one subaltern of twenty-five in command. The Regiment had a bad time, and had to go over 2500 yards of open ground and through three heavy barrages and machine gun fire. Shannon got through all the barrages till the last, when he was hit in the right side by a bullet. He told his men to carry on, when he was again hit by a shell and killed instantly.

Frederick Leycester Barwell (4. 1910–14), killed in action, 29 April 1917:

Later it was discovered through evidence of German prisoners that he had single handed, engaged five or six German planes in a fight which lasted a full-half hour, and was watched by enemy troops in the neighbourhood with intense admiration for the courage of the Englishman, who again and again attacked his opponents. He appears to have brought his machine to within a few feet of the ground when he expired, his machine crashing. The enemy with military honours buried him. His Squadron Commander wrote: It was one of the bravest deeds I have ever heard of, and it shows that the Royal Flying Corps has lost a very gallant officer … He died one of the finest deaths in quite the finest way.

Beresford Winnington Hill (6. 1905–11), killed in action, 4 March 1917:

Beresford Hill gained no distinction in games, but no boy at Malvern, in his day, was better known or more highly respected. He owed his position to his scholarly taste, his genial buoyant temperament, and the obvious uprightness and honesty of his character. Few boys have exercised a wider, certainly none a more wholesome, influence over their fellows, and it is safe to say that no-one came into contact with him that was not the better for it. Let us give him the highest praise at our command, and say that he was one of the finest type of Public School boys. Nothing can be added to that praise.

Reginald Carlton Cross (5. 1906–10), killed in action, 7 June 1918:

A brother officer writes: 'I know you will be proud to hear that he died while carrying back a wounded man from No Mans Land; he was shot through the head and died immediately. He had already carried in one wounded man. I feel no one could wish to die doing a better duty.'

There is also deep poignant sadness and promise unfulfilled:

Reginald Vincent Campbell Corbet (4. 1908–12), killed in action, 14 March 1915:

He was killed in action at the Dardanelles on April 28th. He was a boy of affectionate nature and many sympathies, shown not only among schoolfellows but also in the social work to which he devoted part of his holidays, and his power as a leader combined with a striking natural courtesy rendered him an exceptionally successful Head of his House.

His brother George Frederick Francis Corbet (4. 1912–14) died of wounds, 25 January 1916:

> We share the grief of his parents, who have lost both their sons in the war.

Noel Charles Boosey (5. 1905–10), died of wounds, 22 July 1915:

> Duty first, self last, briefly expressed his character. He was full of life with high ideals, and he had a great sense of humour. He was not cut out to be a soldier, being essentially a man of peace; but when the call sounded, and he thought it was his duty to respond, he did so at once. A fellow officer, and OM, wrote, Noel had the most charming personality of anyone I ever met, besides being a most excellent officer. He was quite the most popular officer in the Battalion. The men all loved him. I think we would have lost anyone rather than him.

Ronald Francis Taylor (3. 1903–07), killed in action, 9 August 1915:

> He took the greatest interest in all that belonged to school life, and his cheerful disposition together with a sense of humour made him a splendid companion. As Head of House in No. 3 he showed the qualities of a real leader; he never spared himself and by his kindness and patience he always got the best out of others … He was killed in Flanders on August 9th aged 27. He met his death while in command of an advanced trench, a shell killing him instantaneously while he was endeavouring to bind up the wound of one of the corporals.

William Stanley Eames (4. 1903–07), died of wounds, 16 February 1916:

> A boy of gentle character, modest, studious and a lover of literature. He was mortally wounded on Feb 15th when he had crawled to the rescue of two men who had been sniped, and spent his remaining strength in shouting to prevent others from attempting to bring him in.

William Andrews St Aubyn Clarke (SH 1911–14), killed in action, 30 December 1917. Charles St Aubyn Clarke (SH 1912–14) survived William by only seven months, dying at Agra, 30 July 1918:

> The two brothers Clarke were boys of high character and distinct promise. Their school career was unavoidably shortened, but they both accomplished enough to prove that they would turn out sound men. Their subsequent career has justified this expectation. Now they are parted for a time. At School they were always together.

Alexis Cowper Honey (2. 1913–17), died of wounds, 10 February 1918:

> A. C. Honey only left School last April – he obtained a commission in the Worcesters and went to the front. He was wounded on November 30th, a bullet passing through his left arm, lacerating the lung and breaking a rib. After ten weeks of patient suffering he died on February 16th. As Alec Honey belonged to the generation of most of the present members of the school his loss will be keenly felt. His shyness and reserve restricted his circle of intimate friends but those who know him best entertained a strong affection for him … He was modest to fault, and could never see any merit in his own performance, although he was a natural and proficient games player.

Ronald William St George Cartwright (9. 1908–10), killed in action, 26 February 1918:

> On leaving school Cartwright took up farming, and eventually went out to British Columbia. He had only been there a few months when war broke out. He joined up immediately in Victoria, and came over with the Canadian contingent early in 1915. After only a few days in England, his company was ordered to the front, and soon came into action. On one occasion Cartwright was buried by a big shell. Shortly afterwards he was invalided home, where he underwent an operation for appendicitis. He suffered from shell shock for eighteen months, but made a marvellous recovery; almost before he was really fit again, he obtained commission on the RFC [Royal Flying Corps] and went to the front in September 1917. He was killed in action on February 26th. Modesty, vivacity, pluck were all strongly marked in him, and he was a general favourite wherever he was.

Given the extent of the horror of this war much thought went into how the dead should be remembered. All over the Empire the rites of mourning found expression in an extraordinary range of memorials in every community and on the recently stilled battlefields. At Malvern a memorial fund was established and plans considered of how best to honour the memory of the fallen. Initially elaborate plans were drawn up to add a memorial chapel and cloister next to the ante-chapel.

This scheme was abandoned in favour of the inspired concept of a triple memorial: a statue on the terrace below the Main Building, oak memorial panels in the Chapel chancel and a Memorial Library. Alfred Drury, the Royal Academician, designed the noble statue of St George in the quadrangle where it still forms the centre of the annual remembrance service.

> As the bugle sounds from the College tower, St George looks out over the bowed heads of the students on the Terrace, over the valley, into the infinite skies beyond. Few statues can express so perfectly the idea of young manhood gone to its last rest. It is simply inscribed 'To Our Brothers'.[6]

The names themselves are written on oak panels on the north side of the Chapel chancel. Both the statue and the panels were unveiled in 1922. Three years later the Memorial Library, designed by Maurice Webb, was opened. Formerly housing books of interest to non-specialists, it is now home to the staff Common Room. In this building is a room set aside for the use of Old Malvernians.[7]

Below: The names of the fallen from the First World War, carved onto oak panels on the north side of the Chapel chancel.

HARRISON AND CARTWRIGHT

Two OMs are known to have had astonishing exploits while escaping from POW camps:

Charles Harrison (SH 1900–02) and Henry Cartwright (2. 1902–05) were both captured in 1914, Harrison having been severely wounded. Together and separately they made repeated breaks from various camps and were recaptured, usually at a Baltic port or on the Dutch border. They endured great hardships on their long and dangerous treks across Germany followed on each occasion by being Court Martialled and sentenced to solitary confinement. They so infuriated their gaolers that both were fortunate not to have been shot in cold blood and, on another occasion, bayoneted – each attack being fended off by unarmed resistance.

Harrison eventually crossed the Dutch border in 1917 and was honoured by a long personal interview with the King before rejoining his regiment and being wounded again. Cartwright also escaped to Holland at his first attempt in 1918 and Harrison, who had been brought back to England, was Best Man at his wedding. They immediately sent a 'suitably inscribed' photograph of the wedding to the Commandant of Magdeburg prison from which they had escaped in 1917, using a key made from an iron bedstead.[i]

Understandably after the war there was a reaction against things military but the Headmaster strongly supported the corps and numbers did not fall too drastically. Joint field days with other public schools resumed, the first being at Chipping Sodbury in 1919. Matters got out of hand when an isolated Malvern platoon found itself charged with fixed bayonets by boys from the Catholic school Downside. In the struggle Sgt Palfreman of No. 4 was run through the hand by a bayonet, but the 'timely arrival of an umpire saved further bloodshed'. The Malvern boys decided to exact revenge. Taking advantage of the fact that the Downside boys had retired for tea, the Malvernians piled their rivals' rifles upside down in the mud and took bolts from a number of their rifles as trophies with which to adorn their Malvern studies. Preston records that he would have ignored the issue had he not received a letter from a friend in the War Office who wrote that unofficially their lordships of the Army Council 'wished to be reassured that there was no religious feeling behind the incident'.

Throughout the inter-war period the annual inspection was a major event when the corps was on public display. The morning of the inspection was taken up with a ceremonial parade on the Senior culminating with a march past of the contingent first in line and then in column, the salute being taken by the inspecting officer.

The Second World War makes its first appearance in the December 1939 edition of *The Malvernian*, which is given over very largely to the move to Blenheim. In the summer of 1940, with the fear of imminent invasion, the Local Defence Volunteers (later the Home Guard) came into being and regular nightly patrols became a feature of life amongst senior boys in Blenheim Park. Live ammunition was handed out although the contingent was left with only twenty rifles – all the other 1917 Lee-Enfields had been called in as temporary issue to the post-Dunkirk army. After the return to Malvern in 1940 there were always two corps parades a week as well as the Home Guard parade each Sunday.

The College was to play a notable, and unexpected, part in the war. After the return from Blenheim the school hoped to return to some degree of normality, but this hope was dashed in 1942 with the move to Harrow so that the College could be used by the TRE which had been evacuated from Swanage to avoid a German attack. The superintendent of this vast scientific undertaking was Dr A. P. Rowe, who has provided an excellent account of the wartime work at the College in his book, *One Story of Radar*.

He describes the physical transformation of the College grounds. Only the Senior Turf remained sacrosanct throughout the war, a touch which is as characteristically English as is the atmosphere in which it was possible for there to be 'a row of Air Vice-Marshalls and Air

Below left: Artist's impression of the ante-chapel considered as a memorial to those who died in the First World War.

Below right: The Memorial Library.

Above: Field Day inspection in the 1930s.

Below: The TRE comes to Malvern.

Commodores sitting at the feet of flannel-bagged lecturers' in the Radar School in the Monastery. The Sixth Form room, which TRE had promised not to convert into a laboratory, was not only the chief superintendent's office, but also the scene of the famous 'Sunday Soviets' – meetings of scientists, university dons, civil servants, service officers and occasionally even cabinet ministers, at which high matters of policy and priority were discussed:

> In the magnificent room at the top of the Tower in Malvern College, entered in the dark by way of a plain, wooden staircase Rowe held meetings of his divisional leaders and into those meetings would come anybody and everybody who was thought to have a really good idea. There would be interminable scientific arguments and discussion and out of these discussions arose in the course of time, that remarkable series of radar devices with the curious code names like G.C.I. A.I., Oboe, H2S, Rebecca, Eureka, gee, window, and the like, which played such a major part in the success of the war in the air.[8]

Big School was used for demonstrating a sample of almost every radar-making device to visiting service chiefs and ministers and to King George VI and Queen Elizabeth when they came on 19 July 1944. The Gymnasium (now the theatre) had been turned into a storeroom and the Memorial Library into a drawing office, Nos. 5 and 9 into hostels, and the other houses into laboratories. 'From almost every College window overlooking the Vale of Evesham could be seen the metal mirrors associated with centimetre radar.' Work on the application of this, the most dramatic weapon in the whole radar arsenal, was done in the Preston Science School and in No. 8.

During this period there was a movement away from the use of radar for purely defensive needs, such as identifying hostile aircraft, to the offensive use of the technology. Among the devices which were developed were 'Oboe', which made possible high-precision bombing or the accurate flare-dropping of the Pathfinders Force; 'H2S', which gave bombers accurate radar pictures of the towns beneath them and therefore made possible the bomber offensive which began in February 1943 that brought the war home to Berlin itself in November of that year; 'Window', the strips of metallised paper which confused the German radar system; the various devices which spelt the end of the U-boat menace and compelled Hitler to announce on the radio in the summer of 1943 that 'the temporary setback to our U-boats is due to one single technical invention of our enemies'; 'Gee', which guided the armada of large and small ships onto the beaches of Normandy in all weathers and which made one naval officer say that that misty day in June 1944 should be called Gee-Day rather than D-Day; and 'Eureka' and 'Rebecca', devices by which the first parachute detachment to be dropped could guide the following troop-carrying aircraft to drop their detachments close to the first.[9]

Work on Oboe and H2S was carried out in the Preston Science School and a range of projects were located around the various houses: the Ground Radar Equipment developed for D-Day in SH; general administration in No. 1; Eureka and Rebecca in No. 2; work on aerials in No. 3; liaison with Bomber, Coastal and Fighter Command was maintained in No. 4; location for reporting back by scientists on effectiveness of equipment on ships and aircraft in No. 6; and Window and other 'counter-measures' in No. 7.

In March 1940 the first names in the new Roll of Honour were recorded and over the next six years the growing list illustrated the locations and fortunes of the conflict which found Malvernians in every theatre of the war. These include Dunkirk and the desperate evacuation, followed by the Battle of Britain – a very large number of Malvernians served in the RAF

Above left: Sunday Soviet in the Sixth Form Room, 30 September 1945.
Above right: Radar experts in the Sixth Form Room in 1944. Dr A. P. Rowe is seated second from right.

Below left: The TRE in Big School.
Below right: HM King George VI and Queen Elizabeth with Sir Stafford Cripps and Dr A. P. Rowe, 19 July 1944.

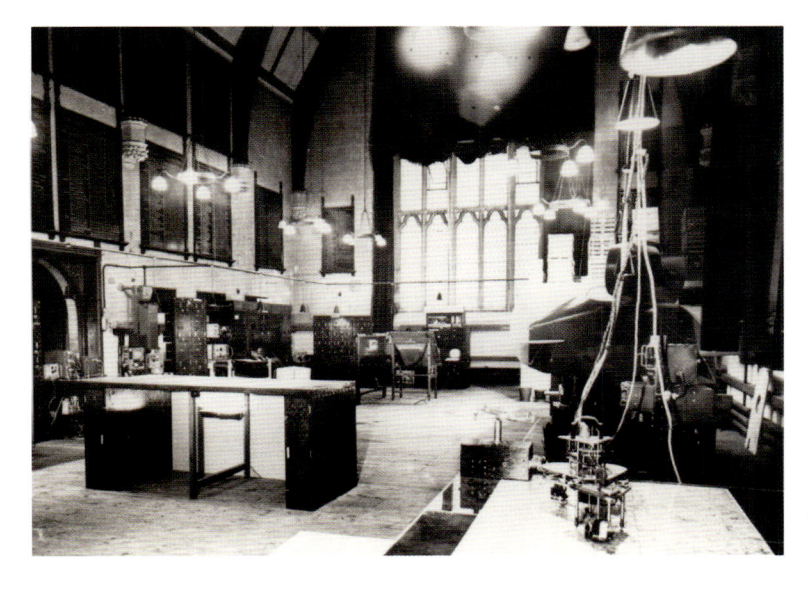

Above left: Dr A. P. Rowe explaining the work of TRE to the King and Queen.

Above right: The 'TRE occupation'.

both as fighter pilots and later in the bombing onslaught over Germany; then the North African and Italian campaigns, leading up to D-Day and the Normandy campaign. There are also references to the conflict in the Far East and to naval action. Bomb disposal and the SOE make their mark. Poignancy and bravery are recorded in these selections from the Roll of Honour:

Patrick Anthony Clement Everitt (SH 1935), died of wounds in Germany and buried with full military honours by the enemy, January 1940:

> 'The Young – the Beautiful – the Brave'. All true of Tony Everitt. His character was as fine as his physical gifts. No mother ever had a more loving or devoted son, no comrade a truer friend. Always smiling, sympathetic, courteous, he was as brave as a lion; and he radiated happiness round him. He had a deep religious sense, and his sympathy with those in sorrow was wonderful to those whom he helped. His life was clean, happy, fine and generous. How sad that such a lovely promise has been cut short.

Harold Graham Porter (SH 1934–38), killed on active service at Dunkirk, May 1940:

> Harold Porter was known to many of us as 'Mercury'. The chemists amongst you will understand why, his initials were H.G. I shared a study with him for a year, and we became good friends, although he had a stubborn streak. He left Malvern at the end of his Hundred year and joined his father's engineering firm. The family had a thirty-foot motor cruiser, and two years later they answered the call for small boats to help in the rescue of the British Army from the beaches of Dunkirk. Twelve times Mercury and his crew of four carried men to transports lying off shore. Intending to make one more journey, their little craft received a direct hit from a dive-bomber and sank without trace.

Above: Blue plaque commemorating Dr Rowe and TRE's work in No. 9 and the College.

William Henry Cromwell Warner (SH 1932–37), missing presumed killed in action, August 1940:

> He took part in the first heavy week's fighting in the Channel off Dover and was shot down over the sea on August 16th. On the previous day his squadron, under his leadership, had destroyed ten of the enemy in the morning and three in the afternoon.

Eric Lawrence Moxey (6. 1907–11), Captain in the First World War; killed on active service, August 1940; posthumously awarded the George Cross:

> Eric Moxey became 'a recognised expert in dealing with unexploded bombs and was constantly called upon for this hazardous work in succeeding months. It was in this way he lost his life in August'. He had four sons at the school.

Nigel Hall Moxey (6. 39), his second son, was killed in August 1940.

George C. B. Peters (6. 1927–30), missing presumed killed in action, September 1940:

> He was killed in a fight over the Irish Sea on September 29th. A list of his victories supplied by his Squadron Intelligence Officer shows that he had destroyed three enemy aircraft certainly, and had to his credit two more probables and other possibles; he also broke up a formation of thirty bombers over Kent on August 31st by making a 'head-on' attack.

Basil H. Way (7. 1931–36), missing presumed killed in action, August 1940:

> It was while leading a flight of Spitfires over the Thames Estuary last June that he was lost in pushing home a bold attack with his small command against overwhelming odds.

Frederick R. Dunton (SH 1935–40), killed in action, October 1944:

> Freddie Dunton and I were exact contemporaries and firm friends. Some of you will know the name through the Dunton Music Prize awarded in his memory. He was clever and won

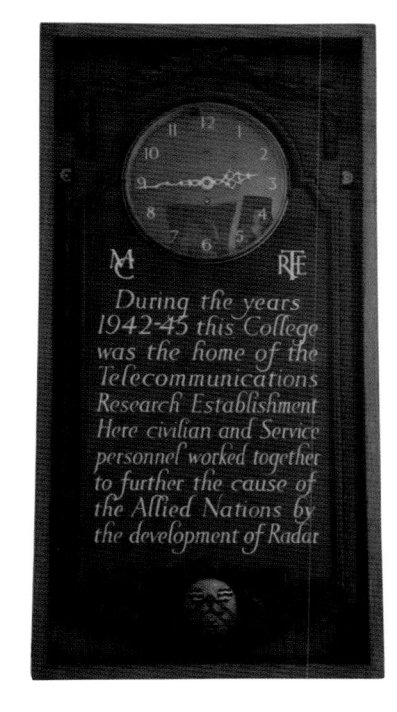

Above: Clock commemorating the role of TRE at Malvern College during the Second World War.

One of the most distinguished Second World War Malvernians was **Sir Denis Crowley-Milling** (4. 1933–37). After serving in support of the British Expeditionary Force in France he returned to England, where:

> He joined Douglas Bader's 242 Squadron and was immediately plunged into the Battle of Britain. Sir Denis was very impressed by Bader's personality and it was the beginning of a warm and close friendship. 242 Squadron very quickly became one of Fighter Command's most successful units. Sir Denis scored his first combat victim in August, the destruction of a Heinkel 111. In the course of the next month he claimed three more victims despite having been shot down and injured on September 6th. Early in 1941 he was awarded his first DFC and in April was promoted as Flight Commander to 610 Squadron flying Spitfires. After several sweeps over France in the early summer of 1941, he was on his second sortie of the day when he was shot down on August 21st. After many adventures, with a false Identity Card and civilian clothes over his uniform, he made his way to Lille, Paris (where he was lodged in a brothel), Marseilles and a trek by foot over the Pyrenees to Spain where he was held prisoner at the Miranda concentration camp. There he contracted paratyphoid and was eventually repatriated by way of Gibraltar and was soon back in command of his flight in 610 Squadron. He was awarded a Bar to his DFC shortly after being involved in sorties for the ill-fated assault on Dieppe. In September 1942 he received his first Squadron command, 181, equipped with the new Typhoon fighter-bombers and the following summer he received command of 16 Typhoon Wing and in the autumn of 1943 he joined the USAAF HQ at High Wycombe to co-ordinate fighter operations with B-17 daylight raids.[i]

(© National Portrait Gallery, London)

LETTER FROM BURMA

Extract from a letter dated 14 October 1942, sent from Burma from P. E. B. Canny (3. 1928–33) to his father Sir Gerald Canny (3. 1894–1900), President of the Malvernian Society:

I also stayed for a time with a tribe of headhunters, delightful people but rather difficult when it came to a choice for the mid-day meal! In spite of several rises I rather enjoyed myself and am a complete expert on crossing crocodile-infested waters under fire and preparing booby traps of the most fiendish patterns. I have been shot at around the clock and it takes more than an earthquake to shake me now. Some of the jungle we have been in is as bad as possible and you wouldn't believe how exhausting and frightening it can be. The lighter side of the picture was very amusing. I met a two-year-old elephant in one spot after I had been stalking what I thought was a Jap for over an hour! The elephant's greeting was to slam me hard in the stomach with its trunk and completely finished my career for ten minutes. Later on I met the head-hunters (Kookies by name) and as I had only had two bananas for 24 hours I thought it might be nice to see what they had in the pot. Unfortunately they were cooking a human head and I didn't feel so well for quite a time.

Above: On 23 September 1950, near Songju, Korea, Major Kenneth Muir (SH 1926–29), The Argyll and Sutherland Highlanders (Princess Louise's), accompanied stretcher-bearing parties to two companies under heavy fire after taking an enemy-held hill. After organising the evacuation of casualties Muir took command of the severely depleted companies. After a requested air-strike disastrously hit their positions, he personally led a counter-attack with the few men left able to fight, retaking the crest. Moving about under fire redistributing ammunition, he was mortally wounded. He was posthumously awarded the Victoria Cross.

a Scholarship to Christ's College, Cambridge, to be taken up after the war. He was also a fine musician, his special instrument being the flute. He volunteered for the Air Force becoming, after some eighteen months, a Lancaster bomber pilot. We used to exchange occasional letters, in his last one he said 'I have put my flute away until after the war and taken up the mouth organ. My crew prefer it and, anyway, the flute was a bit clumsy in the cockpit of a Lancaster'. In the interval between posting the letter and my receiving it, his Lancaster had been blown to pieces over the Baltic.[10]

Three of the fallen were from distinguished Malvernian families:

Maurice F. Beeson (9. 1934–39), killed in action in the Middle East, July 1942, and his elder brother Nigel Wendover Beeson (9. 1932–37), killed in action, August 1944:

> innocent in the best sense of the word and utterly regardless of self. A shell hit his tank and he got out to help the driver. A second shell killed him instantly.

Oscar William Robert Dent (9. 1919–22), killed in Normandy, August 1944[11]:

> Oscar Dent served in the BEF in 1940 and evacuated his arm of the Regiment from Dunkirk with the loss of only two men.

An enjoyable vignette about OM Peter Storie-Pugh (9. 1933–37) is found in *Camera in Colditz* by Ron Baybutt:

> If ever a man deserved to escape from Colditz Castle it was Lt. Peter Storie-Pugh. The slightly built, red-haired officer of the Queen's Own Royal West Kent regiment was captured in May 1940 when German infantry stormed the French village of Doullens and was taken to Colditz that October. Like the vast majority of prisoners of war he was destined to remain there until April 1945. In that time he was involved in no less than twenty-one escape attempts.[12]

The book goes on to explain how Storie-Pugh, because of his intense preoccupation with all matters of subversion, developed a secret code used in letters to his father. The key to the code was his house at Malvern, namely No. 9 of which Frank Hooper had been housemaster. 'In one of his letters Storie-Pugh inexplicably wrote: "The number of letters from Hooper House show all one wants to know". His father eventually worked out the significance of Hooper House and discovered that every ninth word from Hooper onwards spelt a coded message. The code was used throughout the war'.[13]

In total 258 Old Malvernians lost their lives fighting in the Second World War; over a third of these were killed flying with the Royal Air Force. They are commemorated on the Roll of Honour in the ante-chapel. Three of the thirteen masters who had been called up were killed.[14] The College Council launched a war memorial appeal, part of which was used for memorial Exhibitions for the sons of Old Malvernians who had lost their lives in the war. It seems appropriate to finish the account of Malvern's role in the Second World War with the concluding words of an address given by George Chesterton at the Remembrance Day Service in 2009. Having described the lives and loss of five of his friends he reflected:

> Some of these brave men have no known grave, but we must remember them, along with all the tens of thousands of others, who gave their lives for their homelands and their friends. It is thanks to them that all of us sit in this Chapel, from a wide variety of countries and backgrounds and are able to sit together in security and friendship. But there is a little more, please, as daily you walk along the Terrace and pass St. George. Remember, but also regenerate your own faith. That way, we can have hope that there will be need for no more war memorials.[15]

Above: The Second World War Roll of Honour in the ante-chapel.

On 15 September 2010, Battle of Britain Sunday, the College unveiled a plaque to the Malvernians who fought in that battle. George Chesterton gave the address in Chapel on that occasion putting their contribution into its historical setting.[16]

Malvernians have continued to serve with distinction in the many post-war conflicts that this country has been engaged in, and in March 2004 a memorial board was dedicated in the ante-chapel to those OMs who have been killed on active service since the Second World War. This includes Major Kenneth Muir who was posthumously awarded the Victoria Cross for actions during the Korean War.

After 1945 the corps followed the national trend with numbers reduced, length of service almost halved and training given a much less military flavour. Now called the Combined Cadet Force, it was divided into an Army, Royal Air Force and (for seventeen years) a Royal Navy section. In the 1980s a Royal Marines platoon was formed. Possibly the most significant modern development has been the great emphasis on adventure training in the Brecon Beacons. This was one of the reasons for the acquisition in 1962 of Cwm Llwch, a farm cottage in the Brecons. It was used as an essential respite from extreme weather but in time became a popular location for house weekends enabling pupils to enjoy an

Below left: A plaque dedicated to those who fought in the Battle of Britain, on display in the Main Building.
Below right: The board in the ante-chapel dedicated to those killed on active service since 1945.

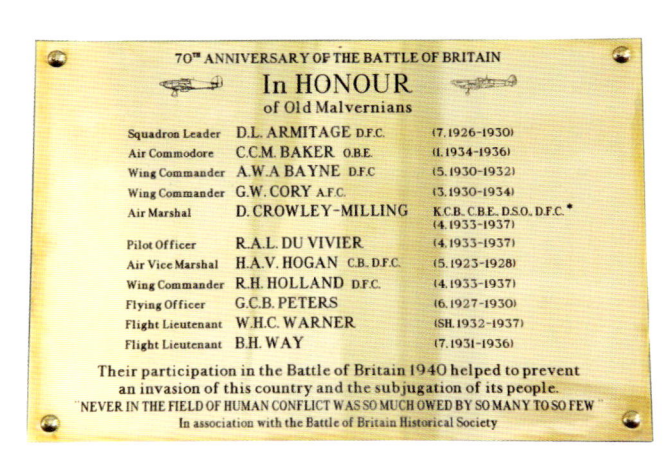

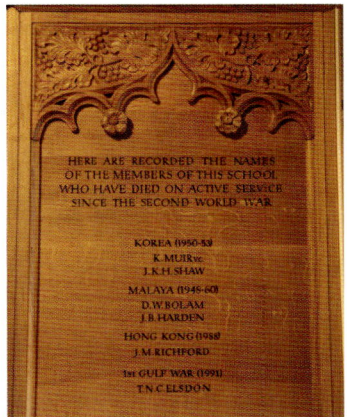

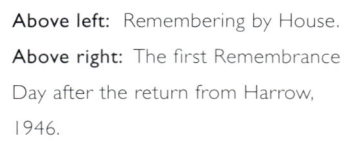

MALVERN COLLEGE

Above left: Remembering by House.
Above right: The first Remembrance Day after the return from Harrow, 1946.
Below: Remembrance: the view from the Tower.

escape to the rugged country.[17] The Army section is particularly popular with the girls and currently there are about 120 pupils in military training.

From 1961 there was a tradition for Malvern College staff and students to take part in self-led mountaineering expeditions. Primarily these fell under the aegis of the CCF but some were in the remit of the Gold Level of the Duke of Edinburgh's Award scheme. By 2006 no fewer than 594 individuals had taken part in these activities and Malvern College developed a national reputation for its unique brand of self-led expeditions. From 1977 parties of Malvernians not only undertook winter mountaineering in the Cairngorms[18] but also, under the leadership of Roger Smith, ventured to Ben Nevis and many completed the MOD's Winter Mountain Proficiency Course. This was also the time when parties went further afield than Scotland in winter, thus starting another tradition.

No fewer than twelve trips were made to the Alps between 1977 and 2005, three to Iceland (1978, 1980, 1989), one to Kashmir (1982), Lappland (1984), Ecuador (1986), Norway (1990) and Alaska (2003). The purpose of these trips was to give individuals the opportunity to climb and explore in a safe manner whilst enjoying a new culture and environment. It is also worth pointing out that on the trips to Iceland (1978), Kashmir and Alaska Malvernians were involved in the first recorded ascents of mountains – a major achievement for school-aged students.

The earliest military engagements in which Malvernians were involved were almost certainly in India during the time of the British Raj and no doubt the defence of the North West Frontier, bordering Afghanistan, was a cause of concern. So perhaps it is fitting to end this chapter with modern Malvernains involved in the same part of the world. A number have served in the current war in Afghanistan. One serving officer assessed the experience as 'an extremely complex and high intensity campaign which has forced the British Army to evolve.' Commanding ninety dismounted infantry, he describes:

> simultaneously trying to win the 'hearts and minds' of the Afghan communities, develop the institutional capability of the Afghan security forces and conduct a high-tech, intelligence driven targeting of the insurgency, designed to isolate the insurgents without alienating the local population. All of this activity is conducted in daytime temperatures that can reach 61°C, with a large premium placed on understanding the local culture and avoiding collateral damage at all costs.[19]

Another veteran of the Afghanistan conflict, Lieutenant Guy Disney (2. 1995–2000), achieved national prominence in April 2011 when, after losing part of his leg in Afghanistan, he raised money for the Walking with the Wounded campaign with a 167-mile trek to the North Pole together with fellow wounded servicemen and their patron Prince Harry. In 2013 they went to the South Pole.[20]

Top left: Sir Steuart Pringle Trophy Competition 2008.
Top middle: Cwm Llwch.
Top right: Naomi Sharpe (8. 2008–12), first female head of the CCF.
Bottom left: CCF Challenge Haute route from Chamonix to Zermatt, 2001, led by Roger Smith.
Bottom right Guy Disney in action. (Courtesy of Walking With The Wounded)

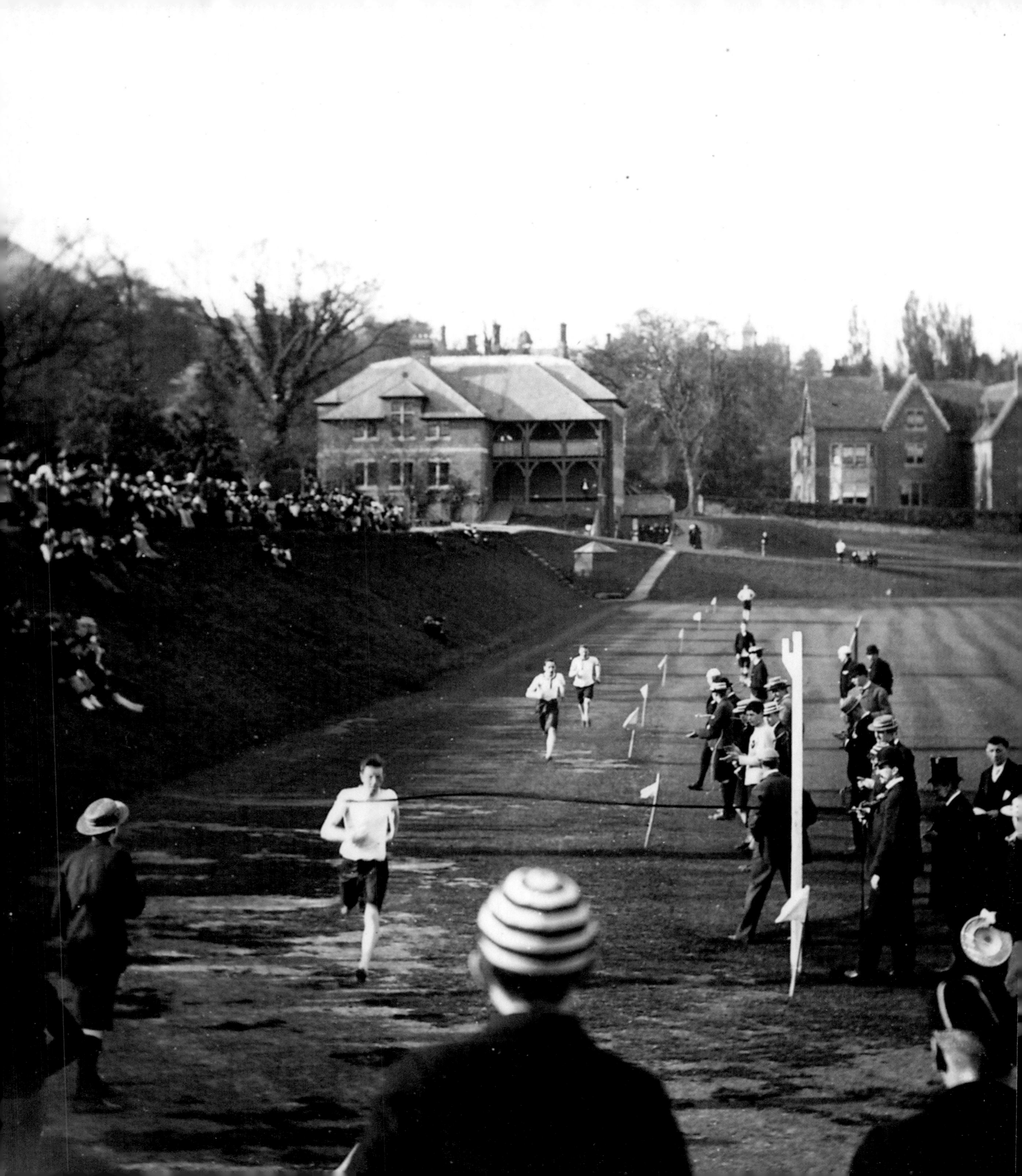

13

The sporting life

The association between public schools and games became inextricably linked in the popular mind during the latter part of the nineteenth century. One social historian states that the 'culture of athleticism steadily came to dominate the whole system of elite education in Victorian England.'[1] A contemporary critic[2] complained of the 'extravagant value set on games' with 'respectable newspapers [devoting] whole columns to reporting the facts of schoolchildren on sports fields'. This marked a dramatic change from the early years of the century when, up to the 1840s, 'sport at public schools was a loose, informally organised affair that had little impact on school lifestyle … characterised by individual sports associated with aristocratic pastimes, such as hunting, shooting and fishing.'[3]

The beginning of change came with reforming headmasters like Arnold who saw organised team games as a way of promoting a healthy and moral education and tackling indiscipline. With the approval of the authorities, games such as football and cricket 'grew at breakneck speed through the second half of the century'. Fives, boating and rackets also became extremely popular. It also fostered strong loyalties and attachments to schools and social units within the schools. A new generation of schoolmasters and parents enthusiastically endorsed athleticism, believing with Charles Kingsley:

> that games conduce … not merely daring and endurance but, better still, temper, self restraint, fairness, honour, unenvious approbation of another's success, and all that 'give and take' of life which stand a man in such good stead when he goes forth into the world, and without which, indeed, his success is always maimed and partial.[4]

The Clarendon Commission asserted that the games fields helped 'to form some of the most valuable social qualities and manly virtues' – the most prized of Victorian attributes. What had started as an aid to discipline had become an end in itself. It also merged with the prevailing enthusiasms of Muscular Christianity and Social Darwinism. Additionally games became inextricably connected to the ideals of imperialism. As the Empire became a dominant theme in British thinking, so public-school games came to be seen as an essential tool 'to train boys in the basic tools of imperial leadership such as courage, control, command and endurance'.[5] A glorious example of this association can be found in the fervent imperialism of the Headmaster of Harrow, James Welldon:

> Englishmen are not superior to Frenchmen or Germans in brains or industry, or the science of apparatus of war … rather, the health and temper which games impart and the pluck, the energy, the perseverance, the good temper, the self control, the co-operation, the esprit de

Opposite: The Senior Mile, Easter 1893. (Courtesy of the Hopkinson family)

Above: First XI cricket colours in 1866.

corps, which merit success in cricket and football, are the very qualities which win the day in peace and war.[6]

We have therefore the development of not just games but a cult to which was attributed manifold virtues. This brings us to one of the most controversial aspects of public school life, one that was strongly represented at Malvern. There is a persistent dichotomy in the experience of past pupils at the school. For some, school really did provide the happiest days of their lives and they speak with real emotion of the joys they had in boyhood games and with profound affection for the masters who encouraged and coached them. However, it was also true that for others the games cult was oppressive, narrow and even brutal. The viciousness of attacks on the boarding-school experience quite often comes back to games. The humiliation of being seen as inadequate in sporting contests – and at a time when self-esteem was often fragile – or the anger at time wasted in playing and the compulsory watching of school sport appear in many memoirs. Perhaps the greatest fury was caused by the sense that skill in games gave an entitlement to power, status and moral authority. It is perhaps easier today to stand back and see the strength of both positions, not least because the sporting life has at last settled into something less than the romantic, heroic vision of yesteryear. It is no longer the case that athletic prowess is the path to all power or indeed to hero worship. It is one among many paths to esteem, and worthy practitioners can receive accolades without the assumptions of moral superiority which so enraged earlier critics.

From the earliest days Malvern was a strong games school, with cricket and football predominant. John Hart recalled that when he started teaching at Malvern in 1963:

> cricket and football were sovereign for the season, then rackets, cross-country, a bit of Fives, and very little else. I was tennis master for a few years and I remember having to manoeuvre against opposition to win approval for the award of tennis colours.[7] Squash was purely recreational, rugby utterly disregarded, badminton and basketball non-existent; as for netball and lacrosse, no-one had heard of them.[8]

Below: Malvern v Rossall, 19–20 June 1891. Malvern won by an innings and 149 runs. P. H. Latham, who is fielding at cover, made 214 for Malvern.

In the subsequent years there were marked changes as the school followed national trends as well as embracing both co-education and a more international intake. Traditional sport still flourished but had to accommodate a diversity and breadth unimaginable to the young Classics master of 1963.

THE SPORTING LIFE

CRICKET

It is no disrespect to the other sports to say that cricket and Malvern have had a very special relationship. For many decades the school was best known for its cricket. P. G. Wodehouse was to write:

> Cricket is the great game at Malvern, and the school has attained that enviable position when anyone who has been a member of the first eleven finds a reputation ready-made on leaving school. 'He must be pretty good. He was in the Malvern team,' is the sort of thing one constantly hears.[9]

In his last contribution to Malvern cricket George Chesterton introduced the 2012 programme for the forthcoming cricket tour to South Africa:

> There can be few more spectacular settings for a cricket ground than the Senior Turf at Malvern. Looking to the east is Bredon Hill, the Severn Valley and the Cotswolds and to the west is the backdrop of the Malvern Hills. Within eighteen months of the school's foundation the first matches were played, but with a distinct advantage to the home side, when local knowledge of the one in sixteen slope paid dividends. 'Like playing on the side of a house', as one opponent said. So, it was not many years before the first terracing took place in 1872. What a labour this must have been, with pick and shovel, and horse and cart. Rather different from the final widening in 1985, when the work was completed with modern machinery in under a week. With a pitch still slightly on the narrow side, the tradition of no sixes has been maintained.[10]

Above: Newspaper board trumpeting Tip Foster's 1903 triumph.

Below: The XI over the years. Top row left to right: 1894, 1935; Bottom row, left to right: 1953, 2013 (Norman Mays Studio).

187

MALVERN COLLEGE

Above: C. J. Burnup (7.1890–94). Blues for Cambridge in cricket and football. Football for England, 1896. Played cricket for Kent 1896–1907. Only one of many cigarette cards to feature players from Malvern.

The first years of Malvern cricket did produce some notable players such as A. H. Stratford who played for Middlesex,[11] J. J. Read who went on to play for Essex,[12] and A. T. H. Newman who represented Gloucestershire and the Gentlemen.[13] The first cricket Blue was P. H. Latham[14] who captained Cambridge in 1894. Despite these successes Chesterton wrote that 'the quality of Malvern cricket languished until the arrival of Charles Toppin in 1885 who for thirty-seven years provided inspirational leadership'. E. W. Swanton attributed to Toppin 'the Malvern style characterised by wristy cover-hitting,[15] to the short square school boundary'. Through his hands passed a procession of fine players including the seven Foster brothers, who dominated Malvern cricket from 1889: except for one year there was a Foster in the XI for fifteen seasons, and they all went on to play for Worcestershire. R. E., known as Tip,[16] was arguably the most talented and certainly the most famous of all Malvernian cricketers. He was a dual international, representing his country in football and cricket – indeed he remains the only Englishman to have captained the national side in both sports. He also entered the record books for an extraordinary innings of 287 on his debut for England against Australia at Sydney in December 1903, which, at the time, was the highest individual score ever by a debutant and the highest by an Englishman in Australia. The bat he used in this innings is on

---

Charles Toppin (1885–1928) was the architect of Malvern cricket. He had a tremendous influence over every boy who played the game during the thirty-seven years that he ran cricket at the College. Described in Wisden as 'the greatest of all public school cricket masters to whom cricket was not just a game but a cult',[i] E. R. T. Holmes wrote in his autobiography *Flannelled Foolishness*:

> No one ever questioned or disputed C.T.'s opinion. If he said anything, it was so … I worshipped him from the moment I first met him. He was approximately fifty-five in 1919 – short and square and very leonine in countenance. He wore gold-rimmed spectacles and invariably (in summer) a straw hat with the Free Foresters ribbon round it. He walked with a stick and a limp and normally assumed a forbidding and rather aggressive demeanour, especially when he was in cap and gown; but when he smiled – and this was very often – it seemed that the whole School did the same, and even the Malvern Hills and Bredon were happy too. I would willingly have died for him.

Holmes recalls that when he took all ten wickets for 36 in a match against the Shropshire Gentlemen in 1922, Toppin invited him to dinner and presented him with a ball which carried a shield recording the event, and said, 'I don't expect that you'll ever do it again; but if you do, and I'm dead and gone, come and whisper it over my grave – I'll hear you.' He went on to predict that Holmes would make his mark as a batsman prophesising that he would make a century in the varsity match. Holmes concluded this reminiscence 'and walking home to my House on that beautiful summer night. I hoped fervently that I would not let him down'.

Donald Knight recalls that Toppin's method 'consisted in exercising his great personality rather than employing actual technical instruction; one felt that one was playing for him and for his approval, and if that was what was earned, it was joy and recompense indeed'.

Behind all Toppin's teaching of cricket, however, there lay a consuming passion, a feeling that cricket was something more than game, that it was a way of life and a test of character by which a boy, a house, and a school could be fairly judged; and if boys went all out for him, it was because they knew how much he cared. His long service at the school was due to end in 1928 and perhaps appropriately for a schoolmaster of such dedication he died in his last term. The Toppin connection continued at Malvern with his daughter Mary marrying J. S. Rambridge. They ran No. 9 for fifteen years after the Second World War, and their son Andrew was a much-liked master and housemaster of SH.

No. 6 house supper, July 1925, when C. Toppin gave up the House after thirty-three years.

PLAYED FOR ENGLAND

R. E. Foster  — G. H. Simpson-Hayward  — D. J. Knight 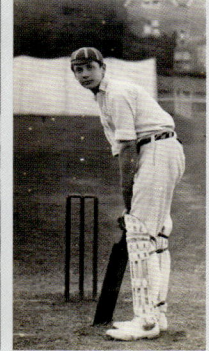 — F. T. Mann  — G. B. Legge  — E. R. T. Holmes  — R. W. Tolchard

display in a glass cabinet in the school Long Room. Sadly business commitments restricted this supremely gifted cricketer to only eight Test matches and 139 First-Class appearances in a career spanning thirteen years.

Amongst many others who came under Toppin's influence was G. H. Simpson-Hayward.[17] He was the last great underarm bowler, although he bowled overarm at school. It is said that he learnt to bowl his savagely spun lobs on board ship, usually on expeditions in search of butterflies, his consuming hobby in which he became an acknowledged expert. He toured with the MCC side to South Africa in 1909 and took 23 wickets in the five Tests, including 6 for 43 in the first innings at Johannesburg. He also toured New Zealand and the USA 'where he was found to be almost unplayable'. Other great Malvernian cricketers include the Day[18] and Naumann[19] brothers, and W. H. B. Evans, later captain of Oxford, whom E. W. Swanton described as possibly the greatest Malvern all-rounder.[20]

Towards the end of Toppin's time Donald Knight[21] was selected for the XI as a new boy and 'his name has gone into legend, as the Malvernian who never watched a first eleven match' – in those days the whole school had to watch the XI play and he played in the first match in his first year. 'He was probably the finest player, on all types of wickets, to learn his cricket on the Senior'.[22] Years later, he played for England against the great Australian side of 1921 and his innings of 38 (run out) in the second innings of the First Test was described 'as the best display of batting in an otherwise lamentable English performance'. F. T. Mann,[23] the captain of Middlesex, led the MCC side to South Africa in 1922, and under his captaincy they lost only one match, winning the series 2–1.

Among the many great names in Malvern cricket, Toppin considered N. E. Partridge to be

Below: 'Father' Tate, cricket professional from 1903 to 1935 with C. A. F. Fiddian-Green, master in charge of cricket (Staff 1923–59), and A. H. Brodhurst, captain of the XI (4. 1930–35).

Right: Match on the Senior.

Above: George Arber, cricket professional 1869–90. He was responsible for levelling the Senior Turf in 1872, owned and ran the first College Store in No. 1, The Lees, and constructed the houses that circle The Lees.

Below: Geoff Morton, cricket professional from 1958 to 1984. He also ran the school store.

the greatest all-rounder the school had ever produced – he scored 229 not out and took ten wickets for 150 in a two-day match against Repton in 1918.[24] He went on to play for Cambridge and Warwickshire. Many other Malvernians went on to play for county sides and for their country: G. B. Cuthbertson (Middlesex and captain of Northamptonshire),[25] C. G. W. Robson (Middlesex),[26] J. A. Deed[27] and C. J. Capes (Kent).[28] The XI of 1922 included six players who would later play First-Class cricket. The greatest of these was E. R. T. Holmes who captained Oxford and Surrey and played for England against the West Indies in 1934 and against South Africa in 1935.[29] G. B. Legge, the captain of the 1922 XI, also captained Oxford and later Kent, and subsequently played for England against South Africa in 1927 and New Zealand in 1929.[30] Toppin retired from running the cricket in 1924 and was succeeded by Charles Fiddian-Green, ably assisted by the coach 'Father Tate'.

In the period following the Second World War batsmen predominated, including R. K. Whiley,[31] Ian MacLaurin[32] and J. W. T. Wilcox[33] who were five years in the school XI, and B. A. Richardson[34] who represented the Old Malvernians ninety times in the Cricketer Cup.[35] The three Tolchard brothers were all outstanding players in the 1960s. Between 1965 and 1983 Roger played 483 First-Class games for Leicestershire (he was captain 1981–83) and in four Tests for England in India.[36] It was during this period that George Chesterton guided the fortunes of Malvern cricket both in the school and in the Cricketer Cup, winning it seven times, second only to Tonbridge.

Alan Duff, an Oxford Blue, took over in 1966 and the highest praise that can be bestowed on his stewardship is that the standards of the Chesterton era were maintained. First-Class cricketers who passed through his hands were Trevor Tunnicliffe, (9. 1963–68; Nottinghamshire), and Ivan Johnson (SH 1966–71; Worcestershire). C. N. Wookey (7. 1966–71) had the unusual distinction of gaining his cricket Blue for both Cambridge and Oxford.

Andrew Murtagh, a former Hampshire player, assumed responsibility in 1980 and tenaciously protected the integrity of the fixture list. The challenges that faced him were considerable – the necessity for greater emphasis on academic results, the expansion of the examination season, a shorter summer term, the proliferation of competing summer sports and latterly the conversion of the school to a fully co-educational entry – but standards were not allowed to slip. Overseas tours were undertaken to the West Indies (twice) and South Africa (thrice) and on two occasions, in 1984 and 2000, the U15s won the Lord's Taverners Cricketer Colts Trophy. Ricardo Ellcock (Worcestershire and Middlesex),[37] David Nash (Middlesex) and Mark Hardinges (Gloucestershire) all became successful county players. Other notable figures were Mark Pougatch, captain in 1985, who became a prominent BBC sports presenter and James Verity, captain in 1991, who was the grandson of the great Hedley Verity, England's premier spin bowler, killed in the Second World War.

Malvern has been fortunate over nearly 150 years in the loyalty and expertise of a handful of professional coaches: George Arber in the early days and 'Father Tate', who bowled endlessly and patiently in the nets for thirty-two years, serving up half volleys in order that the young gentlemen could practise their cover drives, and Bob Beveridge, late of Middlesex, who succeeded him. Then Geoff Morton came to instil generations of Malvernians with skills and impeccable standards of sportsmanship, coupled with his own endearing breed of malapropisms. He in turn passed the mantle on to Roger Tolchard, an outstanding all-round sportsman who added to his knowledge and experience of the game his own particular love of Malvern. His successors, Tim Roberts from Northants and Noel Brett, have continued to offer invaluable expertise.[38] Cricket at the school has always benefited from generous support from the Malvernian Society.[39]

In recent years Malvern has seen the benefits of a partnership with Worcestershire County Cricket Club whereby the county coaches seek to draw talented young cricketers into their academy. If it is appropriate, such a cricketer may also be admitted to Malvern on a Chesterton Scholarship.[40] The first scholar was Tom Köhler-Cadmore (5. 2009–13), a most elegant batsman who became captain of the first XI and, on leaving school, was offered an initial three-year contract by Worcestershire. He certainly fulfilled his promise at school scoring six hundreds, all not out, in his first three years at the school and in his last season scored a record 1,407 runs. He was named Wisden schoolboy cricketer of the year for 2013. The former master in charge of cricket commented that 'four years down the line we are seeing the rewards of the scholarship scheme as not only do talented cricketers come to Malvern but they also attract other good cricketers to the school. Our current first XI is, therefore, exceptionally strong'.[41]

Above: Andrew Murtagh, master in charge of cricket, 1981–2009.

Below left: Cricket tour to South Africa 2012 at Cape Town.
Below right: A record double-century partnership: Tom Köhler-Cadmore (5. 2009–13) and Alex Miltor (5. 2010–14) versus Oundle, 2013.

FOOTBALL

The first Headmaster and three of the original six masters were Wykehamists so until 1873 Winchester football was played. There were no referees and matches between houses were rough affairs, but were taken very seriously. Both Faber and Henry Foster regularly played on opposite sides sending the ball 'soaring with huge kicks from one to the other over the heads of the opposing teams, perhaps half a dozen times in succession.' The Rev McDowall 'normally the most dignified of men with the appearance of a Landseer bloodhound wearing Dundreary whiskers' became so involved in the first match with No. 2, where neither side had the advantage, that he 'jumped up, waving his hat and shouted, 'Go it, my boys, Sausages for tea!' An OM participant recalls that 'the effect was magical. With the war cry "Sausages and Doodles" we simply wiped the floor with old Franky's team and won a goal'. The Winchester form of football did not take root and was replaced in 1873 with Association Football. It is evident from the correspondence in *The Malvernian* that both cricket and football were greatly enjoyed by many and were taken extremely seriously by the boys. The task of junior boys during the football season is evident from a letter written to *The Malvernian* by senior boys who complained about a lack of 'kickers in':

> The field being very slanting, the ball often goes out and then the players have to fetch it, which if there were plenty of kickers-in might be prevented and a great deal of time saved. We all know that it is not pleasant having to stand about on a cold day, but every junior must take his chance, and if they want to warm themselves, they must move about their beat.

Below: Rules of Malvern football in 1868 when the school played the Winchester form of the game, as reflected in Rule 11.

Three Old Malvernians from this period were founder members of Blackburn Rovers and two of them played in the final of the FA Cup Final in 1882. The quartered shirts of Blackburn Rovers were modelled on the old Malvern shirts, with Malvern's green being exchanged for blue.[42]

The earliest football pitches have been described as 'very crude, for although the senior game was played on the Senior Turf, the juniors had a ground that was not free from paths, oak trees and other obstructions, to say nothing of the disadvantages of a considerable slope'.[43] The existing football field, originally 28 acres, was bought in 1895 from Lady Emily Foley for £7,000.[44]

L. V. Bennett played Association Football for Ireland in 1889 and was, according to one account, 'the first Old Malvernian to secure international honours'.[45] The first school to play against Malvern was Bradfield in 1882, and then came Radley in 1884, followed by Repton (1894) and Shrewsbury (1896).[46] These regular fixtures against Repton, Shrewsbury and Charterhouse formed 'one of the corner-stones of traditional school football'.[47] The Malvern–Repton centenary match programme captured something of the significance of their public school contest:

> It has sometimes been said that the golden age of soccer was the period between 1890 and 1914 when the amateur was every bit the equal of many professional players then in the game, and such was the importance and prestige attached to the Malvern v Repton match that in 1913 one of the leading sports' publications of the day referred to its as 'the Derby of Association Football'. During this period Malvern produced no less than eight full international players and seven Malvernians gained Amateur international caps.[48]

R. E. Foster achieved the unique distinction of captaining England in both cricket against South Africa in 1907 and in football against Wales in 1902, and in 1905 both varsity sides were captained by OMs with five others playing in the match. G. N. Foster captained Oxford at football and represented England against Holland and Wales. In 1909 and 1912 the OMs won the relatively new competition, the Arthur Dunn Cup, and in 1911 the AFA Cup.[49] Between the wars football also flourished, with the school winning all matches in 1927 and 1928 and the Old Malvernians winning the Arthur Dunn Cup in 1924, 1925, 1926 and again in 1928.

After the war football Blues were still won, but with the development of professional football the days of players from schools like Malvern performing at the highest club and national level came to an end.

It was Harvey Chadder who was largely responsible for recruiting Denis Saunders to the Malvern staff. 'His influence was immediate' and the 1950s were a vintage time for Malvern football with the XI unbeaten in 1956, 1957 and 1960. An OM captained Oxford in 1960, and the Arthur Dunn Cup was won in 1955 for the first time in eighteen years and then nine times between 1956 and 1978 and again in 1989. Malvern has an enviable record in this competition reaching the final a record 28 times and winning it 17 times, second only to the Old Carthusians. In the late 1950s and early 1960s Malvern benefited from the captaincy of Richard Chadder,[50] who played in nine finals and was captain in four winning sides. The College also figured prominently in the new Arthurian League formed in 1962 for the clubs competing for the cup. One distinguished OM footballer recalled the glory days under Saunders:

Above left: The XI 1875. The College had adopted Association Football rules in 1873, replacing the Winchester form.

Above right: Masters v The School, 1889. Back row: H. R. Smith, E. C. Bullock, R. E. Lyon, J. N. Swann, Dr H. Anderson, Rev T. Spear, C. T. Salisbury, H. K. Foster. Middle row: J. C. Wall, Rev H. Faber, H. S. Pike, Rev M. A. Bayfield (seated behind), C. Toppin, C. H. Watts, H. W. Horsbrough, F. W. Phillips. Front row: W. E. Copleston, R. Neill, L. B. Corbett, W. L. Foster, Rev H. R. Huntington, C. H. Ransome.

Far left: The No. 5 house football team in the 1930s.
Left: Inter-House football in 1979: No. 1 v No. 4.

Above left: A victorious Malvernian team in the 1965 Arthur Dunn Cup. Dick Chadder is holding the cup. (Courtesy of The Arthur Dunn Cup Competition and Replay Publishing)

Above right: In 1954, West Bromwich Albion came to the College to play the 1st XI. At the time West Bromwich Albion were the favourites for the FA Cup. Most of the 550 pupils spent the afternoon watching the match. (Image courtesy of Associated Newspapers / Solo Syndication)

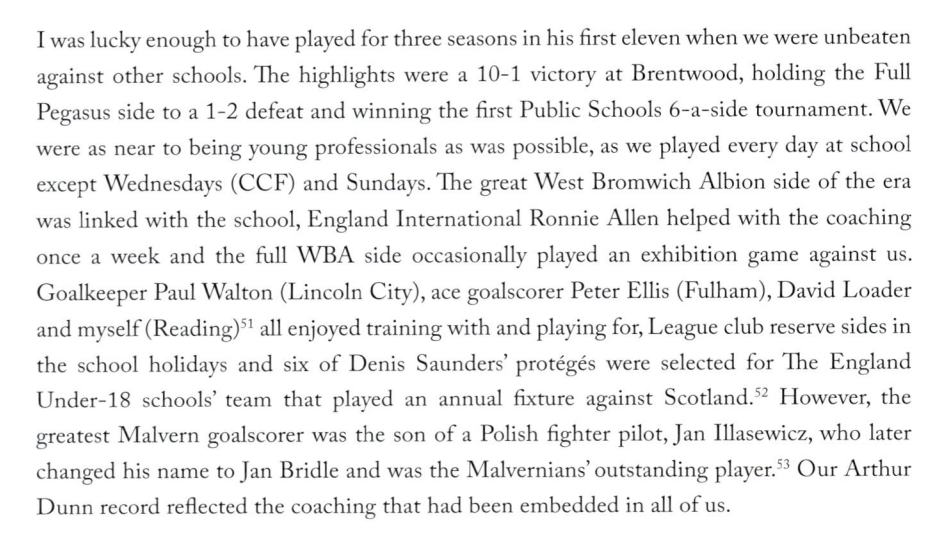

I was lucky enough to have played for three seasons in his first eleven when we were unbeaten against other schools. The highlights were a 10-1 victory at Brentwood, holding the Full Pegasus side to a 1-2 defeat and winning the first Public Schools 6-a-side tournament. We were as near to being young professionals as was possible, as we played every day at school except Wednesdays (CCF) and Sundays. The great West Bromwich Albion side of the era was linked with the school, England International Ronnie Allen helped with the coaching once a week and the full WBA side occasionally played an exhibition game against us. Goalkeeper Paul Walton (Lincoln City), ace goalscorer Peter Ellis (Fulham), David Loader and myself (Reading)[51] all enjoyed training with and playing for, League club reserve sides in the school holidays and six of Denis Saunders' protégés were selected for The England Under-18 schools' team that played an annual fixture against Scotland.[52] However, the greatest Malvern goalscorer was the son of a Polish fighter pilot, Jan Illasewicz, who later changed his name to Jan Bridle and was the Malvernians' outstanding player.[53] Our Arthur Dunn record reflected the coaching that had been embedded in all of us.

After 1974 Mike Percik and then Bob Smith ran the school's football before Syd Hill arrived and ushered in another golden age for the first XI from 1982 to 1984. In addition to the traditional rivals, for a number of years the school played the very strong Manchester Grammar School; Malvern's only victory came from an offside goal by Mark Pougatch. Malvern celebrated centenary matches with their oldest rivals with anniversary matches being played against Repton in 1994 and Shrewsbury in 1995. By the early nineties there was something of a decline. Malvern went fully co-educational in 1992, long before their rivals, obviously reducing the size of the pool of talent available for boys' football. This coincided with a growing localism which affected all boarding schools, with Malvern losing its connections with some of the feeder preparatory schools in London and the north which had provided so many of its finest footballers. Although the first XI maintained its strong reputation, helped in part by the steady arrival of skilled German boys into the Sixth Form, the junior levels declined sharply. There was growing weariness in travelling long distances only to be trounced by schools capable of recruiting from a much wider and deeper pool of talent. Local preparatory schools had developed rugby as their major winter sport – Malvern with its emphasis on football was losing potential pupils as a result. The decision to move football into the Lent term was unpopular with many Old Malvernians, not least because it brought to an end the century-old competition with old rivals, but may well have

Denis Saunders had played football for the RAF in 1946, was an Oxford Blue (1947–51) and had captained the vintage Pegasus side that won the FA Amateur Cup in 1951 and 1953 in front of crowds of 100,000 at Wembley. In the same year he gained his England amateur cap. He ran football at Malvern from 1953 to 1974. He taught geography, was a housemaster of No. 7 and helped to run the RAF section of the CCF. George Chesterton summed up Saunders' extraordinary career in charge of Malvern's football:

(Photograph by A. R. Upex (7. 1966 –70))

> From 1953 to 1974 Denis was in charge of football; the record of the school teams during that period was spectacular; at one stage there was a consecutive run of 23 school matches where they were undefeated. What was his secret? First I suppose there was his own passion for the game, and there was an aura, which surrounded such a great player. He was tactically very sound and his blackboard sessions emphasised the virtue of doing the simple thing, pass the ball the way you are facing, move the ball quickly, and never did he criticise anyone who did his best. He disliked any form of demonstration; I am sure many of you will remember the story of Ian MacLaurin passing to Jock Ellis, who scored against the Centaurs, the two embraced and Denis said, 'Do that again and I'll chop your arms off'.[i]

'Such was Saunders' reputation that in 1984 he was invited by the Football Association to be academic headmaster at their new school of excellence at Lilleshall.'[ii]

Saunders, holding aloft the cup, as captain of the Pegasus side that won the FA Amateur Cup in 1951 at Wembley. (Courtesy of The Arthur Dunn Cup Competition and Replay Publishing)

helped in the increase in enrolment after 2008. Happily as the school approached its 150th, the first XI remained a serious and successful competitor and the junior divisions were expanding and enjoying more success than for many a year.

Girls' football started at Malvern in 2008 and developed steadily with a growing fixture list against other independent schools and local clubs. Among the highlights have been winning the ISFA South-West Schools Sixes at both U18 (2009) and U15 level (2011) and in 2012 competing in the prestigious Donosti Cup in northern Spain, a huge international tournament involving nearly 7,500 players drawn from twenty-three countries. Also in 2012 the U18s competed in an international tournament in Rome, reaching the semi-finals,[54] and in 2013 joined the ISFA Midlands League; they are now competing against the top girls' sides in the independent sector.[55]

Below left: Mercian League champions, 2009.
Below right: U18 girls' football XI, 2012.
Opposite bottom: A. H. Chadder (Staff, 1926–66), master in charge of football 1933–53, as an English Amateur international; by Henry Coller, 'Soccer Celebrities', from the book *To the Palace for the Cup*. (Courtesy of The Arthur Dunn Cup Competition and Replay Publishing))

MALVERN COLLEGE

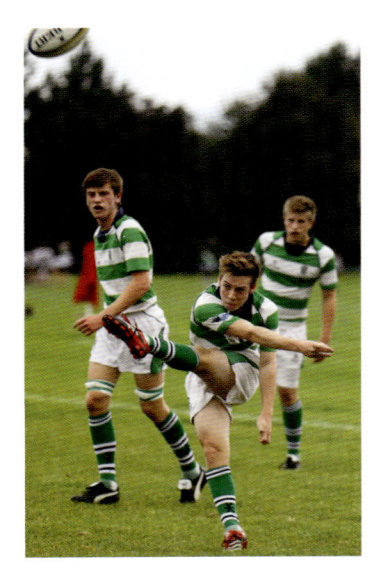

Top left: Kicking for goal.
Above: First XV v Shrewsbury, 1981.
Top right: School House rugby team, winners of the Rugby Cup, 1922.

RUGBY

Rugby has a much shorter history at Malvern than cricket and football. The game was first played in 1910 on an inter-house level and it is clear that many boys greatly enjoyed the game and house matches were, it appears, keenly contested. However, it was not until after the Second World War that rugby fixtures were permitted, the first school match being against Shrewsbury. A controversial engagement, the master in charge, Pat Hooley, was summoned by Donald Lindsay who told him that in no circumstances should the match be reported in the press as it would lead to a tirade of abuse from the football-loving OMs. When the Malvern team arrived at Shrewsbury, Hooley was horrified to find *The Times* rugby correspondent present and had to gain assurance that nothing would appear in the paper. The following day when reporting to the Headmaster that Malvern had won the match Lindsay responded by asking, perhaps facetiously, why this great moment had not been reported in *The Times*. Following national trends rugby became more popular and entrenched in the school, leading to the decision in 2006 to make it the major sport in the autumn term. Recent developments have seen an innovative partnership with the Worcester Warriors.

FIVES

Given the Wykehamist influence three open Winchester fives courts were built in 1867 on the north side of the campus; the Winchester version had its buttress on the left-hand wall. The Eton and Rugby versions of fives became more popular, but Winchester, Bradfield and Radley still play the Malvern version. Given that one court was reserved for prefects and a second for 'inferiors', there 'were vigorous scrimmages round the Fives Court just before 8 a.m. every day; for the only way of booking a Fives Court was to have the name pinned to the door at eight. So a prefect would organise bands of fags to pin his name on the door and defend it against all bands sent by other prefects until the clock struck eight, a procedure known as 'busking.' In 1872 the courts were roofed over and a House Cup competition began.

In 1903 the four existing covered courts were built on the south side next to the Gymnasium (now the theatre). Three were paid for by the Malvernian Society, and the fourth, with its tiered gallery, was the gift of the fifth Headmaster, the Rev S. R. James. Another court is labelled 'Rugby' and reflects the time when the buttress was removed to enable boys to play the more widespread version, but the court was so little used that the buttress was replaced.[56]

Following the Second World War, with a greater variety of sporting activities being available, the three northern courts were closed and the popularity of fives has fluctuated largely depending upon the energy of the master in charge. In the 1950s and 1960s it flourished under Malcolm Staniforth. In the 1970s and 1980s it was taken forward by John Blackshaw, followed by Richard Thurlow, and from 1991 Peter Gray. Matches are still played against traditional rivals: Radley, Bradfield and Winchester, the Jesters, and the Rugby Fives Association. The shortage of available fixtures in the area has become an increasing problem and short tours have been introduced. The fives team has twice visited Ireland to play one-wall handball fixtures against schools, and to try out international handball. In 2006, they travelled to the south-east to play Rugby fives against Alleyn's, St Paul's and Tonbridge. The College has also hosted the national adult Winchester fives championships for both men and women.[57]

RACKETS

Rackets has an unusual pedigree. Thought to have started in debtors' prisons in the mid eighteenth century, it spread to taverns and thence to the emerging public schools of the nineteenth century with a public schools rackets championship beginning in 1868.[58] Considered to be one of the world's fastest ball games, with the ball cracking off the walls at up to 160mph, it is now played in fourteen top British public schools.

In Malvern the first rackets court opened in 1881, with the second being added in 1905. The ubiquitous Henry Foster inspired this addition to the sporting facilities of the College. His seven sons were gifted at both cricket and rackets and in all but five of the twenty-one years[59] between 1889 and 1909 there was a Foster and sometimes two in the Malvern pair for the public school championship. During that period the College won the title three times (in 1892, 1900 and in 1908).[60] Between the wars Malvern won the championship three times, in 1920, 1936 and 1937.[61]

After the war the rackets courts were almost the last of the College buildings to be

Above: Fives rally.

Below left: Rackets 1966. From left: P. F. C. Begg (3.1961–66), J. H. Manners (3.1961–67), R. Hughes, rackets professional, S. J. Broughton (5. 1962–66), P. d'A. Mander (6 1961–66). Begg and Mander won the Public Schools Rackets Pairs Championship in 1966. Only a year after this photograph was taken Patrick Mander was killed in a motor accident.

Below: Congratulatory letter from Prime Minister Stanley Baldwin on the occasion of a Malvern rackets triumph in 1936.

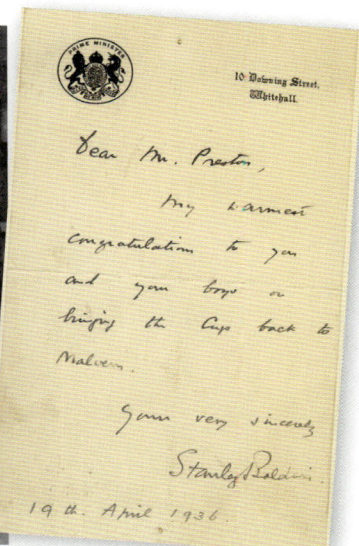

Ron Hughes had been an assistant professional at the Manchester Tennis and Rackets Club since 1935, with a break for war service. Norman Rosser records that 'Malvern's gain in Rackets was a national loss in real tennis' as it was the difficulty of practising tennis whilst at Malvern that led to defeat in New York in 1966 when he was the British challenger for the world title.

Right from the start Ron endeared himself to all Malvernians fortunate enough to play rackets. He insisted on the highest standard of stroke production with his own immaculate style and economy of movement on court providing an example to be imitated. Equally important he made it clear that enjoyment and good manners were essential features of the game, so Malvernians have always had reputations second to none in both respects.[i] He had a gift for making the game enjoyable even for those less gifted players. Bernard Weatherill wrote:

Above all else Ron was a professional – he always said that to be a professional marked one apart from other men; professionals were obliged to conduct themselves to a higher standard because of the example they had to set, both to schoolboys and to amateurs he never let his standards slip, and was a truer gentleman than many who would in the old days have regarded themselves as his betters. We all adored and loved him. He had an incredibly positive influence on generation after generation of Malvernians.

Ron's pastoral care was considered of the highest quality both for its kindness and earthy practical good sense. Norman Rosser recalls:

Much education in the real sense, took place in Ron's room or when travelling to away matches, and Housemasters, faced with a particularly intractable boy, would often say 'I must try and persuade him to play rackets, Ron is the only one who can sort him out.'

Ron Hughes retired in 1986; he and his wife Vera celebrated their diamond wedding anniversary just before his death at the age of eighty-seven. He had made such a deep impression on Malvernians that when the rackets courts were subject to a complete refurbishment they were dedicated to him in 2010.[ii]

Below: Malvern v Eton, 2014.

derequisitioned by the TRE, and being in need of extensive repairs it was not until 1954 that play was possible and a professional appointed. After a fifteen-year break there was little knowledge of the game, and much would depend on the enthusiasm and qualities of the new appointment. Both the game and Malvern could not have been more fortunate. Donald Lindsay, after interviewing Ron Hughes for the job, was heard to say, 'He is the sort of man I would like to have about the place.' He was to more than justify Lindsay's confidence, and his enthusiasm, skill, and professionalism lifted Malvern rackets to the highest level.

By 1966 the game had revived to such an extent that Malvern won the public schools doubles championship. One purple patch was between 1973 and 1977 when Malvern was in five consecutive National First Pair finals, winning three of them.[62] The 1974 finalist Mark Nicholls also won the Foster Cup[63] in 1973 and 1974. He went on to win the Army championship five times with his brother, winning the Swallow Trophy[64] four times between 1979 and 1982. These triumphs were followed by the excellent Mark Hubbard, who won the Swallow in 1997 and went on to beat the world champion, Neil Smith, in the semi-final of the professional singles championship in 1999. Hubbard, with Anthony Scammell, also won the Leonard Cup[65] in 1994 and the Milne Hue Williams Cup[66] in 1997. Hubbard went on to win five professional singles championships. In 2006 he won the British Open doubles crown, and took the world doubles championship the following year partnering the former world champion Neil Smith.[67] The sport owed much to the dedication of Norman Rosser who ran the rackets from 1955 to 1983 and has been described as one of 'the national pillars of the game'.[68] Co-education also opened up this fine game to girls and the College has become known for hosting, with the Tennis and Rackets Association, the Ladies Amateur Doubles. In 2014 Shinan Zhang (No. 8) won The Ladies British Open Rackets Singles Championship Plate competition as one of the youngest competitors.

GOLF

Golf is played at the Worcestershire Golf Club, which has had strong links with the College since 1880. The key figure was the Rev Henry Foster who was honoured with the golf club captaincy three times. As late as 1900 his handicap was 1, 'which even allowing for all the changes that have taken place over the years in such ratings shows that he was considered to be a difficult player to beat'.[69] For some years in the early part of the century the club used to play a match against the Foster family, often on Boxing Day; and the results were generally as close as the one played in 1905, which was narrowly won by the Club 4.5 to 4. S. R. James, Headmaster from 1897 to 1914, was an enthusiastic player and became captain in 1901. In his autobiography he wrote:

> What made my life specially healthy and pleasant at Malvern was the game of golf. I always kept two hours open in the afternoon and I think I must have had a round of golf on average four times a week sometimes oftener. Golf was a godsend largely for the friendly intercourse with colleagues.[70]

With the Headmaster and a number of other masters so keen it was only natural that boys should be encouraged to play. In 1896 they were allowed to play but only with a master, and had to pay 1/- a week or 6d a day for the privilege. In 1906 James thought that convalescent boys could knock a ball around the common as long as they did not get in the way of members. An early enthusiast was W. M. Grundy,[71] described as the best golfer of the three Grundy boys, all of whom achieved golfing Blues; he impressed when, in 1903 playing for his university, he set a course record of 70 playing against the club. In 1904 five of the sixteen players in the varsity golf match were OMs. Frank Preston continued headmagisterial enthusiasm for golf and was invited to be captain in 1921 and 1922 and again in 1928 and 1929.[72]

THE HALFORD HEWITT

The Halford Hewitt was founded by G. L. Mellin in December 1923 when golfers from Eton, Charterhouse, Highgate, the Leys, Malvern and Winchester met to arrange the first competition. Mellin, influenced by the success of football's Arthur Dunn Cup, suggested the idea of creating a similar golfing event to his old friend Halford Hewitt, who agreed to donate a cup and became president of the Public Schools Golfing Society, a post he held until his death in 1949. Mellin became honorary secretary.

The first Hewitt in 1924 had only eleven participants. In 1925 the competition was focused as a three-day event at Deal with the number of schools participating steadily increasing, to forty in 1936 and fifty in 1938. The competition restarted in 1947 after the war and had fifty-six participating schools by 1950. The greater numbers led to Royal St George being used in addition to Deal. The entry is now fixed at sixty-four and the event takes place in early April with some 640 golfers and many supporters creating what is 'possibly the largest and certainly the most enjoyable amateur tournament in the world'. Malvern reached the final for the first time in 1966 and subsequently on no fewer than nine occasions.[i] The long wait for victory finally ended in 2006 when Malvern defeated Sherborne.

Malvern College, the 2006 winners of the Halford Hewitt. Jeremy Lowe (9. 1954–59) is seated second from left.

Above: Playing at Shifnal Golf Club, Telford v Shrewsbury, 2010.
Below: G. L. 'Susie' Mellin with the secretary's Niblick.

Relationships between the club and the College were described as generally happy with just the occasional hiccup when some over-enthusiastic boy had been reported for driving into the back of a not-remote-enough ladies' game. Malvernians have gone on to win Blues and county caps, while a select few have played for their country. The first was G. L. Mellin,[73] a Cambridge Blue for football and golf in 1905, who played golf for England against Scotland in 1922; he was followed by Geoffrey Illingworth, another Cambridge golf Blue, who played for England against Scotland in 1929 and France in 1937.[74] Alan Newey played against Scotland, Ireland and Wales in 1932, and then there was a gap of fifteen years before W. S. Wise,[75] who had left the College in 1918, gained his first cap as a mature player in 1947. 'With competition for top honours in amateur golf becoming increasingly hot, it was not surprising that the next international player did not emerge until 1974 with Rodney James'.[76] When the Club opened the redesigned 18-hole golf course in 1972 and arranged an exhibition match between two professionals and two amateurs, Rodney James was chosen as one of the amateurs.[77] Old Malvernians have had a distinguished record in the university matches between Oxford and Cambridge – to date some thirty-two OMs have played in the varsity match, the most recent being Adrian Barrett Greene in 1982, 1983 and 1984 and Luke Bradley Jones in 1997.[78]

Four enthusiastic golfing Malvernians founded the Old Malvernian Golfing Society in July 1922, which has, with the exception of wartime, come back regularly for matches with the College players.[79] G. L. Mellin[80] became the first captain of the Society. He took over as president in 1925 holding the post until his death in 1961. He was described as 'a wonderful administrator of the game as well as being a fine player and was held in high esteem by his fellow golfers'. In his history of Malvern golf, Robert Beeson[81] credits Mellin and Jeremy Lowe[82] as the two men who 'have done most to ensure the success of the Society'. Lowe has won more OM golfing trophies that any other player and was in addition an 'outstanding administrator', acting as treasurer of the Society for over thirty years.

THE LEDDER

Malvern's most famous sporting event is the eight-mile run across the hills from Ledbury to the College. The origins of the Ledbury Run lie in the early tradition of long-distance paper chases, which provided the staple running experience in the early years of the school. The first mention of the Ledbury paper chase came in 1876,[83] and in March 1879 came the first reference to the run, when 'a goodly number of athletes started for Ledbury by the 2.32 p.m. train, and from thence ran across country to the College steps, a distance of about 8 miles.' In 1881 some twenty-two runners, including the Headmaster Rev Cruttwell, took the train to Ledbury and each had to find their way 'home to the College as best he could. At four o'clock a very large party assembled at the College steps, amidst drenching rain, to witness the arrival of the runners. Cheers announced the arrival of the Rev Cruttwell who was running in excellent form'.

So the great tradition started, frequently beset by problems not least with local farmers. In 1886 the runners experienced 'a slight check owing to some farmers making various demonstrations, one energetic gentleman amusing himself by riding at some of the runners and attempting to charge them over. However, they all managed to reach Malvern unhurt'.

In March 1895 it was decided that the run should finish in the middle of the Senior Turf and from 1896 it became an annual event.[84] There was no formal course at this time and runners

Left: The Ledder, 1950. (Courtesy of Peter Southgate (6. 1946–50))

could make their own choice of route. 'Thus the run became a test of two skills, not just ability at running and perseverance but, often of near equal importance, a sense of "country" and later of map reading'. From the reports on the races of 1896–97 it is clear that nine caps were the norm and by 1899 winning a Ledbury cap was considered to 'bring more honour to the wearer than any other success in the sports'.

There are some notable moments in the history of the Ledder. W. C. M. Berridge (No. 5. 1909–14) gained four caps coming 5th in 1911, 2nd in 1912 and 1913 and finally winning in 1914. One of the closest races came in 1915 when D. C. C. Dickinson won. He was killed in action in August 1918 and his parents presented the Dickinson Cup in his memory; it is still presented to the first No. 5 Ledder cap winner each year. In 1921 C. H. Johnston (3. 1918–21) set a record of 49 minutes, unbeaten until 1956.

A graphic description of running the Ledder in desperate circumstances comes from C. F. G. Pearse with his account of the 1930 race.[85] He awoke on the day of the Ledder, where after heavy snow it poured with rain for the whole day 'so that the conditions became simply appalling'. Having been soaked waiting for a delayed train, the race began:

> The course started up a field about 120 yards long, with a gap in the corner for which everyone races. Thereafter, it climbs steadily for about a mile through woods and fields, and along cart tracks and paths. After that, the way forward lies across nearly five miles of open fields, separated by low hedges and ditches. Under these conditions, the fields were at least half hidden by water, whilst the ditches were raging torrents, knee deep. Twice, when crossing what had been microscopic streams, I was up to above my waist in water, and for the next field I felt absolutely 'done', while my clothes seemed to weigh a ton. However I plodded on and tore my running shorts to shreds on barbed wire.

In 1935, the House Cup was introduced with the number of the places for the first three runners (extended later to four and then to six in 1982) from each house counted and the smallest total declared the winner. In 1951 R. H. Chadder[86] revolutionised the route by crossing the Hills

Below: W. H. Ricardo (6. 1898–1902), winner of the 1902 Ledder with a time of 50.42 – a record which held until 1921, when it was broken by C. H. Johnston.

MALVERN COLLEGE

further north, taking School House with him. Thanks to Chadder's initiative, runners are now spared the final steep and wooded 200 feet of Frith Hill above Ledbury station. In 1956 M. J. Clement (No. 7)[87] clocked 46.48. R. G. Milne's (No. 7)[88] time in his first (1961) win was 46.25, and it remains the fastest ever recorded. Though times in this race are of secondary importance and never a reliable yardstick for comparison, these two performances must be rated outstanding.[89] 1960 saw the third of three remarkable wins by I. G. Campbell[90] a feat that had not been achieved before and as yet has not been equalled. Foot-and-mouth disease caused the only cancellation in 1968, possibly preventing N. G. H. Draffan (No. 1), the winner in 1967 and 1969, from equalling Campbell's record.

Gradually, with the increasing entry and the natural reluctance of farmers to offer wholesale access, the course became more flagged, and from 1961 it has been a fixed route arranged by the master in charge after consultation with landowners. So an eye for country is no longer the valuable asset it used to be.

The 100th Ledder was celebrated in 1986 with an invitation extended to OMs and existing and former members of staff to join the race. *The Malvernian* reported that: 'The response was most enthusiastic and, on the day, 67 guests (including seven past winners) lined up with the 140 boys. The atmosphere was one of excitement, nostalgia, apprehension, but especially of fun!' From 2004 OMs were invited to run each year and in 2005 the Ledder Cap was reintroduced.

The 1987 race saw the first lady runner when Mrs Sarah Fellows (the wife of a master) came 27th, raising over £300 for charity. She improved her position to 15th the following year. This happy precursor paved the way for the participation of girls when the school became co-educational. In 1993 the first three home, all from No. 6, completed the run in just over 82 minutes; in the following year twenty-two girls competed and the leader came in at 56th in just over 66 minutes to win the newly instituted Sarah Fellows Cup. In 2006 Katie Sloan (No. 4) finished tenth out of the ninety runners with a new girls' record. John Makin concluded his history of the Ledder with a speculation that it would not be long before a girl might gain one of the coveted Ledder caps. His prediction came true perhaps rather faster than expected. The master in charge, Richard Hookham, reported on the 125th running of the race in 2012:

Above: D. C. C. Dickinson (5. 1912–16), winner of the Ledder in 1915.

Above: Noah-Vincenz Nöh (No. 5), winner of the 2014 Ledder and the Dickinson Cup.
Right: Modern Ledder.

At Lower Lodge (2 miles into the race) it was Tim Brook (No. 5), Adam Flattery (No. 5) and then Lydia Sharpe (No. 8). Never have I known a girl to be so high up the field at any point in this competition, and certainly none has managed to finish among the boys' Ledbury Cap winners. And it was in exactly the same order that these runners finished, to a mighty roar from a pupil-packed Senior, just a short time later. Tim finished in an excellent time of 52:17, taking over a minute off his winning time of 2011. Adam followed him in with 54:21, easily beating his previous time of 58:35. Then it was Lydia, way up the field, leaving over a hundred boys and girls and every single adult competitor in her wake with her time of 56:20.

Left: Cheering them in: the Ledder, 1999.

Above: Ian Campbell (9. 1955–60), winner of the Ledder 1958, 1959 and 1960.

OTHER SPORTS

The changing nature of the College had profound implications for sport. Although the traditional games were supported and enjoyed with undiminished enthusiasm, co-education saw an expansion in the range of team and individual games. Hockey in particular flourished in the new climate assisted by the influx of keen and talented continentals, and the opening of an all-weather surface. Now the most significant and successful girls' team game it also became a popular boys' sport. Full co-education in 1992 brought in new sports like lacrosse and netball and of course girls' athletics and cross-country. Enthusiastic girls' teams also took to football and cricket. In the summer term tennis was a very popular sport with both sexes.

An account of the school in 1937 stated that 'in athletics Malvern has always enjoyed a good reputation' and its most famous athlete was the remarkable Arnold Nugent Strode Jackson. Athletics took place on the Senior, where there was just room for a straight 200 yards, until 1970 when the Malvernian Society paid for the levelling of the grass track encircling the 1st XI pitch. The first cross-country fixture was in 1956. Steeplechasing round the Firs Estate ended in 1960.

The school's long tradition in shooting emerged from the Officers' Training Corps from the early days of the school, and General Murray presented a cup for a house competition in which all members of each house competed on the miniature range. This range, demolished to make way for the new sports complex, was unique as it had been built as a 50-yard indoor range and then converted into two back-to-back 25-yard ranges, the like of which existed nowhere else in the country. A 'Malvern .22 meeting' was run from 1968 to 2005 and attended by local schools,

Above: Lydia Sharpe (6. 2008–12), who came third in 2012 with a new girls' record, was the first girl to win a traditional Ledder cap.

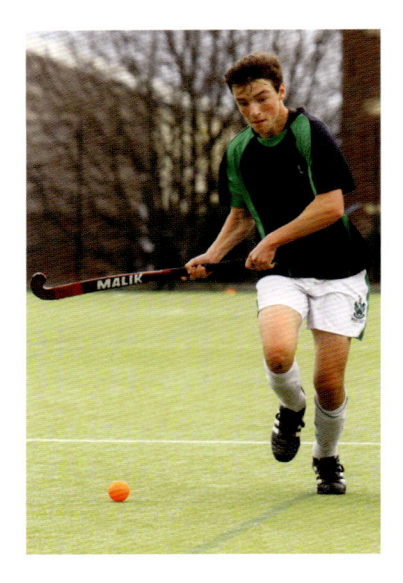

Above left: Boys' hockey.
Above right: Girls' hockey at the Court Road Astroturf.

the home team usually winning the competition. The school is fortunate to have a new .22 range in the Sports Complex.

Malvern first competed for the Ashburton Shield in 1885, when they were one of seventeen competing schools and fired on the ranges on Wimbledon Common with the Martini-Henry rifle. The school had shot 103 times by 2005, after which participation ceased, coming fourth in 1974 (the year the master in charge, Frank Harriss, won The Queen's Prize), second in 1978 (and in two other earlier years) and winning the competition in 1983. More than fifteen shooters have been selected over the years for the British Cadet Rifle Team to Canada (The Athelings). At least six OMs have won Blues in the Oxbridge teams, with three captains, one at each university in 1980 – Rupert Clarke (SH 1973–77) for Cambridge and Carey Wilks (2. 1973–77) for Oxford.

For generations of boys boxing was a major sport in the Lent term with house competitions and the annual Quadruple Tournament, in which Malvern was pitched against Downside, Clifton and Cheltenham. Boxing took place in the old gym (now the Rogers Theatre) but following the national trend provision for boxing was discontinued in the mid 1960s.

Other sports, which have not involved on-site facilities, include polo, rowing and sailing.[91]

Arnold Nugent Strode Jackson (1891–1972) was Head of House and captain of the athletics team at Malvern. At Oxford he won the mile race against Cambridge three times (1912, 1913 and 1914) and was president of the Oxford University Athletic Club.

In 1912 he travelled to the Olympic games in Stockholm and entered himself for the 1500 metres. He had not been selected for the Great Britain team but was able to avail himself of the then custom of private entry – this was the last Olympics where this was permitted. The Americans were the favourite for the medal with no fewer than seven entries for the race. On the final lap three of the Americans ran abreast intending to stop anyone from overtaking, so Jackson had to run wide and went on to win the gold medal in a new world and Olympic record of 3:56.8. The race was described by contemporaries as 'the greatest race ever run'. Winning at only twenty-one, Jackson remains the youngest ever Olympic 1500m champion. A gallant career in the First World War saw him become the youngest brigadier general in the British Army and being awarded the Distinguished Service Order with three bars. Sadly the war brought his sporting career to an end as he was wounded three times and left permanently lame. (Photograph courtesy the Principal and Fellows of Brasenose College, Oxford)

THE SPORTING LIFE

Top left and right: Events from a sports day in the 1930s.
Middle left: Junior steeplechase, early 1950s. (Courtesy of Peter Southgate)
Middle right: Sports Day 2010: the hurdles.
Bottom: Sports Day 2013: the Junior boys' A String 100m.

205

Above left: Netball match play at Malvern.

Above middle: Lacrosse: warming up for a match.

Above right: Mixed doubles.

Right: Programme for an inter-school boxing competition held at Malvern in 1950.

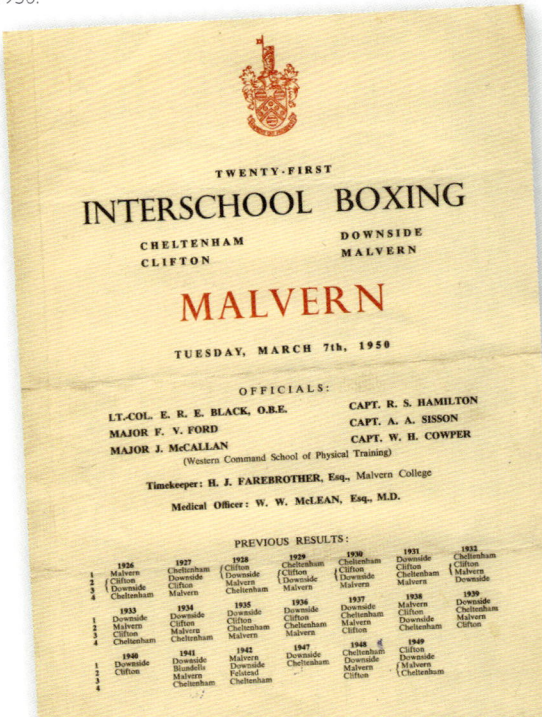

Polo appeared in the early 1990s through the enthusiasm of Pat Hooley and the parents of Roddie Williams[92] which led to Malvern joining with Harrow to compete in the Schools' Polo Championship Rugby[93] and then competing successfully as a full Malvern team, defeating among others Eton. By Easter 1996 they were capable of winning the National Independent Indoor Polo Championship, and then going on to defeat Radley, Marlborough and Wellington to reach the final of the National Schools' Polo Championship, at the Guards Club, Windsor, in which Malvern defeated Eton. The captain and key player was Satnam Dhillon,[94] who was named best player in the tournament, ably supported by Will Bowers, Ricki Watson and Charlie Gundy.[95] In the 1997 final Malvern succumbed to Cheltenham in a rundown but Will Bowers won player of the tournament. Satnam went on to play for England and is now a professional polo player. 1998 saw the first Malvern Girls' Polo team. In recent years equestrian sports have appeared, with Malvern enjoying considerable success.

Old Malvernians have made a significant contribution to the Paralympics movement. Philip Lewis MBE (6. 1952–57, brother of John Lewis, see p.116) was left paralysed after a car accident in 1962. He was treated at the National Spinal Injuries Centre, Stoke Mandeville, by the neurologist Sir Ludwig Guttmann, a Jewish refugee from Nazi Germany, who revolutionised the way paralysed servicemen were cared for and who in 1948 founded the Stoke Mandeville Games, the forerunner of the modern Paralympics. Lewis competed at table tennis in the Tokyo Games of 1964 and went on to win silver in the doubles competition in Heidelberg in 1972. Honoured by the Queen in 1981 for services to sport, he is a trustee of the 'Poppa' Guttmann Trust, which he founded. The main aim of the trust is to advance education of the public in the history of the Paralympics movement and the work of Sir Ludwig 'Poppa' Guttmann in the treatment of spinal cord injuries.

It was a matter of great pride therefore, to the school that two OMs, Rob Richardson (7. 1995–2000) and John Worrall (2. 1996–2001), represented

THE SPORTING LIFE

Team GB in the London Paralympics of 2012 in volleyball. They reached the quarter-finals but were defeated by the reigning world champions, Iran. Robert wrote:

> I was born with a congenital deformity of my right foot and at birth doctors suggested a simple amputation of my right leg below the knee as, in their opinion, I would never be able to walk naturally. Thanks to some fairly stubborn behaviour on the part of my parents, they ignored the medical advice and, sure enough, I was up and walking. Despite a few operations over my early years, a particular low being a painful leg-lengthening procedure of 5½ centimetres, I was mobile and able to do what I wanted: playing football and cricket. By my second year at Malvern a combination of my increasing weight (all those Grub breakfasts!) and the amount of time spent running around the Yard at Number 7 had taken its toll and I was faced with a choice of multiple operations to keep my existing foot or just the one operation, to amputate. I made the decision to have the amputation having asked the doctors which option would get me back in time for the cricket season. It proved to be an excellent decision as Will Stephenson and I enjoyed an opening wicket partnership of 222 during that season. I was especially glad to be back playing football and playing in the First XI remains one of my most satisfying achievements.
>
> I got into Paralympic sport in 2005; on the very day that London won the bid to host the 2012 Games and am now Captain of the Great Britain Paralympic Volleyball team, having been a part of the team since its inception in 2005, amassing 96 caps to date and hope to become the first British athlete to reach 100 caps. As well as competing at London 2012 Paralympic Games, I have also competed at four European Championships and two World Championships – with Great Britain currently ranked 8th in the world, which isn't bad going considering we were 60th when I started. Nationally, I have won the National Championship a record three times and I have been inducted into the Volleyball Hall of Fame and I also sit on the Athletes' Commission for the World Governing Body for Volleyball.

Above left: Queen's Prize winner Captain Frank Harriss, 1974.

Above right: No. 5 shooting squad, winners of the Beechcroft Shield, 1927.

Below: Rob Richardson (7. 1995–2000), right.

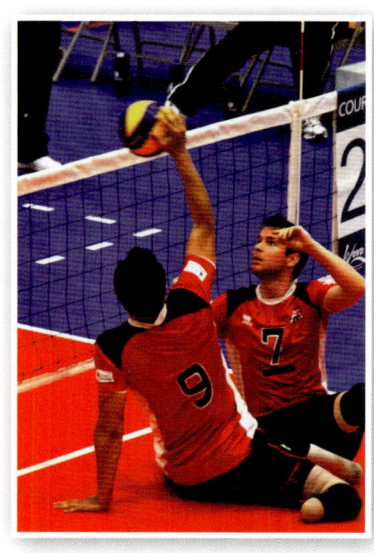

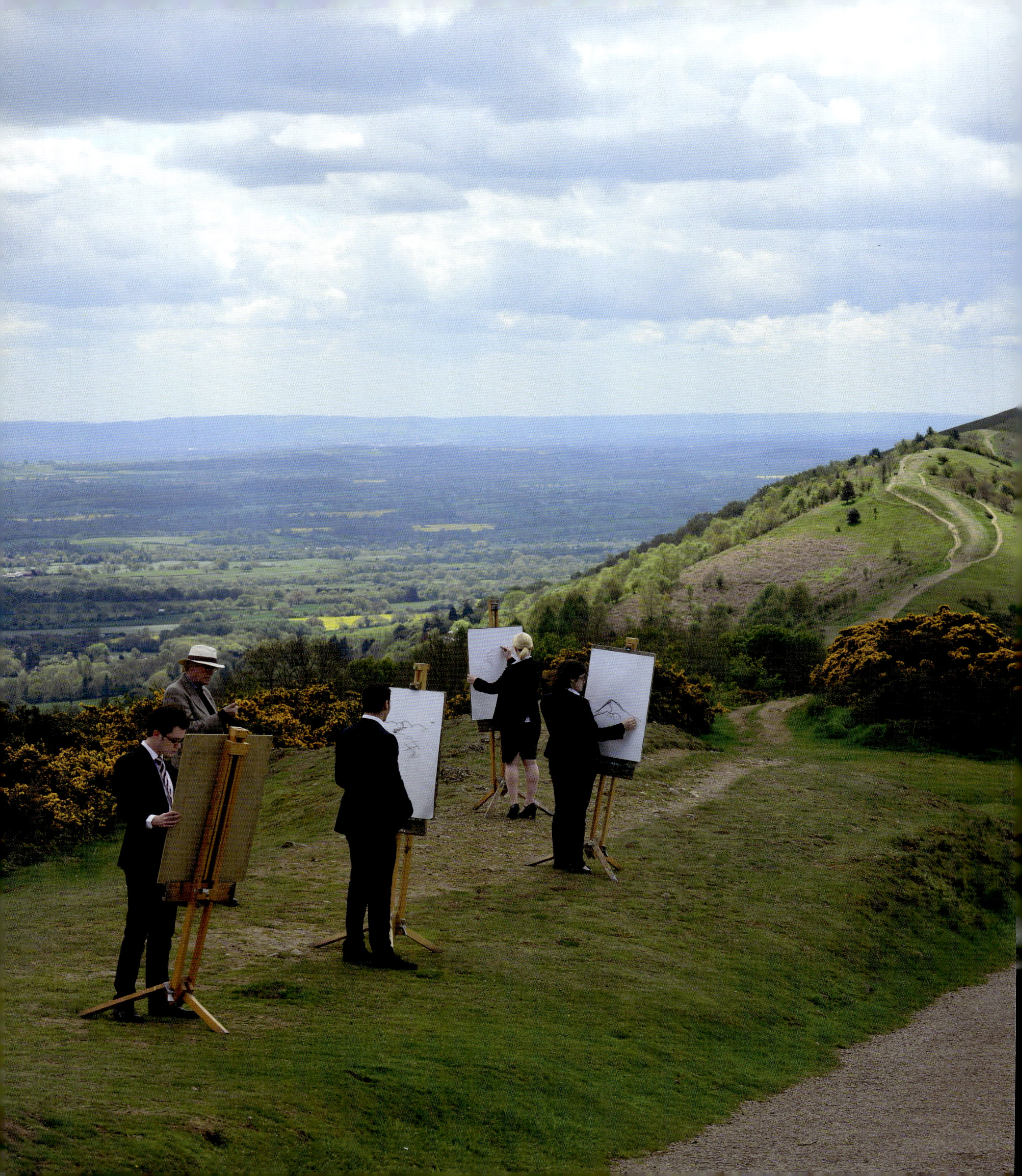

14

Life in abundance

Like all the great headmasters and teachers in Malvern's history Donald Lindsay believed in a fuller life, not one simply dedicated to work and still less to hedonism – hence his dedication to 'life in abundance' in his centenary address, in which he stressed that the arts were essential to developing that fuller life. In the years following his headship his vision has in many ways been fulfilled.

Opposite: Art on the hills: Tim Newsholme, Director of Art from 1988, and pupils. (Photograph by Jon Willcocks)

MUSIC

In the early days there was limited musical activity. Copies of *The Malvernian* reveal termly concerts largely focused on sentimental songs from obscure Victorian composers. We are fortunate to have a vivid account of music in the College in the 1870s:

> About a dozen of us learnt the piano, and one or two the organ, and we were looked upon as rather curious individuals. I do not remember that anyone played the violin or violoncello, and wind instruments were unknown. The only occasion on which I heard an orchestra was when special leave was given me to go for a day to the Bristol Festival for a performance of *Elijah*. At our school concerts the instrumental portion consisted of a piano solo or two and an arrangement of a march or simple overture for two pianos and harmonium. In those dark days the music we were given to play was of an uninspiring order.
>
> But there were some experiences the value and joy of which have remained with me all my life. We had some fine singing. The life and soul of it was Loraine Estridge. He was universally beloved. I count him as one of the greatest friends I ever had, and Mrs Estridge is another. He was in charge of Chapel music and played the organ until he passed it over to me, and I remember the excellence of some of our anthems and of the Hymns and Psalms. I have studied with some of the most eminent men in the musical world, but I doubt whether I learnt as much about what a School music master really requires, for his work with boys, from any of them as I got from Mr Estridge.[1]

In 1906 a more serious departure took place when Lyon launched a series of 'Classical Concerts'. 'Occasionally, the programme was technically quite ambitious; musically it was always safe; and there are OMs with musical sensitivity who suffered deprivations and worse.'[2] Lyon's organ playing in Chapel, wrote one OM, 'perpetuated on a helpless congregation daily improvisations of unsurpassable hideousness.' However, Lyon was generally popular with the pupils and the Chapel choir always did its best for him. An OM recalls a succession of treble soloists 'with

Above: R. E. Lyon, OM (Staff, 1887–1926); Director of Music, 1887–1914.

Below: F. H. Shera, Director of Music, 1914–28. (Brian Iles Collection)

voices like angels, and the singing in unison was terrific'. However, this affection was not universal and one OM from his house recalls a communal act of vengeance on Lyon who had a passion for winning singing cups:

> In my third year at Malvern we lost the cup for singing, which the House had held for several years. This was not surprising as we had conditioned the choir before hand, making it quite clear what would happen to them if they dared win again. When the lost cup was removed from the shelf in the house dining-hall an unknown hand replaced it in the night with a chamber pot.[3]

The emergence of music at Malvern as a serious and stimulating activity can be found, as with so many important innovations, in the Preston years. The acquisition of the Monastery had made possible the provision of more satisfactory practice rooms than the previous accommodation in 4, The Lees.[4] When Lyon left for war service, his place as Director of Music was taken by F. H. Shera, described as 'a man of enormous energy and a genius at inculcating musical appreciation.'[5] Within a year the school orchestra was able, in March 1917, to put on a concert which included Grieg's *Holberg Suite*, Wagner's *Siegfried Idyll*, two short pieces for strings by Elgar and Percy Grainger and Mozart's great G minor symphony. By February 1923 there had been 'no fewer than 100 concerts, or about five a term – this exclusive of the fortnightly organ recital given by Shera in the Chapel'. Between 1922 and 1926, 'under Shera's guidance the boys brought out a magazine called *The Concert Goer*, which appeared five times a term and included programme notes for the forthcoming concerts'. After Shera's departure in 1928, to become professor of music at Sheffield University, J. A. Davison 'carried on the good work. The whole school took part in performances of oratorios, with every boy joining in singing some of the chorales. One such performance, of Bach's *Christmas Oratorio*, was broadcast in 1930.'[6]

> Music flourished: the choral society and the orchestra met weekly and usually gave at least one concert a year. There was even the occasional staged performance in the gym – for example Iolanthe on the 2nd April 1927, noted in my diary as 'a great success'. On these occasions the weaker sections of the orchestra were helped out by professionals from Birmingham.[7]

Despite the privations of war the choral tradition remained strong. Davison's swansong 'was a magnificent performance of the *Messiah* in Oxford Town Hall during the Blenheim days' and Easter Sunday saw the whole school singing the Hallelujah Chorus as the anthem in Woodstock Parish Church. Regarding the former a letter appeared in the *Malvern Gazette*:

> For forty years I have heard these choruses sung by the great trained choirs of the North Country and Wales, but truth to say, I have never heard singing, which thrilled me so much. The fresh and beautiful voices of the boys, controlled so perfectly by the conductor, gave the audience an unforgettable evening.[8]

Davison's successor was a distinguished musician, Julius Harrison,[9] but as he was unable to go to Harrow, Malvern's singing came under the charge of the Harrow master Mr Havergal. Leonard Blake was appointed just before the return to Malvern and he was to guide the musical fortunes of the school for the next two decades.

As with so many aspects of the school it took music a long time to recover from the impact of the war and the post-war problems of recruiting able boys. It fell to Leonard Blake to

Left: The Music School.

mastermind the recovery. In a fine tribute Pat Purcell[10] recalls that Blake started work while the school was still at Harrow when he had 'to disentangle the joint musical activities shared with the host school. He formed an autonomous Malvern choir by arranging separate chapel services, thereby giving the College some musical definition'. Although the choral tradition was to remain strong, orchestral work proved one of the casualties of the war as 'there were simply not enough boys who played an instrument, and especially there was shortage of string players, the backbone of any orchestra'.[11]

The return home brought little comfort for 'in the first term the Music School was still being used by the MOD, and when it did become available there was no basic equipment or furnishing

Left: Leonard Blake, Director of Music, 1945–68. (©Michael Ward / ArenaPAL)

Above: Charles Brett, Director of Music, 1968–76.

Below: Neil Page, Director of Music, 1976–85.

– or assistant staff'. Describing the situation as 'a frightening state of affairs' Blake slowly began the recovery, building 'his formidable reputation as an organiser and teacher.' Thus, in spite of the circumstances, he was able to give a performance of excerpts from Handel's *Samson* in the gym in 1947 but it was not until 1956 that there was a joint performance with Malvern Girls' College: Beethoven's Mass in C. The strength of the choral revival Blake inspired was celebrated in 'a remarkable performance of Elgar's *Dream of Gerontius* in Malvern Priory with the CBSO in his last year as Director of Music. This has long lived in the memory of all who took part.'

The wider challenge of these years is well captured by a description of one of the entrants in the 1948 House Music Competition who was programmed to play the slow movement of Mozart's *Sonata Facile* with the note: RIGHT HAND ONLY.

Pat Purcell summed up Blake's approach and musicality as follows:

> He gave meticulous attention to detail in administration. He was a distinguished pianist and organist, but it was as a choir trainer that he was without peer. Leonard was also a musical scholar of profound depth, and an ideal examiner. This all led to his appointment to the Presidency of The Incorporated Society of Musicians, in 1968, reflecting his skill as a teacher, choir trainer, and church composer. He was always completely true to his beliefs. Not for him the 'pepping up' of Chapel services – nor the cheap surrender to popularity. His musical tastes were catholic on the whole, but occasionally dipped below the plimsoll line of his own standards, perhaps. He was once observed performing a particularly splashy piece of Organ music. When he finished he threw his hands in the air and exclaimed 'Froth! Pure froth of course – but quite fun to play!' Despite his grounding in Bach, Beethoven, and Mozart he was spoken of as a remarkably sensitive duettist in the Romantic repertoire, and one OM tells me that he was lucky enough to witness a revelatory performance of three Debussy preludes.
>
> We have been lucky in Malvern to have enjoyed the presence of some distinguished musicians in charge of the department since Leonard's departure, but I think it fair to say that they worked in more benign and enlightened times. It is a tribute to Leonard that so many OMs and staff remember him with such esteem.

Throughout his long professional life Leonard was ever supported by his wife Maureen, the daughter of Mrs Moore who kept house for C. S. Lewis. A violinist, she inherited the only baronetcy in the United Kingdom that could be held by a female. In the inspired words of Donald Lindsay, at Blake's last Speech Day, she was transformed 'at a wave from the Lord Lyon's wand' from an 'Irish Fiddler into Lady Dunbar of Hempriggs, (with a castle on the north coast of Scotland!)' Leonard Blake left an endowment for Malvern upon leaving and latterly their son, Sir Richard Dunbar, has continued to give to the fund providing a bi-annual 'Blake-Dunbar' scholarship.

Charles Brett was Director of Music from 1968 until 1976. A Wykehamist and choral scholar at King's College, Cambridge, he had taught for two years at Eton before Donald Lindsay appointed him. An excellent counter-tenor, with a growing domestic and international reputation, perhaps one of his strongest fields was his success in developing Oxbridge music scholars. The first of these was John Graham-Hall who has since enjoyed a career as a very successful opera singer. Brett was also a very good keyboard player, both pianist and organist, and a very good accompanist.

Choral music at the College thrived under Brett's guidance, perhaps even more so than the instrumental, although that too improved a lot. His name alone was a very good advertisement and some boys came because of that. Although very much an expert in the somewhat rarified field of early music, his tastes were broad and music was performed from the fifteenth to the twentieth century. Charles' own tastes did not really extend beyond 1945 and he had little interest in 'light music' of any kind. Nevertheless, the atmosphere was a good deal more relaxed than in his predecessor's day. He brought with him from Eton 'a fine violin player and teacher' Timothy Eustace and before long there was a second orchestra. Wind playing was rather better under Jack Hindmarch and when Pat Purcell arrived 'they were given their head and music at last became a joyous experience'.[12]

More adventurous music started to emerge by the 1970s and Pat Purcell's son Simon ran a highly successful band with four of the members – Quentin Hayes, Dave Lee, Max Winter, and Simon himself – going on to 'use their skills in the very tough world of professional music'. Simon received a parliamentary award for his service to jazz in education in the spring of 2006.[13]

Many people, not just pupils, acknowledged a debt to Charles, for learning a great deal about 'music' and singing in general under his baton, both at the College and in the town choral society. There were, too, excellent keyboard performers from his time. Thomas Trotter became the city of Birmingham organist in 1983, and Michael Reed (inherited from Leonard Blake's day) worked for a while with Andrew Lloyd-Webber before becoming a freelance conductor. Two outstanding choral concerts are still remembered from this time. The first was the *Messiah* in Charles' second year when Malvern was introduced to James Bowman's counter-tenor expertise, and a performance of another of Handel's oratorios, *Semele*, with the town choral society.

Above: Isabella Petzinka (6. 2008–12) performing at the annual concerto concert, 2011.

Left: Wind ensemble rehearsal, conducted by Stephen Spanyol (Staff 1990–2012). (Photograph by Jon Willcocks)

Opposite: Aaron King (SH 2009–14). (Photograph by Jon Willcocks)

Opposite far right: The Chamber Choir conducted by Iain Sloan at Upton Parish Church, 2008.

Neil Page (1976–85) came from Hurstpierpoint and brought with him a huge amount of energy and enthusiasm. A good singer with a fine tenor voice he was also a 'brass' man and a very useful performer on the trombone and euphonium. He was for a while a member of the masters' Jazz Band playing the trombone. He certainly meant to 'put Malvern on the musical map' and spent a lot of his time visiting various prep schools, most particularly cathedral schools. From them and other schools he encouraged many talented instrumentalists to come to Malvern, a lot of them as music scholars, exhibitioners or on bursaries. Gradually he built up a body of skilled players able to accept challenges from hitherto untried composers, for example performances of *Rodeo* by Aaron Copeland and *Mass for Choir and Wind Instruments* by Stravinsky.

Page liked to give performances of big works like Verdi's *Requiem* and Carl Orff's *Carmina Burana*. His energetic conducting of the *Dies Irae* in the Winter Gardens caused a rather longer than usual general pause when he accidently catapulted his music and stand into the laps of the first desk of the first violins.[14] In every sense the subject expanded. It was perhaps significant that there were now specialist teachers for all instruments. The Preparatory Schools' Arts Day was started, together with visits by instrumental groups to these schools.

Neil Page was part of the first team (together with Bill Denny and Simon Bennett) to take a production, *The Beggar's Opera*, to the Edinburgh Festival Fringe. The same team were involved in a production of Gilbert and Sullivan's *The Yeomen of the Guard*. Typically he found a song from it that had not been used since Sullivan's day, and put it in the production. After the brief directorship of Michael Brown, who is remembered for a fine performance of J. S. Bach's *St John Passion* in 1987, the baton fell to Rory Boyle who now returned to Malvern,[15] having been originally brought to the school by Charles Brett to be the junior keyboard man (soon joined by Robin Wedderburn, another Etonian, to be head of strings). Another powerful presence, Boyle was popular, full of fun and like Page keen to popularise music in the school. His main interest was in composition, a skill at which he excelled, and some of his pieces were first performed by members of the College and the Malvern Choral Society. He was also engaged in writing music for larger audiences. Although his deepest interest lay in contemporary music, he enjoyed most other types and was a very clear performance-conductor.[16] He had a technique all his own for getting people through the written paper for the Associated Board Grade 5 Theory Exam. It is said that he never had a failure.

Right: *Dido & Aeneas*, 2013.

He was involved as conductor and trainer with the College's musicals *Cabaret* and *Guys and Dolls*, and they were performed with panache and style. Eventually Rory's inner need to compose persuaded him to leave Malvern, and he subsequently settled in Ayrshire where he writes music and teaches composition at The Royal Conservatoire of Scotland in Glasgow.

Boyle's successor was the distinguished singer Iain Sloan, who had studied at Goldsmith's College London and under Dr Paul Steinitz – the Bach specialist – while singing with the London Bach Society. His teaching career started at Christ's College in Blackheath and while there he trained boys for the English National Opera. He subsequently moved to The Downs, Wraxall in Bristol. At both these schools the musical part of the curriculum had to be built up from almost scratch. His move to Malvern accompanied the merger in 1992 when Iain came to teach at Hillstone while also conducting the College Chamber Choir and teaching some GCSE music. He took over from Rory Boyle in 2000. The department was strong, particularly on the instrumental side and Chapel choral tradition. The school choral society, however, had effectively folded and Iain successfully revived it, attracting members from all parts of the Malvern community. It has been of particular value in enabling pupils to play and sing alongside professional musicians. The quality of the musical side of the school went from strength to strength in these years. The range of musical activity could be seen in the number of ensembles. In addition to the Chapel choir there was a chamber choir, a school symphony orchestra, a chamber orchestra, jazz bands, a concert band intermediate ensemble and various Sixth Form small ensembles. Apart from the formal concerts at Christmas, and in the summer, there were a plethora of musical events, one of the most popular being the informal concerts held in the newly refurbished St Edmund's Hall. The annual concerto concert, held at the end of the summer term, comprised performances from the most gifted musical leavers. The standard was immensely high and the repertoire more advanced than in earlier years. A glance through the musical reports in *The Malvernian* show that in addition to the great classical composers there

Above: Rory Boyle, Director of Music, 1988–2000.

Below: Iain Sloan, Director of Music, 2000–14.

Distinguished trumpeter **Michael Laird** (1. 1956–61) studied music at the Vienna Musik Akademie and the Royal College of Music in London. He was a member of the Philip Jones Brass Ensemble before involvement with the Academy of St Martin in the Fields and the English Chamber Orchestra. He has performed and recorded most of the works of Bach and Handel. He is a fellow of the Royal College of Music and was professor there for fifteen years. 'None of this would have been possible for me without Leonard's help. He was an inspiration and I am extremely grateful to him.'

Thomas Trotter (SH 1970–74) went from Malvern to be organ scholar of King's College, Cambridge and since 1983 has been Birmingham City organist and visiting professor at the Royal College of Music, London. He has performed around the world. (Photo by Adrian Burrows)

James Vivian FRCO (2. 1990–92) was a music scholar at Malvern College and organ scholar of King's College, Cambridge (1993–97). After posts at Lincoln Cathedral and the historic Temple Church in London, he became the organist at St George's Windsor.

The baritone **Quentin Hayes** (5. 1972–76) studied at Dartington Arts College, the Guildhall School of Music and the National Opera Studio. From 1999 to 2004 he was on contract as a principal artist at the Royal Opera House, Covent Garden and has undertaken a wide repertoire of roles at leading opera houses and festivals, throughout Europe and the United Kingdom. (Performing in Verdi's *Macbeth*; photograph by Lena Zorn)

Oliver Rundell (3/9. 1991–96) was an organ scholar at Corpus Christi College, Cambridge where he studied music, and trained at the National Opera Studio in London. Since 2002 he has been a full-time member of the music staff at Scottish Opera, and has worked on more than twenty productions.

John Graham-Hall (9. 1969–73) studied at King's College, Cambridge and the Royal College of Music. He sings regularly with all the major British and European opera companies.

were works by Arnold, Bartok, Faure, Finzi, Holst, Shostakovich, Tippett, Vaughan Williams and many more.

A number of innovations further strengthened school music. The introduction of the House Music Competition in 2004 has been very successful, with 200–300 competitors taking part each year. A musicians' dinner was introduced for those who had contributed to the musical life of the school and a number of continental tours took place to Holland, Belgium and to Paris where the choir were able to sing in Notre Dame. The introduction of termly community concerts in 2010, open to local residents, has proved popular, as have the unplugged concerts when pupils are able to play contemporary music. The revived annual Preparatory Schools' Arts Days opened up links between the College musicians and potential scholars in the preparatory schools. The greater role of the arts was well represented by the partnership of the Music and Art departments in support of Drama and especially the major school play. Two much admired musicals were *West Side Story* (described by Iain as a musical voyage of discovery) and *Les Misérables*. Three memorable productions of *Dido and Aeneas* took place with moving portrayals of Dido by Sophie Lerman, Camilla Darlow and Verity Bramson and few will forget the emotional impact of Verdi's *Requiem* in 2009. The Chapel choir and chamber choir have remained strong and the great set pieces in Chapel, like the annual remembrance service and the carol concerts, are consistently outstanding. The College has been blessed with a number of excellent musical scholars in recent years. Between 2001 and 2011 some twenty-two students went on to study music at university or in conservatoires, including five choral scholarships to Cambridge and two organ scholarships. Two of these notable musicians are Edward Nesbit and Alice Howick. Alice has used her musical gifts to great effect:

> During my last year at Cambridge I had the chance, through a friend, to visit Palestine to take part in a Baroque Festival organised by Al Kamandjati music school, a French-Palestinian association which gives music lessons to children in cities, villages and refugee camps across Palestine. Palestinian children grow up in an environment of fear, uncertainty and poverty and I could see immediately the amazing effect that learning a musical instrument had on the children of the school.
>
> I was so impressed by the work that Al Kamandjati was doing that when I discovered that there was a vacancy for a violin teacher there I immediately applied and a couple of months after I left Cambridge I was living in Ramallah, travelling all over the West Bank each week teaching 40 children aged 6–16 to play the violin. I stayed there for two years before moving to Beirut to direct Al Kamandjati's project in the Palestinian refugee camps of Lebanon for a year. I've now been living in London for two years, teaching music in schools and training as a music workshop leader, but have kept very close links with musicians in Palestine, returning several times each year to give concerts and workshops for schoolchildren.

Above left: Edward Nesbit (5. 1999–2004) graduated from Cambridge University in June 2007 with a First in music, scoring the highest mark in the university. This was followed by a masters and a fellowship at the Guildhall. He won the first Verbier Festival Academy Composer Prize, leading to a commission for the Ebene Quartet, premiered in the 2013 Verbier Festival. His works have been widely performed by distinguished orchestras in venues including Wigmore Hall, Royal Festival Hall and Barbican Hall.

Above right: Alice Howick. (4L, 8. 2001–05)

Right: Art in the Main Building, in the 1960s. (©Michael Ward / ArenaPAL)

Far right: Bill Denny, Director of Art 1970–86, with Sir Osbert Lancaster, at the opening of the Lindsay Arts Centre at Commemoration 1974.

ART AND DESIGN

The first significant reference to art in the College in the centenary history comes near the end with a valedictory to H. T. Gillmore, who retired in 1938 after thirty-nine years as art master. Artistically in the tradition of Landseer, he was described as 'a finely built man, with obvious Viking ancestry, fair curly hair, an untidy moustache and [in] his old age he grew a thick beard and looked more of a Highland chieftain than ever. As a young man he ran very wild – wine, women, and song – all of which he enjoyed with uninhibited gusto, and most of all poaching. He loved to tell stories of the tricks he had played on gamekeepers and police in his lusty youth.'[17] He clearly had at least some influence, for *The Malvernian* of 1942 recorded the death of Thomas Edmund Chadwick (SH 1926–30), killed at the battle of El Alamein in October 1942, describing him as 'in all probability the best artist which the school has ever produced'. Chadwick was a

Right: Painting by Ore Adegbola (EH 2009–13).

LIFE IN ABUNDANCE

noted engraver who had won the first prize at the International Exhibition of Lithography and Wood Engravings in Chicago.[18]

During the headmastership of Donald Lindsay, Art achieved a higher status. 'Gillie's' successors Harry Fabian Ware and William Wilkins (OM) enabled an expansion of the subject to include sculpture and pottery. Fabian Ware, Head of Art 1945–63, has been described as 'an archetypal painter, who looked the part of a Bohemian artist, and a great character, inspirational to those boys interested in Art. His own paintings were "bold, fauvist style"'. When Ralph Blumenau began teaching history of art in General periods, 'Harry strongly disapproved of my doing so because I could not paint myself. I was, he said in his usual blunt way, "like a eunuch teaching people how to make love."' But he recalls that the meetings of the Art Society were among the liveliest in the school:

> I only got to know Harry Fabian-Ware and his delightful wife, Armyne, through the Art Society, which met in their house in Abbey Road on certain Sunday evenings. At each

Upper left: Painting by Godfrey Lui (7. 2009–13). (Photograph by Jon Willcocks)

Lower left: Painting by Pia von Oppen (4. 2004–06)

Below: Painting by Margarita Cesar (6. 2008–13).

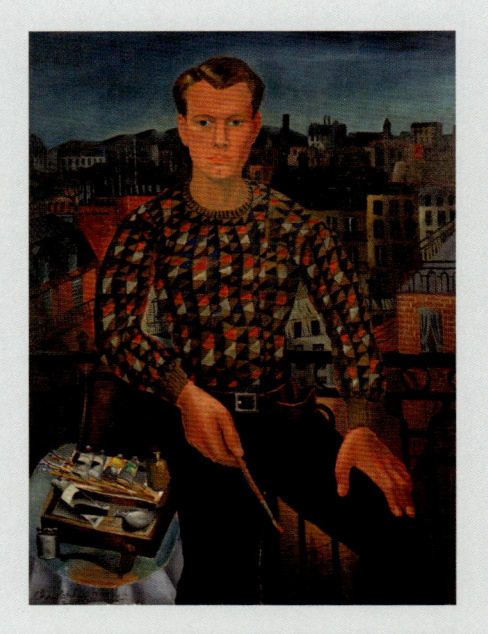

Malvern can claim a very distinguished artist in **John Christopher (Kit) Wood** who arrived in Malvern in 1918, staying for one and a half years. Due to an attack of polio three years before, which had left him with a limp and recurrent pain, John Rothenstein records 'that he was allowed to work in special conditions, lying for instance, on a couch instead of sitting at a desk. No longer able to play cricket or golf, he played the flute and sketched'. After school he set up a studio in Paris where Wood valued his contact with Picasso above everything else. He was closely associated with British avant-garde painting during the 1920s as well as promoting the 'St Ives School'. Although he killed himself at the age of twenty-nine, the body of work he left behind secured him a distinguished place in the history of twentieth-century British painting. He will be best remembered for his poetic series of harbour paintings produced in France and St Ives in the final two years of his life.[i] (Left: *Self Portrait*, 1927, courtesy of Kettle's Yard, University of Cambridge)

'The terrible irony of reading the First World War poets in the environment of the Memorial Library, and the appalling wartime experiences recalled by two OTC instructors, affected **Patrick Hayman** (1. 1929–32) for life. So for a gentle, pacific man began a life-long interest in the realities of war and violence. He lived in New Zealand until 1947 where he was closely associated with a group of young artists who developed New Zealand's first indigenous Modernism. He then alternated between St Ives and London until his death in 1988. Examples of his work are found all over the world.'[ii] Major retrospectives were held at the South Bank Centre in 1990 and 2004.

Above: *Matinee* by Jonathan Wateridge (2. 1985–90).

Above: *The Bend in the River* by Jim Whitty (3. 1984–88).

meeting, at which beer and cigarettes were provided, three members took it in turns to introduce a picture they liked or admired: vigorous debate then followed, often stoked by the strong opinions of Harry, whom Armyne attempted to rein in with cries of 'Oh Harry, Harry…' We talked, of course, about everything under the sun … just like art students or undergraduates and, as we walked back to our houses, we felt exhilarated, free and full of intellectual and creative excitement.[19]

William Wilkins, Head of Art 1963–67, was a striking contrast to Harry: 'neatly dressed in the style of a country gentleman'. Nor was his own style at all fauvist – his own paintings were neat and precise; but he was a fine artist and had some success as such outside the school. He showed an interest in making the subject more appealing to boys who were not already artists. Sculpture began in these years under the direction of Hilary Carruthers, who 'got the boys to produce some fine work'. Her successor Anne Gilmour 'was young and very glamorous, and boys took up sculpture who might not otherwise have done so!'

Towards the end of Donald Lindsay's headmastership the decision was made to build a new art building, to replace the archaic arrangements in which the department was in two locations in the Main Building: painting and graphic design at the end of the Grundy, and

Philip Jones (8. 1946–51) was much influenced by Fabian Ware. He was described by *The Times* as 'one of the most distinguished and individual British painters of the generation born in the 1930s'. His landscapes were part Romantic, part 'free-form' abstraction. He wrote: 'My message is that of what I see beneath the surface, whether in front of, below or above the visual plane. I reflect on the wonders of what we have been given and the landscape both urban and rural at which Turner marvelled in paint and Wordsworth in print'.[iii] (Right: *Broken Landforms*, 1992, courtesy of the family of Philip Jones)

Above right: *Girls Having Coffee* by Julian Bailey (1. 1976–81).

Above: *Burghley West* by Jonathan Myles-Lea (9. 1985–87), distinguished painter of country houses and historic buildings.

Above: *Titan II* by Guy Combes (SH 1984–89), wildlife artist.

ceramics in the other wing next to Big School. Martin Rogers enthusiastically supported the idea and the College Council gave permission for the purchase of Douglas House, a girls' school which had recently closed and which was conveniently situated to the north of the existing campus. It was quickly decided that a new building would best suit the requirements of a modern Art department and the imaginative designs created by Bill Denny, the newly appointed Director of Art, provided the basis for Norton's construction. The building was erected at a cost of £100,000 and opened by Sir Osbert Lancaster at Commemoration in 1974. At the time it was considered to be one of the most impressive artistic facilities in the public-school world. One observer writes:

> In my opinion Art at Malvern only really took off under Bill Denny – his particular genius was in not imposing any particular way of making art: he discovered what was in each boy and helped them to paint what and how *they* wanted to paint. He was not precious either: for example, if boys wanted to copy a picture they saw in a magazine, that was all right with him. But at the same time other boys were producing really original and exciting work, and in an enormous variety of styles.[20]

Right: Yeng Yeng Shang (8. 2008–10) with her painting, which was exhibited in the Tate.

Above: Sculpture by Gabrielle Hogan (3. 2009–12).

Bill Denny had trained at Goldsmith's and taught at Haileybury before coming to Malvern, where he was the first Director of Art from 1970 to 1986. His view of art was catholic and he encouraged a wide variety of artistic forms, including photography and print-making. Under his influence the first art scholarships were offered and history of art was introduced, becoming a very popular A-level option. The annual art history trips to Florence, Venice, Paris and Rome became an established feature of the intellectual and cultural life of the school.

He was ably assisted by Phil Heath, described as 'a very fine potter – making not only very original pottery and porcelain figures himself – his taste was somewhat Victorian and on the sentimental side, but he was a successful artist outside of Malvern College'.[21] Heath was succeeded in 1984 by an outstanding ceramicist Cindy Jones, a gifted teacher with a high sense of her profession. Woe betide any ignoramus who described ceramics as pottery, and at least one senior master was to experience her wrath when he mistook one of her creations for an ashtray when a Common Room party was being held in the art school. Under her influence a series of outstanding ceramic artists were inspired. By the 1980s there was no doubt that the Art department had become one of the most dynamic in the school, attracting large numbers of pupils and producing imaginative work of the highest standard.

In 1986 Bill Denny became the housemaster of No. 9 and, after a brief stewardship by John Brown, Tim Newsholme became Director of Art. Trained at Colchester, Birmingham and East Anglia University, he is a gifted portrait and landscape painter who maintained and built on the fine reputation of the department. Attracted by the outstanding facilities and the high status of art at Malvern, he has been described 'as an English impressionist' with a particular preference for oil painting, although he is also an able exponent of print-making, sculpture and an enthusiast for the history of art. As the school moved into the new century the Art department was clearly popular and had an outstanding reputation for results, particularly in the IB. Work from the school has been placed on their website as exemplars for the world-wide course. A major innovation has been the creation of an artistic 'circus' for the Foundation Year when each pupil spends one term each on history of art, painting and ceramics. For a number of years the subject was in an aesthetic block in which pupils had to study art, music, drama or technology up to GCSE. Although this is no longer compulsory, it performed its central function of establishing the arts as a respected and popular part of the curriculum and the numbers studying these subjects remain very high. The Art department at Malvern had the honour of being the only one in the country allowed to offer a post-A level foundation course performing the same function as similar courses in established further education institutes.[22] The results were spectacular. The numbers going on to art college or following architecture have continued to rise.

Tim Newsholme was also instrumental in acquiring one of the first sets of Victorian frescos for the College. Painted by George Frederick Watts they had been constructed in London and came into the ownership of the Somers family. They were in danger of being moved from their temporary home at Eastnor Castle and Newsholme's effective negotiations acquired them for the College, where they now adorn the walls of Big School. The frescos showing the elements had to be broken apart and reassembled by skilled craftsmen and, apart from their decorative effect, have attracted a series of visitors who enjoy the work of this distinguished artist.

Since the 1970s Malvern has educated a distinguished range of artistic talent. Among the painters have been Julian Bailey, figurative and landscape painter, winner of the Turner Gold Medal at the Royal Academy, and collected by The National Trust and HRH The Prince of Wales; Jonathan Myles-Lea, considered the country's greatest painter of country houses and historic buildings. He is also a broadcaster, and has worked closely with his mentor and friend Sir Roy Strong; Jonathan Wateridge, artist and cartoonist for the *Spectator*; James Whitty; and Guy Coombes.

DRAMA

The dramatic arts had a patchy beginning at Malvern. From early days extracts from English, French and Greek plays were performed on Speech Days but beyond that there was hardly any acting at all. An exception is recorded in 1910 when the boys put on a performance of the melodrama *The Bells* to raise funds for the College Mission.

As with Music it was during the Preston headmastership that regular Drama productions began. After 1918 there were some house plays and other occasional performances which prepared the way for the school plays that began in 1929 – 'cautiously at first, with small casts and the women's parts played by women'. But by 1932, for Shaw's *St Joan*, the main part was played by a boy. These early school plays took place at the Speech Day weekend in the summer term leaving the autumn term free for a masters' play, which also began in 1929. They moved in 1932 to Shrove Tuesday as part of what had always been an evening of entertainment.

Below left: *Henry IV Part 1*, Malvern College Dramatic Society, December 1948. (Courtesy of Peter Southgate (6. 1946–50))

Below right: *L'Avare*, by Molière, June 1949. (Courtesy of Peter Southgate)

Above: Simon Bennett, first Director of Drama 1973–84.

Above: Nigel Turner, Director of Drama, 1984–2003.

As part of the greater role given to the arts in Lindsay's time theatrical activity expanded, partly because Lindsay was himself a great lover of the theatre. A Saturday Night Club produced *HMS Pinafore* in 1953 and the same year saw the start of regular Junior productions. At Easter in 1959 *The Vigil* was movingly performed in Chapel. School House took the initiative of putting on a house play for the whole school, which led directly to the institution in 1960 of the annual House Play Competition in which the entries are entirely the work of the pupils – the first victory went to No. 8 for a play written by its producer. At about this time expeditions to the theatre in Stratford, Birmingham and Cheltenham became a familiar part of the school's programme. Some of the school plays were highly acclaimed; for example, the November 1966 production of *Under Milk Wood*, which was described as 'brilliantly staged and manifestly hugely enjoyed by the actors'. One of those actors[23] recalled another production he was involved in at this time:

> One scene in *Becket* was remarkable in that the Girls' College staff actually allowed it to be performed, since it showed one of their girls playing a French prostitute in bed with King Henry! At the start of the scene, the king and the French girl were hidden behind a scenery cut-out of a tent, and the scene began with Becket entering the tent. As I approached the cut-out it would be pulled up into the flies and then at the end of the scene it would be lowered again. At the dress rehearsal everything went according to plan until we left the tent. As we did so, the cut-out descended with agonising slowness – it seemed to take for ever. John Daniel made it clear that the stage crew had to make sure that it came down much more quickly. The following night the cut-out came crashing down out of the flies, missing us by inches. It smashed into the stage, bounced about 6 inches into the air and split up the middle. The College boys on the stage crew were acting under the supervision of a professional stage hand from the Festival Theatre, whose response when asked about what had happened was 'Well, he said let it go, so I let it go!'

In 1973 Martin Rogers, with the full backing of George Sayer, the then Head of English, was bold enough to appoint Malvern's first Director of Drama, Simon Bennett. The aim was to give drama a higher profile in the life of the College. Some members of staff at that time remained sceptical about its value, although the routine of an early autumn production at the Festival Theatre was well established, as was the house play competition in the early part of the spring term. Over the next ten years the old Gymnasium was converted into an auditorium and stage for drama with an extension to the rear for green rooms and the retention of the spectators' gallery. Raked removable seating was installed, and the new facility was appropriately named the Rogers Theatre. At the other end of the College the space behind Big School was turned into a theatre workshop. These additional facilities enabled the College to widen the scope of the Preparatory Schools' Arts Day, and draw aspiring thespians to stage productions in either of the venues over a long weekend.

Throughout this period, the number of productions at all levels in the school increased, some of which were performed in the open air, and the programme at the Festival Theatre expanded to put on two plays on alternate nights from Wednesday to Saturday in the same week. Among memorable performances were Wilde's *An Ideal Husband*, Anouilh's *Ring Round the Moon*, and Miller's *The Crucible*. Female members of the cast were drawn from Ellerslie or Malvern Girls' College. A production of *Iolanthe* represented the increasingly close cooperation between the Art, Drama and Music departments, and this was reinforced further by a production of Milton's *Comus*, which marked Malvern's debut at the Edinburgh Festival, having been first performed at Eastnor Castle in front of the host family and an invited guest list. Regular meetings of the department heads and other interested staff met in an arts forum aiming to give keen and

Above and left: From the 2014 House Play competition.

talented artists a deserved status in the College. A practical acknowledgement of this was shown in the creation of the arts tie.

Upon Simon Bennett's retirement in 1984 Nigel Turner became Director of Drama and in the following nineteen years was to direct some forty productions, including three that were taken to the Edinburgh Fringe. His philosophy of drama was based on 'its practical significance which balanced the human urge to compete with the need to cooperate; drama was ideally suited to reconcile these instincts, teaching respect for the work of each individual'. Dramatic engagement can be seen as 'an empathetic exercise that extends and deepens our humanity – playing roles is, of course, to gain understanding of the complexity of human feelings and motivations.'[24]

His arrival coincided with the completion of the Green Room extension to the Rogers Theatre. Before this actors had to change in No. 6 and make their way across to the theatre. In the following years, with help from the OM society, the stage lighting system was completely modernised, enabling a greater range of theatrical possibilities. Perhaps the most radical innovation in Nigel Turner's directorship was the incorporation of drama into the timetable. This initiative owed much to Roy Chapman, an enthusiastic supporter,[25] who took the opportunity offered by the introduction of the new GCSEs in 1986 to propose a practical aesthetic block consisting of art, drama, music and technology, with pupils having to study one of these subjects up to GCSE. In preparation for their choice, all first-year pupils would experience each subject in an FY 'circus' – drama for the first time acquired equality with other subjects at this level and proved to be a popular choice for generations of Malvernians.

The house plays continued but after one year Nigel Turner ended the competitive element, the aim being to foster more of a festival approach. Over the years the standard varied and genre and mood changed but by the early 1990s it was widely accepted that the festival was producing drama of real quality, perhaps influenced by the recent arrival of full co-education. It became common for parents to attend which would inevitably produce some tensions when innocent sensibilities were offended by some adolescent indiscretion. In recent years the competitive element has been reintroduced, although without an outside adjudicator and with a number of awards rather than just one cup.[26] Crucially, the annual event continued to be enjoyed by pupils who put great efforts into ensuring that their play won large and enthusiastic audiences. It was pleasing to note that the rather narrow support given in the earlier days of the competition has

MALVERN COLLEGE

given way to a theatrical audience much more interested in quality than simple house loyalty. Turner insisted that each house had to provide its own technical crew, which provided high-quality training for future school productions, and a school prize was introduced for theatre technical work. The festival also revealed unexpected talents both in acting and in play-writing.

The major school production took place four weeks into the autumn term, giving precious little rehearsal time. Nigel Turner negotiated with the Festival Theatre to extend this period to just before half-term and later to a slot in November. The Junior play and the Commem play were now supplemented by major performances from the Lower Sixth, known for a while as the May Plays. These included acclaimed performances of *Equus*, *The Bald Prima Donna* and *Krapp's Last Tape* – directed by Lower Sixth pupils. In 1987 the school took *The Beggar's Opera* to the Edinburgh Fringe followed two years later by *Oh! What a Lovely War*, originally performed as the major school play in 1988. In Turner's opinion this was a most memorable production, not least for the haunting role of Douglas Haig played by Tim Young who effectively recruited in full regalia along the Royal Mile. Other memorable performances came with the Junior production of *The Royal Hunt of the Sun* in 1990 that took full advantage of improved facilities, particularly lighting, to create a stunning stage set. Another memorable production was *Guys and Dolls*, also taken to the Fringe in 1996, staged brilliantly with Jonathan Ellis's imaginative set designs. A second production of *The Beggar's Opera*, this time in the Rogers Theatre, had great poignancy, as it followed a most tragic accident when an Upper Sixth boy, Julian Elwell, had been killed in a car accident. The cast, many of whom were close personal friends of the victim, insisted on dedicating the production to his memory, incorporating a silent tribute without in any way affecting the spirited and bawdy nature of the production.

Following the merger in 1992 another innovation closely allied to drama was introduced, namely lessons in speech and drama. It quickly became a much appreciated addition with fifty or more pupils regularly embracing the varied aspects of the programme: acting, verse and prose and, most popular of all, public speaking. Under the excellent direction of Rosemary Graham, Mary Constable and Rosie Turner, pupils sat the LAMDA examinations and participated at festivals in Worcester and Cheltenham. This area was particularly useful for students for whom English was a second language.

Since Nigel Turner's retirement in 2003, Malvern has been fortunate to obtain the services of two more outstanding directors of Drama: Neil Smith, for an all too brief tenure of four years, and since 2007 Keith Packham. Memorable productions have included *Coram Boy*, *Les Misérables*, *The Boy Friend*, *A Midsummer Night's Dream* and *South Pacific*. Keith Packham has reorganised the dramatic structure of the year to accommodate changing pressures brought on by the examinations industry. In October there is a performance by the Malvern College Dramatic Society – a group of elite actors chosen from the Upper Sixth, and Remove thespians enter the Shakespeare Schools' Festival. The main school play follows this in November, the actors coming from the Lower Sixth and the Hundred. There are productions by the Remove in March and the Foundation Year in June. The house play competition is in February and AS/A2/IB academic drama in April.

There is little doubt that the arts have flourished in the United Kingdom since the Second World War. A combination of generous state subsidies, accessibility through the modern media (particularly the BBC) and a more educated and cultured population has seen an explosion in festivals, exhibitions and musical forms. Malvern has kept pace with this change, and as the school approaches its anniversary the arts have never been more central to the educational life of the College. It is therefore no surprise to find more and more former pupils continuing their cultural education into professional life as artists, musicians and actors and even more into the world of the media and advertising. Preston's wider vision has been in large part fulfilled.

Above: Keith Packham, Director of Drama from 2007.

Opposite from top, left to right,: *A Midsummer Night's Dream*, Senior play 2011; *Daisy Pulls it Off*, Malvern College Dramatic Society production 2012; *South Pacific*, Senior play 2010; *The Sound of Music*, Senior play 2012; *Les Misérables*, Senior play 2008; *Wyrd Sisters*, Foundation Year play 2010; *The Government Inspector*, Remove play 2012; *Nicholas Nickleby*, Senior play 2009; *Private Peaceful*, Foundation Year drama production, 2013.

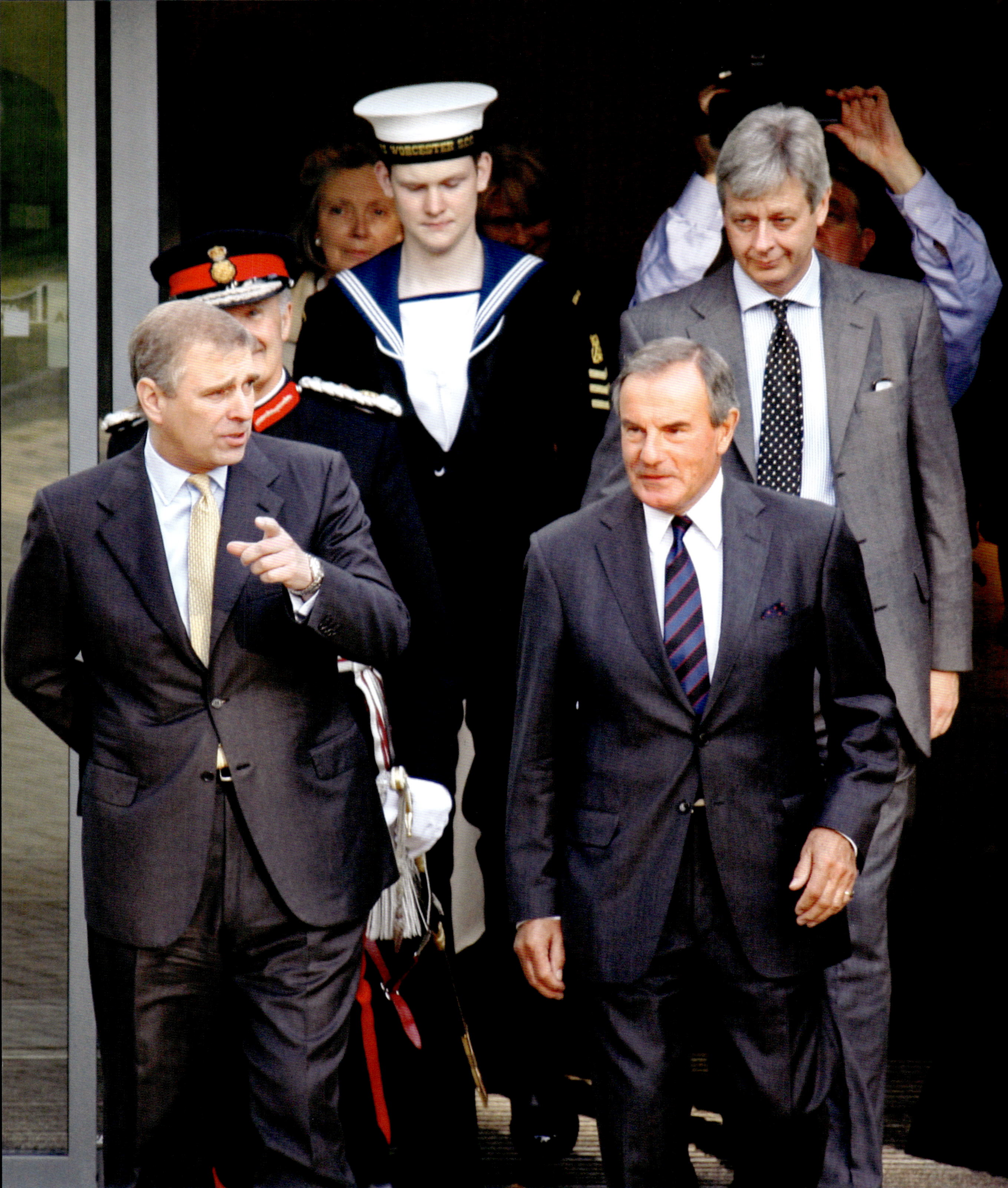

15

Embracing the future

Malvern was fortunate to attract such an experienced headmaster as Antony Clark. Born in South Africa and educated at St Andrew's College, he studied in Rhodes and Cambridge where he met his future wife Brigitte. After an uncomfortable period of national service in the South African army[1] he followed the family tradition of teaching and took a post at Westerford. Following a brief period in the financial world he became Headmaster of St Joseph's College, a Catholic Marist school with a very mixed racial and religious profile, at the very time that the apartheid system was collapsing. After a successful time at St Joseph's he was appointed Headmaster of his old school St Andrew's, where he served for eight years before accepting the post of Headmaster of Gresham's School in Norfolk. Coming to Malvern in 2008,[2] he inherited a school that had been greatly refashioned by his predecessors, but which had experienced some uncertain years in the interregnum following the retirement of Hugh Carson. The new Headmaster made an immediate impression on his new school by his courteous consideration and quiet reflection. Impressive in stature and possessing that indefinable quality 'presence', he commanded the school with apparent ease, although behind the public image was an immensely conscientious and hard-working man.

It was evident that the central concern for the new Headmaster was to focus on rebalancing the intake of pupils to arrest the long-standing decline in Foundation Year numbers. A marketing committee already existed and over the first four years of his headmastership Antony Clark worked closely with this body to pursue a range of initiatives to win support at thirteen-plus. This involved meeting as many preparatory school headmasters as possible, both those new to Malvern and those who had perhaps let the connection wither. Major sporting events like the annual cross-country race and the Preparatory Schools' Arts Day proved popular with potential parents and pupils. Happily, the fruits of earlier planning were now harvested. With the opening of the new Sports Complex in October 2009 Malvern could showcase one of the most impressive facilities in the country. This proved very attractive to potential parents and to preparatory school headmasters. At the same time two new boarding houses were opened with excellent facilities and with an elegant façade that skilfully matched the older campus.[3] HRH the Duke of York opened these new additions to the school on a perfect autumn day to the plaudits of an enthusiastic school. In the evening, following a celebratory dinner in the new Gryphon Room (the former swimming pool converted into an entertaining venue), a number of distinguished sportsmen and women enthralled the guests with anecdotes from their careers. Within four years the numbers in the Foundation Year had reached over a hundred for the first time in twenty years.

The Headmaster sought for greater cohesiveness within what had become a somewhat diverse school, where differences between houses were perhaps too marked. He was concerned

Opposite: Royal touring party at the opening of the new boarding houses and Sports Complex in October 2009. (Photograph by Xin Pang Walker)

Above: Antony Clark, Headmaster since 2008.

Right: Pupils watching Prince Andrew's departure by helicopter following the opening of the new boarding houses and Sports Complex in 2009. (Photograph by Xin Pang Walker)

that all pupils should feel part of the common purpose of the community and encouraged participatory activities such as the Lower School Council, which enabled the younger pupils to express their views. He also actively encouraged the sixth formers in senior positions to be more reactive to matters of social isolation or evident unhappiness. The team of Chapel Prefects, together with the Heads of House and the elected School Council (formerly called the Sixth Form Council), were encouraged to play a much more dynamic role in the affairs of the school. They were left in no doubt that their personal conduct should be beyond reproach and that they had to perform as ambassadors, role models and active agents of social improvement within the school. All pupils who sought high office had to formally apply, their letters of application

Right: Michael Vaughan in the new Cricket Centre. (Photograph by Xin Pang Walker)

Above: The Sports Complex and Gryphon Room. (Photograph by Jon Willcocks)

stating why they wanted such a role and their views on the atmosphere and problems within the school. Candidates were shortlisted and interviewed. Those chosen would then be carefully prepared for their new role with training sessions on leadership, counselling and ways of tackling the myriad difficulties they might encounter. Like Preston and Lindsay, Antony Clark is committed to both academic strength and to an education that develops the full personality. Co-curricular activities have never been so plentiful or so encouraged.

Malvern had prospered as a British school that celebrated its international character. The IB attracted students from all over the world and one of the aims over the next few years was to build on this strength. A key element of this was to be through sharing the experiences and cultures of those who came to study in the school. In the last few years German students performed a play in German, and students have run cafés where their own national food is served. A regular highlight has been Culturama – which developed out of Culture Shock 2000 – an evening 'fair' celebrating cultural diversity through food, drink, dance and song. One current pupil records, 'the very multi-cultural aspect of the College and the diversity within it is what truly makes Malvern a community. To have friendship groups consisting of people from all four corners of the globe is a truly unique experience.'[4]

Below: The new houses – No. 7 and Ellerslie House. (Photograph by Xin Pang Walker)

Malvern had been contemplating links with a school abroad for some time when out of the blue a Hong Kong syndicate approached the College in November 2011. They were seeking a partner for a private school that they were building in Qingdao, in the province of Shandong, China. Early scepticism was overcome when the three leading figures came to Malvern – the Headmaster recalls being impressed by their credentials, personalities and evident vision. In January 2012 the Chinese entrepreneurs contacted the College to say that they had been so engaged by what they had seen at Malvern that they wished to establish their

Right: The Lower Sixth German play, *Die Physiker*, 2010.

Below: Scenes from Culturama.

partnership with the College. The proposal was that the new school, which they were building on a site neighbouring a private university, would franchise the name and seek help in appointments and ensuring 'quality control'. In time the College could expect a sizeable revenue stream from its new partner, and there were many possibilities for cultural interaction. Indeed, in the first academic year two members of the Common Room took up posts in Qingdao,[5] and six former pupils went to assist while also learning Mandarin. In September 2012 the school was formally opened by Antony Clark, who stated that 'it is thought to be the first purpose-built international secondary school for Chinese nationals that is backed by a leading independent UK school and licensed by the Chinese authorities'. Pupils at Malvern College Qingdao take a two-year A level programme as full boarders, following a foundation course, with a view to going on to further education in the US or UK. Subjects offered at the school include maths, further maths, physics, chemistry, biology and economics, with an ancillary liberal arts programme focusing on developing high-level English literacy and language skills. Antony Clark commented at the opening:

EMBRACING THE FUTURE

THE WIDER EDUCATION

(Photograph by Jon Willcocks)

233

MALVERN COLLEGE AND MORGAN MOTOR COMPANY

The College has a long association with the Morgan motor company through William Stephenson-Peach, the first teacher of engineering at Malvern College (1901–18) and a close associate of Henry Frederick Stanley Morgan. Between them, they assembled the first Morgan motorcar in the Engineering Workshops at the College. On 19 April 2009 more than one hundred three-wheelers celebrated the centenary of Morgan with a 'run' from Repton (where Stephenson-Peach had previously taught) concluding at Malvern College (via the Morgan factory). A commemorative plaque was unveiled on the old Engineering Workshops (now the Medical Centre).

The celebratory rally of Morgans, April 2009.

Engineering School, 1907.

Prototype of the Morgan car at Malvern College, 1909.

We know that a high percentage of Chinese parents want to send their children to universities in the US and the UK as a means of enhancing their longer-term career opportunities. We are delighted that Malvern College Qingdao is now formally opened and already providing an outstanding British education for its first cohort of pupils.

Above: *Doors of Malvern*, by Robert Nolan (2. 2005–10).

Meanwhile the plans for the immediate future of Malvern College were clear: the rebuilding and equipping of the science school, a new theatre complex, an all-weather pitch, athletic tracks, and of course a continuous programme of refurbishing the boarding houses and the existing school buildings.[6] The building plans are in furtherance of Lord MacLaurin's declared aim, now enshrined in the mission statement, for 'Malvern to be the best co-educational boarding and day school of its size and type in the country'.

After five years it is possible to give an initial assessment of the current headmastership. Calm, courteous leadership has been Antony Clark's hallmark. Decisions are never rushed but follow a period of considerate consultation. The senior management team has become more prominent with clearly defined areas of responsibility. Happily the school is full, with greater numbers than at any time in its history. New initiatives have been made to identify and stimulate the talented and gifted. Lessons have been lengthened to 55 minutes. Debating is now taught to all Foundation Year pupils and the school debating team has flourished. The growing role of IT is becoming more apparent in teaching as well as administration. The international mix is still

Opposite: Malvern College Qingdao.

Opposite: 'They also serve', the support staff of Malvern College, 2014.

CHAIRMEN OF THE COLLEGE COUNCIL

1863–91	The 6th Earl Beauchamp	1954–64	Admiral Sir William Tennant
1891–1905	G. E. Martin	1964–67	Sir John Wheeler-Bennett
1905–18	The 7th Earl Beauchamp	1967–76	Sir Deric Holland-Martin
1919–41	Lord Justice Lawrence	1976–94	Sir Stephen Brown
1941–49	The 9th Viscount Cobham	1994–2002	Nicholas Morris
1950–54	Sir Gerald Canny	2002–	Lord MacLaurin

there – some forty-one nationalities were studying in the school in 2013 – but with the growing numbers in the Lower School the British identity of the school is more apparent. Sport has been invigorated, not least through such initiatives as the partnership with Worcester County Cricket Club which has enabled a number of talented cricketers to develop, and a similar scheme for rugby players with the Worcester Warriors Rugby Club. The school has never been more aware of the significance of its alumni as a social network, source of stimulus and essential support for developments in the school. The Headmaster stated in 2014:

> The redevelopment of the Science school in particular offers a wonderful opportunity to rejuvenate Malvern's preeminence in science. As a mark of the strong affinity from Old Malvernians, parents and friends towards the College and the crucial role they now play within the school, approximately half of the funds required for this project have so far been obtained through philanthropic gifts. Central to the Science redevelopment was a significant gift from a very generous donor who wished to remain anonymous, made in honour of the Honourable Dato' Sri Mohd Najib bin Tun Haji Abdul Razak, Prime Minister of Malaysia and Old Malvernian (2. 1968–71), and the Razak family.

A Malvern College Parents' Society held its first meeting in June 2011 having been formed by 'a group of enthusiastic parents keen to organise a range of social events and activities to bring together an inclusive group of parents from the UK and overseas with both day and boarding pupils at the College'.[7] Another innovation in 2013 saw a writer in residence spending a week in the College, the first being OM James Delingpole, who gave masterclasses in the art of writing and attended classes, affably provoking debate and discussion.

Below right: Architect's impression of the new Razak Science Centre.
Below: The Honourable Dato' Sri Mohd Najib bin Tun Haji Abdul Razak, Prime Minister of Malaysia, addressing guests at a Malvern College reception held in Kuala Lumpur on 1 May 2014.

What of the current students? The great majority talk warmly of their teachers and lessons, the co-curricular programme and the easy relationships between adults and pupils and between the years in their houses. Generally compassionate, they are prepared to work closely with the staff to assist those in trouble. Tutors, at least in the Sixth Form, are greatly valued and for many become the most significant adult relationship within the school. They are relaxed in their social attitudes and with school going home every three weeks or so, have a social life that their forefathers would find truly astonishing. Inevitably, what criticism there is revolves around the remaining restrictions required by law and for communal living. They overwhelmingly go to university and most follow careers in finance, law and increasingly in the creative arts and media.[8]

So what would our founding fathers think of what we have done with their inheritance? They would rejoice at the health of the school and in its continued commitment to learning, faith and service, and in the celebration of the fuller life through games and the arts. No doubt these visionary and entrepreneurial men would take in their stride the novelties of co-education, changed curriculum and the international mix. They would also rejoice with us in that eternal dynamic of a school: the engagement of enthusiastic teachers with hungry young minds that find joy in sharing the experience of scholarship and enquiry. Their eyes would twinkle at the eternal foibles of the young.

In the centenary history the author hoped that the qualities for which Malvern stood would not fall victim to political attacks. As we reach our 150th anniversary that fear looks less threatening than in the 1960s, but new threats surround us, not least the view that education should only be valued for its economic utility, and an all-pervading culture that devalues the civilised life by being concerned with personal vanity and wealth. Schools like Malvern have to be in this world, for their pupils must be equipped with the skills with which to earn their living, but true educationalists must also counter destructive values, however benign they appear. That was the vision of our founders and the inspiration for generations of teachers who have happily communicated a wider vision to their charges. The loyalty, good works and decency of successive generations of Malvernians pays testimony to their success.

Below: The School House Leavers' informal photograph, 2014. The custom has developed in recent years that, in addition to the formal House photographs, the pupils who are leaving organise what is hoped to be an entertaining memory. (Photograph by Norman Mays Studio)

MALVERN COLLEGE

The Main Building

Ellerslie House
Music School
St Edm Hall
No.9
No.7
Design Tech
Porter's Lodge
School House
Pavilion
No.8
Chapel
Main Building
No.2
Razak Science Centre
Geography
Memorial Library
Preston Building
THE BARKER
No.3
THE SENIOR TURF
No.4
No.6
Rackets Courts
Rogers Theatre
Fives Courts
GYM FLATS
South Lodge
CCF
St George
Cricket on the Senior

EMBRACING THE FUTURE

MALVERN
COLLEGE

Faber Gate

The Broadwalk

The Grub

No. 5

Sports Complex

NIOR TURF

Gryphon Room

Medical Centre

Chapel and Memorial Library

(Map by Roger Ellis)

(Photograph by Jon Willcocks)

239

Appendix 1
The Houses of Malvern College

The Malvern archives do not provide any hard evidence of the reasons for adopting a numbered house scheme as opposed to a named House scheme, except for School House and the day boys' house, during the early years.[1] An examination of some late Victorian and early Edwardian editions of *The Malvernian* show that houses were identified by Malvern's unique House classification system using either numbers or the current housemasters' names (or very occasionally both) mostly for sporting events, leavers lists and for those who served in the Boer War. The allocation of numbers to houses appears to have been in the order of the completion of each house, except for No. 5 and No. 6, which were famously 'swapped' in 1908 to provide Mr C. Toppin with more room for his family in the larger present No. 6 and leaving the bachelor Mr L. S. Milward with smaller, more suitable accommodation in the current No. 5. It is possible to imagine that the earlier houses were referred to by numbers on the original architect's plans for the College for convenience before the original housemasters were appointed, but no one has been able to confirm this, so that the actual origins of the House numbering scheme must remain a matter of speculation.[2]

Below and bottom: School House.

SCHOOL HOUSE

Originally not a boarding house but the residence of Rev Arthur Faber, the first Headmaster, from 1865 to 1871. In the latter year Rev Faber made the present No. 3 into the School House. School House was renamed College House and accommodated assistant masters. Rev A. W. H. Howard began conversion into a boarding house but left because of ill health. In 1877 Faber moved back to the present School House, which had been enlarged to its present size.

Subsequent housemasters:
Rev C. T. Cruttwell, 1881
Rev W. Grundy, 1885
Rev A. St John Gray, 1892
Rev S. R. James, 1897
F. S. Preston, 1914

APPENDIX 1 THE HOUSES OF MALVERN COLLEGE

H. C. A. Gaunt, 1937–42 *(Gaunt ended the custom of the headmaster acting as housemaster of School House)*
D. W. Erskine,[3] 1942
L. R. Dodd (OM), 1956
A. I. Leng, 1960
A. R. Duff, 1975
A. J. Rambridge, 1987
P. D. John,[4] 1995
J. A. O. Russell, 2000

NO. 1
Rev C. McDowall,[5] 1865
Rev T. H. Belcher,[6] 1874
Rev G. E. Mackie,[7] 1881
Rev H. M. Faber, 1887
D. J. P. Berridge, 1913
F. W. Roberts, 1927
In 1940 the House merged with No. 8
H. C. W. Wilson, 1946
N. Rosser, 1962
Rev T. J. Wright,[8] 1977
S. M. Hill,[9] 1986
M. J. Weaver, 1995
Rev A. P. Law, 2005
A. J. Wharton, 2007

NO. 2
Rev F. R. Drew, 1865
C. Graham, 1881
Rev M. A. Bayfield,[10] 1883
J. N. Swann, 1890
W. Greenstock, 1912
P. E. A. Morshead, 1927
In 1940 the House merged with No. 6
R. H. Bolam (OM), 1947
G. V. Surtees,[11] 1960
J. M. McNevin, 1964
M. J. P. Knott, 1979
B. B. White, 1991
W. E. Hyman, 2002
R. G. Lacey, 2003
J. J. W. E. Major (OM), 2014

NO. 3
Rev W. H. Maddock, 1867
Became SH 1871–77 under the headmaster, Rev A. Faber

Rev T. Spear, 1877 *(House again called No. 3)*
P. R. Farrant, 1912
R. B. Porch (OM), 1919
Rev W. O. Cosgrove, 1933
M. A. Staniforth, 1951
A. F. Vyvyan-Robinson,[12] 1966
M. G. Harvey, 1972
A. C. S. Carter, 1984
Became a girls' house
Mrs A. L. Lafferty, 1995–2006
Mrs F. C. Packham, 2006

NO. 4
Rev L. Estridge, 1868
Rev E. L. Bryans, 1878
Rev H. E. Huntington (OM), 1889
H. H. House, 1893
O. Meade-King, 1924
A. H. Chadder, 1938
Rev R. G. Born, 1956
R. P. Hooley, 1965
G. R. Scott, 1969
T. Southall, 1981
Became a girls' house[13]
Mrs H. M. Robinson, 1993
Mrs A-I. Sharp, 2004

NO. 5
Rev H. Foster, 1871 *(in what is now No. 6)*
L. S. Milward (OM), 1908 *(moved into the present No. 5)*
F. U. Mugliston, 1915
H. M. Robinson, 1927
Merged with No. 7
R. T. Colthurst, 1946
J. Collinson, 1949
G. H. Chesterton (OM), 1961
J. B. Blackshaw, 1976
C. Hall, 1988
A. J. Murtagh, 1998
T. P. Newman, 2007

From top: No. 1; No. 2, No. 3; No. 4; No. 5.

NO. 6

Founded in 'Malvernbury' by H. W. Smith in 1891
C. Toppin, 1892
Moved to present site of No. 5 in 1894 and to present No. 6 in 1908
Major H. D. E. Elliott, 1925
J. J. Salter, 1938
H. J. Farebrother, 1956
K. M. Grayson, 1968
R. G. H. Goddard, 1980
Became a girls' house
Mrs J. S. Lamberton, 1992
Mrs G. M. Sloan, 2002
R. T. W. Dain, 2003
Mrs N. J. Cage, 2007
Mrs V. Young, 2011

NO. 7

Founded in 1892 (unofficially 1889)
R. E. Lyon (OM), 1892 (Meade-King *locum tenens* during the First World War)
Rev C. E. Storrs (OM),[14] 1925
R. T. Colthurst, 1930
G. L. M. Smith, 1948
D. F. Saunders, 1962
Dr H. J. C. Ferguson, 1977
A. J. Murtagh, 1989
R. H. Brierly,[15] 1998
P. J. Gray, 2005
D. Eglin, 2008 *(on new site)*

NO. 8

Founded 1895 at 'Malvernhurst'
C. T. Salisbury, 1895
Moved to 'Malvernbury' 1903; Radnor House 1906
W. W. Lowe (OM), 1913
M. C. Nokes, 1932
F. W. Roberts, 1940
House dissolved
G. W. White, 1946
J. L. Lewis (OM), 1961
C. Nicholls, 1976
R. S. D. Smith, 1985
R. A. J. Tims, 1995
Became a girls' house
Mrs P. D. Richardson, 2004
Mrs R. Grundy, 2011

NO. 9

Founded in 1898; started at 'Bryndart', 'Cranhill', Malvernbury 1899; Roslin House 1903
E. C. Bullock (OM), 1898 (G. G. Fraser *locum tenens* during First World War)
G. G. Fraser (OM), 1917
F. H. Hooper (OM), 1927
In 1942 the House was dissolved
J. S. Rambridge, 1946
R. A. Stobbs, 1961
N. I. Stewart, 1974
W. J. Denny, 1986
Dr R. A. Lister, 1998
P. M. Wickes, 2007

ELLERSLIE HOUSE

Mrs E. R. Hart, 1992
Mrs A. L. Lafferty, 1994
Moved to No. 3
Re-established on present site in 2009
Mrs S. Angus, 2008
Mrs B. Swart, 2010
Mrs E. Brown, 2013

From top: No. 6; No. 7; No. 8; No. 9; Ellerslie.

Appendix 2
Wider still and wider

The following list of OMs is intended to be a representative and not exhaustive list of the remarkable contributions that former members of the College have made to national and international life. Careers mentioned in other chapters are not included.

IMPERIAL SERVICE

In the nineteenth century most boys went into family businesses, the armed services and the professions. A significant number emigrated to the Dominions or went into imperial service. H. W. Smith collected the names of forty-eight Old Malvernians who were in the government service in India. Indeed, Ralph Blumenau was able to write in his centenary history: 'it is a fact that Malvern has produced more men of distinction in Colonial Administration than in any other field.' The record began with **Sir Hugh Shakespear Barnes** (2. 1866–70) who entered Malvern when the school was a year old and went on to be Resident in Kashmir in 1894, foreign secretary to the Government of India, 1900–03, and Lieutenant-Governor of Burma, 1903–05. Something of the scope of the imperial adventure can be found in the remarkable destination of other OMs including **The Hon. Sir Eustace Edward Twisleton-Wykeham-Fiennes**, 1st Baronet (5. 1879–81), the Seychelles and the Leeward Islands; **Sir Geoffrey de Montmorency** (SH 1890–95), the Punjab; **Sir Edward Denham** (2. 1892–95), who presided over the destinies of Mauritius, Kenya, Gambia, British Guiana, and Jamaica; **Sir Geoffrey Bracken** (1. 1893–98), Madras; **Sir George Symes** (4. 1896–98), governor of Tanganyika 1931–32; governor general of Anglo-Egyptian Sudan 1934–40; **Sir Robert Reid** (7. 1897–1902), Assam, Bengal, Aden. Perhaps the most famous was **Sir Godfrey Huggins, 1st Viscount Malvern,** (3. 1898–99) Prime Minister of Southern Rhodesia, 1933–53, Prime Minister of the Federation of Rhodesia and Nyasaland, 1953–56. Other post-war administrators included **Sir Andrew Cohen** (SH 1923–28), governor of Uganda, 1952–57; permanent British representative UN Trusteeship Council, 1957–61, director-general of the Department of Technical Cooperation, 1961–64; and **Sir Bruce Greatbatch** (3. 1931–36), colonial service in Nigeria, war service in Burma with Royal West African Frontier Force, high commissioner to Kenya and finally governor of the Seychelles 1969–73. The imperial connection also produced notable careers within the Dominions and later Commonwealth. Two notables from India were **K. S. Digvijaysinhji** (7. 1910–15), Maharajah of Nawanagar 1933, Raj Pramukh of the United States of Kathiawar 1948–56, member of the Imperial War Cabinet, provided refuge for hundreds of Polish refugee orphans; and **General M. S. Rajendrasinhji** (5. 1910–18), first Indian to be awarded the DSO in the Second World War, commander-in-chief, Indian Army, 1952–55.

POLITICS

The school can claim two other prime ministers: **His Excellency Dato' Sri Mohd Najib bin Tun Haji Abdul Razak** (2. 1968–71), Prime Minister of Malaysia from 2009, who introduced the New Economic Model to Malaysia with the objective of creating 'a business friendly environment conducive to economic growth, development and investment'; and **Prince Mikhail Imru**

(4. 1945–47) last Prime Minister of Emperor Haile Selassie of Ethiopia in 1974 and then adviser to the new revolutionary government.

In the UK the most prestigious parliamentary career must be that of **Lord Bernard Weatherill** (6. 1934–38), MP for Croydon North East from 1964, elected 154th Speaker of the House of Commons, 1983–92. MPs have included: **Holcombe Ingleby** (2. 1867–73), poet, and MP for Kings Lynn 1910–18, who had his election challenged on the grounds of his lavish hospitality to his potential constituents; **Lieutenant-Colonel. W. V. Faber** (2. 1869–73), Andover 1906–18; **Sir Thomas Nussey** (SH 1882), Liberal MP for Pontefract 1893–1910; **Lieutenant-Colonel Sir Walter Bromley-Davenport** (8. 1917–21), Knutsford 1945–70, a classic 'Knight of the Shires'. He reputedly lost his junior whip position after kicking the Belgian ambassador whom he had mistaken for a colleague he had thought to be leaving the Commons before a crucial vote. Other Conservatives include **Sir Richard Thompson** (7. 1926–30), Croydon West 1950–55, Croydon South 1955–66 and again 1970–74; **Sir Charles Fletcher-Cooke** (6. 1927–33), Darwen 1951–83, MEP 1977–79; **Sir John Fletcher-Cooke** (6. 1926–28), Southampton Test 1964–66. Two elected as Conservatives 'crossed the floor': **Humphrey Berkeley** (9/4. 1940–44), Lancaster 1959–66, who wrote the highly entertaining *Life and death of Rochester Sneath*; joined the Labour Party, the SDP and then back to Labour; and **Lord Peter Temple Morris** (2. 1951–56), Leominster 1974–2001 who joined the Labour Party in 1998. **John Baker White** (8. 1916–20), Canterbury 1945–53, was an activist against left-wing subversion and amateur spy in Nazi Germany; **M. J. C. Barnes** (SH 1946–51), Brentford and Chiswick, 1966–74; **John Brown** (6. 1952–57), Winchester, 1979–92. **Philip Bushill-Matthews** (6. 1956–62) MEP 1999–2009, was leader of the Conservative group in the European Parliament in 2008. **The Hon. Orville Alton (Tommy) Turnquest** (7. 1973–77), Bahamian MP, was leader of the Free National Movement 2001–5 and minister of National Security, 2007–12. In 1974/5, **Sir Murray Fox** (8. 1926–30) became the 647th Lord Mayor of London.

DIPLOMACY

Malvernian ambassadors include: **Sir Henry Lowther** (2. 1870), Denmark 1913–16; **Lord Harvey of Tasburgh** (1. 1907–1), France 1948–54; **Sir Alexander Clutterbuck** (4. 1910–15), high commissioner to Canada 1946–52, India 1952–55, Eire 1955–59; **Sir John Hutchinson** (3. 1903–09), charges d'affaires, China 1950–51; **Joseph Robinson** (4. 1919–24), Paraguay 1953–57; **Walter G. C. Graham** (1. 1921–24), minister plenipotentiary to Korea 1952–54, ambassador to Libya, 1955–59; **Sir John Nicholls** (9. 1923–28), minister in Moscow 1949–54, ambassador to Israel 1954–57, Yugoslavia 1957–60, Belgium 1960–63, South Africa 1966–69; **Roger Short** (9. 1958–63), ambassador to Bulgaria 1994–98, killed in 2003 in a terrorist attack while serving as consul general in Turkey; **Giles Paxman** (SH 1965–69), Mexico 2005, Spain 2009; **Dr Tej Bunnag** (5. 1957–62), Royal Thai ambassador to France and then the USA, minister of Foreign Affairs, Thailand; **Augustin d'Aboville** (6. 1955–56), French ambassador to Malta; **Andrew Standley** (8. 1969–72), ambassador for the European Commission in Bolivia.

Among notable administrators were: **Sir Gerald Canny** (3. 1894–1900), chairman, Board of Inland Revenue 1938–42; and **Lord Plowden** (3. 1920–22), chief planning officer at the Treasury 1947–53, chairman of the Atomic Energy Board 1954–59. In recent years **Alistair Buchanan** (7. 1975–80), chief executive of Ofgem, regulator of the gas and electrical industries in Britain 2003–13, partner and chairman of KPMG's Power & Utilities practice.

ACADEMIC: SCIENCE AND MEDICAL

The Nobel Prize for Chemistry was won by **Francis William Aston** (2. 1891–93) in 1922 (see p.115). Other notable scientific and medical academics have included **Professor Sir Charles**

Harington (DB 1914–16), Chemical Pathology, London 1931–42, later Director of the National Institute of Medical Research 1942–62; **Professor D. H. Mackenzie** (SH 1929–35), Pathology, Westminster Medical School 1976–; **Hugh de Wardener** (4. 1929–33), professor of Medicine, London University, 1960–81; and **Professor Christopher Whitty** (3. 1979–84), professor of International Medicine and chief scientist at the Department of International Development focusing on reducing childhood deaths from malaria; listed 40th in the Eureka Science 'Top 100 Scientists of the World'; **Dr Dennis Sciama** (SH 1939–44), a leading British physicist and 'one of the fathers of modern cosmology', professor of Astrophysics at International School of Advanced Studies at Trieste, visiting professor at Oxford, supervised doctorates of, among others, Stephen Hawkins; **Professor M. W. Thring** (SH 1928–34), Fuel Technology and Chemical Engineering, Sheffield 1953–64; Mechanical Engineering QMC 1964–81, who was very interested in robotics; **P. D. Storie-Pugh** (9. 1933–37), lecturer Cambridge University 1953–82, president of the Royal College of Veterinary Surgeons 1977; **Oliver Selfridge** (6. 1939–40), a pioneer of artificial intelligence; **Dr John Havard** (2/6. 1938–42), secretary BMA 1979–89; **Geoffrey Chisholm** (1. 1945–49), professor of Surgery at Edinburgh University and a world expert on urology; **Sir Ghillean Prance** (1. 1951–56), prominent British botanist and ecologist; was director of the Royal Botanic Gardens at Kew 1988–99 and involved in the Eden Project. Happy to bridge the divide between science and religion, he was president of Christians in Science 2002–08; **Bertie Blount** (5. 1921–25), a chemist who became Dean of St Peter's Hall Oxford. As scientific adviser to SOE he was the author of various methods of assassinating Hitler ranging from poisoning his drinking water in his train to using anthrax germs; **Edward Eason** (5. 1930–34), who wrote *The Centipedes of the British Isles* and served in the Burma campaign. He responded to Anthony Blunt's comment in 1975, that the brightest undergraduates in his time were Marxists, by recalling that when he was at Cambridge in 1935 'many of my circle were bright, but had any of them expressed Marxist views he would have been debagged and thrown into the Cam';[1] **Mike Hansell** (1. 1954–59), professor of Animal Architecture, Glasgow University until 2005, and published *Built by Animals*; **Professor Jonathan Rawlings** (8. 1974–78), professor of Astrophysics, UCL; **Simon Curry** (5. 1959–64), professor of Computer Science, Quebec 1971–87; **Dr Angus Kennedy** (3. 1976–80), neurologist.

ACADEMIC: HUMANITIES AND SOCIAL SCIENCES

The school has also produced a long line of distinguished literary academics. Apart from C. S. Lewis (see p.114), other distinguished literary academics include: **Lascelles Abercrombie** (4. 1895–1900), professor of English literature, London 1929–35 and one of the Dymock Poets; **Alan Strode Ross** (3. 1920–22), professor of English, Birmingham 1948–51, linguistics 1951–74, the inspiration for Nancy Mitford's 'U' and 'non–U' forms of behaviour and language use.

Notable historians have included: **Sir John Wheeler-Bennett** (5. 1917–20) (see page 77); **Warren Lewis** (SH 1909–13) (see page 114). **Nigel Steel** (SH 1975–80), writer on Gallipoli and head of research at the Imperial War Museum; **Dominic Sandbrook** (1. 1988–93), has written a controversial biography of Eugene McCarthy and then a series on post-war Britain: *Never had it So Good, White Heat, State of Emergency, Seasons in the Sun*. He is a regular columnist on historical matters for major national newspapers and has presented several television and radio programmes for the BBC.

Professor James Meade (8. 1921–26) was described as one of the greatest economists of his generation (see p.117). A significant educationalist and musicologist was **Sir William Hadow** (1. 1871–78), vice-chancellor of Durham University and then Sheffield, the author of the influential Hadow Reports and the *Oxford History of Music*. Other distinguished musicologists were **Alan R. Murray** (SH 1905–10), director of the Royal Academy of Music 1930, and

Richard Rastall (6. 1954–59), professor of Musicology, Leeds University until 2006, specialising in the role of music in Early English Drama.

Notable chairs in Law have been held by: **Ronald H. Maudsley** (3. 1932–36), King's College, London 1966–77, then San Diego. Having achieved Blues against Cambridge in 1946 and 1947 he was known as 'the cricketing don'; **Edward R. H. Ivamy** (4. 1934–39) UCL 1960–86, 'a world authority on mercantile law and a prolific writer of law books'; **Robin Morse** (2. 1960–65), King's College, London, head of School of Law 1992–93, 1997. Other academic chairs have been held by **Anthony D. Fitton-Brown** (7. 1939–43) in Classics at Leicester 1969–89; by **Simon Caney** (SH 1979–84) in Political Theory, Oxford; and by **Dr David J. Steinberg** (6. 1955–56), president of Long Island University 1985–2013.

In architecture **Sir Howard Robertson** (SH 1902–04) designed the British pavilion for the 1925 Paris International Exhibition, an event that helped create the term Art Deco style. He was also responsible for the controversial Shell building in London, and helped design the UN building in New York. He was president of the Royal Institute of British Architects 1952–54. **Aldwyn Douglas-Jones** (7. 1924–27) was professor of Architecture at Bristol 1962–75 and Cornell, and was an author, editor and film maker for the BBC.

LITERARY

The literary tradition of Malvern reaches back to the early years of the twentieth century and has been marked by a number of distinguished writers, many of whom greatly disliked their schooldays. There has been a particular flowering in the last thirty years. Likewise the arts – musical, visual art and drama – have become notably more important as destinations for talented Malvernians.

The earliest notable novelist was **Henry de Vere Stacpoole** (SH 1879–80), author of *The Blue Lagoon*. **Michael Arlen (Dikran Kouyoumdjian)** (5. 1909–13), an Armenian novelist and man of letters, had his greatest success in the 1920s with a series of satirical romances such as *"Piracy"*. **St John Hankin** (Foster 1883–86) was an essayist and playwright and a major exponent of Edwardian New Drama. His most famous and often revived play was *The Return of the Prodigal*. **Raymond Mortimer** (3. 1909–12) was a critic and literary editor of the *New Statesman*; he worked for the BBC and with the Free French in the Second World War. **Ronald Mansbridge** (SH 1919–25) opened the American branch of the Cambridge University Press, presiding over its growth into a multimillion-dollar enterprise; he also worked for Oxford, MIT and Yale University presses. **John Moore** (DB 1921–23) was the author of *Portrait of Elmbury*, the opening novel of the Brensham Trilogy, an early conservationist, and founder of the Cheltenham Literary Festival. **Peter Irwin Russell** (1. 1935–40), poet, writer and editor, prodigious linguist; his most important work was *Elegies of Quintilius*, a lyrical and witty evocation of the decadent end of the Roman Empire, and he achieved a great reputation in Italy, receiving the Dante Alighieri Prize and the Premio le Muse; nominated for Nobel Prize in 2001. **Henry (Harry) Guest** (6. 1946–50) is a noted contemporary poet. **Michael Wilcox** (3. 1956–61), playwright, including the semi-autobiographical *Lent*, scriptwriter and librettist.

Among contemporary writers: **Giles Foden** (8. 1980–85) has greatly impressed with a series of acclaimed novels set in Africa, where he grew up, such as *The Last King of Scotland* (1998, filmed 2006), *Ladysmith* (1999), *Zanzibar* (2002), *Mimi and Toutou Go Forth: The Bizarre Battle for Lake Tanganyika* (2004), *Turbulence* (2010). He holds academic posts at Royal Holloway, London and East Anglia; **Oludiran Adebayo** (3. 1981–86), author and columnist; fellow of the Royal Society of Literature and member of the National Arts Council; author of *Some Kind of Black* and *My Once Upon a Time* and the BBC television documentary *Out of Africa*; named in 2003 as one of London's 100 most influential people by the *Evening Standard*; **James Delingpole**

(9. 1979–83), polemic journalist and author and scourge of what he sees as pseudo-progressive thinking, author of four political books including *How to be Right: The Essential Guide to Making Lefty Liberals History*, and of several novels including *Fin* and *Thinly Disguised Autobiography, Coward on the Beach, Coward at the Bridge*, became famous for his assault on the climate change lobby. **Horatio Clare** (6. 1987–90), columnist, broadcaster and author of *Running for the Hills, Truant: Notes from the Slippery Slope, A Single Swallow: Following an Epic Journey from South Africa to South Wales*; **Miles Hordern** (9. 1978–83), writer of nautical adventures, author of *Voyaging the Pacific: In Search of the South* (2002), *Sailing the Pacific* (2003), *Passage to Torres Strait: Four Centuries in the Wake of Great Navigators, Mutineers, Castaways and Beachcombers* (2006), compared in the *TES* to Joseph Conrad.

THE ARTS[2]

Artistic academics have included: **Dr Denis Wilcox** (SH 1983–88), author of the *London Group 1913–39: The Artists and their Works*, and **Oliver Winchester** (9. 1993–98), now project curator of the Wellcome Trust. Significant artists include **Gareth Cadwallader** (9. 1993–98); **Paddy Troughton** (9. 1986–91); **Robert Beckett** (9. 1976–81) portraiture; **Alistair Laidlaw** (2. 1968–72), photographer; **Alistair Carew-Cox** (7. 1975–80), photographer; sculptor **Ben Carpenter** (9. 1988–93); architect and interior designer **Edward Bulmer** (9. 1975–80). Actors have included **Denholm Elliott** (1. 1936–39), **Brian Aherne** (DB 1917–20), **Peter Bennett** (8. 1931–34). **Alistair Coomer** (1. 1989–94) became casting director at the Donmar Warehouse in October 2012; previously the deputy head of casting at the National Theatre.

THE MILITARY

Among prominent military men we find **General John Fuller** (5. 1893–95), chief of staff of newly formed Tank Corps. He largely planned the Cambrai surprise attack in November 1917 and was an early and leading exponent of the possibility of tank warfare, later developed into the Blitzkrieg tactics used by Germany in the Second World War; he also wrote *Decisive Battles of the Western World*. **Brigadier Ralph Bagnold** (3. 1909–14), the founder and commander of the British Army's Long Range Desert Group during the Second World War. An expert on desert exploration, he wrote *The Physics of Blown Sand and Desert Dunes* (1941), which has been used by NASA for studying sand dunes on Mars. **Peter Morland Churchill** (4. 1923–26), SOE officer in France in the Second World War carrying out a series of important missions to the Resistance, worked with, and later married, Odette Sansom (the only woman to be awarded the George Cross while alive and subject of the post-war film, *Odette*). Among those who served in the Second World War and went on to distinguished post-war careers were **Air Chief Marshal Sir Donald Hardman** (SH 1913–15), commandant, RAF Staff College 1949–51, AOCiC Home Command 1951–52, chief of air staff, Royal Australian Air Force 1952–54; **Major-General Ll. Wansbrough-Jones** (SH 1914–18), chief of staff, Control Commission for Germany 1948–51, Chief of Staff, Western Command 1951–52; **Vice-Admiral Sir Varyl Begg** (3. 1922–26), gunnery officer on a cruiser on the North Atlantic convoys, the Norwegian campaign and the occupation of Iceland, then in the Mediterranean fleet at the battle of Cape Matapan. Commanded a destroyer during the Korean War, Vice-Chief of Naval Staff 1961, CiC Far East 1963–65, Allied CiC Channel 1965–66, First Sea Lord 1966–68, governor & CiC Gibraltar; **General Sir John Mogg** (2. 1926–31), failed at first attempt to get into Sandhurst but enlisted in the ranks of the Coldstream Guards as a gentleman cadet and ended up with the Sword of Honour, commandant of the Royal Military Academy, Sandhurst 1962–64, colonel commandant, Army Air Corps 1963–74, CiC Southern Command 1968–70, ADC to Queen Elizabeth II 1971–74, deputy supreme Allied commander Europe for NATO 1973–76. Described in a

Guardian obituary as probably the British Army's most popular general and finished his career in one of NATO's most influential posts. 'A man of compassion he had a gift for getting on with all nationalities and his relationship with General Haig when Deputy Supreme Commander indirectly proved very useful at the time of the Falklands conflict'.[3] **Major-General Sir Charles Harington** (5. 1924–27), an inspirational commander, he was awarded an MC while with the British Expeditionary Force in 1940 and a DSO in Normandy, commandant of the Staff College, Camberley 1961; CiC Middle East Command 1963–66; ADC to Queen Elizabeth II 1969–71. **James Jesus Angleton** (2. 1933–36) became chief of the CIA's counter-intelligence staff 1954–75. **Major-General Logan Scott Bowden** (2. 1933–38) who carried out a number of secret reconnaissance raids on the Normandy beaches in preparation for the D-Day landings. **Lieutenant-General Sir Christopher Drewry** (5. 1961–65), commander Allied Rapid Reaction Force 2000–03.

THE LAW

Notable legal careers have included **Lord Justice Lawrence** (4. 1876–78) who was Lord Justice of Appeal 1926–38. **Sir Gerald Fitzmaurice** (7. 1914–19), chief legal adviser to the Foreign Office 1959, judge of the International Court of Justice at The Hague 1960–73 and the European Court of Human Rights 1974–82. **Christmas Humphreys** (1. 1915–18), judge in the Central Criminal Court 1968–76, and president of the Buddhist Society. **Sir Derek Hodgson** (8. 1931–35), High Court Judge 1977, who presided over the Blakelock trial in 1987. **Sir Stephen Brown** (5. 1939–42), High Court Judge 1975–, Lord Justice of Appeal and president of the Family Division of the High Court. **Sir Peter L. Gibson** (1. 1946–52), High Court judge 1981, chairman of the Law Commission 1990–92, Lord Justice of Appeal 1993–2005. Appointed Intelligence Services Commissioner 2006 and in 2010 headed Detainee Inquiry. **Hon Judge Ronald Livesey** (8. 1949–54), Circuit Judge, QC and Senior Judge of the Sovereign Base Appeal Court, Cyprus. **Caroline Harry-Thomas** (Ellerslie 1968–75), described in her *Times* obituary as 'one of the most distinguished medical lawyers of her generation who left an indelible mark in the world of medical law'; head girl of Ellerslie and member of the College Council.

THE CHURCH

From its earliest days many Malvernians have entered the Church. The following became bishops: **C. H. Ridsdale** (1. 1886–92), Colchester 1933–46; **H. C. Montgomery-Campbell** (5. 1901–06), Willesden 1940–42, Kensington 1942–49, Guildford 1949–56, and of London 1956–61; **C. E. Storrs** (SH 1902–07) Grafton NSW, 1946–55; **W. G. Sanderson** (8. 1919–24), Plymouth 1962–72; **A. K. Hamilton** (4. 1928–34), Jarrow 1965; **J. E. L. Mort** (2. 1929–34), Bishop of the Missionary Diocese of the Northern Province of Nigeria, 1952–70. In other posts: **H. Costley-White** (4. 1893–97), Headmaster of both Bradfield and Westminster. Dean of Gloucester, 1938–53. **Alfred Dammers** (6. 1935–40), lectured in theology in Birmingham and India and Dean of Bristol Cathedral from 1973, created the Lifestyle Movement based on the maxim 'Live simply, that others may simply live'. Both the Senior Chapel Prefect **J. J. Bamber** (SH 1969–74) and the Junior Chapel Prefect **Alex Pease** (4. 1969–74) from the same year have both trained for ordination, perhaps a first.

PHILANTHROPY

Notable figures in charitable work have been: **Sir Reginald Kennedy-Cox** (7. 1895–90), founder of the Dockland settlements, 1918. **Sir John Reeves Ellerman** (5. 1923–25), ship-owner, wrote an anti-sport novel at Malvern, *Why do they like it?*;[4] a great philanthropist, notably helping

Jewish refugees to escape from Nazi Germany for which he was attacked by name by the infamous Lord Haw Haw, William Joyce. **Sir Tom Shebbeare** (2. 1965–69), director of Charities to HRH the Prince of Wales. **Jenny Henman** (6. 1996–98) founded the charity Plant your Future in the Peruvian Amazon working with smallholder famers to promote sustainable livelihoods and ecosystem restoration. Also promoting sustainable living is **James Strawbridge** (1. 1997–2002) who starred in the television series *It's Not Easy Being Green* and now promotes ecological living; **Ben Keene** (1. 1993–98), founder of *Tribewanted*, which aims to build model communities that 'demonstrate, educate and inspire sustainability.'

COMMERCE, FINANCE AND INDUSTRY

From the earliest days Malvern reflected the commercial interests of many of its clientele. Family businesses predominated in the nineteenth century but opportunities in the imperial territories attracted many Malvernians, and in recent years many found their career in international financial and commercial activity. Among the more significant national figures have been: **G. A. Hunt** (7. 1928–32), managing director of Massey-Ferguson, chairman of Chrysler, UK 1973–77, chairman and president of Peugeot Citroen (UK). **Sir Ross Stainton** (3. 1928–32), managing director of BOAC-Cunard, chief executive, British Airways, chairman, British Airways 1979–81. **R. B. Reid** (8. 1934–39), chairman of British Rail 1983. **Sir Peter Holmes** (2. 1946–50), chairman of Shell 1985–93 who received a tribute from Nelson Mandela for Shell's commitment to South Africa and its work against apartheid. **Lord Inverforth** (Andrew Weir, 9. 1946–50), chairman Bankline shipping company, chairman of the Aldeburgh Festival. **Christopher Reeves** (9. 1949–54), banker who transformed Morgan Grenfell into a major international finance house, later European chairman of Merrill Lynch. **Paddy Linaker** (9. 1948–52), chairman of M&G 1987–94. **Maurice Wilks** (2. 1918–22), chairman of the Rover Car Company 1962–63 who inspired the development of the Land Rover. **Lord MacLaurin of Knebworth** (5. 1951–56), managing director of Tesco, chairman of Vodaphone, chairman of the England and Wales Cricket Board. **Martyn Rose** (7. 1962–66), chairman, Dentons Pension Management. **The Hon. Robert Rayne** (8. 1962–67), chairman, Derwent London plc; chairman, LMS Capital. **David Symondson** (8. 1969–73), deputy managing partner, Electra Partners. **Michael McLintock** (6. 1974), chief executive of M&G, executive director of Prudential and of the Grosvenor Estate. **Charles Delingpole** (1. 1996–2001), founded MarketInvoice. **Rhys Humm** (7. 1993–98), founder and managing director of the Holywell Malvern Spring Water Company. **Ralph D. Oppenheimer** (5. 1954–59), executive chairman of Stemcor, 1982–2013, the world's largest independent steel trader. **Andrew W. L. Wolstenholme** (9. 1972–77), chief executive, Crossrail. **Adrian M. Coleman** (2. 1976–81), CEO and founding partner, VCCP Partnership whose company created the famous 'meerkats'. **John D. Vergopoulos** (1. 1979–84), chairman and CEO of Raphael Group Plc. **Paul C. Nicholls** (9. 1971–76), chairman of Jefferies Hoare Govett. **Mark A. Georgevic** (2. 1975–79), owner Scrivens Ltd. **Christopher Nieper** (9. 1977–82), managing director of David Nieper Ltd. **Tan Sri Lim Kok Thay** (2. 1968–69), chairman and chief executive Genting Group. **James R. Woolhouse** (5. 1978–83), CEO, Condé Nast, Asia Pacific.

THE MEDIA

A profession of increasing significance has been the media. Early examples of Malvernian careers in this area can be found with **F. H. Kitchen** (SH 1882–85), editor of the *Glasgow Herald* 1909–17 and **A. E. W. Thomas** (7. 1910–15), editor of *The Listener* 1939–58. In more recent years: **Ahmed Rashid** (4. 1962–66), columnist and regular broadcaster on BBC and CNN. He has written successful books: *The Taliban* and *Jihad: The Rise of Militant Islam* and has been 'described as the most influential journalist in the world'.[5] He was the guest speaker at

Commemoration in 2003. **Jeremy Paxman** (SH 1964–69), journalist, author and broadcaster, worked for BBC since 1977 and famous for his abrasive style as presenter of *Newsnight*. **Ambrose Evans-Pritchard** (2. 1971–75), columnist on Europe and international business, author of *The Secret Life of Bill Clinton*. **Lloyd Embley** (3. 1979–84), journalist and editor of the Mirror Group newspapers 2012. **Mark Pougatch** (2. 1981–6), sports journalist for BBC radio and television. **Montague (Monty) Don** (6. 1969–71), writer, speaker and television producer on horticulture; **T. G. Cocks** (2. 1989–94), chief correspondent, Reuters, Nigeria.

Some of the most engaging, controversial and entertaining careers do not fit into easy categories: **Henry P. Hansell** (1. 1878–82), tutor to the sons of King George V. **James R. Dennistoun** (House 1898–01), a New Zealander who went to the Antarctic in the *Terra Nova* as a member of Scott's British Antarctic Expedition 1910–13. **William Wilkins** (1. 1951–55), a founder of the National Botanic Garden of Wales. Two esoteric characters dabbled in the dark arts: **Aleister Crowley** (4. 1891–92), English occultist and libertine; and likewise **Cecil Williamson** (SH 1923–26), influential NeoPagan witch who founded the Witchcraft Research Centre, which was part of MI6 in the war against Nazi Germany. He was reputed to have been converted to witchcraft at Malvern following a bullying incident when a woman who lived on the school grounds taught him how to cast a spell, which saw the bully breaking his leg. **Harry Joel** (SH 1909–13), owner and breeder of race horses over fifty-seven years with 780 winners on the flat, winning in his time the Derby with *Royal Palace*, and 294 winners over thirty years in National Hunt racing with *Maori Venture* winning the Grand National in 1987. In shades of *War Horse*, just before the battle of Arras his charger went lame and his father sent him a three-year-old thoroughbred, which survived the war and won two races after that. Much admired for his unassuming manner and total honesty. We will finish with what must rank as one of the more extraordinary OM careers: **Duncan Guthrie** (6. 1925–28) began his career in the head office of the Ionian Bank before moving on to a coffee and sugar plantation in Guatemala. Volunteered for the Finnish Army in 1940, escaping after a series of desperate adventures to Canada. He joined the Canadian Army, transferring later to the Duke of Cornwall's Light Infantry and then seconded to Special Forces in 1944 first in France then in Burma, later described in *Jungle Diary*. When one of his daughters contracted polio in the late 1940s, he became a pioneer in the successful fight against the disease, initiating a fund for research that still exists with an annual income of over £13 million. There is a Guthrie medal in his honour from the British Paediatric Association.

LIST OF SUBSCRIBERS

Malvern College would like to thank the following subscribers:

Katie Adam
S. G. Angus
Jeremy Baker
Jonathan Baker
William Baker
Alasdair P. A. Barley
Victoria E. R. Barley
Adrian Barrett Greene
Mark Bateman
Will Bates
Hugh Beaumont
Sibyl Beaumont
Roger Berkley
Sara Jane Berry
A. E. Bettinson
Penny Bijl
Nicholas C. P. Bird
Robin Black
Richard Böckel
Jonathan C. Bolton
Christopher Born
Peter Bowen-Simpkins
Charles C. G. Bradshaw
Edward William Bradshaw
J. K. Bradshaw
Richard Brinkman
Michael Brocklehurst
Rt Hon Sir Stephen Brown CBE
Georg Christian Bullinger
Julie Burbeck
Michael Burbeck
Burleys (College Hairdresser)
Ana-Zeralda Canals-Hamann
Jack Carlyle
Derek Carmichael
Peter John Cartwright
Claudia Cascon Pulido
Valeria Cascon Pulido
J. P. Chappell
Sumanjit Chaudhry
Alan Edward Clifton Griffith DFM
Danielle Close
Darcie M. Coates
Rebecca Connell
Edward Cooke
Ben Cooke

Stuart Cookson
William Corscadden-Hayward
Paul Courtenay
Simon Cowley
David Crabtree
Abigail G. Cunningham
Catherine Cussans
Helen Cussans
Riccardo D'Amato
Dr & Mrs Jonathan Darby
James Darby
Olivia Darby
Lesley Anne Davies
Brian Davis
Chris Davis
Bertie Davis
Laura Alessandra Dell'Antonio
Bill Denny
J. W. M. Dent
Hilary Dent
Nigel Dickinson
Fiona Doherty
Hugo Douglas-Pennant
Edward Douglas-Pennant
Michael Downey
Dr P. R. C. Dunlop
John S. R. Edge
Jacob J. Edwards
Mike Eglington
Michael Elsom
Marcus Emmerson
His Honour Judge G. A. Ensor
Robin Erskine
Coulman Family
R. H. Farrar
Dr Geoffrey Farrer-Brown
R. W. Farrington
A. W. M. Fergusson
Daniel Ferris
John Flothmann
John Forsyth
Laurent Fourier
Martin Frayn
Adrian Gaynor-Smith
Joy George
K. Gerami

Anthony David James Gilmore
James Glover
Christopher Gobey
Richard Goddard
Edward Goddard
Tristan Griffiths-Hughes
Anna Maria Grill
Matthew Guy
Jonathan Hadley
Richard W. B. Hagar
Mr Chris Haig-Prothero
Clive J. W. Haines
Chris Hall
Roger Hall-Jones
Gaetan Hannecart
Helen Harding
John Hardy
Robin Harrild
Rupert Harris
Jeremy Harris
Kaspar Hartmann
Michael Ian Harwood
Chris Harwood
Simon Harwood
Oliver Harwood-Smith
Tobias Harwood-Smith
Sam Heappey
Lucas Heappey
Richard Hendicott
John Hendicott
Max Hetzler
Anthony R. Higgins
Julian Holdsworth
Chris Hollis
Stephen Holroyd
Sophie Holroyd
Caroline Hopkinson
Peter Hughes
Adam Lee Hutsby
Ian Jamieson
Tony Jemmett
Stewart Johnson
Arthur Jones
Mrs Barbara Jones
Willoughby Jones
Grank Jungmann

Alberto Kechler
Margherita Kechler
Dr Angus Kennedy
Mr Louis Kennedy
Paul & David Kimpton
Nathan King
Aaron King
Michael A. B. Kirk
Jan Kjell Lange
Kaspar Klemm
John Knee
Lindsay Kontarines
Gary Lea
Richard Leitch
Jonathan Lewin
Phillip M. L. Lewis MBE
Jeremy N. S. Lowe
Simon Macdonald
Heather Macdonald
Simon Mander
Verity Manning-Cox
C. St. J. Marlow
Mary Martin
W. Martius
Will Mathews
Dr Marion Matt
J. & D. Mccarry
Ghassan G. Medawar
Kenneth Miles
Charles Miller
Hugh Milway
Natalia Mladentseva
James Moir-Shepherd
Paul Murphy
A. F. O. Murray
R. G. Murray
A. J. Murtagh
Oliver P. L. Nelson
Alexander P. F. Nelstrop
Paul Nicholls
D. R. Nieper
D. H. Nieper
D. C. Nieper
Simon Partridge

Jamie Paterson
Flora Paterson
Alice Paterson
Jonathan Penrice
John Neville Perrins
David Petersen
Christopher Pitchfork
Christian Plump
Nicolas Plump
Martin Porter
Robert Porter
Richard Postins
Clifford A. Poultney
Gilly Poultney
Robyn Poulton
Dani Praag
Stephen Preedy
Patrick Purcell
Professor Rastall
Romney Rawes
James Rawes
Marlies Reibestein
David R. G. Rhodes
Chris Rhodes
Alex Rhodes
Frances Rix
H. M. R. Robinson
M. P. Robinson
Martin Rogers
Martin J. W. Rogers
Charles Rose
Sam Rowe
Chris Rycroft
Katrina Salnikow
Kashe Sambhi
Dr Gabriele Schaudig
Simon J. Shaw
Simon Shenkman
Jonathan A. Smart
Robin C. Smith
Billie Sneath
George Stafford
Fiona Steiger
Nigel I. Stewart

Christopher Stoecker
Jonathon R. Stokes
Richard Stork
Michael A. Taylor
Maximilien Taylor
Louis Taylor
Julie Tegg
Stephen Tegg
Justin Temple
Peter, Lord Temple-Morris
Alexander Ter Kuile
John F. Threshie
Richard Thurlow
M. E. T. Tiley
T. F. T. Tiley
Robert Tims
Heidi Tims
Kate Tripp
Mike Tripp
Emma Tudor
N. R. Tully
Helen van Daesdonk
Angelina von Kalkstein
Amelia Jean Wall
Henry Nicholas Wall
R. S. Waller
Christopher Walsh
Paul B. Warrington
Nigel D. B. Webster
Kenneth West
John Wheeler
Paul M. Wickes
Simon Wilkinson
David Williams
Elwyn Williams
Neil Elwyn Williams
Dr Frank Hugh Williams-Thomas
Jemima Wilson
Amelia Wilson
Paul Winter
J. B. M. Winter
Fiona Carolyn Wood
Nigel Young

ENDNOTES

Chapter 1

1. Jonathan Gathorne-Hardy, *The Public School Phenomenon* (1977), p.69.
2. Ralph Blumenau, *A History of Malvern College, 1865–1965* (1965), p.3.
3. This technique 'can be defined as the use of pure cold water internally and externally to regulate the temperature and perspiration in order to induce stimulation and tranquilization of the nervous system'; Robin Price, 'Hydropathy in England 1840–70', *Medical History* (1981).
4. Walter Burrows, together with his brother, bought out the other partners in the chemist, John Lea and William Perrins, who went on to market the Lea & Perrins brand of Worcestershire sauce from their dispensing chemists on Broad Street, Worcester.
5. Blumenau, op. cit., p.3.
6. Janet Grierson, *Dr Wilson and his Malvern Hydro* (1998). Dr Stummes opened a water cure establishment of his own on what is now the private side of No. 8, which he initially called Priessnitz House, after a well-known German practitioner of hydropathic medicine.
7. The land was acquired from a partial sale of the Mason estate.
8. By 1861 Cheltenham College had 600 boys on its books and had seen the proprietary shares rise in value from £20 to £120.
9. The story is told that Stummes disliked his view of the school being obscured by a row of fine elm trees and despite opposition determined to have them cut down. One Boxing Day he collected a gang of fourteen men and, making the most of Christmas hangovers, the trees were felled before anyone could stop him. In his somewhat broken English he is reported to have said: 'Zey do not like it, but zen zey cannot make me put zem up again!'
10. Now part of Malvern St James School. In September the Company issued 500 shares each of £40.
11. Charles Hansom (1817–88) initially designed the Main Building, School House, and the Porter's Lodge, and later houses 1, 2, 3 and 4. In the local area he also was responsible for the extensions to Little Malvern Court and the Catholic church and presbytery at Hanley Swan.
12. *Berrow's Worcester Journal* (18 July 1863).
13. Ibid. (25 July 1863).
14. Frederick Lygon succeeded his brother in 1866, becoming the 6th Earl Beauchamp.
15. Blumenau, op. cit., p.10.
16. R. B. Grindrod, *Malvern: Past and Present* (1865).

Chapter 2

1. Called 'home boarders' at this time.
2. Now converted into flats.
3. H. R. Wathen (1. 1865–70) written in 1924 and reprinted in the *Old Malvernian Newsletter* (November 1989). All former Malvernians are listed with their house and years at first mention.
4. *Berrow's Worcester Journal* (25 July 1863).
5. Blumenau, op. cit., p.11, quoting from *The Field* (3 December 1910).
6. Wathen, op. cit.
7. This early start continued throughout the year until the headmastership of Grundy (1885–91) when it was ended for the Christmas and Easter terms. Only under the headmastership of Gaunt (1937–53) was it ended in the summer term.
8. Wathen, op. cit.
9. Thomas Arnold, Headmaster of Rugby, promoted morally worthy boys to act as monitors over the younger boys. A major task for these prefects was to ensure good discipline.
10. Blumenau, op. cit., p.18.
11. The dispute emerged from the American Civil War when the United States government claimed compensation for damage caused by the *Alabama* and other ships built in Britain but used by the Confederacy. The dispute was settled amicably in 1872.
12. *Malvern Register*, 1. lvii.
13. Blumenau, op. cit., p.19.
14. Ibid., p.21.
15. This was through the Patteson Society, which was formed in 1878 and named after a missionary bishop in the Melanesian Islands.
16. In 1865 the Building Company had brought Radnor Field from the trustees of E. T. Foley for £4,300 in order to build the south houses. They were designed by Mr Hopkins from Worcester.
17. The most notable of whom was Tej Bunnag, Thai ambassador successively to China, France and the United States, and briefly foreign minister of Thailand in 2008. I am indebted to Ralph Blumenau for this charming anecdote.
18. I am indebted to the editor of the *Old Malvernian Newsletter* of November 1984 for these details of the origins of the school arms and motto. It has also been discovered that Crawford's Whisky used the motto in 1860 allowing the pleasing speculation that Sewell and Faber might perhaps have absorbed the wording while enjoying a convivial evening.
19. All this was acquired for £45,000.
20. F. A. M. Webster, *Our Great Public Schools* (1937).
21. Faber married twice, first to his cousin Maria Sophia Faber in 1854. She died in 1875 and he subsequently married Mary Isabella MacCarthey in 1898. He died in 1910.
22. It appears that Drew refused to implement certain administrative decisions made by Cruttwell.
23. He clearly had the popular touch with boys. In the cricket nets he used to put sixpence onto the middle stump behind him, which went to the bowler who could dislodge them. He regularly lost about half a crown in the process, wrote the son of a boy in his house.
24. This refers to the award of Scholarships and Exhibitions at Oxford and Cambridge as opposed to simply being offered a place. These awards were of little financial significance but were highly prestigious and a method by which schools showed their academic prowess in comparison with their competitors. The old system of Closed and Open awards was abolished by both universities in the 1980s and replaced by scholarships awarded for high achievement once at the universities.
25. Although his personal qualities are well illustrated when he proposed that a tablet should be erected in Chapel in memory of Drew (the schismatic housemaster) who had died in 1883.
26. Rev A. H. James in *The Malvern Register*.
27. Blumenau, op. cit. pp.32–33.
28. By comparison Faber had appointed only nine

laymen in his twenty-five appointments. The change under Grundy obviously expanded the pool of talent from which masters could emerge.

29. The Latin words were written by M. A. Bayfield, the English translation by C. W. Horsburgh, and the music by R. E. Lyon.

Coat of Arms

i. Judging from old guidebooks, the Chalybeate Spring (now lost to sight in the garden of Oakdale), St Anne's Well, and the Holy Well.

Chapter 3

1. Where he saw the numbers expand from fifty-eight to 141.
2. Blumenau, op. cit., p.37.
3. In 1894 nine, in 1895 eleven, in 1896 eight, and in 1897 seven.
4. An attempt by British colonists to undermine Paul Kruger's Transvaal republic by an incursion over the New Year in 1895/6 which was supposed to trigger a rising by British settlers in the Transvaal. It failed but was one of the causes of the later Boer War.
5. Now the Carson Centre.
6. More of this speech is recorded on pp.112–3.
7. Blumenau, op. cit., pp.42–43.
8. By 1894 there were over two thousand OMs and informal reunions were common.
9. Blumenau, op. cit. p.47. In 1958 it again became voluntary but sadly came to an end when changes were made to the timings of Chapel services. The Junior Turf was acquired on a lease in 1890, and its purchase in 1895 for £1,923 involved the closure of a bridle road running diagonally across it. The College was responsible for creating a new road, Woodshears Road, and a new tunnel under the railway at the considerable cost of £2,300. The southern half of the Junior was not properly levelled and seeded until the late 1940s, and in 1985 the Senior was widened westwards by about five yards and its drainage improved.
10. A charming story in James's autobiography attributes his appointment to a letter sent to the Council by a mutual friend in which his chief rival A. H. Cooke was described as 'never really a boy' whereas 'James has never ceased to be one!'
11. Blumenau, op. cit.
12. This comment comes from an article in the *Malvern Gazette* (August 1964). The OM is not named. This legendary story may have its true origins during James's time at Eton.
13. Wodehouse wrote that when he was a small boy he spent part of his summer holidays with an uncle who was the vicar of Upton-on-Severn 'and I played a lot of boys' cricket, some of it on the Malvern ground. From those early years the place fascinated me. I was of course cricket mad in those days, and I can well remember peering in at the pavilion and reading all those illustrious names on the boards'. PG Wodehouse, *Mike at Wrykyn* (Everyman, 2011) p.27.
14. Blumenau, op. cit., p.52. Sausages were clearly something of a treat with breakfast consisting of porridge and bread and butter. A cooked breakfast cost an extra 3 shillings (£1.50) a term.
15. Blumenau, op. cit., pp.52–53.
16. Alister Scott (Toppin, 1905–10) died of his wounds near Ypres on 16 May 1915.
17. Alister McGrath, *C. S. Lewis: A Life* (Hodder & Stoughton, 2013), p.33. Lewis's native clumsiness partly arose from having only one joint in his thumbs, which prevented much success in sport.
18. C. S. Lewis, *Surprised by Joy: The Shape of My Early Life* (1955), p.98. Blumenau, op. cit., p.56.
19. David Lloyd George became chancellor of the exchequer in Asquith's Liberal government in 1908 and his proposals to tax the rich more heavily in his famous People's Budget of 1909 made him a bête noire to upper-class opinion.
20. The retirement of Foster in No. 5 saw a particularly severe drop in numbers.
21. No. 3 House Prefects' Minutes, summer term 1912.
22. Michael Arlen, who at Malvern was D. Kouyoumdjian in his novel *Piracy,* quoted in Blumenau, pp.73–74.
23. James to Fraser dated 8 December 1907. SH archives. Although not certain, this may be G. G. Fraser (Day Boy, 1879–85) who had returned to Malvern as a master in 1901.
24. F. W. Montresor (formerly Rideout) (5. 1898–01) quoted in *OMN* (1985).

The Night Prowler

i. Arlen was a new boy when the event upon which this story is based occurred. Sydney James also gave his version in his autobiography and that account provides for the historical corrections to what today would be called 'faction'.

ii. In reality in order to avoid being identified by his writing he left behind or sent through the post notes laboriously written in pinpricks. James's note read. 'We think your cigars delicious and hope your desk is not much hurt.'

iii. Blumenau suggests that this was probably R. B. Porch who played cricket for Somerset.

The Fosters and 'Fostershire'

i. The news of the royal telegram came from Jay Iliff, 'A sporting hero who would have made sure we won'; *Daily Express* (17 June 2000).

ii. A First-Class cricket match originating in 1806, generally played annually after 1891, when a team of amateurs (the Gentlemen) played a team of professionals (the Players). There were usually two or more games each season. The fixture ended in 1962 when the status of amateurism was abolished.

iii. H. K. 8; B. S. 2.

iv. Apparently this is only one of two occasions in the history of cricket that this happened. The other was by the Chappell brothers in 1974 when Australia played New Zealand at Wellington. Ian Chappell scored 145 and 121 and Greg Chappell 247 not out and 133.

v. Much of the information on the Fosters comes from an article written by George Chesterton in *OMN* (November 1981).

Chapter 4

1. Blumenau, op. cit., p.86.
2. Ibid., p.87.
3. *The Malvernian* (March 1978).
4. Gordon Dashwood (7. 1928–33), *Never a Dull Moment* (1994), p.87.
5. Letter from Captain Lindsay (No. 2), 7 October 1914.
6. Blumenau, op. cit., p.90.
7. F. L. D. Wardle (7. 1916–19), quoted in *Old Malvernian Newsletter* (November, 1985).
8. W. H. Farr (8. 1917–20), *OMN* (November 1985). The housemaster was Walter Lowe of No. 8.
9. Blumenau, op. cit., p.92. A grateful school panelled his old classroom and created a Memorial Exhibition in his memory.

10. This building was originally called Townsend House and was acquired by Dr Grindrod in 1851 for use as a hydropathic establishment. The well-head, known as Dr Grindrod's Fountain, was an important supplier of water from the hills. In 1891 the English Benedictine monks at Douai acquired it. In 1918 they sold the property to Malvern College. The Monastery became the Music School and in 1998 the school was able to purchase, with the help of a generous parent, the now redundant church, which has become a music and lecture venue, with the basement turned into a Sixth Form social centre.
11. The College Council had in 1899 offered £11,000 for SH, but Lord Beauchamp wanted £12,000, so the issue was dropped. In 1920 the long-running battle was brought to an end when the OMS bought SH for £13,500.
12. Later president of the Royal Institute of British Architects.
13. Thus the appellation Ltd disappeared from the official name of Malvern College.
14. A. E. L. Parnis (SH 1924–28), quoted in the *OMN* (November 1987).
15. J. M. Montresor (1. 1925–30), *OMN* (1985).
16. Preston showed that the average age of School House boys fell from 16.1 in September 1931, to 15.6, two years later, when there were only seven boys remaining beyond the age of seventeen. In No. 7 there was not a single boy over sixteen.
17. Preston papers. To put this comment into context, at this time being in the Sixth Form was seen as a mark of academic stature. Most boys were in the Army or Business forms, or left the school earlier.
18. Before 1919 the practice rooms were in 4. The Lees, briefly the home of Edward Elgar in 1889.
19. *The Malvernian* (December 1921).
20. Called for some years the Allison club after its founder.
21. Blumenau, op. cit., p.109.
22. J. M. Montresor (1. 1925–30), in 'Reminiscences from Father and Son', *OMN* (November 1985).
23. Dashwood, op. cit., p.86. On a later visit four boys attended the Duke of York's camp and rejoiced both in the visit of the King and 'official permission to smoke at any time and anywhere except in sleeping marquees.'
24. *The Malvernian* (March 1970). The article noted that Preston was in the same league as Sanderson at Oundle, Vaughan at Rugby, Fletcher at Charterhouse, Norwood at Marlborough and Harrow.

The Malvernian Society

i. Blumenau, op. cit., p.45.
ii. George Chesterton, *A Hundred Pictures of a Hundred Years, The Malvernian Society, 1895–1995* (printed privately).
iii. From 1925 the new OM Club took much of this money to keep separate for tax purposes the work done by the society for the school and that done for its old boys.
iv. See Chapter 15 for further details.

Chapter 5

1. Tom was a nickname by which he was universally known; his full name was Howard Charles Adie Gaunt.
2. Gaunt played for Warwickshire against Worcestershire in 1919 when he was sixteen and 258 days old while on holiday from Tonbridge making 5 and 13 not out. *The Cricketer* (August 1993), in an article about players who made their First-Class debut before their seventeenth birthday; *OMN* (1993).
3. *OMN* (November 1983). Gaunt wrote *The Children's Crusade*, a ballad poem for which he was awarded the Seatonian Prize in 1954. He also wrote hymns and composed hymn tunes.
4. Secrecy was paramount although Gaunt was allowed to inform the chairman of the Council and a little later he was also able to include the Second Master, Major Elliott, in his confidence. Elliott was sent off to make discreet enquiries for alternative accommodation, with Newquay and Llandrindod Wells shortlisted as possible locations. Any quotations on this period, not otherwise acknowledged, are from Gaunt's account.
5. Term was not due to start until 28 September and would be postponed a further two weeks.
6. An allusion to the recently released film *Sixty Glorious Years*, with Anna Neagle portraying Queen Victoria.
7. J. L. Lewis (2–2/6. 1937–42).
8. Blumenau, op. cit., p.129.
9. A. T. R. Jackson (SH 1937–41), written as part of the sixtieth anniversary of transferring Malvern to Blenheim.
10. Gaunt, *Two Exiles* (1946), p.41.
11. J. G. Kelsall (8–1/8. 1938–42)
12. 'The Government will be unable to release, for our use, Houses 1, 2 & 5. It will therefore be necessary to re-organise these houses, so that the whole school may be accommodated in seven houses instead of ten.'
13. The duke and his family had been very hospitable to the College, converting the old riding school into an assembly hall and gymnasium and giving permission for the boys to use the model railway in the Orangery if they could get it working, which they did. He had also entertained staff and senior boys.
14. George Chesterton in an interview with the author.
15. An article in *The Malvernian* (July 1972) put the number who survived at only five.
16. Andrew Murtagh, *A Remarkable Man. The story of George Chesterton*, p.67.
17. Only six boys withdrew because of the move to Blenheim and only seven when the school went to Harrow.
18. Given the uncertainty Gaunt considered what alternatives would be available to the school. Officials tentatively mentioned that Berkeley Castle in Gloucestershire was empty; although it lacked a water supply, the Ministry suggested one might be connected.
19. While awaiting the final decision from London, Gaunt set to exploring the one option offered by the Ministry – a newly built Canadian camp near Hereford, which proved to have so many drawbacks that it would have been a 'desperate proposition'. Approaches were made to Oxford colleges only to discover that every college room was occupied, although the Oxford representative on the College Council suggested the recently evacuated Imperial Service College. This proved impossible as the Army had taken possession.
20. Butler was the president of the Board of Education at this stage.
21. The fact that the City of London School had already located to join Marlborough would have meant uprooting 1,100 boys compared to Malvern's 350 and further investigation found that Marlborough's drainage system was barely adequate for the present inhabitants, and would be quite inadequate for the increased population which TRE

22. Christopher Tyerman, *A History of Harrow School* (2000), pp.432, 524.

23. So No. 3 in Rendalls was Cosgrove's; No. 4 in Westacre was Chadder's; No. 5/7 in Deyncourt was Colthurst's; No. 2/6 in Newlands was Salter's. School House boys were initially distributed in small groups in the Harrow houses until Bradby was freed for their use.

24. Term was supposed to have started on 1 May.

25. One Malvern custom – that of swimming in the nude – was abandoned for good, largely because women who worked in a NAAFI near the pool complained about coming across naked sunbathers. An attempt to revive the custom in 1951 when an outbreak of pink-eye among the boys was attributed to fine fluff from their swimming trunks, was rejected when the School Prefects expressed strong objections on behalf of the school.

26. John Burton (5. 1944–49), letter to the author.

27. Speech to Harrow School, 18 November 1942.

28. Secretary of State for Air and leader of the Liberal Party.

29. Lawyer who advised Edward VIII during the Abdication Crisis and who served the wartime coalition in a number of propaganda posts.

30. MP for Oxford and later long-serving Conservative minister.

31. Burton, op. cit.

32. The custom of banging spoons on tables to celebrate the success of the house, or individuals, in sporting and other activities.

33. This compensation amounted to £150,000 and was paid in full by 1952. Even then the school's overdraft was £28,000.

34. Historian Headmaster of Charterhouse (and later Headmaster of Eton) who was sent as educational adviser to the British zone in Germany to lead educational reconstruction. He played a key role in re-writing Nazi history textbooks.

35. No. 3 Prefects' House Minutes, Lent term 1948.

36. I am indebted to Brian Davis (6. 1949–53) for this anecdote.

37. Gaunt moved to Winchester College where he served as an assistant master and then chaplain until 1963. He became a deacon in 1954 and a priest the following year. In 1963 he became Sacristan of Winchester Cathedral and in 1967 Precentor, a post that he held until 1973. He died in 1980.

38. I am indebted to Geoffrey Farrar Brown for this personal anecdote.

39. Letters of J. T. Williams, kept in the College Archives.

Blenheim diary

i. Colin Silver became Senior Chapel Prefect and worked on breaking Japanese codes at Bletchley Park before going to Oxford in 1945. He then taught, and became a housemaster, at Rugby. He died in 2008 aged eighty-three.

ii. George VI called the nation to prayer at what was seen as a time of dire national emergency with the BEF trapped on the beaches of Dunkirk. In the following days the 'miracle' of Dunkirk occurred when some 330,000 British and French troops were ferried back to England with the help of hundreds of tiny craft.

iii. British Expeditionary Force sent to France at the outbreak of hostilities.

Chapter 6

1. This friend was Errol Holmes who had briefly been Wheeler-Bennett's 'fag' at Malvern (his success in sport exempted him from these duties after one term) and who became one of his lifelong friends. His remarkable cricketing career is described in Chapter 13. The dinner was in April 1954.

2. Recorded by John Wheeler-Bennett, D17, WB papers, SANT, Oxford, quoted in this section by Victoria Schofield, *Witness to History* (2012), p.205.

3. Blumenau, op. cit., p.161. Blumenau also recorded that 'the prefects' minutes show that they found the new Headmaster's dicta irresistible; and it is a loss to the historian that in his second term Lindsay asked that what he said at prefects' meetings should no longer be recorded'.

4. *The Malvernian* (1971).

5. This anecdote was provided by Reg Farrar.

6. I am indebted to Roger Gillard for this delightful vignette.

7. The boy concerned was Peter Bowen-Simpkins (2. 1955–60) who kindly provided this anecdote. Michael McNevin taught chemistry and his lively lessons, often involving explosive experiments, were much enjoyed. He was a much-respected housemaster of No. 2. Norman Rosser provided an academic profile for the Geography Department, which he ran. He was housemaster of No. 1 and master in charge of rackets.

8. Described in the programme as *The Ballet Awful*.

9. The tutor was Roger Gillard.

10. I am again indebted to Roger Gillard for this *Whiskey Galore* moment.

11. I am grateful to Pat Hooley for this wonderful piece of social history. It had, of course, been an assumption in earlier years that masters would have a private income and that their salary was some sort of extra payment.

12. 'Hall' is Malvern jargon for academic preparation time, usually after supper.

13. The school certificate was replaced in 1951 by a two-tier system of public examinations: Ordinary level in a number of subjects at age sixteen, two or three Advanced level subjects at eighteen. The latter would normally be the required route for entry to university.

14. New societies emerged: German, Spanish and history societies, clubs for angling, reels and sailing (whose members built their own sailing site on the Severn near Upton), theatre and jazz. A film club showed classics of the cinema and an 'Anti-Uglies' group photographed eye-sores in the town and sketched suggested improvements. The Natural History Society benefited from the offer to the College of a nature reserve of 26 acres centred on the former home of Elizabeth Barrett Browning at Hope End. The Sixth and Fifth Form discussion groups became the Socratic Society and Forum, which in turn generated discussion groups in the houses.

15. Another description of this derivation comes from the 1965 *Age Frater:* 'the aptness of the name was confirmed when the habits of this animal were investigated: they are inquisitive and courageous and, when left to their own devices, will gorge themselves – then fall asleep for long periods.'

16. Address by Ian Beer (Headmaster of Harrow) at the service of thanksgiving for Donald Lindsay, 8 March 2003.

17. Blumenau, op. cit., p.170. A fine collection of nineteenth-century watercolours was presented to the College in 1961 by Mrs E.

P. Higgins in memory of J. C. P. Higgins (SH 1927–32), who had originally formed the collection. In 1982 a small gallery was created at the entrance to the Grundy to exhibit them.

18. Peter J. Pegrum (8.1954–58) in a reminiscence in the *OMN* (May 2004) following Donald Lindsay's death in 2003.

19. There are many versions of this story and I greatly indebted to Martin Knott for what seems to be the most accurate account.

20. Ralph Blumenau writing in *Warwickshire & Worcestershire Life* (October 1970).

21. The Headmasters' and Headmistresses' Conference represents some 250 of the leading independent schools in the UK.

22. These proposals would have seen public schools being forced to accept 50 per cent of their intake as state-assisted pupils from a much wider range of academic ability. Lindsay represented the view that such schools would be perfectly happy to take up to 25 per cent of state-assisted pupils but that the exact proportion should remain within the choice of the individual school, and that special provision would have to be created for any less academic pupils.

23. Address by Ian Beer at the service of thanksgiving for Donald Lindsay, 8 March 2003.

24. After retiring as headmaster Donald Lindsay became the first director of the Independent Schools Information Service (ISIS). *The Times* obituary recalls: 'the heads of some of the most famous schools felt little need for such an association, and some of the backwoodsmen of the Headmasters' Conference did not want to be allied with girls' schools and prep schools but Lindsay persuaded them that the whole of the independent sector should work together and that individual schools would have additional muscle when represented by a national organisation'. *The Times* (3 December 2003).

25. *The Malvernian* (March 1965).

26. James Stredder in a letter to the author. Eb Kennedy, who started teaching at the College in 1928, retired in 1965. I am grateful to Richard Thurlow for the following: '"ECK" edited half a dozen Latin and Greek texts and literature compilations for use in schools. His notes on the various Classical authors were always clear, informative and scholarly – and perfectly pitched for their "target audience". I remember using his *Two Centuries of Latin Poetry* (first published 1964) and *Latin Unseens from Roman History* (first published 1951) with GCSE classes at Malvern in the 1980s and 1990s. The book he wrote with G. W. White is called *SPQR* (first published 1943). It's a succinct 'Cook's Tour' of the history and social life of Ancient Rome and is aimed at Lower School "amateur Latinists" (as John Hart would have called them)'.

27. Lewis Dodd was an Old Malvernian who started teaching in 1948. Sadly injuries sustained in the war curtailed his housemastership of SH. He retired in 1966, and taught for two years in Budo College in Uganda before running a bookshop in Newport in Wales. The qualities mentioned come from Ralph Blumenau.

28. Malcolm Staniforth came to Malvern to teach geography in 1938. For many years he ran the cricket and was housemaster of No. 3 during its golden age of sporting triumph. He retired in 1976.

29. Ralph Blumenau, 'Look Outward, Look Ahead', *Warwickshire and Worcestershire Life* (October 1970).

30. The CCF responded to a decision by the armed services to reduce numbers by deciding that boys should only serve for three years rather than four or five. Therefore from 1963 the military obligation only began in the third year at school with the new boys studying arts and crafts and the second year given over to the Pioneers – since 1956 a training in rope-climbing, map-reading and field craft.

31. Kevin Walton certainly had a distinguished career and as an engineering officer on the *Rodney* took part in the pursuit of the *Bismarck* before his remarkable contribution in keeping the *Onslow* afloat after it had been holed in action against the *Admiral Hipper* and *Lützow*. For this action he was awarded the DSC, and then mentioned in despatches for his service on the North Atlantic convoys. He subsequently was greatly involved in Antarctic research and was awarded the George Cross in 1946 for rescuing a fellow member of an expedition from a crevasse. Another rescue in South Georgia led to the Queen's Commendation. His schoolmastering career started at Oundle and he came to Malvern in 1969 where he started the Penguin sailing club referred to by Dr Taylor, as well as attempting to foster an understanding of engineering among the pupils. He died in 2009 aged ninety.

32. Dr Michael Taylor.

33. In the same year Donald Lindsay replied to a request from a correspondent in *The Malvernian* to see more of the headmaster as follows: 'If I am invited I will certainly accept. Of course, one must always remember that sometimes absence makes the heart grow fonder and that ignorance of each other may be bliss'.

34. This engaging story comes from Norman Rosser who recalls that the Common Room was delighted to hear the whole escapade and as far as he could remember 'the punishments were not too draconian'.

35. Jeremy M. Lewis (1. 1955–59), *Playing for Time* (Collins, 1987), p.213.

36. Jeremy M. Lewis, private letter to author.

37. Andrew Lowcock (9. 1963–68), letter to the author.

38. Both had been abolished at Westminster.

39. He was seconded as a Nuffield research fellow to the Nuffield Chemistry Project from 1962 to 1964 and as Salter's Company Schoolmaster Fellow at the Department of Chemical Engineering, Imperial College, London in 1969. Among his publications are: *John Dalton and the Atomic Theory* (1965), *Chemistry and Energy* (1968), *Chemistry: Facts, Patterns and Principles* (1972) (co-author), and *Francis Bacon and the Birth of Modern Science* (1976). He edited the Nuffield O-Level Sample Scheme (1965), the Foreground Chemistry Series (1968) and the Farmington Papers from 1993 to 2001.

40. Martin Rogers, interview with author (October 2010).

41. This appeal for £500,000 was reached ahead of schedule in July 1983.

42. Adam Pharoah (SH 1976–81) in a letter to the author. Adam associated this end of beating with EU directives but they did not come into force until much later. It seems more likely that the custom fell into disuse with changing generations of housemasters. With the demise of caning the usual punishments for misbehaviour became 'gating', when a pupil was banned from a range of social activities and had to have a gating card signed every hour, or rustication, when a pupil was sent home for a number of days. The ultimate sanction of expulsion continues to be used sparingly for very serious offences.

43. Pat Hooley chaired the working party that

44. Ralph Blumenau, Head of History 1958–85, in a paper on *Coeducation at Malvern before the Merger*.
45. No. 3 under the housemastership of Michael Harvey. A fuller account of these changes can be found in Chapter 10.
46. Initially eight assisted places would be offered at eleven-plus enabling boys to go to a local preparatory school before coming to Malvern, and a further eight places would be available for entry to Malvern at thirteen.
47. This featured an extension at the south end that included a green room, changing rooms and access round the back of the stage. It was opened on 23 November 1984 by Martin Rogers and was named after him as a tribute to his encouragement of the arts during his headmastership.
48. Interview with Martin Rogers, *The Malvernian* (June 1982).
49. So called because the initiator and first host Michael Harvey covered the costs of hospitality by putting it down under the fuel allowance for the house lawnmower. The housemasters' wives, not to be left out, created the Strimmers 'which was described as dealing with the bits that the Flymos could not cope with' (my thanks to Julia Knott for this engaging description).
50. Martin Rogers retired from the headmastership in 1991 and was appointed as director of Farmington Institute for Christian Studies in Oxford.
51. *The Malvernian* (June 1982).
52. Sir Stephen Brown (5. 1939–42) in the *OMN* (November 1982).

Sir John Wheeler-Bennett

i. Probably influenced by a neighbour of the family, Arthur Boosey, founder of the music publishers Boosey & Hawkes, who was educating his boys at the College.
ii. Schofield, op. cit. p.9.
iii. Many readers will be familiar with the invaluable relationship between George VI and Logue which formed the central theme of the film *The King's Speech* (2010).

George Sayer

i. Robin Clark (SH 1970–74) from an article entitled 'A guide to Punctuation & Spelling'.
ii. Hugh Pullan (8. 1956–62) from Alan Carter's tribute to Sayer in the *OMN* (April 2006).
iii. Philip Bushill-Matthews, MEP (6. 1956–62).

The Duke of Edinburgh Award Scheme

i. Richard Goddard taught history and politics, was housemaster of No. 6, and subsequently an assistant bursar. His dry humour and considerable wit was a delight to both pupils and colleagues. On the occasion of a departmental inspection he reassured a nervous new master (the author) by announcing that he was going to give his class a reading period!

Chapter 7

1. The International Baccalaureate requires the study of six subjects: three at Higher level and three at Standard and students have to balance English, mathematics, languages, sciences and humanities. In addition they have to study a course on the theory of knowledge, write a 4,000-word extended essay and fulfil a programme of creative, sporting and service activities.
2. I have been told that Tony Leng had pioneered this some years earlier when his own daughter was taught at the College living, of course, at home, and thus could be considered a member of SH.
3. Malvern Girls' College, Ellerslie, St James and Lawnside.
4. Professor Davey had been on the College Council since 1986 and was vice-chairman 1994–2006. He taught at the School of Public Policy at the University of Birmingham (UK) from 1969 to 2000. His posts included Professor of Development Administration; director, Institute of Local Government Studies; and head of school. After the collapse of the Communist regimes in Eastern Europe he became a key adviser on the establishment of local government to the new democracies.
5. 'Hundred' is Malvern jargon for Year 11 or the GCSE year. The first year is called the Foundation Year and the second year the Removes. In earlier years the first year was called the Shell.
6. It was discovered that the prep school could be comfortably accommodated in the other old Ellerslie buildings, leaving Hampton to could accommodate both Pre-Prep and the boys of No. 6.
7. Martin Knott in an interview with the author.
8. Frank Harriss in an interview with the author.
9. I am indebted to Sue Lamberton for this account of the early days of the merger.
10. Angela Lafferty in letter to author.
11. Richard Goddard, housemaster of No. 6, had, of course, been informed about the fate of his house much earlier and carried out the school's policy with a heavy heart. When he told the boys in his house a number were in tears.
12. The following presided over Hampton House (for boys displaced by conversion of their house for girls) until it became the Pre-Prep for Hillstone: R. G. H. Goddard, 1992; T. Southall, 1993; R. G. Witcomb (OM), 1995–97.
13. Chaired by the master diplomat and Director of Studies Frank Harriss.
14. Headmaster's speech at Commemoration, 1986.
15. Interview with Hugh Carson by Philippa Lambert, *The Malvernian* (1996).
16. The boy was Kaspar Hartmann (2. 1998–2000). The tutor was the author!
17. ISC Inspectors' Report (November 2005).
18. Frank Harriss, *The Malvernian* (2006).
19. Hugh Carson, headmaster's report in the *OMN* (May 2000).
20. This building now contains the classrooms for maths, languages and Classics.
21. ISC Inspectors' Report (November 2005).

Chapter 8

1. From the eighth annual report.
2. That is until they were abolished in the 1980s.
3. E. L. Bryans, *Malvern Register*, I xxxviii.
4. H. C. Minchin, *The Malvernian* (March 1925).
5. Sir John Wheeler-Bennett, '*Groves of Academe*'. D17, WB papers, SANT, Oxford quoted in Schofield, op. cit., p.9.
6. Ibid. p.12.
7. Ibid. p.11.
8. Preston's comments are from his unpublished memoirs of his time as headmaster.
9. A military college for preparing artillery and engineering officers. It was merged with Sandhurst after the Second World War.

10. The architect was an Old Malvernian, P. W. Hubbard.
11. Malvern science had seen the service of some distinguished teachers in this period. John Lewis singles out Douglas Berridge, Freddie Hare and Malcolm Nokes.
12. November and December 1938 editions of *The Malvernian*.
13. George Chesterton quoted in Murtagh, op. cit., p.58.
14. Ibid., p.66.
15. Reg Farrar in an interview with the author.
16. *OMN* (November 1983).
17. Martin Knott remembered that Ralph Cobb, apart from being a brilliant teacher for sixth-form mathematicians, 'was the problem-solving bureau of the Mathematics Association dealing with requests from teachers all over the country confronted with difficult examination questions'.
18. *Malvernian* tribute in 1983.
19. 'The pioneer work done in Malvern in the 1960s on the teaching of modern Physics included the study of radioactivity, which resulted in its inclusion in all GCE syllabuses from then onwards. Preliminary work in this area was undertaken by M. C. Noakes who taught in the Science Department from 1922 to 1946'. *OMN* (1983).
20. Named after J. J. Salter, former Head of the Chemistry department and housemaster of No. 6, who died in 1960.
21. *The Malvernian* (March 1965).
22. James Stredder writes: '"Viv-Rob", pioneering the study of Geology at the school, put its Victorian collection of fossils, rocks and minerals into our hands; revealed to us the extraordinary geological riches of the Malvern Hills and their immediate surroundings; took us on field-trips in a minibus to locations miles away from Worcestershire; made us feel the excitement of what was, after all, a very new science, so much so that I felt a direct connection with the founding fathers of the subject, which, I decided, I would read at university.'
23. Alan Duff won a special teacher's award from the Association of Science Education for his outstanding teaching of Nuffield Physics.
24. By complete coincidence and, of course, before he came to Malvern as headmaster.
25. Arnold Darlington was Head of Biology from 1965 to 1973 having spent much of his career at Bishop's Stortford.
26. In 1989 Malvern submitted a team of three boys for the Young Scientist of the Year competition with a project on the geology of the Malvern Hills. They were selected from several hundred schools to appear in the BBC television programme; they won their heat and were runners-up to the eventual winners in the final, but of sufficient merit to go to Eindhoven for the European final.
27. This initiative came through the good offices of Mr G. Farrer-Brown who encouraged an interest in a paper by a Malvern master lamenting the limited linguistic opportunities for non-specialists.
28. Michael Wilcox, *Outlaw in the Hills: A Writer's Year*, p.86.
29. This was proposed and run by Michael Harvey who actively promoted the educational value of art.
30. James Stredder in a letter to the author. The housemaster was John Collinson.
31. He also gave his name to an important legal ruling in Hart v Pepper, 1992. See p.122.
32. The Lower Sixth and the Upper Sixth were called 'VIC' and 'VIB' in those days.
33. Ralph Blumenau in a paper on *Coeducation at Malvern before the Merger*.
34. Rather less well known was his encyclopaedic knowledge of murders.
35. Martin Frayn went on to have a most distinguished career at the College. As a first-class teacher, and Head of the Economics and Politics department, he greatly increased both the popularity and academic status of the subject. As Head of the Sixth Form he stood firmly for high standards and both in that role and as a tutor greatly influenced the evolution of Malvern's pastoral system.
36. See Chapter 14 and Appendix 2 for career details.
37. In earlier years there was a rather chaotic allocation of administrative jobs and the evolution of academic policy was rather haphazard. The remarkable Simon Wilkinson had done much to bring order out of chaos but after his departure to become headmaster of St Alban's School fragmentation reappeared.
38. IB numbers gradually increased from 16 in 1995 to 36 in 2000, and then considerably reaching 106 in 2011. Malvern acquired an enviable reputation of being one of the best and most established IB schools in the country.
39. A good score in the IB (around 38 points) can lead to a full year's credit at some American universities.
40. In the opinion of the IBO this forms the core of the whole programme, in which students are encouraged to examine 'how' they know what they think they know in the different disciplines. It is examined by an essay and in a class presentation.
41. Moritz Liebelt (1. 2009–12).
42. The English teacher was Katie Adam, the instructor Justin Major.

Harry Hammond House

i. Blumenau, op. cit., p.118.

Harry Wakelyn Smith

i. C. S. Lewis, *Surprised by Joy*, p.85–6.

The Lewis connection

i. Alister McGrath, *C. S. Lewis: A Life* (Hodder & Stoughton, 2013). McGrath records that as early as 1903 Lewis rejected his Christian name, Clive, in favour of Jack for reasons that remain obscure.

ii. His historical works include *The Splendid Century: Some Aspects of French Life in the Reign of Louis XIV*.

iii. McGrath, ibid. p.37.

John Lewis

i. James Stredder in a letter to the author.

ii. This organisation brings together the Royal Society, the American Academy of Science, and the Russian Academy of Science.

iii. A morris dancing troupe which would tour regularly in the summer months and became an extremely popular social activity with a number of John's former pupils.

Reg Farrar

i. Alan Carter in a retirement tribute, *OMN* (November 1985). The final comment referred to Reg's love of school gossip and his categorisation for who should be granted the latest information. If I remember correctly 'in strictest confidence' meant that you had to wait until you heard someone else repeating the story, before passing it on!

Ralph Blumenau

i. Tony Leng in a retirement tribute in 1985.
ii. Ahmed J. Rashid (2. 1962–66), letter to the author 14 October 2012.
iii. Ralph Blumenau papers.

Alan Carter

i. Dale Vargas came from Harrow and Cambridge to teach maths at Malvern for a few years. He returned to Harrow to teach, become a housemaster and later rose to be deputy head, and then chair of the Harrow Association.

Chapter 9

1. In 1891 Sir Arthur Blomfield had been responsible for the construction of Eton College Lower Chapel.
2. Better known as M. R. James the author of a number of classic ghost stories. He had played a leading role in the restoration and rearrangement of the medieval glass in Malvern Priory.
3. From the *Kempe Society Newsletter* quoted in George Chesterton's *History of Malvern College Chapel*.
4. Simpson, *Aspects of Malvern College Architecture*, pp.3–4.
5. Brigadier F. M. Montresor, MC (formerly F. M. Rideout) (5. 1898–1901) quoted in *OMN* (1985).
6. John Baker White (7. 1916–20), *True Blue: An Autobiography 1902–39* (Frederick Muller, 1970), pp.81–82.
7. The work was carried out by Mr W. J. Blomfield.
8. A. M. Field (SH 1924–28), *Before the Memory Fades: The Life Story of Colonel Arthur Maurice Field OBE. MC, Late Royal Engineers* (printed privately, 2005). Arthur Field had a distinguished military career winning the MC in Pakistan and serving with the Indian Army and in Korea. He was on the staff of Supreme Headquarters Allied Powers Europe (SHAPE) and commandant of Joint School of Nuclear and Chemical Ground Defence 1958–60.
9. *OMN* (November 1983).
10. Donald Lindsay's address was reprinted in the *OMN* (May 2000).
11. Silviana Ciurea Ilcus (8. 2010–12), now studying at Stanford, in a letter to Dr Robin Lister (October 2012).
12. Robert Porter (SH 2011–).
13. Andrew Law, the current chaplain, in a letter to the author.
14. From T. S. Eliot, *Little Giddings* from *The Four Quartets*.

Chapter 10

1. Michael Arlen, *"Piracy"* (1922).
2. Wyvern was Lewis's barely concealed name for Malvern in his autobiographical *Surprised by Joy*. Bloods was a nickname for the sporty senior boys who were often the subject of hero-worship from the younger boys.
3. C. S. Lewis, op. cit.
4. Blumenau, op. cit., pp.75–76.
5. The infamous brutal school in Dickens' *Nicholas Nickleby*.
6. A. M. Field (SH 1924–28), *Before the Memory Fades* (printed privately, 2005), p.37.
7. Lt. Col. A. A. Mains (1. 1927–32) 'From Fag to Prefect', *OMN* (December 1990).
8. C. E. S. Gillyatt (5. 1921–26), 'Fagging – Exploitation or Training?', *OMN* (November 1995).
9. Blumenau, op. cit., pp.110–11.
10. Dr Finlay Murray (9. 1986–91).
11. Robert Heussler, *Yesterday's Rulers: The Making of the British Colonial Service* (1963) quoted in Dr Finlay Murray, 'School and Empire: British imperial service and the public schools between the wars', *Inklings* (Malvern, 2001).
12. According to Anthony Kirk-Greene's *Britain's Imperial Administrators, 1858–1966* (2000) quoted in Murray op. cit., between 1926 and 1956 Malvern sent out twenty-one colonial administrators, the same number as Eton.
13. D. R. Erskine, son of the housemaster of School House (30 September 1951).
14. The rule at the time was that the last boy to appear got the job and then did not have to answer another fag call for the following week; so the little boy used for this demonstration got off lightly – by just appearing, he was free for the next week.
15. Robin Harrild (7. 1959–64), letter to author.
16. In one of the official publications for the centenary, *Age Frater*, a highly critical article appeared attacking the whole concept of fagging. The author suggested that all boys below the rank of prefect should perform general domestic duties. The author took particular umbrage to personal fagging 'with prefects being allotted other boys to clean their shoes, brush their jackets and wash their games clothes, all activities to bolster up any feelings of superiority they may already possess.'
17. Ralph Blumenau's tribute to Donald Lindsay in the *OMN* and *The Malvernian* (2003).
18. School Prefects' minutes, May 1961.
19. George Chesterton and James Stredder have different versions of the incident 'up-town' but the key issue was the response.
20. George Chesterton to the author.
21. James Stredder, interview with the author.
22. *The Malvernian* (March 1967).
23. *The Malvernian* (December 1972).
24. Alan Duff, housemaster of SH, 1975–87.
25. Martin Knott, housemaster of No. 2, 1979–91, interview with the author.
26. Michael Harvey was Head of German and together with his wife Suse acquired a great loyalty from the boys in their house. A remarkable intellect, Michael additionally came to teach history of art and religious studies. No man thought more deeply about the nature of education. He was also immensely entertaining and his wide circle of friends greatly enjoyed hilarious evenings at the Harvey table.
27. Michael Harvey, *Christian Leadership: A Formula for Boarding Education* (unpublished paper).
28. The College employed John Adair, formerly in charge of leadership training at Sandhurst and subsequently first professor of leadership at Surrey University. He was the pioneer 'of action centred leadership'.
29. I am indebted to Mr Andrew Walker for forwarding this fascinating description of how house fagging came to an end in No. 8.
30. It was perhaps of some significance that Mark was an American.
31. Letter dated 1 September 1980 from Mark Hardiman to Andrew Walker.
32. Chris Rycroft (6. 1978–83), *A Walk on the Hills – a Personal Reflection on his Time at Malvern* (private publication).

33. Eighteen were invited to apply for the academic year 2013/14.

34. Susie Cromme (4. 1998–2003). Susie gained a Masters in Management at St Andrews and subsequently a Masters in Psychology at the LSE. In 2009 she started work for the Boston Consulting Group in Germany.

35. Arthur Wakeley (2. 2006–11), Senior Chapel Prefect 2010–11, then read history at Lincoln College, Oxford.

George Chesterton

i. Being an Anglican school it was expected that all masters should be available to teach divinity, as religious studies was then called. This expectation weighed heavily on many who had a limited grasp of elementary theology or who feared mobbing by an unruly class who would quickly delight in their teacher's uncertainty.

Chapter 11

1. Apparently the suggestion came from Mr Foster and the original intention was to assist the continuation of Bishop Patterson's work in the Melanesian Islands.

2. According to Alana Harris this was part of continued interest in 'the condition of England' question. This ongoing debate had been a major literary and religious issue since the 1840s.

3. *The Malvernian* (1894), p.508.

4. Ben. T. Tinton, *War Comes to the Docks* (Marshall, Morgan and Scott, 1941), quoted in Peter Watherston, *A Different Kind of Church* (Marshall Pickering, 1994).

5. It cost £350.

6. *The Malvernian* (1894).

7. *The Malvernian* (1896).

8. Basil Kentish (3. 1890–95), *This Foul Thing Called War: The Life of Brigadier General R. J. Kentish CMG, DSO, (1876–1956)* (The Book Guild Ltd., 1997).

9. Reginald Kennedy-Cox, *Docklands Saga* (1955), p.30, quoted in Peter Watherston, op. cit.

10. *The Times* (21 October 1927). Quoted in Dr Alana Harris, 'Building the Docklands Settlement: Gender, Gentility and the Gentry in East London, 1894–1939', in *Material Religion: Journal of Objects, Art and Religion* (Spring 2013).

11. Alana Harris, op. cit.

12. Kennedy-Cox was knighted for his efforts in the East End. A block of flats in Cooper Street today is named after him.

13. Kennedy-Cox, op. cit.

14. Mike Tiley in letter to the author who also met presumably the same men when they visited Malvern.

15. In a letter to Mike Tiley from Bill Hurn.

16. David Warren, report in *The Malvernian* (May 1975).

17. When pupils can wear their casual clothes rather than the normal school uniform. It is not unusual for some pupils to 'try it on' by wearing outlandish costumes, so teachers have to be prepared to judge whether a rugby player in drag or a girl in a bear outfit is conducive to disciplined learning.

18. Homes for Kids in South Africa. This charity is run by a great friend of Antony and Brigitte Clark.

19. Moritz Liebelt (1. 2009–12), in a letter to the author.

Chapter 12

1. The award of Younger's VC came nearly two years after his death; at the time the Victoria Cross was not awarded posthumously, and instead it was noted in the *London Gazette* that he would have received the VC had he survived. In April 1902 Victoria Crosses were given to the families of six men who had performed acts of valour in South Africa that would have entitled them to be recommended for the VC had they survived. Younger was one of the six. M. J. Crook, *The Evolution of the Victoria Cross* (Midas Books, 1975).

2. This institution went through a series of different forms: 1883–1909 as an artillery unit; 1909–41, the Infantry Officers' Training Corps (attached to the Worcestershire Regiment); 1941–48 the Junior Training Corps and the Malvern College Flight ATC, and finally the Combined Cadet Force.

3. *The Malvernian* editorial (August 1914).

4. *The Malvernian* editorial (November 1914).

5. One feature that is apparent from the over 400 obituaries is the sizeable number of OMs who came back to fight for Britain from the Dominions, particularly Canada. It is also striking how many of those who paid the ultimate price had been wounded before returning to combat.

6. Blumenau, op. cit., p.90.

7. As part of the commemoration of those who had died the Malvernian Society created a series of memorial books called *Our Brothers*, which is why there is so much material readily available on those OMs who fought, and died, in the Great War.

8. Extracts from J. A. Radcliffe's address at the Memorial Service for A. P. Rowe. John Ashworth Ratcliffe, FRS (1902–87), was an influential British radio physicist. He and his University of Cambridge group did much pioneering work on the ionosphere, immediately prior to the Second World War. He was one of many leading radio scientists who worked at the Telecommunications Research Establishment during the Second World War.

9. An interesting aside to these developments comes from an account of a Luftwaffe pilot, Hubert Gangl, who survived the shooting down of his Junkers Ju88 bomber over Malvern in July 1942. Revisiting the town in 1962 he met Dr Rowe who told him that the shooting down of his aircraft 'was the first successful use of a new kind of radar apparatus designed for night-fighters'. He thought it appropriate that this should have happened over Malvern, the centre of the country's radar research (*Malvern Gazette*).

10. Comments from George Chesterton's Remembrance address, 2009.

11. No fewer than eight members of the Dent family have been to Malvern including Oscar Dent's sons, grandsons and great-grandson, who was Head of House in No. 9 in 2012–13.

12. Ron Baybutt, *Camera in Colditz* (Hodder and Stoughton, 1982).

13. Quoted in *OMN* (November 1982). This story featured as a plot line in the BBC television series *Colditz*.

14. Gerry Chalk, who had been in charge of Malvern cricket from 1935 to 1937 and had then left to become captain of Kent; A. M. McClure, whose arrival at the College in 1938 had galvanised the Art School; and H. B. E. Mills.

15. George Chesterton's sermon for Remembrance Day 2009 from the *OMN* (2010).

16. The original plaque contained seven names but subsequent contacts from OMs has brought the number up to eleven.

17. The cottage has also been used by OMs for holidays and for leadership training schemes.

18. An annual pilgrimage was made in the Easter holidays to the Cairngorm Mountains of Scotland. Under the leadership of Dick Grant (Royal Marine), Kevin Walton (British Antarctic Survey), Michael McNevin, Simon Partridge, Trevor Southall and Martin Knott (MC staff) groups camped out in full winter conditions and completed an arduous traverse of the Cairngorm range. In the later years an element of winter climbing was introduced to the course by Trevor Southall.
19. Nick Stafford (5. 2000–05), Captain, 2nd Royal Tank Regiment.
20. Lieutenant Disney of the Light Dragoons was commanding a troop of armoured vehicles. Quote from McCrum, Mark, *Walking with the Wounded* (Sphere, 2011)

Harrison and Cartwright

i. I am indebted to P. J. Horsey (4. 1938–42) for this account that appeared in the *OMN* (November 1989). Mr Horsey wrote that the 'full account of their experiences is in their book *Within Four Walls* and other references to them is in *Cage Birds* by M. E. Hervey'.

Sir Denis Crowley-Milling

i. These biographical details of Sir Denis' wartime adventures comes from an obituary written in the *OMN* (November 1997). Crowley-Milling, KCB, CBE, DSO, DFC and Bar (4. 1933–37) was a loyal OM arranging flights for the CCF, acting as liaison officer with the service and representing the MOD on the College Council. He also served as president of the Malvernian Society.

Chapter 13

1. Richard Holt. *Sport and the British: A Modern History* (Oxford, 1989), p.74, quoted in Stephen Hill, 'Malvern College and the Victorian "cult of games"', *Inklings* (2006), based on University of York degree dissertation.
2. Frederic Harrison quoted in Simon & Bradley, *The Victorian Public School: Studies in the Development of an Educational Institution* (Dublin, 1975), p.3.
3. Ibid.
4. Charles Kingsley, *Health and Education* (London, 1887), p.85, quoted in Hill, op. cit.
5. Hill, op. cit. p.21.
6. This view found support from foreign observers; Baron de Coubertin, founder of the modern Olympics, thought that encouragement of 'physical vigour and group cooperation in games had played an important part in the acquisition of the British Empire'.
7. Early maps show numerous lawn tennis courts in the grounds. At one stage each house had their own.
8. J. T. Hart, 'Then and Now', *OMN* (November 1995).
9. P. G. Wodehouse, 'Malvern College', *Public School Magazine* (November 1900).
10. The tradition of no sixes was one of the things that Antony Clark, Headmaster and great cricket enthusiast, remembers when he came on tour as a boy to the UK with St Andrew's College, Grahamstown.
11. Alfred Stratford (2. 1870–73) He also played football for England v Scotland in 1876.
12. John Read (1. 1872–75).
13. Arthur Newman (4. 1874–79) played for Gloucestershire. He was an interpreter in Russian for the Intelligence Service.
14. P. H. Latham (3. 1887–91) Cambridge v Oxford, 1892–94 and was captain; he became a schoolmaster at Haileybury.
15. Known as the 'rackets shot'.
16. 'The origin of the nickname has been lost in the mists of time', Andrew Murtagh.
17. George Simpson-Hayward (1. 1889–94) played football v Cambridge 1896–98.
18. Samuel Day (Lyon 1893–98) made a century in his first county match while still at school, held Blues in cricket and football v Oxford, and played football for England 1906; Arthur Day (Toppin 1898–04) played for the Gentlemen and for Kent.
19. Frank Naumann (3. 1907–11), Blue in cricket v Cambridge 1914 and 1919; John Naumann (3. 1908–12) Blue in cricket v Oxford, 1913 and 1919.
20. *Illustrated Sporting and Dramatic News* (7 June 1935). Blumenau, op. cit., p.51. William Evans (6. 1896–01) Blues v Cambridge in cricket 1902–05 (captain) and football 1902–05. Played for the Gentlemen. Killed when flying with Colonel Cody in August 1913. Memorial window in Chapel.
21. Donald Knight (9. 1908–13), cricket v Cambridge 1914 and 1919.
22. G. H. Chesterton in an article on OM cricket, *The Malvernian* (1977).
23. Francis Mann (6. 1902–07), played cricket and rugby v Oxford.
24. Norman Partridge (6. 1914–19).
25. Geoffrey Cuthbertson (2. 1915–18).
26. Clayton Graeme Robson (8. 1915–20).
27. John Deed (2. 1915–20).
28. Charles Capes (7. 1912–16).
29. Errol R. T. Holmes (5. 1919–24) had a reputation as a fine, hard-hitting batsman and as a captain disapproved of a negative or defensive attitude. He toured the West Indies in 1934 and in the second test was top scorer with 85 not out, the match being lost on the last ball but one in a nail-biting finish. England lost the series, the first time they had done so in the West Indies. Holmes played in 1935 in the Lords test against South Africa and led a successful MCC tour to New Zealand and Australia in 1935 although there were no Test matches. As captain of Surrey in 1934 and 1935 he did much to pull his county around after a difficult period. He was able to return to help re-build Surrey fortunes as captain in 1947 and 1948.
30. G. B. Legge (7. 1916–22) made little impression in the 1927 tour of South Africa but in 1929 when touring New Zealand, he played 'the innings of a lifetime' scoring 196 in only four hours and forty minutes, 'driving and cutting with great effect' His test average was 59.8 and he also topped the bowling average for the tour as a whole taking 200 wickets at eleven apiece. Legge was killed flying with the Fleet Air Arm in 1940 (Baker White, p.78).
31. Richard Wiley (9. 1949–54) played for Dorset.
32. Ian MacLaurin (5. 1951–56) played for the RAF and Kent.
33. John Wilcox (3. 1954–59) played for Essex.
34. Bryan Richardson (3. 1957–62), brother of Peter and Dick, the only pair of brothers to have played for England in the same Test. GHC reckoned that Bryan was the most talented of the Richardson brothers but after a few games for Warwickshire the call of business lured him away from the First-Class game.
35. The Cricketer Cup is a competition for some 32 independent schools old boys' clubs. It is now sponsored by Investec Wealth & Investment. It was inaugurated in 1966 and Malvern is second only to Tonbridge in its

number of victories.

36. Roger Tolchard (4. 1960–64). Andy Murtagh comments, 'he would undoubtedly have played more Tests had his career not coincided with Alan Knott and Bob Taylor.'

37. Ricardo Ellcock was selected for the England tour of the West Indies in 1989/90 but back injuries limited his participation and led to a premature ending of his cricket career. He subsequently became an airline pilot.

38. Much of this information about Malvern's cricket history comes from two articles written by George Chesterton, the first in *The Malvernian* (1977), and the second, just before he died, for the December 2012 First XI tour of South Africa.

39. Examples of this generosity are: nets and matting £608 in 1951; a roller £886 in 1970; sight screens, wicket covers, and artificial wicket £2,500 in 1987; a bowling machine £959 in 1989; and an electronic scoreboard, the gift of Mrs Deed, in memory of J. A. Deed (2. 1915–20). The score box, a replica of an earlier one, was given in 1949 by D. J. Knight (9. 1908–13) and J. A. Deed. A terrace for spectators was built in memory of A. R. Duff, master in charge of cricket 1966–80, and in 2003 a cricket net was installed in honour of G. H. Chesterton (SH 1936–41; master in charge of cricket 1951–65), the gift of an appreciative parent.

40. It was started in 2009 by Steve Rhodes – Director of Cricket – and Damian D'Oliveira (son of the famous Basil D'Oliveira) – director of the academy. The boys have to pass a test in English, maths, and science.

41. Tom Newman, currently housemaster of No. 5, to whom I indebted for the details of this scholarship.

42. The three Malvernians were F. W. Hargreaves (1. 1875–77), J. Hargreaves (1. 1875–79) and D. H. Greenwood (1. 1877–78). The latter was injured and thus unable to play in the Cup final.

43. Webster op. cit.

44. A further 16 acres were purchased to the south in 1922, but this was compulsorily purchased for the Telecommunications Research Establishment (radar) in 1949. It was replaced by 11 acres towards Barnards Green (£2,643). A further three acres in the south-west corner were compulsorily acquired by TRE in 1942 and its successor QinetiQ plans to build houses on it.

45. Lionel Bennett (SH 1880–83).

46. The annual match against Shrewsbury started in 1896 and the first fifty years were dominated by the Salopians who won nine engagements to Malvern's three. By 1939 Malvern had achieved 13 victories to Shrewsbury's 24. But after the Second World War fortunes were reversed. Between 1948 and 1970 saw 16 Malvern wins to their opponent's 2. Since 1970 the contest has been very even (Shrewsbury 10 to Malvern's 8).

47. In *The Malvernian* of December 1894 it was suggested that the new fixture with Repton came about because 'for some time past we have wished to test our old rivals of the cricket field in the Football Fields, so that they should they again reel off an unlimited number of victories at cricket, we should at any rate have a chance of wiping off some of these defeats at football. Both schools are heartily glad that such a match has been arranged, and long may it be an annual fixture'.

48. From the Malvern v Repton centenary match programme, September 1994.

49. The Arthur Dunn Cup was inaugurated in 1903 to be contested by clubs made up of former pupils of public schools and colleges. The competition was named in honour of the Arthur Tempest Blakiston Dunn, a noted amateur footballer and Victorian philanthropist who founded the Ludgrove School in Cockfosters in 1892. Dunn played in two FA Cup finals for Old Etonians – who still enter the Cup today – and also represented England on four occasions. In 1913 the competition was oversubscribed to such an extent that a second competition, the Old Boys Cup, was introduced for those clubs not already entered into the Arthur Dunn.

50. R. H. Chadder (SH 1945–51).

51. P. A. Walton, (5. 1952–7), Blue v Cambridge 1957 and 1958. P. D. Ellis (5. 1952–56). H. D. Loader (7. 1952–57). Tony Williams (6. 1952–57).

52. Paul Walton, David Marnham (who was probably the finest schoolboy defender coached by Denis) Michael Costeloe, Mike Theobald, David French and Tony Williams, who provided this information.

53. J. W. Illaszeicz Bridle (5. 1956–61). Tony Williams to the author May 2013.

54. Four girls were selected to represent the South-West Schools in the Independent Schools Football Association (ISFA) U18 inter-regional tournament in March 2012, one of whom was subsequently named for the ISFA national squad. In 2012 the U18s had their most successful ISFA cup run to date, reaching the quarter-finals.

55. I am greatly indebted to my colleague Joe Gauci for the information on girls' football. As master in charge he has been the inspiration and driving force behind this popular and highly successful activity.

56. Fives has always enjoyed the support of the Malvernian Society. For example, in 1899 they lent £250 at 3 per cent for repairs, and after the Second World War they gave £341 for lighting and repairs to the present courts, which they had initially funded. In 1984, the lighting was further improved at a cost of £2,094 from a bequest by a former master in charge of fives, E. C. Kennedy (1928–65).

57. In the summer of 2006 the three original courts, used for storage in recent years, were demolished to make way for a two-storey extension to the pavilion block to house fourteen Modern Languages classrooms.

58. Lord Aberdare, *The J. T. Faber Book of Tennis and Rackets* (Quiller Press 2001) p.119, writes: 'The truth is that Rackets started in the debtors prisons, the Fleet and the King's Bench, in the mid eighteenth century'. Gentlemen imprisoned for debt and familiar with tennis would persuade friends to bring their rackets 'to the prison to while away the tedious hours. They found the high prison wall ideal for this purpose'.

59. In one of those years Malvern did not enter.

60. The most gifted was Harry Foster who reached the amateur singles final the year after leaving school and then won it for the next seven years and for the eighth time in 1904. He also won the amateur doubles eight times between 1894 and 1903 with a variety of partners including his brothers Wilfred and Basil. Basil was amateur champion in 1912 and 1913 and the doubles champion five times (once with brother Harry and once with Wilfred).

61. The star player was Desmond Manners (3. 1932–38) who played in the school pair for five successive years reaching the final three times and winning twice with Nigel Beeson (9. 1932–37).

62. In 1974 with brothers Mark (9. 1970–74) and Paul Nicholls (9. 1971–76); in 1975 with Paul Nicholls and Martin Tang (9. 1971–76); and

in 1977 with Philip Rosser (6. 1972–77) and Andrew McDonald (1. 1972–77). The latter became the first pair to win schoolboy titles at every age group.

63. Named after H. K. (Harry) Foster and awarded for the public schools singles championship.
64. For under-24s open singles.
65. Under-21 open doubles.
66. Public-school old boys under-24 doubles.
67. In this period Malvern provided no fewer than three contemporary school rackets professionals – Hubbard at Radley, Philip Rosser at Rugby and Roger Tolchard at Malvern.
68. Aberdare, op. cit., p.271.
69. I am very grateful to the late Garnett Scott for this information on Malvern golf. Garnet taught at Malvern from 1957 to 1984; he ran the school golf team for 15 years and was captain of The Worcestershire Golf Club twice – in 1975 and again in 2000. Generations of Malvern golfers owed a great deal to Garnet's encouragement and expertise.
70. Rev S. R. James quoted in Robert Beeson's *Malvern Golf, 1865–2007* (Witley Press Ltd, 2007).
71. Son of the third Malvern headmaster.
72. Eleven members of Common Room having been captains.
73. Gustave Lassen Mellin (Spear, 1897–1902).
74. Geoffrey Illingworth (SH 1920–25).
75. William Wise (5. 1915–18).
76. R. D. James (7. 1956–61).
77. One of the professionals due to play in that match was the OM A. G. Grubb who unfortunately was unable to play. He had had a distinguished career winning the PGA Close Championship in 1964 and coming very close to getting into the Ryder Cup team.
78. A. A. Barrett Greene (SH 1976–81). L. Bradley Jones (1. 1989–94).
79. The information on the OMGS is from Beeson, op. cit.
80. Known as Susie, for some inexplicable reason.
81. R. J. Beeson (2. 1955–59).
82. J. N. S. Lowe (9. 1954–59).
83. This account of the history of the Ledbury Run owes much to an article written by G. L. M. Smith in the *OMN* (March 1980).
84. It is remarkable that, since 1896 when records proper began, the race has been run from Ledbury every year except six: 1940 when it took place 'midst the mysterious spires of Blenheim Park to the accompaniment of fighter planes training above and members of the Marlborough household riding behind'; 1943–46, at Harrow on the Moor Park golf course; and 1968 when it was cancelled because of an outbreak of foot-and-mouth disease.
85. C. F. G. Pearse (SH 1926–31), from his diary dated 15 March 1930 and published in the *Old Malvernian Newsletter* of December 1980 and again in John Makin, *A History of the Ledbury Run, 1865–2006* (Aspect Design, Malvern 2008).
86. Son of A. H. C.
87. Michael Clement (7. 1952–56).
88. Robin Milne (7. 1956–62).
89. An article for *The Malvernian* in December 1932 had a detailed history of the race contributed by T. Aubertin (7. 1897).
90. Ian Campbell (9. 1955–60).
91. The sailing club was most active in the 1960s. E. H. Milvain (SH 1926–30) donated a 14-footer, and under the guidance of S. G. Partridge the boys built a jetty and landing stage at Defford, and shared the clubroom with the Avon Boating Club.
92. Pat Hooley tells me that Nick and Ginny Williams were unstinting in their support for Malvern's entry into polo, providing training facilities and coaching for boys who had no experience of the sport.
93. In 1992 the competition moved to the Guards Club.
94. Satnam Dhillon (5. 1991–96).
95. William Bowers (5. 1992–97). Ricki Watson (7. 1993–98), and Charlie Gundy (1. 1993–98).

Charles Toppin

i. *The Birmingham Post* (8 December 1951) in a series on Midland public schools.

Denis Saunders

i. From an address in Chapel for Denis Saunders' funeral in February 2003.
ii. Roy, Bevan, Hibberd & Gilbert, *The Centenary History of the Arthur Dunn Cup* (Replay Publishing Ltd, 2003).

Ron Hughes

i. A valedictory tribute to Ron Hughes by Norman Rosser in the *OMN* (1986).
ii. The refurbishment means that the courts are now of tournament quality and amongst the best in the country. The College celebrated the refurbishment with its first major tournament in January 2011, the Professional Singles Championship, involving players from Britain and North America.

The Halford Hewitt

i. These were in 1966, 1984, 1986, 1990, 1992, 1996, 2004, 2006, 2008, 2011.

Chapter 14

1. A. B. N. Johnson (4. 1875–79) in an article 'Musical Memories' written in 1926 and reproduced in the *OMN* (November 1995). Mr Johnson became Director of Music at Eton and examiner for the Royal College of Music. Johnson recalled, 'Loraine Estridge took holy orders when he left Malvern and became a canon of Truro. His death which occurred in 1903, was the result of a bicycle accident.'
2. Blumenau, op. cit., p.62.
3. J. Baker White, *True Blue: An Autobiography 1902–1939* (Frederick Muller, 1970), p.76.
4. Edward Elgar had lived there for a few months in 1889.
5. Blumenau, op. cit.
6. Blumenau, op. cit., pp.105–06.
7. A. E. L. Parnis (SH 1924–28) in *OMN* (November 1987).
8. *The Malvernian.*
9. A notable composer and conductor, Julius Harrison was Director of Music at Malvern College from 1940 to 1942. He then accepted a post as a conductor with the BBC Northern Orchestra in Manchester.
10. Pat Purcell, a gifted oboe player, arrived in 1966 to teach wind instruments together with his wife Eunice who would teach the piano and cello. Pat had served for nine years in the Band of the Irish Guards and a further five years as an orchestral player in London.
11. Blumenau, op. cit., p.156.
12. Ralph Blumenau in a letter to the author.
13. He has been Head of the Jazz Department at Trinity College of Music from 2005.
14. I am indebted to Martin Frayn for this

15. He had been Head of Music at Walhampton.
16. His composition of a marimba concerto for Evelyn Glennie received its world premiere in Malvern.
17. Blumenau, op. cit., p.158.
18. Member of the National Society of Painters, Sculptors and Engravers; elected Member of Royal Society of British Artists, 1935.
19. James Stredder, letter to the author.
20. Ralph Blumenau to the author, March 2013.
21. Ibid.
22. Tim Newsholme has subsequently become a governor of Hereford Art College.
23. Andrew Locock, (9. 1963–68), letter to the author.
24. Nigel Turner in an interview with the author.
25. Martin Frayn recalls that Roy Chapman's 'own appearance in a staff review as a leather-clad motorbike rider to the tune of *Leader of the Pack* was electrifying'.
26. Cups are awarded for Best Play, Best Entertainment, Best Director, Best Actor, Best Actress and Best Technical Design.

Artists

i. Denys Wilcox, 'Christopher Wood: A Malvernian Painter in Picasso's Paris', *Inklings* (2000). See also Sebastian Faulks's *The Fatal Englishman*, and Richard Ingleby, *Christopher Wood: an English painter* (1995).
ii. G. H. Chesterton in *OMN* (2003)
iii. Obituary in *OMN* (April 2009).

Chapter 15

1. Antony Clark recalls that he was the only member of his platoon who opposed the apartheid system. Fortunately his cricketing prowess enabled him to play for the army cricket team, thus avoiding some of the more grisly actions in the protracted conflict in Namibia.
2. The new Headmaster had first visited Malvern in 1973 when on a school cricket tour.
3. The new girls' house, Ellerslie, revived the name of the school lost in the merger. The second house, for boys, provided a new location for No. 7.
4. Joseph Zivny (SH 2010–) who 'was originally French' but has Australian citizenship and currently is living in the United States.
5. The school is managed in partnership with the Chinese firm Babylon Education and the school's headmaster, the first being Ross Hunter. In 2014, one of these former members of the Common Room, Mrs Lorraine Atkins, was appointed head.
6. One enforced improvement came in No. 6 where a serious fire destroyed most of the private side in April 2010. For the following year the girls were accommodated in the old No. 7 – fortuitously now empty – while the damaged house was rebuilt.
7. Clifford Poultney, chairman of the MCPS 2013, writes: 'A new innovation for the school, to date the society has successfully organised theatre visits, picnic walks and weekly hockey, tennis, raquets and badminton clubs attended by a growing number of parents. Recognising the wide range of skills and expertise within the parents of children at the College, a careers evening was organized to enable pupils of all ages to glean advice and guidance from parents working within their chosen professions in a wide range of careers options. This event generated a huge amount of positive feedback from pupils and parents alike. More recently, a music and supper evening was enjoyed by 130 parents and friends entertained with rock, pop and jazz performed by children from the school.'
8. A rather unscientific survey of recent OMs revealed liberal social attitudes but strong hostility to the use of drugs. The sample showed considerable appreciation for the academic, pastoral and co-curricular aspects of their education at Malvern.

Appendix 1

1. The day boy housemasters were: L. S. Milward, 1893; H. E. Cookson, 1908; F. Brayne-Baker, 1913; Major D. S. M. Tassell, TD, 1926–33.
2. I am grateful to Michael Tiley (5. 1960–64) for sharing his research into this question. He also writes: 'It is widely believed that Malvern and Roedean School share the distinction of being the only independent schools in the UK which have numbered boarding houses. It appears to be more than a coincidence that the two schools adopted their house numbering schemes as the three founding sisters of Roedean, Penelope, Dorothy and Millicent Lawrence, had a distinguished Old Malvernian brother called Sir Paul Ogden Lawrence (4. 1876–78) who was a High Court judge and later served as chairman and President on the Council of Roedean. Although there are no formal records to prove that Sir Paul suggested that Roedean should number their houses, it seems quite likely that he was the one to do so, based on his previous experience at Malvern.'
3. Later rector of Dundee High School.
4. Later Headmaster of King Williams, Isle of Man and then Greshams.
5. Later Headmaster of Highgate.
6. Later Headmaster of Brighton College.
7. Later Headmaster of Godolphin School.
8. Later Headmaster of Sir John Lyon School.
9. Later Headmaster of Ellstree Preparatory School.
10. Later Headmaster of Christ's College, Brecon and then Eastbourne College.
11. Later Headmaster of Rishworth School, Halifax.
12. Later Headmaster of the Royal Masonic School, Bushey and then Woodbridge School, Suffolk.
13. Cherbourg in Ellerslie briefly served as another girls' house under Mrs A. Tattersfield, 1992–93, before moving to No 4.
14. Later Bishop of Grafton, New South Wales.
15. Later Headmaster of Heathfield School.

Appendix 2

1. *OMN* (May 2000).
2. In addition to those noted in Chapter 14.
3. Obituary, *OMN* (May 2002).
4. Under the pseudonym of E. L. Black.
5. In an article in *The Daily Telegraph* when Rashid was interviewed by Alex Spillius.

BIBLIOGRAPHY

Aberdare, Lord, *The J. T. Faber Book of Tennis & Rackets* (Quiller Press, 2001)

Arnell, Henry, *An Account of the Old Malvernian Golfing Society, 1922–1992* (The Old Malvernian Golfing Society, 1993)

Baker White, John, *True Blue: An Autobiography 1902–39* (Frederick Muller, 1970)

Beeson, Robert, *Malvern Golf: An Account of Old Malvernian Golf and the Old Malvernian Golfing Society, 1865–2007* (Witley Press, 2007)

Blumenau, Ralph, *A History of Malvern College, 1865–1965* (Macmillan, 1965)

Chesterton, George, *A History of Malvern College Chapel, 1899–1999* (printed privately, 1999)

Chesterton, George, *A Hundred Pictures of a Hundred Years: The Malvernian Society, 1895–1995* (printed privately, 1995)

Chesterton, George, *Malvern College: 125 Years* (The Malvern Publishing Company Ltd, 1990)

Dashwood, Gordon, *Never a Dull Moment* (printed privately, 1994)

Field, A. M., *Before the Memory Fades* (printed privately, 2005)

Gathorne-Hardy, Jonathan, *The Public School Phenomenon, 597–1977* (Hodder and Stoughton, 1977)

Gaunt, H. C. A., *Two Exiles: A School in Wartime* (Sampson Low, Marston & Co Ltd, 1948)

Gray, Peter, *No 7: Records and Reminiscences 1892–1977* (printed privately in Malvern College)

Grierson, Janet, *Dr Wilson and his Malvern Hydro* (Cora Weaver, Malvern 1998)

Grindrod, R. B., *Malvern, Past and Present* (Malvern, 1865)

Harris, Dr Alana, 'Building the Docklands Settlement: Gender, Gentility and the Gentry in East London, 1894–1939', in *Material Religion: Journal of Objects, Art and Religion* (Spring 2013)

Holmes, E. R. T., *Flannelled Foolishness: A Cricketing Chronicle* (Hollis & Carter, 1957)

James, Sydney Rhodes, *Seventy Years* (Williams & Norgate Ltd, 1926)

Kennedy-Cox, Reginald, *Reginald Kennedy-Cox: An Autobiography* (Hodder and Stoughton, 1931)

Kentish, Basil, *This Foul Thing Called War: The Life of Brigadier General R. J. Kentish, CMG, DSO (1876–1956)* (The Book Guild Ltd, 1997)

Lewis, C. S., *Surprised by Joy* (Fount Paperbacks, Harpers Collins, 1998)

Lewis, Jeremy, *Playing for Time* (Collins, 1987)

Lewis, Jeremy, *Grub Street Irregular* (Harper Press, 2008)

Lewis, John, *John Lewis* (John Goodman & Sons (Printers) Ltd)

McGrath, Alister, *C. S. Lewis: A Life* (Hodder & Stoughton, 2013)

Makin, John, *A History of the Ledbury Run, 1865–2006* (Aspect Design, Malvern, 2008)

Mangan, J. A., *Athleticism in the Victorian and Edwardian Public School* (Frank Cass, 2000)

Mann, Phyllis, *Collections for a Life and Background of James Manby Gully, M.D.* (Bosbury Press, 1983)

Murtagh, Andrew, *A Remarkable Man: The Story of George Chesterton* (Shire Publications Ltd and Malvern College, 2012)

Rowe, A. P., *One Story of Radar* (Cambridge University Press, 1948)

Roy, David et al, *The Centenary History of the Arthur Dunn Cup* (Replay Publishing Ltd, 2003)

Schofield, Victoria, *Witness to History: The Life of John Wheeler-Bennett* (Yale 2012)

Simpson, Matthew, *Aspects of Malvern College Architecture* (Malvern College Press, 1984)

Tyerman, Christopher, *A History of Harrow School 1324–1991* (OUP, 2000)

Smith, Brian, *A History of Malvern* (Leicester University Press, 1964)

Watherston, Peter, *A Different Kind of Church* (Marshall Pickering, 1994)

Webster, F. A. M., *Our Great Public Schools* (Ward Lock, 1937)

Wilcox, Michael, *Outlaw in the Hills: A Writer's Year* (Methuen, 1991)

Wodehouse, P. G., *Mike at Wrykyn* (Everyman's Library, 2011)

OTHER SOURCES

Ralph Blumenau papers

Frank Preston, account of Malvern years

Roy Chapman, account of the merger

Michael Harvey, Christian Leadership

John F. Nasmyth-Miller (9. 1948–52), memoirs of Malvern from autobiography

Chris Rycroft, *A Walk on the Hills*

Papers of the 6th Earl Beauchamp

The History of Ellerslie School, 1922–1992

Letters to the Council from Gaunt, Lindsay, Rogers, Chapman, Carson

College records 1924, 1949, 1977

Archives of *Inklings*

Archives of *The Malvernian*

Archives of *Old Malvernian Newsletter* 1979–

School Prefects' Minutes

Index

References to images are in *italics*; references to notes are indicated by n.

A levels 79, 92, 95–6, 101, 120, 122, 125
Adebayo, Oludiran 124
Admiralty, the 56, 61
Afghanistan 183
Andrew, Prince, Duke of York *228*, 229
Arber, George *190*, 191
architecture 131
Arduous Training 80
Arlen, Michael (né Dikran Kouyoumdjian) 37, 38
Army class 28
Arnold, Dr Thomas 143, 185, 253n.9
Art 81, 86, 121, *208*, 218–23
   and Hilary Carruthers 220
   and Bill Denny 221–2
   and Anne Gilmour 220
   and Phil Heath 222
   and Cindy Jones 222
   and Tim Newsholme 222–3
   and William Wilkins 219–20
Artillery Cadet Corps 25, 169
Ashton, Francis William *115*
Assisted Places 92, 97, 105, 107
Athletics 203, *205*
Attlee, Clement 69

Bailey, Julian 124, 223
Barwell, Frederick Leycester 172
Bazaar 31–2
Beacon, The 48, 51
Beer, Ian 83
Beeson, Maurice F. 180
Beeson, Nigel 180, 263n.61
Bennett, L. V. 192
Bennett, Simon 224, *224*
Beveridge, Bob 191
Big School *22*
Billière, Sir Peter de la 103

Biology 121, 232
Birley, Robert 72
Black, Robin 108
Blackburn Rovers FC 192
Blackshaw, John 47, 97, 98, *101*, 197
Blake, Leonard 114, 210–12
Blenheim Palace *4–5, 54*, 56–62, 116–17, 175
Blomfield, Charles 136
Blomfield, Sir Arthur 32, 132, 136
Blumenau, Ralph 17, 28, 33, 51, 84, 120, 219
   and centenary history 7, 84
   and fagging 82–3
   and Donald Lindsay 76, 121
   and Preston 53
Blunkett, David 109
Board of Education 115
Boarding houses 14–15, 19, 24, 63–4, 92
   see also individual Houses
Boarding School Allowance (BSA) 97
Boer War 39, 133, 169
Boissier, A. P. 66
Bolam, Jim 123
Boosey, Noel Charles 173
'Bottling' Club 78
Boxing 206
Boyle, Rory 214, 215, *215*
Bradfield 12, 197
Brett, Charles 212–13
Brett, Noel 191
British Army 63, 181, 183
British Empire 11, 12, 90, 148, 150, 174, 185–6
Brown, Michael 213
Brown, Sir Stephen 97
'Buggy's Bower' 21
Building Company 14, 15, 25
Bullock, E. C. 28, *53*
Bullying 21, 143, 154
Burke, Edward William 171
Burleys, the 108

Burma 180
Burrow, John 12, 13
Burrow, Rev H. H. 13, 14
Burrow, Walter 12, 13

Cadet Corps 31, *33, 170*, 175; *see also* Combined Cadet Force
Cambridge University 27, 86, 92, 101, 111, 115, 121, 122, 123
Campbell-Ferguson, James 121
Campbell, Ian *203*
Caney, Simon 124
Canning Town 32–3, 53, 81, 161–2
Canny, P. E. B. 180
Canny, Sir Gerald 180, 236
Carmen Malvernense 27, 28
Carruthers, Hilary 220
Carson, Hugh 105–6, *106*, 107–8, 109, 141, 229
Carter, Alan 123
Cartwright, Henry 174
Cartwright, Ronald William St George 174
CCF *see* Combined Cadet Force
Chadder, A. Harvey *53*, 193, *194*
Chadder, Richard H. 'Dick' 73, 193, *194*, 201
Chadwick, Thomas Edmund 218–19
Chapel 14, 19, 93, 141
   and architecture *130*, 131–2, 136, 138–9
   and First World War 136–8
   and funds 31, 32
   and windows 134–5
Chaplains 140
Chapman, Roy de Courcy 95, *95*, 96–8, *100*, 101, 103, 104–5
   and Drama 225
   and prefects 157
Chapman Technology Centre 96, *96*, 125, *126*
Chappell, Peter 127
Charity 165–7; *see also* Missions
Charterhouse 12, 192

267

Cheltenham 12, 13, 25
Chemistry 111, 121, 124, 232
   and James Campbell-Ferguson 121
   and Michael 'Jock' McNevin 121, 253n.7
   and John Nicholls 121
Chesterton, George 47, 89, 95, 150–2, *151*, 181
   and Chapel 139
   and cricket 73, 187, 188, 190
   and Second World War 63, 116–17
China 127, 231–2, *234*, 235
Choral Society 121
Christian Fellowship 63
Christianity 12, 86, 93, 103, 161; *see also* Chapel
Churchill, Lord Randolph 28
Churchill, Lady Sarah, 62
Churchill, Winston 56, 59, 69–70, 83, 86
Cigarette cards *39*, *188*
Clare, Horatio 124
Clark, Antony 109, *159*, 229–30, 231, 232, 235
Clarke, Ambrose Childs 171
Clarke, William Andrews St Aubyn 173
Classics 14, *110*, 111, 115, *121*, 122
   and John Hart *110*, 122
   and Harry Hammond House 112
   and Richard Thurlow 127, *127*
   and George White 118, 257n.26
Clifton 12, 14, 25, 31
Co-education 91, 95, 96–8, 100–1, 203
Coat of arms 25, 26, 48
Cobb, Ralph *53*, 118
'Cold War warriors' 76
College Council 26, 27–8, 48, 55, 64, 236
   and IB 96
   and merger 98
   and salaries 79
Colonial service 147, 148
Combined Cadet Force (CCF) 44, *76*, 77, 86, 87, 88, 181–2
Commemoration (Commem) 31, *83*, *104*, *109*
Common Room 78, *92*, 93, 107
Constable, Mary 227
Coombes, Guy 223
Corbet, George Frederick Francis 173
Corbet, Reginald Vincent Campbell 172

Coronation 73, 75
Corporal punishment 19, 28, 34, 38, 81–2, 89, 147, 148
Council Room *113*
Coursework 122
Coventry Cathedral 86
Cricket 23–4, *25*, 28, *29*, 31, 34–5, *36*, *186*, 187–91
   and Donald Lindsay 87, 88, 91
   and Charles Toppin 188
Cricket Pavilion *30*, 31, *32*, 61
Cross, Reginald Carlton 172
Crowley-Milling, Sir Denis 179
Cruttwell, Rev Charles 26–7, *27*, 111, 200
Culturama 231, *232*
Culture Shock 2000: 106
Curriculum 12, 112, 115–16, 123–4, 125–7; *see also individual subjects*, A level subjects; International Baccalaureate
Cwm Llwch 181–2, *183*

Darlington, Arnold 121
Davey, Ken 98
Davison, J. A. 210
Day boys 19, 25, 93
Debating Society 21, 23, 28, 31, 37, 50
   and First World War 44
Delingpole, James 124, 236
Denny, Bill *218*, 221–2
Dent, Oscar William Robert 180
Dickinson, D. C. C. 201, *202*
Diphtheria 31
Discipline 28, 34, 44, 95, 104, 143, 158
Discussion Society 51
Disney, Lt Guy 183, *183*
Disraeli, Benjamin 23
Divinity/Religious Studies 96, 124, 125, 151
Docklands Settlement 24, 53, 69, *160*, 162–5
Dodd, Lewis 86
Donaldson, Poppy *129*
Dormitories *45*, 49, *82*, 89
Dowdles, David 109, *109*
Downs School 107, 108
Downside 175
Drama 51, 73, 81, 86, 88, 121, 217, 223–7
   and Simon Bennett 224
   and Nigel Turner 225
   and Neil Smith 227

   and Keith Packham 227
   and Neil Smith 227
Drew, Bob 24, *24*
Drew, Rev Francis 19, 26, *26*
Drury, Alfred 174
Duff, Alan 121, 154, *154*, 190
Duff, Sir Patrick 56
Duke of Edinburgh Awards 80, 86, 90, 182
Duke of York's camps 52
Dunton, Frederick R. 179
Dyslexia 129
Dyson, Rev Frank 13

Eames, William Stanley 173
Economics and Politics 123, 127, 232
   and Jim Bolam 123
   and Martin Frayn 123
   and Stephen Holroyd 123
   and Simon Wilkinson 123
Edinburgh Festival Fringe 213, 224, 225, 227
Education 88, 89
Eglington, Michael 47
Eliot, T. S. 63
Elizabeth, HM the Queen Mother 74, 84, *84*, *85*, 176, *177*, *178*
Elizabeth II, Queen 75
Ellcock, Ricardo 191
Ellerslie 97, 99, 108
Ellerslie House 96, 98, *231*
Engineering 44, 86, 234, *128*
English 51, 96, 111, 114, 122, 124
   and Alan Carter 123
   and Peter Chappell 127
   and Douglas Mensforth 123
   and George Sayer 80
   and John Venning 123
   and Harry Wakelyn Smith 113
Entry standards 78, 79
Eton 12, 102, 206
Eustace, Timothy 213
Everitt, John Paxman 171
Everitt, Patrick Anthony Clement 178
Examinations 20, 111, 117, 256n.13
Expulsions 28, 38, 101

Faber, Rev Arthur 14, *15*, 19–20, 21, 23, 26, 84–5, 111
   and cricket 24
   and football 192
   and motto 25
   and prefects 143
Fabian Ware, Harry 219, 222

Fagging 21, 82, 83, 88, 143–7, 148–50, 153, 155, 156
Farebrother, John 77
Farrar, Reg 119, 121
'Father Tate' *189*, 190, 191
Fees 19
Fellows, Sarah 202
Ferrets 79–80
Fiddian-Green, Charles *53*, 190
Filho, René 96, *97*, 123–4, 125
Finances 25, 26, 28, 91, 97, 107–8
 and OMs 46
Fire-fighting 68–9
Firs Estate 48
First World War 39, 44–5, 46, 112, 169–75
 and Chapel 136–8
Fives 197
Flymo meetings 93
Foden, Giles 124
Food 20, 21, 44, *79*
Football 24, *33*, 35, 73, 87, 88, 91, 192–5
Foster, B. S 'Basil' 40–41, 169.188
Foster, G. N. 'Geoff' 40–41, 188, 193
Foster, H. K. 'Harry' 28, *29*, 40–41, 188, *193*
Foster, M. K. 'Maurice' 40–41, 188
Foster, N. J. A. 'Johnnie' 40–41, 188
Foster, R. E. 'Tip' 35, 40–41, 188–9, *189*, 193
Foster, Rev H. 23–5, 40, 134, 169, 192, 197, 199
Foster, W. L. 'Bill' 40–41, 169, 188, *193*
Foundation Year 122, 222, 229, 258n.5
Frayn, Martin 122, 123, 259n.35
Free French Army 63, *64*
Fuge, Adam 102, *104*

Games 23–4, 34–6, 73, 80–1, 185–6;
 see also Sport
Gauci, Joe 124–5
Gaunt, Tom 55–6, 58–9, 69, 70, 71, 73
 and Blenheim Palace 61–3
 and Harrow 65–7
 and prefects 148–9
 and teaching 117–18, 121
GCSE curriculum 96, 101, 124, 222–3, 225
General Purposes Committee 98
Geography 77, 99, 151, 195
 and Norman Rosser 77–8, 256n.7
George V, King 169
George VI, King 176, *177*, *178*

German pupils 72, 96, 103, 127–8, 158, 231
Ghana 166–7
Gifts 46–7
Gillard, Roger 100
Gillett, Rev Gresham 161
Gillmore, H. T. 218
Gilmour, Anne 220
Girl pupils 91, 93, 96–8, 100–1, 122–3
 and football 195
Girls' schools 81, 88, 97
Gladstone, William 23
Goddard, Richard 90, *90*, 101, 258n.i
Godsland, Paul 123–4
Golf 35, 199–200
Graham, Rosemary 227
Graham-Hall, John 212, 216
Gray, Rev Arthur 31, 32–3, 131–2, 141
Gray, Peter 125, 197
Grayson, Ken 121
Great Depression 50
Grub Shop 31, *49*, 61
Grundy, Rev William 27–9, *29*, 111, 199
Grundy Library 14, *29*, *113*, *128*
Gully, Dr James 12, *12*, 13, 14
Gun squad *34*
Gunster, J. H. 24
Gymnasium 31, 46, 92, 176, 224

Haakon, King of Norway 69
Haileybury 12
Halford Hewitt 199
Hall, Chris 121
Hampton 101
Hansom, Charles 14, 131
Hardiman, Mark 156
Hardinges, Mark 191
Harrison, Charles 174
Harrison, Heath *26*
Harrison, Julius 210
Harriss, Frank 124, 204, *207*
Harrow 12, 14, 65, 66–71, 117, 175
Harry, Prince 183
Hart, Eirian *102*
Hart, John *110*, 122, *122*, 186
Harvey, Michael 154–5, *155*, 260n.26
Harvey Jones, Sir John 103
Harwood, Simon *165*
Hayes, Quentin 216
Hayman, Patrick 220
Heath, Phil 222
Hellyer, Sidney Hannaford 171
Help for Heroes Endurance Challenge *165*

Higgins, Alison *129*
High Church 12
Hill, Beresford Winnington 172
Hill, Syd 47, 194
Hillstone 96, 97, 98, 100, 108
Hindmarch, Jack 213
History 14, 111, 120, 123, 126
 and Ralph Blumenau 120, 121
 and Alan Smith 126–7
History Society 103
Hockey 203, *204*
Hodgson, Rev Tom 103
Hogg, Quintin 69
Holmes, E. R. T. *189*, 190
Holroyd, Stephen 123
Holyrood House 19
Home Guard 59, 175
Honey, Alexis Cowper 173
Hookham, Richard 124, *124*, 202–3
Hooley, Pat 103, 196, 206, 257n.43
Hop-picking 53
Hopkinson, J. G. *34*
Hordern, Miles 124
Hoskins, Wilf 24, *24*
House, Harry Hammond 112
House colours 26
House Play Competition 81, 224
Housemasters 19, 26, 64, 66–7, 88, 157
 and pastoral care 91, 92, 102, 154
Howick, Alice 217, *217*
Hubbard, Mark 198
Huggins, Sir Godfrey *73*
Hughes, Ron 198
Hundred, the 122, 227, 258n.5
Hunt, Sir John 90
Hunter, John 97
Hunting *45*

IB *see* International Baccalaureate
Illingworth, Geoffrey 200
Immorality 37–8
Industry 93, 122
Inklings 106
INSET training 129
Inspections 79, 109, 115, 117–18
International Baccalaureate (IB) 95, 96, 98, 101, 106, 125, 231
 and charity 165, 166
 and René Filho 96

Jackson, Arnold Nugent Strode 35, *39*, 203, 204
Jacomb, Brian 47
James, Rodney 200

James, Sydney Rhodes 34, 35, *35*, 36, 37, 38, 39
   and Chapel 132–3, 136
   and mission 162
   and sport 199
Jones, Cindy *138*, 222
Jones, Philip 221
Junior Turf 254n.9
Juniors *33*

Kempson, Henry 46, *46*
Kennedy, Eb 86
Kennedy-Cox, Reginald 53, 162–3, 165
Knee, John 123, 125
Knight, Donald 189, *189*
Knott, Martin 154, *154*
Köhler-Cadmore, Tom 191
Kontarines, Lindsay 101, *101*

Lace, Cyril 47
Lacrosse 203, *206*
Lafferty, Angela 101, *103*
Laird, Michael 216
Lamberton, Sue 100–1, *103*
Lancaster, Sir Osbert *218*, 221
Lancing 12
Latham, P. H. 28, *29*, 188
Latin 19
Law, Andrew 126
Lawrence, Sir Paul 46
Lea, John 13, 15, 17, *17*
Learning support 129
Lechmere, Sir Edmund 13, *13*, 25
Ledder 73, 200–3
Lees 48
Legge, G. B. 190
Leng, Tony 118, 121
Lewis, C. S. 36, 37–8, *44*, 114, *114*, 143–4
Lewis, John 79, 116, 118–21
Philip Lewis 206
Lewis, Warren 114
Lindsay, Donald *74*, *75*, 75–7, 78, 80, 82, 84–5, 86, 87–8, 164
   and arts 209, 212, 219, 220–1, 223–4
   and co-education 91
   and games 80–1
   and politics 83
   and prefects 150
   and religion 138, 139–40
   and sport 196, 198
   and staff 79
   and teaching 118–19, 121

Lindsay Art Centre 92, 121, 221
Lister, Dr Robin 126
Literary Society 28
Loh, Tim *140*
Long Room Club 86
Lowe, Jeremy 200
Lowe, W. W. *53*
Lower School Council 230
Lucretian Society 103, 106
Lygon, Frederick 13–14, 15, 17, *17*, 25
Lyon, R. E. 36–7, 209–10, *210*

McDowall, Rev Charles 19, *19*
MacLaurin, Lord 108, 109, *159*, 235
Macmillan, Harold 84, 85, *85*
McNevin, Michael 'Jock' 77, 121, 253n.7
Main Building 14, *15*, *16*, 61, *94*, 131, *239*
Malvern 12, *13*
Malvern Carmen, The 27, 28
Malvern College:
   and Blenheim Palace 56–62
   and centenary 84–5
   and China 231–2, *234*, 235
   and Diamond Jubilee 48
   and establishment 12, 13–14, 19
   and Harrow 66–71
   and leadership 106–8, 124–5
   map *238–9*
   and merger 97–8, 100–1
Malvern College Qingdao 232, *234*
Malvern Conference 63
Malvern Proprietary College Company 13–15, 17
Malvernian, The 21, 33, 51, 69–70, 73, 81, 103–4, *107*, 109
   and co-education 98
   and fagging 153
   and First World War 44, 169–70
   and missions 162
   and Second World War 175
   and sport 23, 28, 192
Malvernian Society 33, 46–7, 48, 72, 133, 200
Marlborough, John Spencer-Churchill, Duke of 56, 62
Marlborough 12
Masters' Common Room *37*
Mathematics 26, 44, 96, 111, 115, 118, 122, 123, 124, 125, 166
   and China 232
   and Ralph Cobb 118

and Reg Farrar 119
and John Knee 123
Matthews, David 124
Mauler, The 104
Meade, James *117*
Mellin, G. L. 199, 200, *200*
Memorial Library *42*, 46, 174, *175*, 176
Mensforth, Douglas 124
Merchant, Moelwyn 103
Metelman, Henry 109
Ministry of Works 56, 63, 65
Missions *see* Canning Town; Docklands Settlement
Modern Languages 14, 53, 96, 123, 124, 127, 232
   and René Filho 123
   and Paul Godsland 123–4
   and Richard Hookham 124, *124*
   and Tony Leng 118, 121
   and David Matthews 124
Monastery 48, 50, 61, 210, 255n.10
Monckton, Sir Walter 69
Montgomery, Field Marshal Bernard 72
Morgan Motor Company 73, 234, *234*
Morrison, Herbert 69
Morton, Geoff *190*, 191
Mountaineering 182–3
Moxey, Eric Lawrence 179
Moxey, Nigel Hall 179
Muir, Kenneth *180*, 181
Murtagh, Andrew 190–1
Music 36–7, 50, 73, 81, 86, 88, 121, 209–15, 217
   and Leonard Blake 201–12
   and Rory Boyle 214–15
   and Charles Brett 212–13
   and Timothy Eustace 213
   and Jack Hindmarch 213
   and Neil Page 214
   and Pat Purcell 213, 264n.10
   and F. H. Shera 210
   and Iain Sloan 215
Myles-Lea, Jonathan 223

Nash, David 191
National Curriculum 124
Natural History Museum *39*
Natural History Society 37
Nesbit, Edward 217, *217*
Netball 203, *206*
New College, Oxford 13, 14

Newey, Alan 200
Newsholme, Tim *209*, 222, 223
Newsom, John 83
Nicholls, Colin 121, 156
Nicholls, Mark 198
Night prowler 37, 38
No. 1 House *25*, 60, 63, 70, 87, 100, 157, 177, *193*, 241
No. 2 House 19, 60, 63, 157, 177, 192, 241
   and Francis Drew 26
No. 3 House 24, *27*, 63, 68, 86, 101, *142*, 154, 155, 156–7, 177, 241
   and discipline and fagging 154–5
No. 4 House 24, *26*, 63, 101, 158, 177, *193*, 241
No. 5 House 24, 25, *33*, 40, 87, 107, 146, 150, 152–3, 169, *193*, 203, 241
   and discipline 152–3
   and Rev Henry Foster 24
   and Second World War 60, 63, *64*
No. 6 House 24, 25, 63, 70, *70*, 72, 77, 96, 149, 152, 177, 202, 225, 242
   and fagging 149–50
   and girls 98, 100–1
No. 7 House 25, 45, 63, 138, 150, 157, 177, 202, *231*, 242
   and Denis Saunders 195
   and fagging 150
No. 8 House 25, 63, 70, 78, 107, 156, 157, 176, 224, 242
   and abolition of fagging 156–7
   and John Lewis 116
No. 9 House 25, 70, 153, *178*, 180, 188, *222*, 242
Nöh, Noah-Vincenz *202*
Nuffield Science *79*, 116, 119, 121

O levels 79, 92, 122
Ogilvie, Ian 93
Olympic Games 35
Oxbridge *see* Cambridge University; Oxford University
Oxford University 27, 86, 92, 101, 111, 115, 121, 122, 123

Packham, Keith 227, *227*
Page, Neil *212*, 214
Paralympics 206–7
Parents' Society 236
Parish of All Saints, Haggerston 24, 161
Partridge, N. E. 189–90
Pastoral care 91–2, 102, 109, 154

Paxman, Jeremy 103, 109
Penter, David 121
Pepper v Hart 122
Percik, Mike 194
Peters, George C. B. 179
Philip, Prince, Duke of Edinburgh *90*
Philosophy 120, 125
Philpott, Dr Henry 14
Physics 116, 118–19, 121, 232
   and Alan Duff 121
   and Ken Grayson 121
   and John Lewis 79, 116, 118–21
   and Fred Vivian-Robinson 121
   and Richard Walwyn *117*, 121
Politics 21, 23, 31, 37, 50, 83, 105
Polo 206
Porch, R. B. *34*, *44*, 47, *47*, 53
Porter, Harold Graham 178
Porters 24
Porter's Lodge 61
Pougatch, Mark 191, 194
Prance, Sir Ghillean *106*
Prayers 21
Prefects' room 38
Prefect system 12, *32*, 38, 44, 102, *142*, 143–59, *144*, *146*, *152*, *153*
   and Harrow 67
   see also fagging
Preston, Frank Sansome 43–4, *44*, 45, 50, 51, 52, 53, *53*
   and curriculum 112, 115–16
   and drama 223, 227
   and music 210
   and sport 199
Preston Science School 50, *51*, 56, *79*, 115, 118, 119
Prince's Trust 167
Proprietary schools 12–13
Prosser, Frederick 24
Public schools 11–12, 13, 21, 78, 88, 96, 105
   and commission 83
   and prefects 147–8
   and sport 185–6
Pupil numbers 19, 21, 25, 26, 28, 37, 48, 72
   and Great Depression 50, 64
   and Martin Rogers 93
   and Sixth Form 96
Purcell, Pat 213, 264n.10
Purcell, Simon 213

Qingdao 231–2, *234*, 235

Rackets 24–5, 31, 35, 87, 197–8
Radley 12, 13, 197
Railways 12, *13*, *73*
Razak, Hon Dato' Sri Mohd Najib bin Tun Haji Abdul *236*
Razak Science Centre 236, *236*
Reed, Michael 213
Remove, the 101, 122, 258n.5
Repton 24, 28, 192, 194
Richardson, Robert 206–7, *207*
Roberts, Tim 191
Robertson, Howard 48
Robinson, Francis Edward 170
Robinson, Helen 101, *102*
Rogers, Martin 75, 88, 89, *89*, 92–3, 122
   and arts 221, 224
   and prefects 155
Rossall 12
Rosser, Norman 77, 78, 198
Rowe, Dr A. P. 175–6, *177*, *178*
Royal Charter 48, 98
Rugby 35, 44, 91, 196
Rugby School 12, 65, 143
Rundell, Oliver 216

Sailing 86, 87
St Edmunds church 106
St George 46, *48*, 70, *137*, 139, *168*, 174, 181
Salaries 78, 79
Salmon, H. G. C. *53*
Sanatorium 19, 31, *38*
Sandbrook, Dominic 124
Saunders, Denis 193–4, 195
Sayer, George 79, 80, 121, 224
Sayers, Dorothy 63
Sayle, Gladys 99
Scholarships 26
School Certificate 117
School Council 102, 157–8
School crest 48
School customs 70–1
School House 14, *19*, 21, 25, 35, 49, 67, 70, 99, *196*, 202, *237*, 240–1
   and drama 111, 224
   and sale 48
   and war 56
School motto 25, *38*
School routine 20–1, 48–50
School rules 28, *144*
School trips 109
Science 50, *114*, 115, 118–21
   and Michael Shepherd 121

Scriven, Tim 97
Second World War 25, 55–71, 116–17, 175–81
  and Chapel 138
  and Docklands 164
Senior Mile *184*
Senior Turf 24, 34, 37, *71*, 175, 192
Shannon, Richard Bernard, Earl of 171–2
Shang, Yeng Yeng *222*
Sharpe, Lydia *203*
Sharpe, Naomi *183*
Shebbeare, Sir Tom 167
Shepherd, Michael 121
Shera, F. H. 210, *210*
Shooting 203–4, *207*
Shrewsbury 12, 24, 192, 194, 196
Simpson, John 109
Simpson-Hayward, G. H. *25*, 189, *189*
Sinclair, Sir Archibald 69
Sixth Form 27, 79, 86, 89, 91–2
  and Centre 106
  and Council 95, 102, 157–8, 165–6, 230–1
  and entry 103
  and numbers 96
Skiing *81*
Sloan, Iain 215, *215*
Sloan, Katie 202
Smith, Alan 126–7
Smith, Bob 194
Smith, F. 'Charlie' 24
Smith, Harry Wakelyn 'Smugy' 28, 45, 113, *113*, 114
Smith, Neil 198, 227
Southall, Trevor 101
Spanish influenza 45, 48
Spanyol, Stephen *214*
Speech and drama 227
Speech Day 28, *31*, *50*, 51, 52, *68*
Sport 90–1, 103–4, 203–7, 229, 236; *see also* Cricket; Football; Golf; Ledder; Rackets; Rugby
Sports Day *205*
Squash 48
Staniforth, Malcolm *61*, 77, 86, *86*, 197
Stephenson-Peach, William 234
Storie-Pugh, Peter 180–1

Stredder, James *152*, 153
Study bedrooms 89, *89*
Stummes, Dr Leopold 13, 14, *14*, 23–4
Swimming 25, 256n.25
Symonds Yat 93, 155–6

Taylor, Ronald Francis 173
Teachers 112, 116–17, 121, 127–8, 129
Team games 12
Technology 96, 124, 125, 222, 225
Telecommunications Research Establishment (TRE) 65–6, 67, 71, 175–7, *178*
Temple, William, Archbishop of Canterbury 63
Tennis 48, 87, *206*
Tent-pitching *39*
Terrace *83*
Thai students 24
Thurlow, Richard 127, *127*, 197
Tinton, Capt Ben 162
Tolchard, Roger 191
Toppin, Charles 28, 188, 189, 190
TRE *see* Telecommunications Research Establishment
Trotter, Thomas 213, 216
Turner, Nigel *224*, 225, 227
Turner, Rosie 227
Tutorial system 102, 155, 237

Uniforms *19*, *23*, *25*, 48–9, *49*, 82–3, 87, *107*, 145
  and restrictions *49*, 70, 145, 146–7, 150
United States of America (USA) 126
Universities 28, 31, 51–2; *see also* Cambridge University; Oxford University

Vaughn, Michael *230*
VE Day 69–70
Venning, John 123
Verity, James 191
Victoria, Queen 31
  Diamond Jubilee 31, 169
Vincent, Mark *36*
Vivian, James 216
Vivian-Robinson, Fred 121

Volleyball 206–7
Voluntary service 81, 86, 165

Wachter, Dr Oswald *21*
Walton, Kevin 86
Walwyn, Richard *117*, 121
Wanklin, Alan 24, *24*
Warburton's 14
Ware, Kalistos 103
Warner, William Henry Cromwell 178
Wateridge, Jonathan 124, 223
Wathen, H. R. 19
Way, Basil H. 179
Weatherill, Sir Bernard 98, *104*
Weatherill Society 103
Webb, Maurice 174
Welch, Sarah 109
Wellington 12
Wheeler-Bennett, John 51, 75, 77, 84, *85*, 112, 119
Wheeler-Bennett Society 77, 106
White, Brian 157
White, George 118
Whitty, Christopher 124
Whitty, James 223
Whyman, Ernie 24, *24*
Wilkins, William 219, 220
Wilkinson, Ellen 71
Wilkinson, Rev Keith 102
Wilkinson, Simon 123
Wilson, Dr James 12, 13
Winchester 14, 197
Wings of Hope charity *166*
Wise, W. S. 200
Wodehouse, P. G. 34, 187, 254n.13
Wood, John Christopher 'Kit' 220
Worcester Warriors Rugby Club 236
Worcestershire County Cricket Club 191, 236
Worcestershire Golf Club 199–200
Work experience 103, 122
Worrall, John 206
Wright, Tim 93

'Young Malvern' 103
Young, Sir Roger 103
Younger, Captain David Reginald 169, *169*

MALVERN COLLEGE No 6
NEW CHAPEL

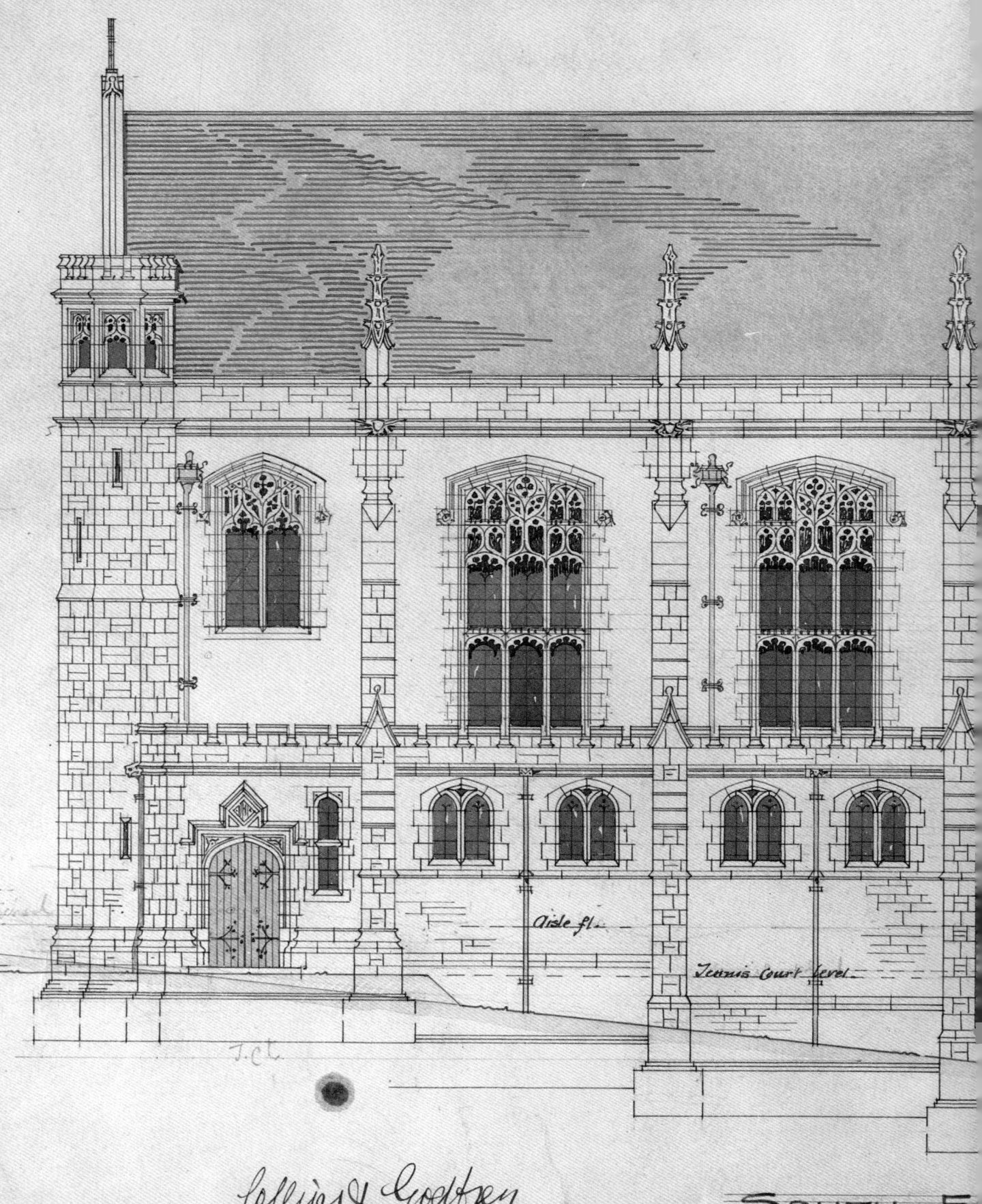

Terrace level
Aisle level
Chapel floor level

Aisle fl.

Tennis Court level

Collins & Godfrey

SOUTH E